The Rise and Decline
of
Western Liberalism

ANTHONY ARBLASTER

The Rise and Decline
of
Western Liberalism

Basil Blackwell

First published in 1984 by Basil Blackwell Publishers
Ltd., 108 Cowley Road, Oxford OX4 1JF.

Basil Blackwell Inc.
432 Park Avenue South, Suite 1505,
New York, NY 10016

British Library Cataloguing in Publication Data

Arblaster, Anthony
The rise and decline of Western liberalism.
1. Liberalism—History
I. Title
320.5'1'091821   JC571

ISBN 0-85520-765-5

Typeset by System 4 Associates, Gerrards Cross
Printed and bound in Great Britain by
Bell and Bain Ltd, Glasgow

Contents

PART II   THE EVOLUTION OF LIBERALISM

Preface

The origins of this book go back more years than I care to remember. My original intention was to write a book about Cold War liberalism — at that time a more influential intellectual current than it is now. As will be seen, this makes up only a small ingredient in the present work. I then had the idea of writing an analytical study of liberalism, but became convinced that a completely ahistorical analysis was also inadequate. Hence the present hybrid volume, which attempts to combine analysis with criticism and history.

The result is a book which is longer than I would have liked, for who, after all, has the time to read long books? Considering its scope, however, and the range and complexity of the materials I felt had to be considered, experts in any of the several fields into which I have trespassed will be more likely to complain of its brevity and superficiality. Even so, of course, it is in no way comprehensive in its coverage. What I am offering is a perspective on, or an interpretation of, liberalism as a whole, which I have tried to support with enough argument, analysis, evidence and example to make it plausible. To adapt G. K. Chesterton, my excuse is that this was worth doing, however sketchily, rather than it not being done at all — and in fact full-scale studies of liberalism are remarkably thin on the ground at present.

This interpretation will not please everyone, and certainly some liberals will be unhappy with it. But the fact is that much of the analysis and history of liberalism has been written by the liberals themselves. Liberalism has therefore had, in my view, a rather better press than it deserves. I have therefore wanted to tip the balance the other way by bringing out some of those darker and harsher aspects of liberalism which liberal writers have naturally tended to gloss over.

Acknowledgements

The business of writing a book is, usually, the work of a single person. It is so in this case, and I alone am responsible for the opinions expressed here. The *creation* of a book is, however, a far less individual matter, and it is a fact that many people, both known and unknown to me personally, have contributed to the evolution of this text. Many intellectual debts are acknowledged in the citations and footnotes. But some others are not. I would like to thank my friend and one-time history tutor, Christopher Hill, for his encouragement, and also my post-graduate teachers in the Philosophy Department, University College London, Richard Wollheim and Jerry Cohen, who taught me what philosophy I know, and did their best to nurture in me a more rigorously analytical frame of mind.

I must also thank Elizabeth Thomas, literary editor of *Tribune* in the 1960s, who generously allowed me to air in a column on books some of the ideas which reappear here, as well as Richard Clements, the editor. Journalism as it is practised has many faults, but it can provide the would-be writer with an invaluable training, from which one learns that writing is not simply a matter of self-expression, but also essentially of communication with others.

I could not have written this book without having available the resources of a good library. I have made extensive use of the Sheffield University Library, and am grateful to its staff for the good and helpful service they provide, under the difficult circumstances of heavy cuts in funding, at both the governmental and university levels.

Among friends and colleagues at Sheffield University, I must thank Geraint Williams, with whom I have had many valuable discussions about liberalism, both in public and private, and Andrew Gamble, who kindly read several chapters of the book and made some most useful criticisms. David Beetham and Raymond Plant both read almost the whole manuscript, and made many useful suggestions which I have generally tried to take up. I am most grateful to them.

I am also grateful to the staff of Basil Blackwell for their commitment to this book.

One friend who has taken a consistent and helpful interest in this work over the past ten years is Clifford Owen. I am grateful to him, and also to Patricia Stubbs, who gave much help and support in the book's earlier stages. But probably my greatest debt is to Steven Lukes, with whom I have discussed most if not all of the themes of this book over many years, and who read and commented valuably on the first part of the book. My wife, Lynda, deserves most thanks, for she has not only read the manuscript and made many useful criticisms, especially on matters of style, but has also given much invaluable help in the lengthy practical business of typing, re-typing, indexing, and preparing the work for publication.

The dedication of this book hardly needs any explanation, but it ought to be said that, like the children of loving and encouraging parents everywhere, I owe an incalculable debt to them for all their encouragement and support, especially in the years of my full-time education. That was the basis on which everything has subsequently been founded. I recall it with love and gratitude.

Anthony Arblaster
Sheffield, January 1984

For my mother
and in memory of
my father.

PART I

The Analysis of Liberalism

1

Liberalism — Alive or Dead?

Is liberalism alive or dead? That is not an easy question to resolve. As a distinctive, organized political tendency, liberalism in the late twentieth century survives only precariously, even in the Western capitalist societies which have been its historic home. For the most part explicitly liberal political parties do not flourish. Two major exceptions to this rule might possibly be the Democratic Party in the USA and the Canadian Liberal Party. But in other cases, such as Japan, Australia and Italy, the party called Liberal is a party of the right or even the extreme right. North America is the only area of the developed capitalist world in which liberal parties have not been replaced on the left by social democratic (labour) or communist parties in the twentieth century. Liberal 'revivals', of the kind seen in Britain over the past 20 years, express the negative of dissatisfaction with the major parties of right and left, rather than a positive commitment to liberalism.

Globally, the present and future prospects for liberalism look even less encouraging. Authoritarian regimes, whether of the left or right, provide the dominant pattern. The parliamentary-democratic constitutions which the withdrawing colonial powers sometimes left behind in the Third World have hardly anywhere survived. In many countries the military have taken over — including some, such as Chile and Uruguay, where the liberal constitutional tradition seemed to be well established. Where civilian rule still exists it usually takes the form of a one-party state.

In societies of mass poverty and hunger, all those who are not committed to the preservation of exploitation and privilege are necessarily preoccupied with urgent material questions — with the political strategies which will most effectively challenge injustice and exploitation, and make possible substantial improvements in the lives of the masses of the urban and rural poor. To them liberalism appears to have little or no relevance, and the word 'liberal' is likely to be used as a term of contempt. The question of a person's freedom, as it is understood by the liberal, is secondary to the question of his or her sheer survival, and the politics of hunger and poverty are first of all the politics of survival. Even Western liberals recognize this in principle:

> It is true that to offer political rights, or safeguards against intervention by the state, to men who are half-naked, illiterate, underfed, and diseased is to mock their condition; they need medical help or education before they can understand, or make use of, an increase in their freedom. . . . First things come first: there are situations, as a nineteenth-century Russian radical declared, in which boots are superior to the works of Shakespeare; individual freedom is not everyone's primary need. . . . The Egyptian peasant needs clothes or medicine before, and more than, personal liberty . . .[1]

In practice, however, the priorities of liberalism have been rather different. Western liberals have typically shown themselves more interested in issues of civil liberties in the Third World than in the extent to which its societies fail or succeed in making social and economic progress. They have labelled countries like China, Cuba and even Chile under Allende, as 'totalitarian', and therefore to be condemned. They have represented the transition from Batista to Castro in Cuba, and the replacement of the Caetano regime in Portugal by a brief period of rule by the armed forces as being no more than the substitution of a left-wing or communist dictatorship for a right-wing one, as if both were equally obnoxious from a liberal point of view. The immense changes that the Cuban revolution has effected in the lives of the Cuban people, in terms of eliminating hunger and disease, illiteracy and extreme poverty — these are disregarded, or treated by implication as secondary to the great liberal issue of political freedom. As a consequence, rightly or wrongly, this liberal order of priorities is seen by radicals and revolutionaries in the Third World as misguided and irrelevant.

And that is the most charitable judgement on liberalism that they are likely to make. Many of them regard liberals and liberalism with undisguised contempt. Whether this contempt is justified or not, it is important to understand the reasons for it. The Western liberal is suspected of hypocrisy, and of being inconsistent even in the application of his/her own professed standards:

> In relation to Africa, Asia and Latin America, the European and American liberal has too often been — and is perhaps increasingly — a false friend. Typically, in welcoming the new independence of, say, the African countries, he has warned them lest they fall under the far greater tyranny of communism, and he tends to identify communism with indigenous left-wing movements, thereby consciously or unconsciously identifying liberalism with, for example, the Emirs of Northern

Nigeria. . . . His moral worries about forms of government in African countries are unevenly distributed along the political spectrum.[2]

Western liberals, including social democratic politicians, verbally condemn apartheid in South Africa, as they did the rule of white racists in Rhodesia, but the British Labour Government did not send in troops when the white racists staged their rebellion in 1965, nor does the liberal West operate effective sanctions against South Africa. They preach to others the virtues of peace and non-violence, but liberals and social democrats in both Europe and America widely supported the American war in Vietnam, at least until it became clear that the USA could not win. This may be a biased and jaundiced view of the moral and political character of contemporary Western liberalism, but it appears less so from vantage points outside the West, and it is widely held, even by some people in the West: 'Liberal values, tarnished by the spurious tributes of the rich world's media, today make the rich world yawn and the poor world sick.'[3]

In the West, too, authoritarian tendencies are gaining strength, as they have done in earlier periods of capitalist crisis, and a period of liberal political equilibrium has come to an end. The immense preponderance of economic power on which regimes of relative freedom and tolerance were founded has vanished, and the harsher climate in which capitalism now fights to hold 'its own' may not indefinitely allow what many people now ominously refer to as the 'luxury' of political freedom. Attempts to place, or replace, severe restrictions on trade unions and on working-class industrial action are the most obvious sign of this new situation. The revival of liberal economics has been conspicuously *not* accompanied by any comparable commitment to liberal politics: the 'free' economy is, in a seeming paradox, tied to the strong state.[4]

So liberalism and liberal institutions appear to be in retreat, most plainly in the non-Western world, but also in the West itself. Should we then conclude that liberalism is dead, and therefore that any study of liberalism must of necessity be an obituary or epitaph, melancholy or triumphant according to the political inclination of its author?

This would be premature, I think. It is obvious, first of all, that liberalism as an issue is far from dead. No creed or doctrine could attract the kind of fierce, vital hostility which liberalism often stimulates were it a complete anachronism. Totally dead doctrines — those with no significant hold over people's minds — do not attract that type of hostility. They are simply ignored. No one in the West today would bother to mount a passionate attack on the doctrine of the Divine Right of Kings, or the belief in witches. But people do bother to attack liberalism, from both the Left and the Right. The presumption must be, therefore, that liberalism is alive enough to be worth attacking, or defending.

And this is surely correct. For although liberalism no longer takes the form in most countries of a separately organized political movement, that is partly because it has no need to do so — in the West at least. Its major battles — for certain forms of political freedom and tolerance and for lawful rather than arbitrary government — have been fought and won. And with its crusading days in the past it exists for the most part now as a widely diffused ethos, or ideology — vague and somewhat directionless, no doubt, but nevertheless influential in determining attitudes and outlook at the most fundamental level, the level of assumptions which are so deeply ingrained that they are hardly ever made explicit, or argued for or over.

Here lies both the strength and weakness of contemporary liberalism. Assumptions that are essentially liberal, rather than, say, Christian, or feudal, or socialist or anarchist, lie buried deep in the common social, political and economic attitudes of people in the West. And they are not primarily assumptions of an overtly political nature. As with every major political tradition, at the heart of liberalism lie a number of ontological premises, about the world and about human nature, which determine and underpin the explicitly political values. It is the liberal world-view, rather than that of traditional conservatism or revolutionary socialism, which is the most generally shared in the West today.

Liberalism is the dominant ideology of the West — dominant, not in the sense that it is explicitly and deliberately imposed, as what passes for Marxism is imposed in many communist countries, but in a more subtle, and probably therefore a more effective manner. Liberalism in its contemporary form is not so much a set of ideas or doctrines to which people subscribe by conscious choice; it is a way of seeing the social world, and a set of assumptions about it, which are absorbed by the individual in so natural and gradual a manner that he or she is not conscious of their being assumptions at all. Liberalism makes up a large part of the intellectual air we breathe — so much so that the very word 'intellectual' is misleading if it is taken to mean available only to those who are intellectuals by profession or training. Liberal assumptions are far more widely diffused than that. They are among the commonplaces of our time and society. This is the present stage of what has been a long and complex historical development, for, as Harold Laski rightly said at the opening of *The Rise of European Liberalism*, 'liberalism has been, in the last four centuries, the outstanding doctrine of Western civilisation . . .'[5]

Recently, too, there has been something of a revival of liberal economic philosophy, in the various guises of monetarism, 'Thatcherism' and 'Reaganomics'. This revival is clearly connected with the general crisis which overtook the world capitalist system in the mid-1970s, in which the generally unprecedented combination of inflation with economic decline and high unemployment suggested that the prescriptions of Keynesian or post-Keynesian economic management were no longer working very effectively.

The very fact that this particular current of liberalism has shown itself to have been dormant rather than dead bears witness to the persistence of liberalism. The revised social-democratic version of liberalism, which is suited to capitalism in its periods of growth and stability, yields place to a more oldfashioned, nineteenth-century version of the creed at moments of crisis. At those moments, a robust defence of the old liberal values of property, initiative and 'free enterprise' is what capitalism requires; and the old ideology of *laissez-faire* is there, in a suitably updated form, to meet this need. What this suggests is that so long as capitalism survives, so will liberalism in its various alternative forms.

It is worth considering briefly at this point one or two examples of the pervasiveness of liberal assumptions. Let us consider the concept of the individual. At first glance this looks simple enough: by 'the individual' we mean the single human being. Everyone is an individual, and the term emphasizes the fact that he or she is who he or she is, and not something or someone else. Thus it stresses the uniqueness of each human being, what differentiates one person from another rather than what they have in common with each other. Thus Isaiah Berlin writes of Herder: 'For him men are men, and have common traits at all times; but it is their differences that matter most, for it is the differences that make them what they are, make them themselves, it is in these that the individual genius of men and cultures is expressed.'[6]

But this is already contentious, and tendentious. Why is the essence of a person defined by what she does *not* have in common with others, rather than by what she does? Suppose that someone suggests that 'the individual' is threatened by 'mass society', or that 'there is no room for the individual', in, say, communist China? Or when Virginia Woolf, peering into the 'economical, powerful, and efficient future', sees 'disappearance and the death of the individual'[7] — what does she mean? Clearly they are not saying that people, as people, cease to exist in such societies, but rather that a certain kind or kinds of person cannot exist in such a context. They want to suggest that human diversity is being threatened, that variety and eccentricity and what is (tendentiously again) called 'character' have no scope for expression and expansion in such societies. A speech by the American liberal politician, Adlai Stevenson, Democrat candidate for the presidency in 1952, is typical of this way of thinking about 'the individual': 'What is the nature of the threat which communism brings to the free world? It is the threat of an all-powerful state, dedicated to the extinction of individual dignity, and individual freedom — individualism, in short. To put it more simply, communism is the death of the soul. It is the organisation of total conformity . . .'[8] This is, obviously, very different from talking about the survival of the human being as such. Built into the everyday uses of the term 'the individual' are certain assumptions about the naturalness and rightness of human diversity, and the desirability of allowing deviance and eccentricity to flourish. They are so widely accepted that they lurk concealed and undiscussed beneath the surface of our ordinary, apparently non-ideological language. But they are at least debatable; and the very concept of the individual, which is central to liberalism, is far from being universally accepted and non-contentious. It is, in fact, a comparatively recent historical conceptual development, and an essentially Western one as well. As Colin Morris has pointed out: 'Western individualism is therefore far from expressing the common experience of humanity. Taking a world view, one might almost regard it as an eccentricity among cultures.'[9]

Consider next an obviously value-laden set of terms such as 'free', 'freedom', 'independent', etc. What do people mean when they refer to a 'free press', as something that exists in Britain or the USA, but not in the Soviet Union, or Chile since 1973? They mean that it is free from direct control or censorship by the Government or the state. They certainly do not mean that the press is free from constraints which may be placed upon it by its owners — constraints which, in terms of the opinions which can be expressed and the 'slant' which must be given to news coverage, can be extremely restrictive. Nor do they mean that it is free from the pressures resulting from the financial need to obtain large quantities of advertising. Such pressures undoubtedly exist, and restrict the freedom of editors and journalists. Yet they are not generally seen as negating, or even seriously limiting, the freedom of the press. In this particular everyday instance freedom, which is a general term, is habitually identified with one specific kind of freedom, namely, freedom from the state. And this is an essentially liberal habit of thought, as Professor Maurice Cranston has made clear: 'The liberals were proud to admit that they believed in freedom. But freedom from what? The answer to that question must hold the key to the intelligibility of any sort of liberalism. The answer of the English liberal is unequivocal. By 'freedom' he means *freedom from the constraints of the state.*'[10]

The word 'independent' is frequently used in the same way. 'Independent' television in Britain is not independent of the commercial interests from whose advertising it derives its revenue. But it is seen as independent of the state in a way that the BBC is not; although it is an open question whether the pressures placed upon it by the constant need to satisfy its paymasters the advertisers are more or less restrictive than those inherent in the ambivalent semi-official character of the BBC. The 'independent' schools are so called for the same reason. It is in cases such as this that we can see how the liberal conception of 'freedom' or 'independence' is built into our everyday language so thoroughly that the words used are not seen by most people as being political or ideological or tendentious in any way.

To treat liberalism as an ideology may be controversial, since contemporary liberals sometimes claim it as one of the merits of liberalism that it is non-ideological — and indeed anti-ideological. Those who in the 1950s and early

1960s announced 'the end of ideology' were concerned not merely to proclaim an event — a non-event, as it turned out — but also to celebrate it. But what they understood by ideology was something different and narrower than what is meant here. By ideology they meant an explicit, comprehensive political creed or dogma implying a programme of wholesale political and social change. They intended a contrast between this 'doctrinaire' attitude, which seeks to reshape reality to conform to certain principles or 'dogmas', and a liberal 'empiricism' in politics, which eschews programmes and blueprints, and seeks rather to provide specific remedies for specific evils as and when they occur. Writers like Karl Popper, Isaiah Berlin, J. L. Talmon (a conservative), Bernard Crick, and many others, associated ideology both historically and conceptually, with totalitarianism. Their case against 'ideological' politics had earlier been summed up by E. M. Forster in three words: 'Programmes means pogroms.'[11]

The liberals have successfully popularized this conception of ideology; but it is a much more restricted conception than that developed by Hegel, Marx and the 'classical' theorists of ideology. As a liberal writer on the subject, John Plamenatz, pointed out:

> . . . the word 'ideology' is not used to refer only to explicit beliefs and theories. Those who speak of bourgeois ideology . . . often mean by it beliefs and attitudes implicit in bourgeois ways of speaking and behaving, and sometimes they speak of bourgeois theories and doctrines as if they did little more than make explicit these beliefs and attitudes.[12]

It is in this sense that liberalism can fairly be described as an ideology. By contrast with the liberals' own notion, it is not necessary for ideology thus understood to take the form of an explicit and conscious political creed, or a comprehensive political programme. Indeed it is far more common for ideological assumptions to be concealed and implicit — often so effectively that it is only with the advantage of historical hindsight that they are brought to the surface at all. My examples are intended as a preliminary illustration of how this has happened in the case of liberalism.

This, then, is the strength of liberalism: its rooted pervasiveness. But this is also its weakness. Whereas in the past it was concentrated in a specific political form, today it is diluted and diffused. The very fact that liberal assumptions and attitudes can apparently be shared by conservatives and social democrats bears witness to the dominance of liberalism, but also to the limits of that dominance. Liberal principles no longer provide the main thrust of major political movements and parties. They have been absorbed into other traditions. In the process those traditions have themselves been altered, but liberalism itself has been weakened by amalgamation and dilution. Conservatives and social democrats may protest that they value freedom and tolerance as much as Voltaire or John Stuart Mill, but their order of priorities among political values which inevitably come into competition with each other at times is unlikely to be that of classical liberalism. Despite their protestations, they will be more willing than genuine liberals to sacrifice freedom and tolerance to the (to them) more insistent requirements of order and stability on the one hand, or of equality and rational planning on the other.

The vague unspoken consensus in the West as to the virtues of liberalism has induced complacency. Liberal principles, apparently, do not have to be fought for. Our societies, after all, *are* the liberal democracies. Consequently liberal principles can in practice be steadily and stealthily undermined while the public chorus of self-congratulation rolls on. The very banality of liberalism is what weakens and endangers it. It is a small step from yawning to falling asleep. Liberalism has become, or is in danger of becoming, through its very acceptance, a 'dead dogma' rather than a 'living truth'; and that is a dangerous state for any belief or truth to fall into.

So to the question with which we began we can reply that liberalism is alive, certainly, but judged by the standards of one of its leading protagonists, John Stuart Mill, it is in dubious health. (It was, of course, Mill who suggested in *On Liberty* that any truth which is not discussed and challenged, is likely to end up as a 'dead dogma' rather than a 'living truth'.) Liberalism, in the form of certain widely held ideological assumptions, provides a consensus outlook in the West sufficiently pervasive and persistent to be the object of equally persistent attack; even if its banality, its diffuseness and lack of political edge, look like the tell-tale signs of a doctrine in decay and perhaps retreat. Those who remain firmly committed to liberal principles, even while recognizing their limits and inadequacies, must be anxious about their prospects for survival. If liberalism as a whole is 'bankrupt', nevertheless there are elements which need to be salvaged from the wreckage. Hence an examination of liberalism is more than a purely academic or historical exercise. It is a live political issue. We in the West can hardly avoid the impact of liberalism, and it is therefore important to have the fullest possible understanding of it. This book is intended as a contribution to that process.

ON DEFINING LIBERALISM

So far I have referred to liberalism without defining it. I have traded on the familiarity of the term, as if we know what is meant when liberalism is referred to. But we need a reasonably clear idea of what liberalism is before discussion can go much further. The question of definition is, however, anything but simple. Dictionaries can be called in aid, but they cannot be expected, or indeed allowed, to resolve what are unavoidably complex conceptual and methodological issues.

There is a sense in which any book about liberalism in general is bound to be a book exploring the definition, or the concept of liberalism. This is particularly true of this book. For one of its central contentions is that liberalism should be seen, not in fixed and abstract terms as a collection of unchanging moral and political values, but as a specific historical movement of ideas in the modern era that begins with the Renaissance and the Reformation. As such it has undergone many changes, and requires a historical rather than a purely conceptual and inherently static type of analysis. Hence the picture of liberalism which I want to present should emerge from the historical sketch traced out in the book as a whole.

Nevertheless, to call such a sketch a study of liberalism does imply that there are certain continuities and common threads running through the history. We do not escape all the problems of definition by adopting a predominantly historical approach. But the most common way of defining and discussing political 'isms' tends to focus exclusively on on those common threads, while treating change and development as essentially marginal or superficial. A political doctrine such as liberalism is usually seen in terms of a collection of loosely related moral and political values, or even in terms of a single dominant value. Thus it has been said frequently that socialism is 'about equality', and it has been suggested that liberalism, interpreted 'rather narrowly', can be described as 'the belief in the value of the liberty of the individual'. [13]

To start with definitions as general and abstract as these is an invitation to ahistorical eclecticism. Whenever one of these values, or an exponent of them, crops up in whatever historical context, the episode or the individual is promptly incorporated into the liberal 'tradition', or the 'history' of socialism. This approach can produce some extraordinary results. It is possible to produce entirely serious books with titles like Alexander Gray's *The Socialist Tradition from Moses to Lenin*, [14] although it would be hard to think of two more unlikely political partners; while F. J. C. Hearnshaw traced the ancestry of conservatism back even further, to the Garden of Eden. [15]

In the case of liberalism the attempt to produce unifying generalizations which will cover the variety of particular forms actually taken by the creed has also had some bizarre consequences. Alan Bullock and Maurice Shock, in the Introduction to their anthology of British liberalism, *The Liberal Tradition*, offer 'the belief in freedom and the belief in conscience as the twin foundations of Liberal philosophy and the element of continuity in its historical development'. [16] The oddity of citing 'belief in conscience' as something distinctively liberal is partly explained by the fact that they have in mind the British Liberal Party, which was in some respects the political expression of the Nonconformist conscience in the nineteenth and early twentieth centuries. But the extreme broadness of these 'foundations' reflects the authors' historical awareness that it is easier to see the differences between such diverse figures as Fox, Bentham,

Gladstone, T. H. Green, Lloyd George and Keynes, than to discover what it is that allows us to call them all liberals.

The most blatant example of what might be called the Moses-to-Lenin syndrome is the anthology of liberal utterances put together by Professor J. Salwyn Schapiro.[17] The first two figures in his collection are — Socrates and Peter Abelard! Schapiro explains that 'Liberalism as an attitude towards life — sceptical, experimental, rational, free — was given expression by extraordinary individuals long before the Modern Age' (p. 14). Socrates was 'a notable liberal in ancient times', who also qualifies for inclusion because he was 'a martyr to the cause of intellectual freedom' (p. 94). Then 'in medieval times another liberal voice was heard, that of Peter Abelard' (p. 14).

Given the generality of Schapiro's definition of liberalism as 'an attitude toward life', to call Socrates and Abelard liberals is defensible even if implausible. And it might be objected that it is only the excessive vagueness of the definition that is at fault: all that is needed is a stricter definition. But as the case of Bullock and Shock makes plain, even when you start, not from a definition but from history, the effort to arrive at a sufficiently inclusive formula is still likely to end with generalizations so broad as to be virtually useless. The vagueness is inherent in the approach. It is the habit of defining political doctrines in terms of abstract values that is at fault.

The value-definition approach has two major defects. The first is the failure to connect the values with the world-view which underpins them. For the values themselves are not usually a haphazard collection, but a *set*, whose coherence is derived from the metaphysic or ontology lying behind them. In particular there is at the base of every major political doctrine a distinctive conception of man, or human nature, and a general theory of human society logically related to that conception. It is the failure to perceive, or to bring out, this relationship between values and world-view which is largely responsible for the vagueness and abstractness of the attempted definition. And this is often compounded by a further failure to recognize that the values themselves are not seen by adherents of the doctrine or creed in question as being all of equal importance. They are invariably ranged in an *order* or *hierarchy of importancce*. And it is the *relative* weight given to these values in relation to each other which often distinguishes one political position from another. Liberals and socialists may both claim to believe in freedom and equality, for example. But we cannot conclude from this that they 'really' agree on fundamentals. What matters, and what is likely to divide them, is whether they will give the claims of equality precedence over those of freedom, or vice versa, and how they weigh the claims of these values in relation to other values to which they may also subscribe, such as justice, or security, or the rights of property.

The second defect of the value-orientated approach is one of which some examples have already been given: it can set no realistic historical limits to the doctrine in question. Just because it is seen as a collection of values or principles, it is all too easy to discover its traces in the most unlikely places. Hence we find liberalism being traced backwards as far as Pericles and Democritus, in much the same way as Whig historians used to discover the beginnings of English liberty in Magna Carta, or even in 'that good old constitution which took its root in Saxon times', as Gladstone once called it. [18] Such anachronisms can hardly be avoided unless the abstract values are placed firmly within the context of the theory of man and society which gives the doctrine its power and coherence; and unless the doctrine in turn is situated within its proper historical and social context. This is, in fact, part of what is implied in describing liberalism as an ideology.

Our definition of liberalism must therefore be one which specifically seeks to remedy these two defects of the value-orientated approach. First, then, liberalism *is* more than a set of values. Liberalism is a more coherent, more comprehensive view of the world than many people, including many liberals, have recognized. Its values do not stand on their own metaphysical two feet, as it were, but derive from a theory of human nature and society. And in this respect liberalism simply conforms to the general pattern of the major political doctrines. This relation between political and moral values and ontological or metaphysical theory is not always made plain. Not many political theorists are as systematic as Hobbes, or Bentham (who admired Hobbes). But Bentham makes the structure of the argument clear beyond doubt:

> Nature has placed mankind under the governance of two sovereign masters, *pain* and *pleasure*. It is for them alone to point out what we ought to do, as well as to determine what we shall do. On the one hand the standard of right and wrong, on the other the chain of causes and effects, are fastened to their throne.

The celebrated opening sentences of the *Introduction to the Principles of Morals and Legislation* start the book where it needs to start, with Bentham's conception of human nature, as it is governed by nature as a whole; and it is on this would-be empirical foundation that he constructs his entire utilitarian argument.

It is the lack of comparable explicitness in so many other political thinkers which generates so much scholarly debate as to their conceptions of human nature and of the relation of man to society. But what is significant for our present argument is the assumption underlying the debate — that such conceptions do exist and are crucial to their political theory as a whole. Hence our first task, in developing an adequate conception of liberalism, will be to uncover and describe the theory of man and society which supports the political values of liberalism, and to elucidate those values. The first part of the book is devoted to this. Our second task is to identify the specific historical character of liberalism as a movement of ideas and as an ideology — to place liberalism in its proper historical context, tracing the evolution of liberal ideas, noting both the changes and the continuities within the overall tradition. This is what the second and larger part of the book is about.

2

The Foundations of Liberal Individualism

The metaphysical and ontological core of liberalism is individualism. It is from this premise that the familiar liberal commitments to freedom, tolerance and individual rights are derived. As has already been noted, liberals do not have a monopoly of commitment to these values. They do not belong exclusively to the tradition of modern liberalism. Bhikhu Parekh has pointed out that 'As with any body of beliefs, many of its basic values long preceded its birth.' But, he went on, 'What distinguishes Liberalism and makes it a unique 'historical individual' is not its belief in these values but the way it redefines and rearranges them within the bourgeois individualistic conception of man.'[1] Individualism is a familiar term, but not a self-explanatory one. The word has not one, but several meanings, albeit related and overlapping.[2] Liberal individualism is both ontological and ethical. It involves seeing the individual as primary, as more 'real' or fundamental than human society and its institutions and structures. It also involves attaching a higher moral value to the individual than to society or to any collective group. In this way of thinking the individual comes *before* society in every sense. He is more real than society. In the quasi-historical theories of the social contract developed by Hobbes, Locke, Paine, and others, he is seen as existing before society temporally as well. Finally, his rights and demands come morally before those of society. And ontological individualism provides a philosophical basis for ethical and political individualism. (The male emphasis, on 'man', 'mankind', etc., has usually been more than a verbal habit. Women have, until comparatively recently, been generally regarded as not full 'individuals'. This is one of the term's many half-concealed difficulties.)

As we have already seen, the concept of 'the individual' is both ambiguous and question-begging. Meaning at its simplest no more than 'the single human being', there is almost invariably an additional weight of emphasis on the aspect of singleness, on what separates or distinguishes one person from another, rather than on what one person has in common with his or her fellow human beings. The concept itself leans towards seeing the single human being in isolation, with society or the universe treated as background or context. It tends therefore to impute a high degree of completeness and self-sufficiency to the single human being, with the implication that separateness, autonomy is the fundamental, metaphysical human condition. To the liberal this looks like an inescapable fact:

> . . . as for individualism — there seems no way of getting off this, even if one wanted to. The dictator-hero can grind down his citizens till they are all alike but he cannot melt them into a single man. That is beyond his power. He can order them to merge, he can incite them to mass-antics, but they are obliged to be born separately, and to die separately. . . . The memory of birth and the expectation of death always lurk within the human being, making him separate from his fellows and consequently capable of intercourse with them.[3]

Significantly, though, this theme of birth and death, which Forster interprets as proof of the separateness of human beings, prompted quite the opposite reflections in John Donne three centuries earlier. He saw death as an event which brings human beings together in a common realization of their common fate: 'any man's *death* diminishes *me*, because I am involved in Mankinde . . .'; and 'that privat and *retirid* man, that thought himselfe his owne for ever, and never came forth, must in his dust of the grave bee published and (such are the *revolutions* of the *graves*) bee mingled with the dust of every high way, and of every dunghill. . . .'[4]

FACTS AND VALUES:
THE SEPARATION OF 'MAN' FROM THE WORLD

Writing in the early seventeenth century, Donne was implicitly opposing the rising tide of individualistic thought at that time. For Donne was a contemporary of Francis Bacon. And if individualism stresses the separateness of person from person, it also stresses the separateness of man from the natural world, thus reflecting the development of the orthodox outlook of modern science. What is important in the scientific outlook for the individualistic theory of morals is the stress on the moral neutrality of the world of scientific facts, as well as the concept of the person as the detached observer of those facts. For if the world of facts, the world studied by science, is devoid of (or deprived of) any moral dimension, what happens to morality? Where do values go when they are excluded from the empirical world of science? The answer of modern liberal moral theory is that they become a matter of individual choice and commitment. Iris Murdoch has vividly summarized this process: ' "Value" does not belong inside the world of truth functions, the world of science and factual propositions. So it must live somewhere else. It is then attached somehow to the human will, a shadow clinging to a shadow.'; and 'Values which were previously inscribed in some sense inscribed in the heavens collapse into the human will. There is no transcendent reality. The idea of the good remains indefinable and empty so that the human choice may fill it.'[5]

It would be perfectly consistent with acceptance of the fact/value distinction to allow a church or a religion the prerogative of deciding in matters of morality. However, the rise of modern science was paralleled by — and connected with — the development of a religious individualism which claimed that each should follow, not the decrees of an external, institutional religious authority, but the inner voice of God speaking directly to him through his conscience. In the secularized form of protestantism which has now largely replaced the Christian version it is conscience alone — although no longer the voice of God — which retains its pre-eminence. In principle at least, liberalism respects the moral obligations, and hence the moral right, of the individual to follow the dictates of his or her own conscience — so long as the consequences are not too drastically anti-social.

So the liberal conception of the moral life is essentially individualistic. Values are not woven into the fabric of the universe, as they had been by Aristotelianism and medieval Christianity. Nor can they be laid down by any form of traditional or institutional authority, whether secular or religious. From the beginning liberalism disputes the right of priests or kings to force conscience. The individual must choose his values for himself, and construct his own morality. Certainly he should do this in a rational manner. Like the scientist, he should assess the factual situation as objectively as possible. But the facts cnanot, and will not, tell him what he ought to do. If he believes that they do, that is because he has confused fact and value, and that is logically inadmissible. Between the facts and the moral evaluation of facts there lies a gulf which no logic can bridge. A starving child crying for food, a wounded man screaming in agony — these are facts. But to say that they are bad facts, as most people would, is not to describe them, but to evaluate them. To say that someone is starving is to say nothing about whether that is a good thing or a bad thing. That is a matter for the moral judgement of the individual, and in such matters disagreement is always in principle possible. If there is a disagreement as to whether the child is starving, or whether it is in pain, those are issues which can in principle be resolved by empirical investigation. But no amount of investigation will resolve the question of whether starvation is to be called good or bad. That is not a question of fact, but of value or moral judgement. Hume's argument in Book III of *A Treatise of Human Nature* is essentially similar to this; and to it he appends his celebrated observation about the disjunction between 'is' statements and 'ought' statements. This is an elaboration of the fact/value distinction in terms of linguistic analysis, and since these terms are so congenial to contemporary philosophy, Hume's observation, like the fact/value distinction itself, has become part of the orthodoxy of modern liberal philosophy. This development in itself reflects the historical growth of individualism and the increasing atomization of bourgeois societies in the early modern period. Alasdair MacIntyre has written, with reference to Hume, that 'as shared ideals and accepted functions drop away in the age of individualism, the injunctions (of morality, that is) have less and less backing. The end of this process is the appearance of a ''You ought . . .'' unbacked by reasons, announcing traditional moral rules in a vacuum so far as ends are concerned, and addressed to an unlimited class of persons.'[6]

The distinction between facts and values is important to liberalism in two ways. First it enables liberal moral theory to coexist with science and positivism. Indeed it is sometimes claimed that more than mere compatibility is achieved. It is argued that liberal moral theory is as scientific as it is possible for such a theory to be, since, like science itself, it insists on a respect for the facts. Objectivity is a requirement of morality as it is of science. It is the duty of the individual, when forming a moral judgement or opinion, first of all to observe, assemble and examine the facts in exactly the way that a scientist would do. And he or she should also take the greatest care to allow no taint of evaluation to infect the factual description of the situation. If this essentially scientific method is followed, it should be possible for all concerned to agree on the facts of the situation, and thus narrow the area of potential disagreement down to the question of evaluation. Such an approach will greatly increase the chances of reaching a moral consensus, since many apparently moral disagreements spring from ignorance of the full facts, and will therefore disappear when a more rational and scientific approach to the formation of moral judgement is widely adopted.[7]

Liberal morality can be made still more empirical and scientific if the fundamental premises of utilitarianism are accepted: namely, that human behaviour is basically determined by human desires and appetites, and that the wisest and most realistic course is to recognize, and accept, that each person calls 'good' what he or she desires. If the moral legitimacy of human desires and aversions is accepted, then, as Bentham saw, the substantial problems of morality are reduced to two: the weight or importance of one desire or aversion relative to others, and the adjustment of each person's satisfaction to those of all the others. Given the possibility of translating all desires and aversions into terms of sensations of pleasure and pain, then both of these questions become matters for essentially empirical and quantifiable calculations. And that is what the bulk of Bentham's *Introduction to the Principles of Morals and Legislation* is given over to, once the matter of first principles has been — fairly briskly — disposed of. The sovereignty of felt personal desires is also an important part of liberal individualism, as we shall see.

The second way in which the supposed fact/value distinction plays a key role in liberal moral theory is in the support it provides for the idea of the moral autonomy of the individual. One condition of this autonomy is that the individual is not required or expected to accept the moral decrees of institutions, whether religious or secular. The other condition is that the individual's judgement is not restricted by any moral implications inherent in the facts themselves. Facts are facts, and no more. They do not have in themselves a moral dimension which can limit the independence of the moral choices and commitments made by the individual: 'there is a picture of the individual standing before the historical events of his time, able to pass judgment on them exactly as he pleases. His values are for him to choose; the facts in no way constrain him.'[8] In this way, as MacIntyre has pointed out, liberal morality differs from both Marxism and traditional Christianity, which share the belief that questions about the nature of the world and of human beings have to be asked and answered before it is possible to answer the question 'But how ought I to live?'[9]

For the liberal this is to confuse facts with values. And that, he argues, is not only illogical; it is also morally and politically sinister, because it represents an attempt to shift the load of moral responsibility from the shoulders of individuals (which is where it belongs) onto such inanimate entities as nature and history. This lightening of the burdens carried by the individual conscience can then make it that much easier for the dictator, the party or the totalitarian regime to commit their terrible crimes against humanity. For they will argue that these crimes express, not the will of responsible individuals, but the necessities of God, or nature or history. Hence moral theories which deny or limit the responsibility of the individual are politically as well as logically objectionable. Both the logical, and moral and political cases against such theories are passionately set out by a representative contemporary liberal writer, Isaiah Berlin, in his well-known lecture-essay on 'Historical Inevitability'.

Existentialism, too, objects to any attempt to shift moral responsibility away from the individual. Within the moral philosophy of Sartre in his early existentialist phase such attempts are seen as classic examples of bad faith, of the kind of self-deception through which men and women try to conceal from themselves the inescapable existential necessity of making their own moral choices: 'Since we have defined the situation of man as one of free choice, without excuse and without help, any man who takes refuge behind the excuse of his passions, or by inventing some deterministic doctrine, is a self-deceiver.'[10] Existentialism carries the emphasis on the individualistic character of the moral life to its furthest point, where even the Kantian notion of moral rules is rejected. Sartrian existentialism places a far greater stress on the absolute uniqueness of each moral dilemma faced by the individual. This uniqueness makes it impossible to generalize in the way required by neo-Kantian morality: 'No rule of general morality can show you what you ought to do: no signs are vouchsafed in this world.'[11] The burden of choice placed on the individual is thereby increased still further, since we are unlikely to find in the choices of others any useful guidance in our own individual dilemmas. This it was that led Burke, who had the normal conservative's conviction of human weakness, to place so much stress on the value of tradition, habit and prejudice as guides to action, easing the burden of choice in particular situations.

At first sight it may seem odd to link liberalism and existentialism, particularly to Anglo-Saxons, who are apt to see a great difference in styles of thought between their own supposedly practical and empirical liberalism, and the grandiose metaphysics of continental strains such as phenomenology and existentialism. However the often unsystematic character of Anglo-Saxon liberalism does not always disguise the fact that its basic assumptions have much in common with existentialism. Hence Albert Camus's synthesis of existentialism with political liberalism in *L'Homme Revolté (The Rebel)* presents far fewer problems than Sartre's attempts to integrate existentialism and Marxism.

Existentialism from Kierkegaard and Dostoevsky to Heidegger and Sartre, can be seen as in many respects part of a prolonged revolt against positivism and the hegemony of the scientific outlook. Nevertheless some versions of existentialism accept the positivist division between the human world of (essentially subjective) values and the non-human world of objective facts. Indeed Sartre's novel *Nausea* insists quite brutally on the absolute indifference of the non-human world to human hopes, fears and feelings. Part of the misery of Roquentin, the novel's central figure, is that the normal consolations of anthropomorphism are inaccessible to him. He is not merely alienated from both his fellow human beings and the natural world. He actually experiences the latter in particular as overwhelming him by its omnipresence and so threatening his very identity. His experience can be seen as the dark side, or nightmare, of modern positivism; just as Pascal's famous observation: 'The eternal silence of these infinite spaces frightens me', expresses the agony of the religious man contemplating a universe which, in Lucien Goldmann's words, 'has ceased to present the existence of God as either certain or probable.'[12] The astronomers, followed later by Newton, had finally banished the old interventionist God of signs and miracles, leaving a universe which was marvellously rational but morally and spiritually a void. And so, for Pascal, human dignity necessarily consists in the capacity for thought, since in every other respect we are dwarfed by the spatial and temporal dimensions of the world which science had revealed: 'in point of space the universe embraces me and swallows me up like a mere point: in thought, I embrace the universe.'[13]

The moral emptiness of the world constitutes the metaphysical gulf which lies beneath liberal morality. Consciousness of this gulf has increasingly haunted liberalism as positivist confidence has waned. But for the most part liberalism has seen in the separation of human values from scientific facts only a great rational achievement, and hence a source of pride. What may now appear as one aspect of the alienation of man from the natural world, was and is still seen by liberalism and positivism as part of the triumph of the rational and scientific outlook over the backward anthropomorphism of primitive super-stitions and obscurantist religion.

THE ISOLATION OF HUMAN BEINGS FROM EACH OTHER

The isolation of the individual from nature implicit or explicit in the liberal conception of morality is compounded within liberalism by a similar isolation of each human being from his/her fellows. Each of us is, as Forster suggested, ultimately alone, above all before the fearful fact of death. This separateness is again most vividly expressed in the novels of modern existentialism, such as *Nausea*, and Camus's extended soliloquies, *The Outsider* and *The Fall*. The separate floating consciousness of the various figures — they are hardly *characters* — in Virginia Woolf's *The Waves* convey much the same impression. This is the fiction of solipsism, in which the characters seem to be imprisoned within their own heads. These novels may be taken as representing the individualism which was inherent in the novel from its beginnings pushed to its furthest point, the point at which it threatens to 'finish off the novel', to borrow a phrase from Cyril Connolly, by dissolving its essential social dimension. Woolf, it is fair to point out, was well aware of the dangers inherent in her chosen method, writing in her diary: 'I see immense possibilities in the form I hit upon more or less by chance two weeks ago. I suppose the danger is the damned egotistical self; which ruins Joyce and [Dorothy] Richardson to my mind. . .' [14]

But for all that the concept of the individual has always been central to the novel as a form. With a few recent exceptions, as well as some novels by the revolutionary socialist writer Victor Serge — which may be a pointer to the future of fiction — it is hard to think of many novels which do not hinge on the possibility of singling out individual men and women and tracing their development and experience in some degree or other separately from the collective history of their society or community. In the novel society provides the 'setting', and the changes in the personal, social and financial fortunes of individuals provide the theme. 'Leaving home, improving on the lot one was born to, is a vital feature of the individualist pattern of life' writes Ian Watt — and hence a central feature of the novel itself. [15] The emergence of the novel reflects the development of a society in which individual social mobility was a key experience. And from the beginning too there is a tendency to abstract the individual from the social context, and thus to emphasize his proud self-sufficiency and defiant aloneness.

Defoe's *Robinson Crusoe* is one of the first classic examples of this tendency.

To mention the novel and its links with the growth of social mobility may serve to remind us that individualism is, historically, a comparatively recent development, and one for which a word was not found until the early nineteenth century. As de Tocqueville observed: 'That word "individualism", which we have coined for our own requirements, was unknown to our ancestors, for the good reason that in their days every individual necessarily belonged to a group and no one could regard himself as an isolated unit.'[16] No doubt de Tocqueville was over-simplifying. He was naturally inclined to romanticize the stability and integration of pre-revolutionary society. Nevertheless, he was right to connect the concept of the individual with the increasing atomization of society.

Until the later medieval period it was usual to see human beings as incorporated within society and the order of the natural and supernatural worlds. The concept of society or a community as a body is, of course, a metaphor. To Bentham it was therefore also a fiction: 'The community is a fictitious *body*, composed of the individual persons who are considered as constituting as it were its *members*.'[17] 'As it were' — Bentham had a sharp eye for a tendentious metaphor. But there was no degree of make-believe in this way of thinking for classical Greeks or medieval Christians. For them this metaphor expressed a fundamental truth about the structure of the world and man's place within it. The pattern of the relationship between the physical body and its members was one expression of what was the proper and natural relationship intended by nature or God to subsist between society and the single human beings who belonged to it. What this implied was that each person on his or her own was radically incomplete and inadequate. Like limbs, they only achieved life as parts of a larger whole.[18] Aristotle is absolutely explicit on the question of self-sufficiency. The normal human being is not self-sufficient. Any being that is, and 'needs nothing from the state', like a god, cannot be part of the community at all. Hence autonomy for the individual human being was not an ideal, because it was not seen as possible, let alone desirable. Wholeness and completeness belonged to the community, the *polis*, not to the separate human being, whose dependence upon others and upon society was recognized and accepted.

Here then, in the central tradition of thought of classical Greece and medieval Christianity, especially in the neo-Aristotelian form associated with Thomas Aquinas, we have a way of seeing man and man's relation to society which is clearly opposed to that of individualism. The same is true of Burke's type of conservatism, as epitomized in his famous sentence: 'individuals pass like shadows; but the commonwealth is fixed and stable.' The contrast helps to bring out the distinctive character of modern Western individualism. For Aristotle it is axiomatic that the community is by its nature prior to the individual. For modern liberalism the opposite axiom holds good. And this fundamental difference of perspective affects every aspect of liberalism — its conception of human nature, of the relation of man to society, its social goals and political values, and finally its practical policies and specific choices.

THE SEPARATED CONSCIOUSNESS

Just as the separation of 'man' from nature finds its philosophical form in the separation of facts from values and of 'is' from 'ought', so the separateness of human beings from each other also finds philosophical expression — in the philosophy which makes the experience of the individual the ultimate touchstone of truth. Montaigne was one of the first to express not merely a curiosity about, but also a faith in the value of his own experience, and Montaigne has since become a prominent figure in the liberal pantheon. But it was Descartes who first gave systematic philosophical expression to this position. He decided that the one thing he could not doubt was that he existed as a thinking entity capable of entertaining doubt. It is the existence of the thinking being, or soul, of which Descartes is most certain. He has greater difficulty in convincing himself of his existence as a bodily being. In his scepticism about the knowledge that can be derived from sense-experience, and in his emphasis on the critical role of the mind, or understanding, in testing the validity of this knowledge, Descartes proclaims himself a rationalist. And the distinction betwen rationalism and empiricism with its belief in sense-experience as the prime source of knowledge, is philosophically of great importance.

Nevertheless we find that for Descartes, as for the empiricists, the starting point in constructing a theory of knowledge or truth is the experience of the single individual. Guarantees of truth offered to the individual from outside by society or by a church are no longer to be relied on. Philosophy shares in the liberal individualist revolt against the authority of kings and priests. Henceforth the individual's own experience provides the touchstone by which the validity of theories old and new are to be tested.

It is striking to find Sartre, more than three centuries after Descartes, taking the *cogito* as his starting-point for the development of the existentialist philosophy of *Being and Nothingness*,[19] and reasserting this in the brief account given in *Existentialism and Humanism*:

Our point of departure is, indeed, the subjectivity of the individual; and that for strictly philosophic reasons. . . . And at the point of departure there cannot be any other truth than this, *I think, therefore I am*, which is the absolute truth of consciousness as it attains to itself. . . . Before there can be any truth whatever, then, there must be absolute truth, and there is such a truth which is simple, easily attained and within the reach of everybody; it consists in one's immediate sense of one's self.[20]

Sartre, however, follows Husserl in arguing that all consciousness is consciousness *of* something,[21] and thus he escapes the danger of solipsism which lurks behind Descartes' *cogito*: I may be convinced of my own existence but how can I be equally convinced of the existence of others? But for all that it may be said that solipsism, the imprisonment within the self experienced by Sartre's own Roquentin, is an endemic threat in a philosophy which places so much stress on the isolated consciousness of the single individual — just as cosmic emptiness is the nightmare of positivism.

Locke, the most influential of empiricist philosophers, is less troubled by the problem of certainty than Descartes, or at least treats it less penetratingly, for he more or less takes for granted exactly what Descartes had arrived at only through deep questioning:

> As for our own existence, we perceive it so plainly and so certainly, that it neither needs nor is capable of any proof. For nothing can be more evident to us than our own existence. . . . If I doubt of all other things, that very doubt makes me perceive my own existence, and will not suffer me to doubt that. . . . Experience then convinces us, that we have an *intuitive knowledge* of our own existence, and an internal infallible perception that we are.[22]

Of our own existence we can be sure. It is a matter of intuitive certainty. But what of the existence of other things, not to say other beings, outside ourselves? The danger of solipsism bulks even larger in Locke's epistemology than it does in Descartes', for Locke argues that the mind can know nothing directly, but only through the medium of its own ideas. How can we be sure that these ideas correspond to the existence of real objects in the real world, particularly when it is possible to have ideas, or mental impressions, such as dreams and hallucinations, which clearly are not the direct transmissions of external realities?

> whether there be anything more than barely that idea in our minds, whether we can thence certainly infer the existence of anything without us, which corresponds to that idea, is that whereof some men think there may be a question made; because men may have such ideas in their minds, when no such thing exists, no such object affects their senses (Book IV, ch. 2, p. 14).

This is a real difficulty, but it is clear from his tone that Locke is determined to brush it aside. 'Some men' may think 'there may be a question made' of it;

but not Locke, who at this point simply resorts to bluff common sense and rhetorical questions: 'For I ask any one, whether he be not invincibly conscious to himself of a different perception, when he looks on the sun by day, and thinks on it by night; when he actually tastes wormwood, or smells a rose, or only thinks on that savour or odour.' The philosophical feebleness of this is significant, but it is less important to our argument than the fact that at this crucial point in his argument Locke places all his reliance upon the individual's own senses — and sense. In the *Essay Concerning Human Understanding*, empirical sense-experience is added to Cartesian individualism and the rational certainties of logic and mathematics. There are then, on Locke's account, three kinds of knowledge; our intuitive knowledge of our own existence, the demonstrative knowledge of logical thought, and sensory knowledge of the external world.

Empiricism reinforces individualism because it argues that the first source of each person's knowledge of the world is his or her own senses. Of course that sense experience will be supplemented and corrected by the accumulated experience of others and by the rational, organizing activities of the mind. Or, as Bacon put it: 'It is the duty and virtue of all knowledge to abridge the infinity of individual experience, as much as the conception of truth will permit. . .'[23] But theories, hypotheses, principles and what Locke terms 'maxims' should not command 'our blind assent'. We should 'take care that the name of *principles* deceive us not, nor impose on us, by making us receive that for an unquestionable truth, which is really at best but a very doubtful conjecture'. Such general propositions about the world should be tested by reference to sense-experience, for 'No existence of anything without us, but only of God, can certainly be known further than our senses informs us.' The evidence of the senses is a sure touchstone, for whatever we may *want* to see or perceive, 'what a man sees, he cannot but see; and what he perceives, he cannot but know that he perceives.'[24] The 'true way' of arriving at the truth, says Bacon, is to derive 'axioms from the senses and particulars, rising by a gradual and unbroken ascent, so that it arrives at the most general axioms last of all.'[25] Have faith in your own experience of the world, and be healthily sceptical of traditional wisdom and accepted truths — they may only be prejudices. Baconian and Lockean empiricism implies both a confidence in the individual's experience and powers of reasoning, and a corresponding lack of deference to the authority of tradition. What was originally a Protestant individualism is here given a philosophical shape and basis.

LIBERALISM AND SCIENCE

Like the fact/value distinction, confidence in individual experience and the empiricist method of testing general propositions by experiment and comparison with personal sense-experience, serve to align liberal individualism with the outlook and principles of modern science. Indeed, it is often claimed by liberals that among political movements liberalism enjoys a unique affinity with science. It is argued that liberalism embodies the scientific approach and extends it to the realm of politics. Thus Leszek Kolakowski has written that according to 'the classical liberal conception of the university' one of its tasks is 'the teaching and spreading of certain values that are applicable not only in scientific matters, but in all fields of social life, including the political: these values include impartiality in judgement, tolerance, criticism, obedience to logical rules.'[26] Science is committed to reason, questioning, criticism and the advance of knowledge through trial-and-error experiments. Liberalism represents the application of these rational and pragmatic methods to the ordering and government of human society. This is the argument of Karl Popper in both *The Open Society and Its Enemies* and *The Poverty of Historicism*.[27] And the same case is put more succinctly in an essay, 'Philosophy and Politics', by Bertrand Russell, which owes something to Popper's arguments:

> The essence of the Liberal outlook lies not in *what* opinions are held, but in *how* they are held: instead of being held dogmatically, they are held tentatively, and with a consciousness that new evidence may at any moment lead to their abandonment. This is the way in which opinions are held in science, as opposed to the way in which they are held in theology. . . . The scientific outlook, accordingly, is the intellectual counterpart of what is, in the practical sphere, the outlook of Liberalism.

And of Locke he says: 'Both in intellectual and practical matters he stood for order without authority; this might be taken as the motto both of science and of Liberalism.'[28] These claims for a 'special relationship' between liberalism and science are open to criticism on several grounds. But historically it is undoubtedly true that the growth of modern science and the emergence of liberalism are overlapping developments; and several of the most important philosophers and writers of the seventeenth century, such as Bacon, Descartes, Hobbes, Spinoza and Locke, make major contributions to both traditions. Empiricism, the weight given to individual experience, and the scientific picture of the world as a neutral, value-free collection of facts — these are elements common to both traditions.

The atomistic assumption is also ubiquitous. It is an ontological conception as well as a simply physical one. At one level the world is seen as composed of discrete particles of matter. At another it is seen as a collection of distinct and separable facts and events. As Bacon put it: 'nothing exists in nature except individual bodies, exhibiting clear individual effects, according to particular laws, . . .'[29] Hobbes, too, held that there was 'nothing in the world

Universall but Names', for the things themselves, grouped under general names 'are every one of them individual and singular'.[30] Leibniz gave the most powerful philosophical expression to this outlook in his theory of monads. These, according to him, were the 'true atoms of nature'. These are the 'simple substances' from which the compound phenomena of the world are built up. They are impregnable and immune to attack or impact from outside themselves. They are absolutely self-contained: 'they have within themselves a certain perfection; they have a certain self-sufficiency which makes them the sources of their internal activities, and, so to speak, incorporeal automata.'[31] It is not difficult to see here an exact philosophical analogue to the liberal ideal of the individual person, who either is, or ought to be, self-sufficient and the source of his or her own activities exactly as Leibniz's monads are. Philosophical atomism is reflected in the conception of society as a collection of separate self-moving individuals — human monads, or would-be monads, depending on whether you take the view of Hobbes and Bentham, or the view of Spinoza.

SELF-POSSESSION

It is a short step from the notion of self-containment to that of self-possession, using the term here not in its usual sense, but with its liberal meaning of owning oneself. Ideas of ownership and property figure largely in political and economic liberalism, of course. What is still more striking is that they should penetrate so deeply into the liberal philosophy of the self. From the seventeenth century onwards we find expressions of the central belief of possessive individualism, the idea that a man's life 'belongs' to himself. It is his property, to do with as he likes, not the property of God, or society, or the state. (The masculine idiom is particularly appropriate here, since it did not occur to anyone except a few radicals and 'extremists' that such principles might also apply to female human beings.)

This possessive aspect of individualism has become so much of a commonplace that, like the body and members metaphor to which Bentham drew attention, we hardly realize that this is a metaphorical way of speaking, let alone sense anything odd in talking of life, and work, as forms of property. As C. B. Macpherson has shown, this idea of the individual as proprietor of himself is explicit in Locke: 'Man (by being Master of himself, and *Proprietor of his own Person*, and the actions or *Labour* of it) had still in himself *the great Foundation of Property*.'[32] Nor was Locke the first to articulate this idea. Richard Overton, the Leveller pamphleteer, had said much the same thing more than 30 years earlier.[33]

Thus to possess material property is really the expression in concrete terms of that ownership which we already have of ourselves and our 'own' actions and industry, and even the man who owns no material property still 'owns' his body, skills and labour.

THE SOVEREIGNTY OF DESIRES

Finally, in our rough sketch of the philosophical foundations of liberal individualism, we must enquire what resources are available to the individual to enable him to achieve the autonomy and self-sufficiency which feature within liberalism as both the natural and the ideal state of the single person. I think the answer to such an enquiry falls into two parts. First, the liberal conception of human nature sees human beings as driven actively from within by the natural energy of innate desires and appetites. And second, the individual is guided in the pursuit of the gratification of these desires and appetites by the crucial faculty of reason, which is in some degree, the universal possession of human beings. Let us consider first the liberal view of human desires.

The desires or appetites which animate the individual are not mere passive wishes, or faint aspirations of the 'it would be nice if . . .' type. They are power-ful enough to set the individual off in pursuit of satisfaction. They are what make human beings active rather than passive, creatures in movement rather than at rest. This is particularly clear in Hobbes: 'Life it selfe is but Motion, and can never be without Desire . . .'; and 'to have no Desire, is to be Dead . . .';[34] but it is also a fundamental assumption in Hume and Bentham, and is, indeed, one of the commonplaces of the eighteenth century. The action and behaviour of the individual is naturally inspired by passions, appetites and desires which are fundamentally selfish, in that the individual naturally seeks his or her own happiness, pleasure and gratification. Here is the source of the dynamics of human action.

The idea of human desire acquires an exceptional strength within the liberal conception of human nature. For Hobbes, Hume and Bentham they enjoy a kind of sovereign independence which places them outside the province of morality. Desires are essentially given and unalterable facts of human nature to which morality must accommodate itself. For Bentham what a person desires is therefore by definition good — for that person at least. Hobbes takes much the same view,[35] and such is the strength, in his view, of the most basic and widespread human appetites that the business of both morality and politics must be restricted to ensuring that men, in pursuit of their own satisfactions, do not produce a chaos of insecurity in which their own aims are totally frustrated. There has to be regulation of the incipient conflicts between these atomic individuals each intent on his own gratification. The desires of each have an equal legitimacy with the desires of every other. But laws and rules must be devised which prevent people from pursuing their own satisfactions at the expense of others, and they must be penalized when they do. These are the necessities of civilized life; they derive from the principle of the equality of rights of individuals. They do not imply any criticism of the desires themselves. In the twentieth century Freud has outlined a similar conflict between basic human instincts and their need for gratification, and the fundamental requirements of civilization, which is founded necessarily on the repression of those same instincts. [36]

Desires are taken as given. This assumption is also embodied in the structure of liberal economics, in which 'revealed preferences', as expressed in the market in terms of what people buy and what they will pay, are taken as given and beyond discussion; it being the business of the market simply to minister to those preferences:

> Observable market behaviour will show what an individual chooses. Preference is just what the individual under discussion prefers; there is no value judgement involved. Yet, as the argument goes on, it is clear that it is a Good Thing for the individual to have what he prefers.

But, as Joan Robinson goes on to point out, in reality the issue is not so simple: 'drug-fiends should be cured; children should go to school. How do we decide what preferences should be respected and what restrained unless we judge the preferences themselves?' [37]

Liberalism which, as we have seen, likes to identify itself with the critical, questioning, sceptical outlook, adopts a strikingly uncritical and unquestioning attitude towards the desires. It seldom asks where those desires come from, or how they may have been formed. The complex processes and experiences through which a child is adapted and adapts itself to the demands and limitations of a particular culture and society — the whole process of socialization — is generally ignored by liberal theory. Implicitly it assumes that a person's desires, wishes and aspirations are simply *there*, a part of a man's or woman's fundamental nature. This, too, has been incorporated in liberal economic theory: 'For Jevons, and in his less cautious moments for Marshall, the consumer is 'a man' a Robinson Crusoe, an individual with his tight, impermeable, insulated equipment of desires and tastes.' [38] But this picture, too, owes more to myth than to reality. To portray beings whose desires and tastes derive wholly from their own characters, and are formed independently of every external pressure, is to portray beings who are impervious to education and upbringing, to culture and customs, history and fashion, to say nothing of that whole industry of advertising and public relations which has been created specifically for the purpose of moulding tastes and awakening latent desires. The implausibility of this needs, for the time being, no further comment.

Nor has liberalism usually accepted the possibility of a gap between people's

'real' or fundamental desires and aspirations and their expressed desires —
that is those desires which are clearly reflected in their actions and choices,
and, to a lesser extent, in their words. For actions speak louder than words
to the empirical liberal, let alone speculations about what people *might* want
under certain other ideal (and therefore unlikely) circumstances. For liberals,
people's apparent desires are also their real desires and should be respected
as such. Translated into terms of buyable commodities, these desires are then
seen as dominating the market economy. Today most 'moderate' liberals would
have some doubts about the market as a full and undistorting mirror of human
preferences. But this loss of confidence has not led to any more extensive
rethinking about the relation between expressed preferences and possibly hidden
hopes and aspirations. Liberals remain suspicious of any more general attempt
to discredit the reliability of expressed desires as indicators of basic aspirations.
It is still axiomatic for liberalism that people do know, and can express, what
they want and what is in their own interest. Any suggestion to the contrary
is treated not only as non-empirical, but also as potentially elitist and anti-
democratic. Bentham made the point with his usual directness: 'Generally
speaking, there is no one who knows what is for your interest so well as yourself
— no one who is disposed with so much ardour and constancy to pursue it.'
John Stuart Mill was content to follow in his steps, and endorse

> the popular dictum, that people understand their own business and their
> own interests better, and care for them more, than the government does,
> or can be expected to do. This maxim holds true throughout the greatest
> part of the business of life, and wherever it is true we ought to condemn
> every kind of government intervention that conflicts with it. [39]

Who has the right to suggest that people 'really' want something other than
what they say and think they want? It is, in Berlin's words, a 'monstrous
impersonation'. Each individual must be taken as the most reliable judge of
his or her own desires. Once that principle is abandoned the way is open to
the despotism of some kind of enlightened minority which claims to know better
than people themselves what it is they really want and yearn for. [40]

So the liberal faith in the individual's ability to know and express his own
desires is a political and not merely philosophical issue. And so, therefore, is
the liberal suspicion of any intellectual developments which question this, or
suggest that the social conditioning of individuals extends as far as the shaping
of their wants and aspirations. A desire is in itself authentic, and legitimate.
The potentially awkward implications of this belief were brought out in one
of the challenging aphorisms of Bentham's contemporary William Blake:
'Sooner murder an infant in its cradle than nurse unacted desires.' It was
another and far more scandalous contemporary of Bentham's, Sade, who

exposed the full anti-social implications of this doctrine of the legitimacy of desires. In one of two philosophical dialogues, *Dialogue between a Priest and a Dying Man*, the priest urges the dying man to repent of his sins, to which the other replies that he does indeed repent:

> By Nature created, created with very keen tastes, with very strong passions; placed on this earth for the sole purpose of yielding to them and satisfying them, and these effects of my creation being naught but necessities directly relating to Nature's fundamental designs . . . I repent not having acknowledged her omnipotence as fully as I might have done. I am only sorry for the modest use I made of the faculties (criminal in your view, perfectly ordinary in mine) she gave me to serve her; I did sometimes resist her, I repent it. Misled by your absurd doctrines, with them for arms I mindlessly challenged the desires instilled in me by a much diviner inspiration, and thereof do I repent . . .[41]

The dialogue — like nearly all so-called dialogues since Plato, it is a very one-sided affair — ends with the priest joining the dying man in an orgy of sensual pleasure with six women whom the latter has 'reserved . . . for this moment'. The other dialogue is *La Philosophie dans le Boudoir*, the dedication of which opens with the following words:

> Voluptuaries of all ages, of every sex, it is to you only that I offer this work; nourish yourselves upon its principles: they favor your passions, and these passions, whereof coldly insipid moralists put you in fear, are naught but the means Nature employs to bring man to the ends she prescribes to him; harken only to these delicious promptings, for no voice save that of the passions can conduct you to happiness.[42]

Sade differs from Hobbes and Bentham in seeing sex (not sexual relationships, or love) as the chief source of pleasure and happiness for human beings, and in interpreting the desires which animate both men and women as being overwhelmingly sexual in character. But he shares with them the belief that desires implanted by nature provide the dynamics of human action. He accepts the sovereignty of desires, and is much more radical than them in attacking every kind of moral philosophy and human institution which stands in the way of the gratification of those desires. And, except in so far as the satisfaction of one person's (sexual) desires may involve the suffering of others — as Sade accepts that it may — what objection can there be to that, from the point of view of Bentham or Berlin? I indicated above that it is sex, and not any kind of relationship, which Sade identifies as the source of pleasure; and in this, too, he is close to Bentham, for like Bentham he is identifying pleasure with the experience of certain (essentially bodily) sensations of pleasure.

It is the great merit of Sade to bring out into the light some of the crucial problems and weaknesses in the liberal theory of human desire. Thus Hobbes and Bentham, having put forward the idea that human beings are motivated by desires which are fundamentally egotistical and selfish, are faced with the problem of explaining how such radically atomistic and anti-social beings can ever live together in society. Sade underlines the dilemma by stressing the futility of denying nature, and the frustration and unhappiness which must result from attempts to do so. And if happiness is the aim of the individual, how can he, and why should he, be expected to suffer such frustration?

Sade's protracted sexual fantasies also bring out the extent to which the pursuit of pleasure or satisfaction necessarily involves treating other persons as objects, mere means to one's own ends. In the *Dialogue between a Priest and a Dying Man* the 'six women lovelier than the light of day' figure as no more than objects to be used, waiting in the 'next room' until summoned by a bell. Of course this availability is a stock feature of male sexual fantasies, but in this respect such fantasies are only extreme versions of the attitude toward others which is the logical result of acting out basically egocentric desires. From this point of view other people, other beings, are seen either as means or hindrances to our own gratification. And they, because the same self-love animates them, will view us in the same fashion. [43]

Here we encounter one of the major contradictions within liberal individualism. On the one hand individualism is usually taken to imply a principle of equality. If each man — and sometimes each woman too — is seen primarily as an individual rather than as a social being with a fixed role and position in society, then as an individual he will possess certain rights equally with all other individuals. This principle is expressed by radicals during the 1640s, the period of the English Revolution. But it does not emerge in its full clarity until the late eighteenth century, in the form of the doctrine of the rights of man. It is at this time that Kant enunciates the principle that 'every man is to be respected as an absolute end in himself' and not 'as a mere means to some external purpose'. This principle of respect for each human being as an end in himself is often seen as central to liberal individualism.

Yet at the same time there is another strand within liberalism which asserts and reasserts that the individual is naturally egoistic, and therefore tends, as Wolff has rightly pointed out, to treat other individuals not as ends, but as means to his or her own ends. And both these strands are present in some of the most important theorists of liberalism, such as Hobbes, Locke, Bentham and even J. S. Mill. Of course it is possible to resolve this contradiction by jettisoning one or other of the two elements. But an individualism or egoism, which abandons the principles of equal rights and respect for the human person, such as we find in, say, Max Stirner or Nietzsche, is certainly no longer liberal.

While on the other hand the abandonment of psychological egoism requires a reconstruction of the theory of the personality and human motivation which liberalism has never undertaken. So the contradiction remains.

But it has not always been as sharply posed as my account of it may have suggested. Hobbes's pessimistic account of human appetites and their potential for conflict was never popular, and within liberalism it was supplanted by more optimistic pictures of human nature. It was generally accepted that it was the passions or appetites which provided the driving force behind human action. It was also accepted that these passions were for the most part egoistic, although most writers followed Locke who, by making a distinction between the state of war and the state of nature ('men living together according to reason, without a common Superior on Earth'),[44] asserted that men were social by nature: they did not, as Hobbes suggested, enter into society for purely selfish reasons. What the eighteenth century called 'benevolence' was held by many to be the product of natural inclination as well as calculating self-interest. Hence it was not necessary to follow Hobbes to his gloomy conclusion that only the absolute, unquestionable authority of a single sovereign could prevent human societies from disintegrating into their constituent atomic individuals. Nature herself had provided safeguards against the potentially destructive power of human egoism.

First there was the notion of what came to be known by a phrase of Adam Smith's, the 'hidden hand'. This was the belief that the mass of individuals, each pursuing his or her own interests regardless of all others, far from coming into unavoidable conflict with each other, as Hobbes had believed, automatically harmonized with each other and coalesced to produce the general good. This hypothesis, in its general non-economic form, was not, of course, Smith's invention. More than 40 years before *The Wealth of Nations* (1776), Pope had explained in the *Essay on Man* how

> . . . God and Nature link'd the gen'ral frame,
> And bade Self-love and Social be the same.
> (Epistle III, 317—8)

It was a commonplace of the age. But Bernard Mandeville went further, and suggested that what might, according to conventional Christian morality, look like wicked or selfish behaviour, could nevertheless work to the general good. 'Private Vices, Publick Benefits' was the motto of his celebrated *The Fable of the Bees* (1705, 1714). Dr Johnson, who admired Mandeville, further developed this theme by arguing that apparently self-indulgent luxury benefited the poor more than apparently unselfish charity, because the production of luxury consumer goods gave the poor employment.[45]

This was the paradox of which Smith evolved an economic version, when he observed that he had 'never known much good done by those who affected to trade for the public good', while on the other hand the individual (Smith uses this term) who seeks 'his own advantage . . . and not that of the society' discovers that 'the study of his own advantage naturally, or rather necessarily, leads him to prefer that employment which is most advantageous to the society.' Although 'He generally, indeed, neither intends to promote the public interest, nor knows how much he is promoting it.' Yet 'he is in this, as in many other cases, led by an invisible hand to promote an end which was no part of his intention. Nor is it always the worse for the society that it was not part of it. By pursuing his own interest he frequently promotes that of the society more effectually than when he really intends to promote it.'[46] It is the market mechanism which ensures this happy result; the manufacturer and trader can only benefit themselves by producing and marketing goods which other people will buy — and if they buy them it is clear that they want them. Hence the supplier benefits himself by meeting the wants of others. He is not required to display selflessness, or benevolence.

It was never clear how convincingly the market model could be applied to all social relationships. But two considerations encouraged the wider application of Smith's model. First, as we have seen, the notion of a more general harmony between individual egoism and the common good preceded Smith. Secondly, it was assumed that the independence which individuals were held to possess within the context of the market was an attribute which also protected them in other situations. Just as no producer or trader was supposed to be able to persuade you to buy something that you didn't really want, so how could anyone, short of using brute force, get someone else to do anything that he or she didn't want to do? Given that government was necessary to prevent the arbitrary and indiscriminate use of force and violence, it could be assumed that for the rest the individual could look after himself. The individual's best insurance against being used as a means or an object by others was his sound sense of what his own wants and interests were.

But in speaking of 'sound sense' we have wandered in the direction of a second, and still more important bulwark which, in the liberal view, nature has provided against the potentially destructive chaos of conflicting individual desires. This second force is reason, or rationality. Reason both complements and regulates the powerful but erratic energies of the appetites and desires, teaching them how to obtain the greatest amount of gratification by the most economical of means: 'nature provides a remedy in the judgment and understanding, for what is irregular and incommodious in the affections.'[47] For the possession of a desire or appetite, and of the energy to seek its satisfaction are not in themselves enough to ensure success. We may have a clear idea of what we want, but suffer endless frustration in trying to attain it by inappropriate and ineffective methods. How can this be avoided?

VERSIONS OF REASON

Among the capacities which the individual of liberalism must possess in order to conform to the model of self-sufficiency and self-direction, quite the most important is reason, or Reason. Classical liberalism assumed that the individual was in some sense rational. But there's the rub: in *some* sense. 'Reason' and 'rational' are terms at least as difficult and ambiguous as the concept of 'the individual' itself.

The individual as seen by Hobbes, Hume and Bentham is not rational in the sense that it is reason which selects his aims and purposes. On the contrary, it is the passions, the desires, the appetites and aversions, which animate the individual, providing the impetus to move in one direction rather than another. Given this account of human dynamics, reason can only be the servant, or, to use Hume's word, the 'slave' of the passions or desires. Within this model of the relation of human purposes to reason and feeling, reason can be applied only to means, and is therefore essentially calculation. Reason cannot tell us that one end is more rational than another. Any desired end or object is good simply because it is desired. The function of reason is to work out how desires can be satisfied, how one desire can be reconciled with another, or with the desire for the same thing on the part of someone else. It is assumed by Hobbes, Bentham, and by liberals generally, that each person is sufficiently well endowed with this capacity to calculate and think clearly to be able to pursue his or her own interests effectively. It is this capacity which saves normal adult human beings from the distressing frustration of the child, or the foolish or ignorant person who knows what he or she wants but cannot work out how to attain it.

Liberal faith in the individual and his autonomy is bound to assume this much. And it may be thought that it is not, after all, very much to assume. Yet, as with other attributes of the individual, it is not clear whether this reasoning capacity, even if innate as potential, requires to be developed through processes of education and guidance, and is therefore a social rather than a purely natural and individual endowment.

But there was a more positive, optimistic strain of liberalism which is associated particularly with the Enlightenment and its inheritors. These liberals were convinced that both individual and social life could be based on an ideal of reason which was more than calculation and logic. It was irrational for the individual or society to be guided by uncontrolled passion or unanalysed prejudice, habit or tradition. The rational approach was to formulate general principles, based upon an understanding of nature and human nature, which would apply universally and which would be the most conducive to the progress and happiness of mankind.

This concept of reason tied it to humane values; but it also continued to regard it as a faculty or potentiality inherent in each person which, under favourable circumstances, would guide his actions in a way which would simultaneously advance his own and the public good. Spinoza and Kant certainly did not equate reason merely with the ability to calculate and think clearly. For them the rational man is not the one who merely *uses* reason to guide and assist his desires. He is the man who through reason liberates himself from the tyranny of appetite and desire and lives according to general principles. But they agree with Hobbes and the English liberal empiricists in seeing reason also as a natural potentiality which is indispensable to the autonomous, self-directing individual, whether that is seen as the natural or the ideal condition of the single human being.

This ambiguity, between the real and the ideal, between the descriptive and the prescriptive, is one that is constantly met with in liberal discussion of individualism and the individual. Autonomy is sometimes presented as a description of the basic natural state of man, sometimes as an ideal to be aspired to; and the distinction between the two is not always clear. Some of the ambiguity undoubtedly springs from the difficult, inherently ambiguous concept of what is 'natural'. But however objectionable this confusion may be from a logical point of view, it is a normal and indeed justifiable feature of any substantial political theory. For what it points to is the attempt to base the ideals or values of a political creed on a related conception of human nature. And unless an attempt *is* made to show that these ideals or values represent the fulfilment of fundamental human needs, desires and aspirations, then, inevitably, these ideals or values appear to be totally arbitrary to those who do not already share them. Thus, if autonomy is the ideal condition of the individual, it is important to show that he or she has both the ability and the need to achieve this ideal. Then the ideal turns out to be the realization of the true nature and potential of the single human being. As a result the gap between fact and value, description and evaluation, which (as we have seen) liberal philosophy characteristically views as an impassable logical gulf, is constantly being crossed — or by-passed — by the liberals themselves. Except from their own point of view, this is neither surprising nor reprehensible. But it is significant that liberalism is unable to follow its own methodological precepts, and falls instead into the common pattern of political and moral theories, in which the empirical and the evaluative are inextricably bound.

Spinoza at least was clear that autonomy was an ideal exceedingly difficult to attain, involving a struggle to emancipate oneself from enslavement to natural appetites and desires. This sets him apart from the mainstream of the liberal philosophy of the self, which sees autonomy as the natural state of man as well as a personal and political ideal,[48] and which does not share Spinoza's moral criticism of the natural appetites and desires. Let me briefly recapitulate this liberal view of man. The foundations of this philosophy were laid down in the seventeenth century, in general harmony with the principles which were evolved as the basis of the modern scientific attitude. The autonomy of the individual was established by the separation of human and moral values from the outer world of value-free facts: the individual was no longer constrained or limited in his choice of values by anything inherent in the world itself. This freedom to choose was at first hailed as a great liberation. But in the twentieth century, existentialist writers have tended to portray this freedom as a burden, and choice as an obligation. The moral emptiness of the world has come to look more like a nightmare than simply a liberation from old ghosts and superstitions.

The separation of man from the natural world was paralleled by the separation of man from the human and social world. At the most fundamental ontological level a man can be certain only of his own existence — which means that solipsism is an ever-present threat in this philosophy. And in forming his view of the world the individual must trust primarily his own experience, conveyed to him through his senses — empiricism and individualism go together. Just as the individual is essentially isolated in his unique conviction of his own existence, and in the process of learning about the world, so he is isolated from others by his self-possession, by the idea that he owns his body and faculties, and may therefore do with them what he wills.

When we turn to the consideration of human motives and desires we discover that once again each person is separated from all others, because each is animated by appetites and passions which are essentially selfish and egoistical. Each seeks gratification for himself — or herself. This means not only that the human world is composed of discrete atoms, each pursuing their own satisfactions, but that from the point of view of each of these atomic individuals, other people tend to appear as objects, neutral when they do not impinge upon us in any significant way, but otherwise serving as helps or hindrances to the realization of *my* purposes and the satisfaction of *my* desires.

Considering that liberalism is often thought of as an optimistic creed, with strong ties to the belief in progress, this is a surprisingly bleak picture. It is mitigated, however, by the belief, most widely and confidently held in the eighteenth century, that these independent atoms cohere, like the physical atoms of Newton's cosmology, into one orderly and harmonious system. And the anarchic tendencies of men's selfish desires are held in check by the all-important guiding and restraining power of reason:

> Two Principles in human nature reign:
> Self-love, to urge, and Reason, to restrain:[49]

Thus coexistence and co-operation between individuals becomes possible. But they remain separated and self-contained in their aims and purposes. What kind of society can be constructed on this atomistic foundation?

3

The Individual and Society

So far discussion has centred on individualism as an ontological theory, but inevitably it has strayed frequently into discussion of individualism as a moral and political principle. Ontological individualism often provides an explicit basis for ethical and political individualism. From seeing individuals as primary and society as secondary, from seeing individuals as more 'real' than society and its institutions, it is not a great step to seeing social institutions as 'logical fictions', possessing no existence beyond that of the individuals who collectively compose them.

For Bentham, as we have seen, the community is a 'fictitious body', and therefore 'the interest of the community' is no more than 'the sum of the interests of the several members who compose it'. If the community is a fiction, except in so far as it is conceived of as the mere arithmetical sum of its individual members, it follows that no rational person could elevate the supposed interests of a fiction above the real interests of real individual people: 'A people cannot be punished, a people cannot be free, a people doesn't exist except as an abstract conception; the only realities are the individuals who actually make up "the people".'[1] The solid and palpable existence of individuals provides the ground for preferring their rights and interests above the claims of fictitious entities such as 'the community', 'society' 'the state', 'the nation', 'the party', and all the other social institutions which sometimes claim a moral and political precedence over individuals — real people.

This is a recurring them in liberalism. In the 1940s and 1950s it was revived by F. A. Hayek, Karl Popper and others in the modernized form of 'methodological individualism'. Hayek argued that 'such collectives as "society" or "the economic system", "capitalism" or "imperialism" are no more than provisional theories, popular abstractions' which the social scientists 'must not mistake for facts'.[2] Popper had the same message:

most of the objects of social science, if not all of them, are abstract objects; they are theoretical constructions. (Even 'the war' or 'the army' are abstract concepts, strange as this may sound to some. What is concrete is the many who are killed; or the men and women in uniform, etc.)[3]

Hayek, Popper, T. D. Weldon in *The Vocabulary of Politics*,[4] and Isaiah Berlin in 'Historical Inevitability' (1954), all attach importance to this principle of analysis, not just for methodological reasons, but also because they associate it with liberal moral and political values. Berlin attacks the belief that human behaviour and history are determined by impersonal factors and entities such as class or nation or capitalism, as 'a pseudo-sociological mythology which, in the guise of scientific concepts, has developed into a new animism' that undermines the belief in individual freedom and personal moral responsibility.[5] Popper contrasts methodological individualism with its opposite, 'holism', which holds that 'the objects of sociology, social groups, must never be regarded as mere aggregates of persons.'[6]

Holism is not only unscientific, in Popper's view; it also provides a basis for political utopianism, which 'aims at remodelling the "whole of society" in accordance with a definite plan or blueprint', and is therefore potentially, and perhaps inevitably, totalitarian.[7] The immense political importance which Popper attaches to the conflict between individualism on the one hand, and historicism, holism and utopianism on the other, can be seen in the dedication of *The Poverty of Historicism* to the 'memory of the countless men and women of all creeds or nations or races who fell victims to the fascist and communist belief in Inexorable Laws of Historical Destiny'. Thus the link between different ways of seeing the relation between the individual and society, and the opposed political values of liberalism and totalitarianism (to use the liberals' own blanket term), has been strongly insisted on by many contemporary liberals.

FROM NATURE TO SOCIETY

It is time to look in a little more detail at the effects of individualistic thought upon liberal social and political theory. Within traditional political theory the habit of thinking of individuals as primary and society as secondary found expression in the pseudo-historical scenario of man's supposed progress from the state of nature via some form of social contract into society.

This scheme is presented with the greatest clarity by Hobbes, who portrays individuals in the state of nature as already equipped with their animating passions and desires, then coming together in a rational way to set up society and authority, but each acting solely for his own benefit and no one else's. For Hobbes, man, like other natural beings and even objects, is an entity whose natural condition is not rest or equilibrium — as was believed by medieval Christians — but motion. And the motion which impels him is called appetite or desire (when directed towards something), or aversion (when in flight from something). Appetite and desire are basic to man's existence whether or not he lives in contact with other human beings:

> Life it selfe is but Motion, and can never be without Desire, nor without Feare, no more than without Sense.
> Nor can a man any more live, whose Desires are at an end, than he, whose Senses and Imaginations are at a stand.

Hobbes explicitly rejects the Aristotelian view that men are naturally social creatures, and contrasts human beings with 'certain living creatures, as Bees, and Ants, who live sociably one with another'.[8] Society and government are mechanisms set up by individuals acting collectively but still only out of self-interest. This is expressed through the idea of contract — an essentially business relationship, limited in character, and entered into by all parties for their own advantage. The term 'mechanism' is appropriate here, because this kind of account is intended to stress the fact that government and society are human inventions rather than, as in Aristotelian and Greek thought, a part of the natural condition of human beings. They are devices or tools, more complex, no doubt, than the spade or the waterwheel, but standing in the same relation to human beings, as things, to be used or manipulated. As Hobbes put it, 'we make the commonwealth ourselves.'[9] The same relationship is implied in the phraseology of 'social engineering' used extensively by Popper in his political writings.

Such an approach to the relation between man and society could be, and was, liberating in profoundly important ways. To think of society as in principle controllable, as existing for the use of all men rather than for the inscrutable purposes of God, or the not-to-be-questioned policies of kings and emperors, was a great, potentially democratic, advance. But the possibilities of a society collectively determining its own destiny, implicit in this approach, were for the time being negated by the individualistic, atomistic conception of society to which it was then tied.

With the possible exception of Locke, none of the theorists of the social contract were ever quite happy about the quasi-historical structure of the theory, which was apt to lead people to peer backward into the mists of pre-history to find out what life had 'really' been like in the state of nature 'before' society had been invented. The 'condition of warre', which Hobbes saw as the natural condition of mankind, he recognized 'was never generally so, over all the world'. It was a condition into which men fell when governments were weak or non-existent, rather than a purported description of the life of primitive man.

But these qualifications in no way affected the potency of the myth itself. Men — and women too, sometimes — as individuals fully equipped with desires, aspirations, faculties and rights, came first, society afterwards.

This way of thinking long outlived the demise of contract theory itself. Thus Mill wrote, critically, that

> Bentham's idea of the world is that of a collection of persons pursuing each his separate interest or pleasure, and the prevention of whom from jostling one another more than is unavoidable, may be attempted by hopes and fears derived from three sources — the law, religion, and public opinion. [10]

But his own 'idea of the world' remained closer to that of his mentor than perhaps he was willing to admit. 'Men are not, when brought together, converted into another kind of substance', he wrote; to which E. H. Carr has retorted appropriately: 'Of course not. But the fallacy is to suppose that they existed, or had any kind of substance, before being "brought together".' [11]

The same pattern, of individuals with an existence and rights prior to society, is articulated in Hazlitt's essay (1828) 'Project for a New Theory of Civil and Criminal Legislation':

> Society consists of a given number of individuals; and the aggregate right of government is only the consequence of these inherent rights, balancing and neutralising one another. How those who deny natural rights get at any sort of right, divine or human, I am at a loss to discover; for whatever exists in combination, exists beforehand in an elementary state. The world is composed of atoms, and a machine cannot be made without materials. [12]

This passage encapsulates several aspects of liberal individualism — the conception of society as a collection of individuals; the extension of the methods and metaphors of atomism to social life, and the consequent assumption that complex or 'combined' phenomena can always in principle be separated out into their constituent atomic parts; finally the notion of government as a 'machine'. What Hazlitt terms 'the will' of the individual has a right or authority which is only circumscribed by the equal rights of other individual wills:

> each man's will is a sovereign law to itself; this can only hold in society as long as he does not meddle with others; but so long as he does not do this, the first principle retains its force. . . . Thus, in a desert island, it is evident that my will and rights would be absolute and unlimited, and I might say with Robinson Crusoe, 'I am monarch of all I survey.' [13]

ANTI-SOCIAL 'MAN'

These passages from Hazlitt's essay also illustrate another important facet of liberal individualism — its tendency to stress the inherently anti-social, or at least, non-social character of the human being. The condition of Crusoe may be a lonely one, but it is also profoundly satisfying in that it involves none of the normal social constraints upon the naturally egoistic will of the individual. Given the nature of the individual will, the restraints which social life imposes are inevitably experienced as irksome and frustrating, and tension between the individual and society is thus unavoidable.

In the twentieth century it is Freud who has written most eloquently about this tension, which he, too, sees as inevitable — the necessary price which men and women pay for the benefits of civilization. In his later general essays on culture, society and the individual, Freud restates the Hobbesian version of traditional contract theory:

> Human life in communities only becomes possible when a number of men unite together in strength superior to any single individual and remain united against all single individuals. . . . This substitution of the power of a united number for the power of a single man is the decisive step towards civilization. The essence of it lies in the circumstance that the members of the community have restricted their possibilities of gratification, whereas the individual recognized no such restrictions.[14]

Freud, like Hobbes, argued that 'every individual is virtually an enemy of civilization', and that as a result 'civilized society is perpetually menaced with disintegration through this primary hostility of men towards one another.'[15] This pessimistic view is often seen as an essentially conservative argument in favour of order and authority — or, in Freud's case, repression — but the premise of the argument is not original sin, or some other hypothesis of man's natural wickedness or malevolence. Human beings are anti-social not because they are wicked, but because they are naturally separate, self-moving and self-interested. Hobbes's dourly anti-social characterization of human nature is, in other words, an extreme version of the liberal concept of the individual rather than something qualitatively different.

Many liberals, from Locke to Mill, rejected both the Hobbesian pessimism and the authoritarian political consequences he deduced from it. But they did not renounce the belief that man is naturally self-interested. They simply denied that self-interest necessarily ruled out either individual benevolence or the possibility of social harmony. Just as Hobbes argues that the results of unrestrained individualism justify, and indeed require, strong government, so the far more popular hypotheses of a natural harmony between the interests of individuals became the basis of the liberal case *against* government interference with the spontaneously beneficial workings of society and the economy. Liberal hostility to the state, and the liberal case in favour of limited government, were not based exclusively on abstract constitutionalism or the theory of natural rights, contrary to what liberals themselves sometimes like to suggest. It was also supported by this popular and optimistic account of the relation of the individual to society. But the currently relevant point is that the difference between, let us say, Hobbes and Adam Smith is not over the essential characterization of human nature. They are agreed in thinking of man as naturally non-social and egoistic. They disagree over the social consequences of this characterization. We may consider Hobbes to be, in this respect, more realistic, less self-deceiving than his more sanguine successors in the liberal tradition. But it is easy to see why it was the optimistic version which enjoyed the greater influence and popularity.

'THAT PRIVATE AND RETIRED MAN'

This emphasis on the asocial egoism of the individual plays a permanently important part in liberalism. Without taking it into account it is impossible to understand the importance which liberalism attaches to the principles of personal freedom and privacy.

Freedom would be of no value to a being that did not have the ability to make good use of it. And the classical assumption is that freedom does *not* leave the individual disorientated and at a loss, as writers like Burke and Durkheim believed. On the contrary, freedom is the condition which each person needs in order to fulfil himself. The thoroughgoing integration of the individual into the collective life of society must result in the cramping and distorting of the personality. But give the individual freedom and privacy: set her free from the pressures of state and society, and she will find within herself the resources to make the most of the opportunities freedom offers. We are still not far from the basic assumption made by Hobbes and Smith and Bentham and Godwin and Paine: that each individual is prompted primarily by self-interest. Leave him alone, and he will pursue these promptings with a good chance of success.

Within liberalism, freedom and privacy are closely related concepts. For from at least the time of Mill onwards, liberals have tended to think of freedom in terms of an 'area of non-interference' within which the individual is left completely to his or her own devices, 'a circle around every individual human being which no government, be it that of one, of a few, or of the many, ought to be permitted to overstep',[16] but also in which the individual is free from any kind of restrictive social pressure: 'privacy in its modern sense — that is a sphere of thought and action that should be free from "public" interference — does constitute what is perhaps the central idea of liberalism.'[17]

Why is this so important to modern liberals? It is because it is within the private sphere that the individual human being is expected to find the greatest degree of happiness and fulfilment. This is not merely because the public sphere is seen, by contrast, as a rather barren area of self-denial and boring duties. It is because man is not seen as a primarily social animal, finding meaning and fulfilment in social or collective activities, but as self-contained and self-sustaining, needing a private area of withdrawal from society, not merely for rest and refreshment, but as the essential condition of self-realization. From this view of the relation of the individual to society springs contemporary liberal resistance to the idea or ideal of participation, as expressed, for example, by a social democratic writer like Anthony Crosland:

> experience shows that only a small minority of the population wish to participate in this way. I repeat what I have often said — the majority prefer to lead a full family life and cultivate their gardens. And a good thing too, for if we believe in socialism as a means of increasing personal freedom and the range of choice, we do not necessarily want a busy bustling society in which everyone is politically active and fussing around in an interfering and responsible manner, and herding us all into participating groups. The threat to privacy and freedom would be intolerable. [18]

Once again, it is worth noting here the contrast between liberal individualism and the social ideas of classical Greece. In the classical Greek view it was the private sphere, the household (not 'the home'), which was the realm of necessity, as opposed to the public sphere, which was the realm of freedom. It was not by escaping from the 'pressures' of society into the private area of non-interference that human beings found fulfilment. It was by participating in the public, collective life of the *polis*. Thucydides put these words into the mouth of Pericles: 'Here each individual is interested not only in his own affairs but in the affairs of the state as well . . . we do not say that a man who takes no interest in politics is a man who minds his own business; we say that he has no business here at all.'[19] Because the Greeks saw man as essentially a social creature they attached no importance to privacy. Privacy is important within liberalism because liberalism does not see human beings as essentially social, as members of a coherent community, in the same way.

Both views are naturally related to the actual social experience of their times and cultures. It was when the relatively homogeneous city-states went into decline in the Hellenistic period that we find the development of philosophies closer to liberal individualism, stressing the futility and degrading character of politics and the virtues of withdrawal and self-cultivation. The modern liberal feeling that, as Auden put it:

Private faces in public places
Are wiser and nicer
Than public faces in private places.

similarly reflects a society in which public life and politics have become specialized professions in which ordinary human qualities are at a discount. The division of labour elaborated under capitalism does not apply only to productive activity. It is possible that this decay in public life could be mitigated, if no more, by movement towards direct, participatory democracy. But then, as we have seen, it is an article of faith with contemporary liberals that most people 'don't want' to participate in politics. They 'naturally' prefer the private life.

THE SOCIAL ROLE OF THE INDIVIDUAL

Society is composed of individuals, and has no existence, and therefore no claims, beyond or above those individuals. Its function is to serve individuals, and one of the ways in which it should do this is by respecting their autonomy, and not trespassing on their right to do as they please so long as they can do so without harm to others. So far the emphasis is negative — on the need to protect the always vulnerable individual against the power and the bogus claims of the state and society. But liberals also emphasized the positive contribution which 'the individual' can make to society, and claim that many things *should* be left to individuals to undertake rather than being made the object of collective or corporate action. In *On Liberty* Mill gives three reasons for opposing 'government interference'. The first is that some things are best done by the individuals most directly concerned. The second is that there is a positive virtue in allowing scope to individuals to use their powers of invention and initiative. The third is 'the great evil of adding unnecessarily' to the power of government.[20] These are all respectable liberal arguments.

But it must also be said that Mill is concerned to attack not merely governmental action, but also any kind of action in which individuals band together and act as a collective body:

The greatness of England is now all collective; individually small, we only appear capable of anything great by our habit of combining; and with this our moral and religious philanthropists are perfectly contented. But it was men of another stamp than this that made England what it has been; and men of another stamp will be needed to prevent its decline.[21]

This patriotic tub-thumping is hardly Mill at his best, of course. But it is revealing. Liberal individualism has generated a widespread, and often rather silly, suspicion of all forms of collective action, as if individuals, and individualism, were somehow diminished by the very act of working together. Mill believed that collective action implies smallness on the part of individuals, rather than the largeness and power of the institutions they band together to oppose.

This was not the only reason why nineteenth-century liberals came to think that, as E. H. Carr has put it, 'combination was in principle something bad'.[22] It was held that 'combination', or organization, distorted the natural balance which obtained between equally free individuals in society, and gave an unfair advantage to the organized group. Thus liberals viewed trade unions with suspicion on these grounds, and some, such as Hayek, continue to do so. They threatened the free contracts which were made between the employer and each of his employees, both sides being assumed to be equally free to negotiate such contracts — a fiction which was attacked by 'New' liberals in the last quarter of the nineteenth century, as well as by socialists. But the suspicion remained. And it was reinforced by the belief that collective action and organizations involved the risk, or even the likelihood, that the private and authentic judgement of the individual is swamped by the pressure of majority or group opinion. Mill believed that this was already happening in the increasingly democratic England of the mid-nineteenth century:

> But society has now fairly got the better of individuality; and the danger which threatens human nature is not the excess, but the deficiency, of personal impulses and preferences. . . . I do not mean that they choose what is customary in preference to what suits their own inclination. It does not occur to them to have any inclination except for what is customary. Thus the mind itself is bowed to the yoke.[23]

Conformity, and *a fortiori* unanimity, are always suspect. They suggest to the liberal that people are merely following convention or fashion or the crowd, rather than acting out their own independent and spontaneous inclinations. We meet here once again the characteristic individualist stress on the *differences* between people rather than on what they might have in common. It is assumed that a variety of opinions, beliefs, etc. is 'natural', and that therefore conformity or unanimity can only be the results of some kind of pressure or manipulation which destroys variety and forces opinions and personalities into a single mould.

These suspicions help to explain why the device of the secret ballot is so central to liberal political mechanisms. The isolation of the voting booth extends privacy into the public sphere, and is supposed to guarantee that the individual can there make his or her own independent, unpressured choice. By contrast, forms of collective decision-making such as the mass meeting — which, it should be noted, was a central feature of direct democracy in classical Greece, as well as of much contemporary working-class and radical decision-making — are viewed with dislike and suspicion. In such circumstances, it is held, the individual is under pressure not to dissent. The secret ballot reflects the picture of society as a collection of individuals. The mass meeting, with decision-making following upon collective discussion and debate, reflects the idea of society as having some corporate identity, and of the single human being playing a role as a member of that body.

Mill's individualism is inspired not only by a concern with the rights of the individual, but also by the belief that individuals rather than groups or combinations, are the originators of social progress: 'The initiation of all wise or noble things comes and must come from individuals; generally at first from some one individual.' But those who are capable of such initiatives are nevertheless a minority: 'There are but few persons, in comparison with the whole of mankind, whose experiments, if adopted by others, would be likely to be any improvement on established practice. But these few are the salt of the earth; without them, human life would become a stagnant pool.' Eighty years later another English liberal, E. M. Forster was writing in remarkably similar terms: 'I have no mystic faith in people. I have in the individual. He seems to me a divine achievement and I mistrust any view which belittles him.' And Forster, too, places his faith in a minority of the human race 'an aristocracy of the sensitive, the considerate and the plucky . . . They represent the true human tradition, the one permanent victory of our queer race over cruelty and chaos.' It is only to be expected, though, that the twentieth-century liberal is far less hopeful than his predecessor about the possibility of this enlightened minority leading the rest of mankind in the right humane direction: 'With this type of person knocking about . . . the experiment of earthly life cannot be dismissed as a failure. But it may well be hailed as a tragedy, the tragedy being that no device has been found by which these private decencies can be transmitted to public affairs.'[24] This belief in the vital historical and ethical role of exceptional individuals is the positive side of the liberal picture of the relation between individuals and society. Society needs, for its own health and continued progress, to offer the maximum scope for individual initiatives in its collective life.

A further, and very popular development of this belief is the highly personalized approach to history in which 'great men' — and a few 'great women' — hog the limelight while collective actions and impersonal forces recede into a shadowy background. It is typical of a society saturated with individualism that it prefers to absorb its history in the highly tendentious form of biographies of the 'great' rather than in more general and analytical terms.

So, as Mill argued, freedom is important, not simply in terms of the rights of individuals, but also for social progress. Freedom is the condition in which originality and creativity can flourish and make their indispensable contribution to the progress of mankind. In this way Mill hoped to reconcile his commitment to freedom with the utilitarian ethic, which required that such a commitment be justified in terms of human happiness. How far he succeeded has been a matter of debate ever since.

This faith in the social role of the individual, with its accompanying distrust of combinations and 'the people' exposes with particular sharpness certain difficulties and ambiguities in the liberal concept of the individual. First there is the contrast between individual action and collective action which, if it were not so commonplace, would surely be seen as odd. For in what way do individuals cease to be individuals when they combine, or work together rather than separately? There is in fact a contradiction here, for if, as Mill, Bentham and others constantly insist, society *is* nothing but a collection of individuals, how can 'the individual disappear' into collectivities which are simply names for such collections? And how can 'the individual' be counterposed to 'society' or 'the people' in the way that it so often is?

What this contradiction points to is the central ambiguity in the very concept of 'the individual', between its simple meaning of 'the single human person', and its concealed, subsidiary meaning, whereby 'the individual' really means 'the exceptional individual' or 'the isolated individual'. What often occurs, certainly in *On Liberty*, is an unnoticed, and probably unconscious, slide from the one meaning to the other. This has obvious political advantages. Everyone is anxious to support the rights of the individual, meaning the rights of the person, and it is therefore easy to overlook the fact that we are sometimes being asked to endorse something rather different — a belief in the special virtues, and often the special status, of a minority of the exceptionally talented, or sensitive or enlightened. Because of this ambiguity, the concept of the individual, which in its simple form is clearly egalitarian, can become the vehicle of elitist and anti-egalitarian attitudes. This is abundantly clear in Mill, who makes a sharp distinction between the great mass of 'average' men capable only of 'mediocrity', and the minority of the 'more highly gifted and instructed', who should be allowed to play the leading role in society:

> No government by a democracy or a numerous aristocracy . . . ever did or could rise above mediocrity except in so far as the sovereign may have let themselves be guided (which in their best times they always have done) by the counsels and influence of a more highly gifted and instructed *one* or *few*. The initiation of all wise or noble things comes and must come from individuals; generally at first from some one individual. The honour and glory of the average man is that he is capable of following that initiative.

They also serve, no doubt, who only stand and wait.

Mill, and many others, have undoubtedly overrated what it is possible for the single and supposedly isolated individual, however remarkable, to achieve. This is still a common enough tendency, but it is not as plausible as it was a century ago. It is no longer possible for the serious student of history to see, say, scientific innovators or inventors as solitary geniuses working in an intellectual and social vacuum. Historical research and changing perspectives have revealed how much those whose names are commonly associated with some dramatic leap forward have owed to those before them who groped their way painfully towards a new theory or a new discovery, but never quite reached the final goal. But it is an indication of the pervasiveness of individualism that it has been, and is still, so easy to exaggerate the isolation and independence of the 'great man' and the innovator. Brecht made the necessary point in a fine poem, 'Questions from a worker who reads':

> The young Alexander conquered India.
> Was he alone?
> Caesar beat the Gauls.
> Did he not have even a cook with him?
> Philip of Spain wept when his armada
> Went down. Was he the only one to weep? . . .
>
> Every page a victory.
> Who cooked the feast for the victors?
> Every ten years a great man.
> Who paid the bill?

THE INDIVIDUAL VERSUS THE STATE AND SOCIETY

I have suggested that there is a contradiction between arguing on the one hand that society and its institutions are no more than collections of individuals, and claiming on the other that 'the individual' is at odds with society, and that there is a qualitative difference between collective action and action by individuals. If society is no more than a collection of individuals, then any conflict between society and 'the individual' is a conflict between some individuals and others, not between two qualitatively different entities, of which one enjoys an automatic ethical priority over the other. And in fact many such conflicts, which are presented in the terms of liberal individualism as epic contests between the state (that impersonal monolith), or society (that agent of collective tyranny), and the individual (lonely, embattled, heroic), are in reality less ethically simple. They are conflicts between the rights and interests of various groups of individuals. What are often tendentiously labelled as the demands or interests of the

state or society are not necessarily completely divorced from the real interests
of real people.

Sometimes, of course, they are. The very facility with which phrases like
'the public interest' or 'the national interest' or 'the will of the people' are
invoked in support of policies which are clearly unpopular, or whose advantages
to real, identifiable people are hard to perceive, makes liberals — and not only
liberals — suspicious. This is the process through which the real interests of
real people are sacrificed to what look like abstractions; and it is this which
makes some sense of the conventional antithesis between the state, or society,
and the individual. It also explains Forster's famous declaration of faith,
delivered on the eve of the Second World War:

> Personal relations are despised today. They are regarded as bourgeois
> luxuries, as products of a time of fair weather which is now past, and
> we are urged to get rid of them, and to dedicate ourselves to some move-
> ment or cause instead. I hate the idea of causes, and if I had to choose
> between betraying my country and betraying my friend, I hope I should
> have the guts to betray my country. [26]

This is certainly justifiable as an intended challenge to the unthinking patriotism
and nationalism which have driven so many millions of men and women to
useless deaths. Frenchmen, Belgians, Germans, Austrians, Britons, and many
others died willingly in millions in the 1914—18 war for their respective
'countries'. But who actually benefited, or could have benefited, from that mass
slaughter?

On the other hand Forster was wrong if he believed that 'my country' or
a 'cause' never signifies anything but some abstraction empty of human content.
There are, clearly, innumerable occasions on which to betray a country or a
cause must involve doing great harm to human beings whose lives and rights
are not less valuable than one's friends simply because one does not know them
personally. Whether such betrayals are right or wrong is another matter, but
it is only rarely that such decisions are morally simple choices between human
loyalties and allegiance to inhuman Molochs.

Despite this, Forster's way of thinking is characteristic of twentieth-century
liberalism. The old liberal tradition of suspicion of the state and its power and
purposes has not died. Originally this tradition was founded on the liberal faith
in the ability of individuals to look after their own interests, and in the self-
regulating capacity of society: 'Great part of that order which reigns among
mankind is not the effect of government. It has its origin in the principles of
society and the natural constitution of man. It existed prior to government,
and would exist if the formality of government was abolished.' [27]

It was reinforced by experience of the feudal-absolutist or Whig-aristocratic states of the eighteenth century, which convinced liberals and radicals that the state was little more than a conspiracy of the aristocratic minority to provide for themselves and their followers at the expense of society as a whole.

These misgivings obstructed, but could not finally prevent, the immense growth of state economic intervention and welfare provisions, which were accompanied by the attempts of English liberals like T. H. Green, Arnold Toynbee, L. T. Hobhouse, and others, to develop a liberal theory which gave a positive rather than merely 'nightwatchman' role to the state. But in the twentieth century the old suspicions of state power have been revived in a new and more topical form: the idea and fear of 'totalitarianism'. Under the single head of totalitarianism the theory lumps together authoritarian regimes of both Left and Right, Stalin's Russia and Hitler's Germany, ignoring their great differences in favour of what they are held to have in common: the attempt to establish total control over society through the apparatus of the state. Implicit, and sometimes explicit, in this typology of modern regimes, is the argument that the important distinction to be made is not between conventional Left and Right, but between totalitarian regimes of all kinds and liberal-democratic political systems. And since the essence of totalitarianism is the attempt to give the state total control over society, it must follow that the power of the state must be severely limited within the liberal framework. Hence it has been possible for liberals to interpret the increasing activity of the state in both the economy and the sphere of welfare as carrying with it the danger of a steady drift towards totalitarianism. One (then) Labour politician even suggested that too high a level of public spending would destroy 'the values of a plural society'. [28] Samuel Brittan has argued that 'A liberal democracy is subject to unbearable tensions if the public sector and thus the area of political decision is stretched too far.' [29] In this way, to the liberal mind, even the limited style of interventionism associated with social democracy is associated with the spine-chilling horrors of state domination. Thus both poles of the conventional antithesis between the individual and the state are still sustained in liberal thought. Individualism still thrives, and so does suspicion of state power.

Yet, as Mill and Forster make plain, their defence of 'the individual' involves an assault not merely upon the state, but also on a wider range of targets: all those supposed abstractions — causes, parties, nations, classes, movements, society, the community — to which the interests and even the lives of real people, living individuals, are so readily sacrificed by tyrants, fanatics and even seemingly well-meaning idealists. And so one of the recurring themes in contemporary liberal writing has been the need to oppose the anti-individualistic character of 'utopian' politics. Isaiah Berlin quotes Bentham with approval in this context: 'Individual interests are the only real interests . . . can it be conceived that there are men so absurd as to . . . prefer the man who is not to him who is; to torment the living, under pretence of promoting the happiness of them who are not born, and who may never be born?' 'This passage', adds Berlin, 'is at the heart of the empirical, as against the metaphysical, view of politics.'[30] The essential moral claim of empiricism is that because of, not despite, its modesty, it is actually more humane, more solicitous of the individual, than the lofty utopian dreams of complete equality, and an end to oppression and exploitation. 'The practical consequences of reactionary and Utopian theories are societies like those of Hitler and Stalin', writes Bryan Magee in his adulatory study of Sir Karl Popper. Whereas on the other hand what he calls 'the Popperian approach', 'instead of encouraging one to think about building Utopia . . . makes one seek out, and try to remove, the specific social evils under which human beings are suffering . . . . It starts from concern with human beings' — unlike, we are meant to think, political utopianism or radicalism.[31]

Obviously behind such a reaction lies all the heavy weight of the incalculable suffering and cruelty of the era of Hitler and Stalin, and the necessary determination that such horrors should never be repeated. But it is one thing to share that determination, and quite another to conclude that political utopianism was the root cause of the trouble, and that humane values are to be identified with political empiricism. In fact the admirable directness of Bentham's rhetorical question exposes the weakness of this position. For, of course men and women *are* frequently 'so absurd as to . . . prefer the man who is not to him who is'. Every family that saves money or means to provide for as yet unborn children or grandchildren is guilty of this absurdity. So is the man who spends money and effort planting trees whose sight and shade he will never live to enjoy. So are states and societies which tax and levy the living in order to build homes, schools and hospitals for future generations, or operate pension schemes for an old age which many of the contributors to the scheme may never attain. And most people would think it almost criminally negligent of the state *not* to make such provisions.

Policies which involve the sacrifice of the well-being, happiness and even the lives of the living for the sake of some future advantage are certainly not the monopoly of either socialist or totalitarian regimes. Any war involves just such a sacrifice. The liberal democracies did not hesitate to demand such sacrifices from millions of their citizens when they went to war against Nazi Germany. Nor did liberal empiricist America draw back from sacrificing the lives of 55,000 of its own citizens, and an unknown, but far larger number of Vietnamese and Cambodian lives for the sake, it was claimed, of the *future* freedom of South Vietnam, Cambodia and the *future* people of those countries. The American intervention in South-East Asia suggests that liberal democracies are not obviously more scrupulous in this respect than more authoritarian regimes. Barrington Moore has fairly commented:

The calm confidence — or ecstasy — of the political leader who sends masses of humanity to their death for the sake of a shining distant future is indeed abominable. Equally abominable is the complacency of those liberals willing to rain terror from the skies while they prate about the virtues of pragmatic gradualism.[32]

Yet despite such ominous examples, virtually any modern government is expected, and therefore obliged, to make some provision for future generations, and thus to transgress Bentham's rule, by imposing some degree of privation on the living. In opposing this in principle, liberal individualists are not, as they like to claim, being more humane than their opponents. They are simply putting the claims of existing human beings above any claims made on behalf of future generations, who, barring some planetary catastrophe, *will* exist, despite Bentham's pedantic effort to make this appear a matter for doubt.

It is one of the most significant limitations of liberal individualism that its time-scale is narrowly confined to the present and immediate future. As we have already seen, reliance upon the past, upon the inherited weight of tradition, is frowned upon as an illegitimate attempt to shuffle off the responsibility which the individual has for forming his own opinions and making his own choices. Now it seems that a concern with the future is also suspect, as likely to generate an inhuman, anti-empirical utopianism. Thus a dramatic narrowing of the time perspective is produced, as Bhikhu Parekh has pointed out:

> the range of humans whose well-being moral conduct is supposed to seek has shrunk. . . . The future is hypothetical, non-existent, and therefore is considered morally important only as the future of those alive, and not as signifying countless generations yet unborn. Thus the three-dimensionality of time has collapsed into the present, and morally only the claims — present or future — of those alive are taken into account.[33]

I have tried to show in this chapter how the emergence of moral and political individualism has been tied logically and historically to the development of an analytical individualism which was used to interpret the natural physical world as well as the world of man. The very concept of 'the individual', with all its significant complexities and ambiguities, is a comparatively recent one. But it is the key to the understanding of liberalism. All the characteristics of the abstract individual — his separateness from the natural world and from his fellow human beings, the fundamentally anti-social egoism of the desires which animate him, the autonomy of his will and his reason — all these are carried over into liberal social, economic and political thought. The individual is the fixed point of reference in the liberal world. He or she is real, concrete, in a way which larger social entities cannot be. He has a unique authenticity: his

C

desires and inclinations are 'his own', reflecting his nature quite directly. Consequently liberalism has traditionally been resistant to any kind of social theory which emphasizes the influence of society over the individual and his nature and desires. Berlin's remarks about a 'new animism' are representative of this anti-sociological strand in liberal individualism.

If the individual enjoys this kind of ontological and moral primacy over society, it is only logical that liberalism should make the individual the focus of its values. And this is so, both negatively and positively. Negatively it seeks to protect the rights and freedom of the individual against both the power of the state and the (to Mill and others) no less oppressive and more insidious influence of society, or 'public opinion'. Positively, it asserts that it is to the individual that we must look for leadership and salvation, for 'the initiation of all wise or noble things'. Liberalism is profoundly and instinvctively anti-collectivist, and, as we shall see, various attempts to change this state of affairs have only succeeded in leaving liberal theory and liberal political practice in a state of embarrassed confusion.

It is at this point that we encounter most directly the notorious ambiguity in the concept of the individual between its ostensible meaning, 'the single human being', and its half-hidden meaning, 'the exceptional human being'. It is this ambiguity which enables liberalism to move in the direction of an elitism to which some liberal writers, including Mill, have wanted to give institutional expression. This is only one of the difficulties and even contradictions within the liberal world-view.

Because the moral and political principles of liberalism have their ontological or metaphysical basis in individualism, it has hardly been possible to discuss individualism without also discussing the values of liberalism. Untidy as this is, it does at least illustrate how closely interwoven are the different elements in a comprehensive political philosophy. Nevertheless, having outlined what I take to be the ontological foundations of liberalism, we must now look more specifically at its values, or principles.

4

Liberal Values

There has never been much disagreement as to what the principal 'official' values of liberalism are. Pre-eminent among them is freedom or liberty. And with freedom are connected certain other values, such as tolerance and privacy, which are in essence deductions from, or extensions of, the idea of freedom; while the liberal commitments to constitutionalism and the rule of law are seen as the practical and institutional principles by which the freedom of the individual or citizen is protected and guaranteed. Reason or rationality in some sense, is, as we have seen, important to liberalism, and with it we should associate the identification sometimes made between liberalism and the spirit of science. It is often assumed that liberalism and democracy are natural and harmonious partners, but, as will be seen, the relationship is more complex and ambiguous than that. These are some of the values and principles most commonly credited to liberalism. They are not the only ones to be mentioned, nor, of course, are they exclusively associated with liberalism.

But liberalism has, or has had, other less well-advertised commitments, some of which are at least as important, historically and conceptually, as the publicly proclaimed values of the creed. These half-hidden attachments essentially concern the relationship between liberalism and capitalism. They involve the awkward issues of class, and property, matters which were not, of course, always as embarrassing to most liberals as they are today.

The relative importance of these various strands within liberalism has varied greatly from period to period and culture to culture. Some older elements, such as *laissez-faire* economics, fell into disrepute and were generally jettisoned, while new ideas were taken on board. Among the latter probably the most important was the commitment to political gradualism and empiricism. Traditionally the empirical or pragmatic approach to politics has been regarded by both its friends and enemies as the prerogative of conservatism.[1] But in the twentieth century it has been made common ground between conservatives, liberals and many social democrats.

A mere list of values does not, however, define a political doctrine, or distinguish it from others. What matters is the world-view through which they are linked to each other, and the order or hierarchy in which they are arranged. Terms like freedom, reason and democracy are now so universally prestigious that nearly all political movements and regimes find it necessary to use them. But this does not indicate any wide measure of agreement. Definitions of such inspiring but vague terms naturally vary, as does the priority given to these values in relation to other political commitments.

FREEDOM

Liberalism distinguishes itself from other political doctrines by the supreme importance it attaches to freedom, or liberty. So much so, that, as we noted earlier, it is even possible for liberalism to be 'narrowly defined' by sympathetic commentators in terms of this one principle alone. This is familiar, but it is worth noting the distinctiveness of the preoccupation. The idea of freedom does not feature very prominently in European political thinking of either the classical or the medieval eras. Even in the modern period it has had to compete with other principles to which many have attached greater importance: happiness, or equality, or social justice, or democracy, or the maintenance of continuity, or social order and stability. But within liberalism none of these principles rivals the commitment to freedom: 'Liberty is not a means to a higher political end. It is itself the highest political end.'[2] This opinion of Lord Acton was echoed more recently by Stuart Hampshire: 'I believe that the extension and safe-guarding of every individual's equal freedom to choose his own manner of life for himself is the end of political action.'[3] Not one end among others, be it noted, but *the* end.

Freedom is not a self-explanatory term, and liberalism has its particular conception of freedom which again helps to distinguish it from other political tendencies. To speak of freedom immediately invites at least three questions, Freedom from what? To do what? And for whom?

The liberal definition is normally couched in terms of 'freedom from' rather than 'freedom to'. It usually defines freedom negatively, as a condition in which one is *not* compelled, *not* restricted, *not* interfered with, and *not* pressurized. Hobbes offers a definition of this kind: 'By LIBERTY, is understood, according to the proper signification of the word, the absence of externall Impediments: which Impediments, may oft take away part of a mans power to do what hee would.' Later he enlarges this definition a little, by distinguishing between freedom and power:

> LIBERTY, or FREEDOME, signifieth (properly) the absence of Opposition; (by Opposition, I mean externall Impediments of motion) . . . But when

the impediment of motion, is in the constitution of the thing itselfe; we use not to say, it wants the Liberty; but the Power to move; as when a stone lyeth still, or a man is fastned to his bed by sickness.

And according to this proper, and generally received meaning of the word, a FREE-MAN, is he, that in those things, by which his strength and wit he is able to do, is not hindred to doe what he has a will to.[4]

It is consistent with Hobbes's incorporation of human beings in the whole order of nature that he should offer a definition of liberty which is designed to apply to other beings besides man. But most theories of liberty concentrate more specifically on man, and also stipulate that the 'external impediments' which restrict a man's freedom must themselves be man-made, as in this statement by Isaiah Berlin:

> I am normally said to be free to the degree to which no man or body of men interferes with my activity. Political liberty in this sense is simply the area within which a man can act unobstructed by others. If I am prevented by others from doing what I could otherwise do, I am to that degree unfree. . . . Coercion implies the deliberate interference of other human beings within the area in which I could otherwise act.

This is freedom defined as an 'area of non-interference'. According to this view, as Berlin says, 'the wider the area of non-interference, the wider my freedom.'[5] And the threats, or 'impediments', to freedom must be both external, and man-made. Berlin goes even further by stipulating that coercion must involve *deliberate* human interference. It would follow from this that no one's freedom could be restricted or denied as the accidental or unintended consequence of human action.

Within the mainstream of liberal thought freedom is carefully and insistently distinguished from power or ability. Berlin follows Hobbes in this as in other respects, and Maurice Cranston, working within the conventions of post-Wittgensteinian linguistic analysis, also stresses the importance of this distinction:

> In the conventional use of our language, there *is* a difference between *being free to* and *being able to*, and it is not a difference we can afford to ignore . . . a man does not say he is free to do a thing simply because he possesses the power or faculty to do it. . . . He says he is free to do it only when he wants to refer to the absence of impediments in the way of doing it.

In answer to the objection that 'freedom is "empty" without power', he concedes that 'there is little point in "being free to" unless we "have the power to''', but insists that 'it certainly does not follow from this that the one is identical with the other.'[6] Put another way, we can say that this conception of freedom implies the absence of obstacles, and so perhaps the presence of opportunity, but not necessarily of the means to make use of the opportunity.

Thus this conception of freedom is essentially negative, in that it is usually couched in terms of freedom from, or the absence of, external hindrances or obstacles. (Given the use Berlin makes of the supposed distinction between 'negative' and 'positive' liberty, there is, for liberals, nothing pejorative about the term 'negative' in this context.) As for 'freedom to', it is either said (by Cranston) to be merely a more confused way of talking about 'freeedom from', or else it is presented (by Berlin) as an alternative and potentially far more dangerous way of thinking about freedom.

But freedom from what? What does liberalism point to as the sources of those restraints and obstacles which menace or restrict freedom? According to Cranston: 'The answer of the English liberal is unequivocal. By "freedom" he means *freedom from the constraints of the state.*'[7]

We have already seen how individualism and the individualistic analysis of society generate a suspicion of the state and of the claims made in its name. The liberal way of thinking about freedom enhances this suspicion. Liberal thought is characteristically political, rather than social and economic. When it thinks of power, or authority, it thinks of *political* power or authority. It thinks of laws and the state apparatus, rather than of the economic power of employers, monopolies and cartels, or of the social power of the owners of land, or of the means of communication. Even Mill, 'the man who . . . founded modern liberalism',[8] who in *On Liberty* is as concerned with the restrictive pressure of society as with the power of the state, did not really succeed in deflecting liberalism from its obsession with the state as the primary enemy of the freedom of the individual. Liberals continue to cite their hostility to the increase of state power as a critical difference between them and socialists.[9] So freedom, for liberals, continues to mean, above all, freedom from control, compulsion, restriction, and interference by the state.

As to the question of *whose* freedom, the short answer is that it is the freedom of the individual with which liberals are principally concerned.

By the freedom of the individual is normally meant personal freedom. And, as with the concept of the individual itself, the emphasis is on the single human person on his own. The individual must have the right to believe what he chooses to believe, to express those beliefs publicly and to act in accordance with them, in so far as such rights are compatible with others holding and exercising the same rights, and with the existing framework of laws and lawful institutions. But if the individual should want to band together with other like-minded individuals, to organize and act collectively, then he will need more than individual freedom. There must also be rights for political organizations and trade unions; he will need to use also the freedom to publish opinions and produce newspapers. These freedoms are not synonymous with the freedom of the individual, although it might well be argued that that freedom would be extremely restricted without them. Liberals are usually committed to these institutional freedoms as well. But that has not always been the case in the past, and if liberals have often been unsympathetic or hostile to the long working-class struggle to secure recognition for trade unions and their rights, that is partly because the individualistic bias of liberalism has led them to see trade unions, in common with other institutions and collectivities, as threats rather than supports to the rights and freedom of the individual. The crown of martyrdom which the media automatically confer on the person (the individual) who refuses to join a union, or who is 'sent to coventry' for non-participation in a strike, or whatever, reflects this individualistic bias in its crudest form. Different freedoms and rights do not necessarily harmonize with each other. When they clash, the instinct of the liberal is to be on the side of the single individual rather than the collective organization or institution.

JUSTIFICATIONS OF FREEDOM

To define the kind of freedom you are interested in is not the same thing as to justify it. We still have to explain exactly why liberalism attaches such overwhelming importance to the freedom of the individual, beyond all other political values.

A number of different justifications are put forward, some of them more fundamental than others. Some of the less fundamental are contingent upon the truth of certain broadly empirical generalizations. One of these is the argument put forward by Mill, and many others, that there is a necessary link between creativity and originality and the freedom of the individual. It is pleasant, and to the Western world gratifying, to think that the arts and sciences flourish most healthily in the pure air of freedom and tolerance; while under any form of tyranny, social or political, these plants will sicken and die. Ringing declarations to this effect are the common currency of liberal rhetoric. Camus, for example, declared, after the abortive Hungarian uprising of 1956, that 'Without liberty, there is no art. Art lives only by the limits which it sets for itself. It dies from all others.'[10]

Is this in fact true? Not even Mill's most ardent admirers have been able to accept his hypothesis without considerable qualifications, to say the least. Thus Berlin has written:

No one would argue that truth or freedom of self-expression could flourish where dogma crushes all thought. But the evidence of history tends to show . . . that integrity, love of truth, and fiery individualism grow at least as often in severely disciplined communities, among, for example, the puritan Calvinists of Scotland or New England, or under military discipline, as in more tolerant or indifferent societies; and if this is so, Mill's argument for liberty as a necessary condition for the growth of human genius falls to the ground. [11]

It is clear that the all-embracing cultural dictatorship exercised by the Nazi and Stalinist regimes was generally disastrous for the arts and many of the sciences — although even with such extreme cases there are some complexities. Shostakovich wrote one of his finest symphonies, the Fifth, in the late 1930s as, in his own own words, 'a creative response to just criticism' after official disapproval of his Fourth Symphony and an opera. On the other hand, no one would suggest that the last century of Russian Tsarism was a period of enlightenment and tolerance either, yet it was a golden age for Russian literature and music. Like the French *philosophes* of the eighteenth century, Russian writers of the nineteenth seemed to have thrived — artistically, that is — on their necessarily oppositional role. Evidently a high degree of individual freedom in the conventional political sense is not an indispensable precondition of great artistic or scientific or intellectual creativity, even though such activities may be more easily pursued in conditions of political freedom. So as a justifying argument for individual freedom this is too tenuous to provide key support for the liberal case.

Another argument put forward by Mill in *On Liberty* also turns out to be rather vulnerable. This is the argument that the truth is only arrived at through open debate between opposing viewpoints — and that such debate is only possible in the condition of freedom. To Roman Catholics, biblical fundamentalists, and some other religious groups, this argument is misplaced, since their belief is that fundamental truths are not discovered, but revealed, through a chosen institution, a chosen people, or a chosen book. Hence the hostility of a Catholic like John Henry Newman towards liberalism:

> by Liberalism I mean false liberty of thought, or the exercise of thought upon matters, in which, from the constitution of the human mind, thought cannot be brought to any successful issue, and therefore is out of place. Among such matters are first principles of whatever kind; and of these the most sacred and momentous are especially to be reckoned the truths of Revelation. Liberalism then is the mistake of subjecting to human judgement those revealed doctrines which are in their nature beyond and independent of it. [12]

Since views of this kind are probably held now only by a minority of conventionally educated persons, it might be thought that they could be ignored.

This would be easier if it were not that this confidence that there are truths which lie beyond debate, is shared to some extent by the more positivistic advocates of the scientific approach, including Mill himself. The positivist camp does not, of course, believe in revelation, or deny the function of debate as a means of arriving at the truth. What it does suggest, however, is that once we *have* arrived at the truth, debate ceases: 'As mankind improve, the number of doctrines which are no longer disputed or doubted will be constantly on the increase; and the well-being of mankind may almost be measured by the number and gravity of the truths which have reached the point of being uncontested.'[13] The conviction that the truth *can* be arrived at with a high degree of certainty thus imposes some limit on the freedom to debate and question. And although scientists may allow in principle that their fundamental assumptions or hypotheses are always open to question, in practice the range of permissible views is always limited by what are taken to be virtual certainties.

It may be said that this is not a very serious limitation, since the important disagreements occur in areas where scientific certainty is in principle impossible or improbable. But where is the line to be drawn between the debatable and the non-debatable? This is a vital question, and it is significant that Mill himself seems to have been confident — at least at times — that the advance of knowledge will steadily narrow down the area of the debatable. Thus he opens his essay on *Utilitarianism* by lamenting 'the little progress which has been made in the decision of the controversy respecting the criterion of right and wrong'. This he takes as symptomatic of 'the backward state in which speculation on the most important subjects still lingers'. What is, today, so striking is that he should regard such a controversy as one capable of being 'decided' at all. But, as the essay makes plain, Mill believes that there is a 'science of morals'. For although 'questions of ultimate ends are not amenable to direct proof', we can have good reasons which are 'equivalent to proof'. It is of course perfectly true that in *On Liberty* Mill also argues passionately in favour of treating virtually all issues as open to debate. My only point here is that in so far as Mill shared the positivist belief that definitive and final truths could be arrived at in both the natural and human sciences, he weakened his own case in favour of liberty of thought and discussion.

A much stronger argument in favour of freedom of opinion can however be found in a qualified form in *On Liberty*. That is the argument from scepticism, or from human fallibility. As Mill says: 'we can never be sure that the opinion we are endeavouring to stifle is a false opinion' — though he partially undermines this by adding 'and if we were sure, stifling it would be an evil still.' I have already suggested why this second proposition can have only a limited appeal. The first is much more coherent; and undoubtedly the intellectual plausibility and political attractiveness of a basically sceptical, relativist and hesitant approach to knowledge and belief have increased enormously in the century and more since Mill was writing. A whole range of intellectual developments, and above all the realization that ideas, and what we take to be truth, do in fact have a history, have helped to create a climate of greater caution. Freedom of opinion is endorsed just because we can recognize the possibility of being wrong or mistaken even on those issues about which we have least reason to suppose that we are.

A particularly relevant form of this argument was put forward by Stuart Hampshire in two articles published in *Encounter* in the 1950s: 'In defence of radicalism' (August 1955), and 'Uncertainty in politics' (January 1957). Hampshire argued that traditional pictures of a universal human nature have broken down, and that it is no longer possible to generalize confidently about human wants, beliefs and aspirations. Hence the kind of 'utopian' planning and blueprints which such confident generalizations allowed are no longer possible. Instead the one overriding political goal must be freedom for each individual equally. But in whatever form, scepticism about final truths provides a much more substantial justification for freedom than more positivistic views which accept the possibility of reaching conclusions which are beyond doubt or dispute.

Political events, as well as intellectual developments, have reinforced the appeal of scepticism to twentieth-century liberals. What Russell called 'liberal tentativeness' has seemed to many people a more humane as well as a more rational attitude than any kind of 'dogmatic' certainty. From this point of view the greatest horrors of this century are directly due to the quasi-religious fanaticism with which the propagators of the political creeds of our time — principally fascism and communism — have implemented and imposed their programmes, regardless of the cost in human suffering. What this leads to, in Berlin's words, is 'the vivisection of actual human societies into some fixed pattern dictated by our fallible understanding of a largely imaginary past or a wholly imaginary future. To preserve our absolute categories or ideals at the expense of human lives offends equally against the principles of science and of history.' It follows that 'What the age calls for is . . . less Messianic ardour, more enlightened scepticism.'[14] Scepticism, and the freedom of opinion which must logically accompany it, is thus held to be a more humane as well as rational approcah to politics than the self-proclaimed idealism of the visionaries and fanatics.

The last of the justifications of freedom within liberalism is also the most fundamental and important. It is that which is based directly on individualism itself. At its simplest and most fundamental it asserts that every individual's life 'belongs' to himself — or herself. Every one has a fundamental and final right to live, think and believe as he or she wishes, always provided that in doing so one does not hinder or prevent others from exercising the same right equally.

As we have seen, there is a great weight of individualistic thinking behind such a principle. It may be supported by the belief in the ontological primacy, the greater 'reality', of 'the individual' as opposed to society and its institutions. It may be supported by a Spinozistic belief that autonomy is the condition to which each individual naturally aspires. Most commonly, perhaps, it has been expressed in terms of rights: natural rights, or the rights of man.

The doctrine of rights articulates the possessive character of liberal individualism with particular clarity. The individual owns his or her life, and possesses rights in much the same way: 'Rights are typically conceived of as *possessed* or *owned by* or *belonging to* individuals, and these expressions reflect the conception of moral rules as not only those prescribing conduct but as forming a kind of moral property of individuals to which they are as individuals entitled.'[15] But rights are not bits of material property; they are concepts. In what sense can we possess concepts? The metaphor of ownership, despite its familiarity, is a source of great difficulties, and it is not surprising that some contemporary liberals, influenced by the philosophical modes of logical positivism and linguistic analysis, have dismissed the notion of natural rights as 'metaphysical' — their ultimate term of condemnation.[16]

Nevertheless the notion of human or natural rights retains a strong appeal, despite philosophical objections, and it is not difficult to see why. First of all, if the notion is abandoned, we are deprived of one useful yardstick by which we may measure and criticize the actual rights which particular governments and societies allow to their citizens. No one wants to be in the position of having to accept that her only rights are those allowed to her by the government of the day. It would be the same if the idea of justice was identified with that of actual law, so that we were deprived of the possibility of saying that particular laws, or legal decisions or penalties, were just or unjust. Concepts like 'rights' and 'justice' afford some defences against the monopoly of morality as well as power to which most governments aspire. What is more, they are exceptionally valuable just because they make exceptionally strong moral claims.

But it may be suggested that to say that someone has a moral or human or natural right is to say no more than that you believe that he ought to be allowed to do or say something, or that he ought not to be treated in some particularly arbitrary or repressive way. And if that is so, then the issue is open to the normal kinds of ethical argument, since it is in principle possible for reasonable people to disagree on such matters. But such a translation of the language of rights and justice seriously weakens the position. Human rights are not so widely respected and so secure that we can afford such a weakening, even if the philosophical arguments for it were very powerful. But in fact this translation not only weakens the case: it does so by eliminating what is really the core of the argument. For what the notions of rights and justice imply is a conception, not necessarily made explicit, of what it is that human dignity and a respect for human beings require.

The most fundamental justification of freedom is that which argues that freedom is the logical political consequence of a respect for the value and dignity of each individual human being. This does not necessarily mean mere 'non-interference' — just 'leaving people alone'. It need not imply indifference to what people make of their lives. It may well imply positive action and planning to ensure that the means and opportunities exist to enable people to make the most of their own abilities and inclinations. But it also implies an ultimate rejection of all patronizing or contemptuous views of the capacities and qualities of the mass of mankind. Under present conditions these abilities and qualities may not have the room to grow and flourish. In many societies they may only be latent and hidden. To change these conditions may need long and sharp struggle and a great deal of positive activity. Nor need it be assumed that freedom, in the conventional liberal, political and legal sense, is the only, or even the most important, condition necessary for this flowering of human potentialities. Nevertheless, the most fundamental case for freedom is that which maintains that men and women are not toys or dolls, incapable of an independent, self-directing existence, and therefore available for unlimited manipulation.

It may be that in past or present societies people *are* conditioned and manipulated, and the ease with which this can be done then convinces the advocates of paternalist or authoritarian politics that this is the way people naturally and invariably are. They need to be, or are only fit to be, controlled and manipulated. The believer in freedom rejects this conclusion on three grounds. First of all he does not accept that men and women do not possess the capacity for shaping their own lives. Within classical liberalism this takes the form of the belief in the universal possession of reason, together with the belief that each person is the best judge of his or her own self-interest.

Secondly, everyone possesses not only the capacity for independence, but also the right to it; and the notion of 'right' here expresses a radical sense of human equality; each man or woman is a person of equal value; each of them is unique, not replaceable by any other. So from where can any individual or group or institution derive the authority to place themselves above the rest of the human race, to presume to shape the lives and determine the futures of others, to treat other human beings as means rather than ends? And this conviction that people have not only the capacity for independence but also the right to it, is greatly strengthened by the scepticism discussed above. For when fundamental beliefs about the world and human nature and right and wrong change so much through history and vary so much from society to society and even within societies, it is hard to make out a convincing claim for the right of any elite, or church, or party or institution, or temporary majority, to impose its metaphysical and moral beliefs on anyone who would not or does not voluntarily embrace them.

It is true, however, that the actual connections between freedom on the one hand, and human happiness and self-realization on the other, have been insufficiently explored within the liberal tradition. As Iris Murdoch once put it: 'Our central conception is still a debilitated form of Mill's equation: happiness equals freedom equals personality.'[17] Matters are, obviously, a great deal more complicated than that. It has often been remarked that urban life, the life of the individual in big cities, is much freer than life in small and comparatively close-knit communities. It is freer in exactly the way that concerned Mill particularly: the individual's style of life is less likely to be constricted by social pressures in favour of conformity to orthodox patterns. This is one reason why many young people, particularly those whose sexual or political life-style is unconventional, try to move from small communities into the big cities where they are less likely to be the victims of gossip, censure and intolerance.

But this greater freedom has its costs and disadvantages. Loneliness is often the price which has to be paid; less often, perhaps, by the young than by the old, the widow or the widower living alone, barely knowing the shifting population of the rooms or flats next door, sometimes even dying unnoticed. Such people might prefer to pay the price of community, a certain loss of freedom and privacy, rather than that of urban freedom. As Philip Toynbee once remarked: 'A raging libertarianism can easily forget that there is a degree of applied freedom beyond which the desolation of man is increased rather than reduced.'[18]

Self-realization is also a goal whose relation to freedom is more complex than has sometimes been supposed. The natural tendency of liberal individualism is to think of the individual as separate and self-sufficient. But of course people seldom find fulfilment in isolation, but through involvement with others at a variety of different levels from casual acquaintance to lifelong love. Even creative artists who, it might be thought, represent the extreme of isolated self-fulfilment through their work, have often stressed the importance to them of rootedness and attachment. 'Thank God I am not free, any more than a tree which has roots is free', declared the restless D. H. Lawrence. And Robert Paul Wolff, in his penetrating critique of liberalism, has contrasted 'Mill's equation', as Iris Murdoch calls it, with Durkheim's analysis of suicide:

> It seems, if Durkheim is correct, that the very liberty and individuality which Mill celebrates are deadly threats to the integrity and health of the personality. So far from being superfluous constraints which thwart the free development of the self, social norms protect us from the dangers of anomie; and that invasive intimacy of each with each which Mill felt as suffocating is actually our principal protection against the soul-destroying evil of isolation.[19]

Liberalism has not usually included the notion of community among its ideals.

A partial exception to this is the 'New' liberalism associated with T. H. Green, L. T. Hobhouse, J. A. Hobson, and many other less well-known figures, which flourished in the period between 1880 and the outbreak of the First World War. Green, an Hegelian liberal, rejected the ontological individualism of the classic liberal tradition from Hobbes and Locke to Mill, and asserted the mutual dependence of society and 'the individual', or 'persons' (see chapter 16 below); while Hobhouse, similarly, asserted that 'freedom is only one side of social life', and that 'the theory of collective action' was 'no less fundamental than the theory of personal freedom' (*Liberalism*, chapter 6). There was, they believed, an 'organic' relationship between society and individual human beings. Significantly, however, this tendency never succeeded in displacing the dominant individualism. Its ideas, and several of its leading exponents, were eventually absorbed into the mainstream of social democracy.

Liberalism continued to treat the idea of community with some suspicion, as a source of restrictions on the individual and his free development. And this may well be seen as a critical weakness in liberal thought about man's life in society. It is also true that the liberal conception of freedom remains essentially and primarily political and legal rather than social and economic, despite not only the 'revisionist' efforts of Green, Hobhouse and others, but also Mill's stress on the social pressures which he saw as threatening individual freedom. But when every allowance has been made for these and other possible limitations, the liberal will always want to assert that freedom, however subtly and comprehensively defined, is the only political principle compatible with a respect for the dignity and capacities of human beings and an awareness of the limits of human knowledge and understanding. What the general principle of freedom has concretely meant at different stages in the historical development of liberalism is something that will be explored in the second part of this book.

TOLERANCE

Some of the other values identified with liberalism are, in essence, extensions or elaborations of this central commitment to freedom. Tolerance is such a value, whether it is thought of as a public policy or a personal virtue. Tolerance is the duty, on the part of state, society or the individual, of allowing and not interfering with activities and beliefs which, although they may be disliked or even disapproved of, do not in themselves make any infringement on the equal right of others to act and believe as *they* choose. Tolerance may be seen as a makeshift, second-best expedient, if the ideal is either homogeneity of belief and practice within society, or if people are expected, not merely to put up with their neighbours, but to love them. Hence Forster raised two, but not three, cheers for democracy. But love is a counsel of perfection which many liberals, including Forster, priding themselves on their 'realism', reject as inapplicable to the human condition as it is. Tolerance however, demands something, but not too much, of people.[20] The pragmatic case for tolerance accepts that differences in belief and behaviour exist, and cannot be eliminated, whether or not it is in principle desirable that they should be so eliminated. A more affirmative attitude regards such differences as positively desirable, as does Mill, for example, so that tolerance is converted from a sensible but grudging recognition of reality, into a barometer of social health.

Wolff has argued convincingly that the liberal case for tolerance has been reinforced, though also significantly altered, by the rise of the modern pluralist conception of society. There is a shift in emphasis from the diversity of individuals to the diversity of groups. Pluralism stresses the natural disunity of society, its lack of any general will or common interest: '[the] common good is itself the process of practical reconciliation of the interests of the various "sciences", aggregates, or groups which compose a state; it is not some external and intangible spiritual adhesive or some allegedly objective "general will" or "public interest".'[21] Society is not homogenous; it is a mosaic of groups, large and small, all with particular interests to promote. When such interests conflict, the appropriate outcome is a compromise rather than a victory for one party, because it is accepted that all these groups and interests have at least a measure of legitimacy. The principle of tolerance is the recognition of that legitimacy: 'Tolerance in a society of competing interest groups is precisely the ungrudging acknowledgement of the right of opposed interests to exist and be pursued.'[22] But Wolff points out that it is fairly easy to envisage such acceptance when it is only a conflict of *interests* that is supposedly involved. Compromise between interests seems sensible and practical. But when the issue is seen as a conflict of *principles*, compromise will be more difficult and is not necessarily desirable. As between those who wanted to exterminate the Jews and those who opposed anti-Semitism, what compromise was possible, or desirable? It is not persuasive to argue for compromise as a *general* rule in the world of morals and principles.

Is tolerance, then, connected with moral indifference or neutrality? Some of its protagonists argue strenuously that it is not. Crick has argued that there is no sense in saying that we are tolerant when we are in fact indifferent to what is going on. Tolerance, on this reading, implies an effort. It is only meaningful to talk about tolerating what we don't like or don't approve of. 'I disapprove of what you say, but I will defend to the death your right to say it.' But even a formulation such as the one sometimes attributed to Voltaire makes a tolerance sound morally easier than it actually is. It is not difficult to tolerate the expression of even the nastiest opinions so long as they are demonstrably uninfluential. When they are effective the situation is more complex. A racist speech is not merely the expression of an opinion: it is a potent political act. And, as Mill himself said in *On Liberty*: 'No one pretends that actions should be as free as opinions. On the contrary, even opinions lose their immunity when the circumstances in which they are expressed are such as to constitute their expression a positive instigation to some mischievous act.'

Many such speeches have been followed by attacks on black people and their homes. Should state or society tolerate acts (speeches) which lead to acts of intolerance or worse?

Racist speeches and even actions are tolerated by the British state because they are popular, and attempts to use the law against them would probably make matters worse for the black minority. Irish Republicanism, on the other hand, is understandably not popular in mainland Britain and, since November 1974, not only have Republican organizations been illegal, but so has the expression of verbal support for Republicanism.

I mention these two cases not only because they show how muddled and inconsistent the behaviour of a supposedly liberal state can be. They also illustrate some of the practical problems of tolerance as a policy — the difficulty of distinguishing between opinions and actions; and the difficulty, too, of deciding what actions ought to be tolerated, since, despite what Mill says, it is clearly a mockery of tolerance or freedom to suggest that once an opinion becomes influential we are no longer bound by any general principle of tolerance.

The case of Irish Republicanism also points to the link that in practice does often tie tolerance to indifference. Until the crisis which began in 1968 it would have been thought pointless to outlaw Republicanism because no one much cared about it one way or another. Generally a belief or movement or group can only be sure of being tolerated when its existence is, for most people, a matter of indifference. There is a clear connection between the growth of religious toleration in Europe in the early modern period and the spread of an attitude of indifference towards the content of the various religious disputes over which so much blood had been shed. As Butterfield said: 'toleration emerges with the return of religious indifference.'[23] In practice the most tolerant society is likely to be also the one which is the most aimless, and the most tolerant individual is probably the one who believes nothing very strongly and leans towards universal scepticism.

Individuals and societies may find it difficult to practise the virtue of tolerance. It may indeed require positive effort to do so. Many liberals would attribute this to the persistence of fundamentally illiberal attitudes. Intolerance of black people, or Irishmen or Jews, is the product of bigotry, which can only be eliminated by the spread of knowledge and rationality. Religious or political intolerance is the product of dogmatism, an intellectual over-confidence which can only be corrected by a more relativistic and sceptical awareness of the variety of human beliefs and the impossibility of certain knowledge in such areas. Within liberalism, tolerance is linked to rationality, and, like freedom, is powerfully supported by scepticism. The enemy of liberal tolerance is fanaticism. Two lines of Yeats have been repeatedly quoted by liberal apologists in recent years:

> The best lack all conviction, while the worst
> Are full of passionate intensity.   ('The Second Coming')

It must be agreeable to have no convictions, yet be able to acount oneself among 'the best'. What the endorsement of these lines indicates is that liberalism inclines to tentativeness (to use Russell's word) and even uncertainty, and is suspicious of too strong convictions. There is further support for this attitude in another poem of Yeats', 'A Prayer for My Daughter':

> An intellectual hatred is the worst,
> So let her think opinions are accursed.

If we want a tolerant society, then uncertainty, indifference and even apathy are preferable to having too many people with too strong opinions. [24]

It is with tolerance as it is with freedom: the most fundamental and radical case is one which rests on some conception of human rights, of what basic human dignity and respect for persons require in terms of both laws and collective and individual attitudes. What this implies is that if arguments about tolerance, or toleration, are couched in terms of whether society or the state should or should not tolerate this group or that belief, this already concedes to government or society an authority to which they have no moral right. Radical liberals saw this very clearly. In 1791 Paine wrote:

> The French constitution hath abolished or renounced *Toleration*, and *Intolerance* also, and hath established UNIVERSAL RIGHT OF CONSCIENCE.
>   Toleration is not the *opposite* of Intolerance, but it is the *counterfeit* of it. Both are despotisms. The one assumes to itself the right of withholding Liberty of Conscience, and the other of granting it. [25]

Similarly, Shelley in his *Address to the Irish People* wrote: 'I propose unlimited toleration, or rather the destruction both of toleration and intolerance.' [26]

Tolerance on the part of state, society and individuals, is undoubtedly necessary if liberal freedom is to be made a reality, and it can be seen as the practice of that respect for persons upon which the principle of freedom itself rests. Tolerance in practice may require an effort of self-discipline; yet it is in some ways a minimal and negative virtue. It means not interfering with people, leaving them alone. But leaving them alone can mean neglect as well as tolerance, and if indifference is often the soil in which tolerance grows, indifference can also shade off into callousness.

PRIVACY

The importance which liberalism attaches to privacy illuminates the specific nature of the liberal idea of freedom. In classical and neo-classical conceptions the freedom that mattered was freedom within the public sphere. What was important was that men (but not women, and not all men, for that matter) should be free to express their opinions and act politically within the processes of collective decision-taking. The idea of being 'left alone', or an area of non-interference, did not form part of these older ways of thinking.

Liberalism shifts the balance of thought on to the opposite scale. Not only is the individual no longer seen as essentially a part, or member, of some larger social body. Such ideas are now regarded as illiberal and even potentially totalitarian. Even the thought of large-scale popular involvement was suspect to Anthony Crosland, as we have seen.

But Crosland's view, which is a representative one, raises many problems. He doesn't explain why people should be more secure in their privacy when politics are left in the hands of the professional minority. He also appears to assume that the private sphere, the sphere of home and local life, as it actually exists, offers people the scope they need for self-fulfilment. No doubt, if challenged, he would have agreed that the private sphere is at present more cramped and restricted than ideally it should be. But then the question arises of how that sphere is to be enlarged, if not by political action? And how is such action to be taken if people do not, by participating in politics, make plain their dissatisfactions with the present limited scope of private life?

A belief in the value of privacy need not imply that people have no public obligations, not that it is positively ominous if they participate in large numbers in public life. Yet in practice the liberal elevation of private life has been accompanied by a disparagement of public life — as in the lines by Auden quoted earlier. It has developed into a mood, and even an ethic, of withdrawal prompted by disillusion, which received classic expression in Matthew Arnold's 'Dover Beach':

> Ah, love, let us be true
> To one another! For the world, which seems
> To lie before us like a land of dreams,
> So various, so beautiful, so new,

Hath really neither joy, nor love, nor light,
Nor certitude, nor peace, nor help for pain;
And we are here as on a darkling plain
Swept with confused alarms of struggle and flight,
Where ignorant armies clash by night.

The impulse to withdraw recurs in twentieth-century writers like Forster, Orwell and Angus Wilson. Forster said of his own work that 'my books emphasize the importance of personal relationships and the private life, for I believe in them.' The obverse was a strong disbelief in public and political action: 'In the world of politics we see no salvation.'[27] Thus privacy becomes even more important because it is only within the private sphere that the values of liberalism and humanism can be preserved. Liberalism in this latter-day form has withdrawn almost entirely from the public world in despair. All the remains of the earlier campaigning and crusading liberalism are a few faint stirrings of the political conscience, a vague uneasiness:

. . . All right, it's late.
But, Angus: though it lies in wait
With terrible reproaches, fate
    May yet forgive
Our scared retreats, both small and great,
    And let us live.[28]

John Fuller's verse 'Letter to Angus Macintyre' perfectly catches this mood of uneasiness in seclusion. Liberalism has lost hope of gaining acceptance for its values in the public sphere, and so reconciles itself to preserving them in the few refuges and enclaves of privacy where Forster's 'aristocracy' of civilized people hold out against the surrounding barbarism. The defence of privacy need not be a sign of retreat and defeat, but in much contemporary liberalism it has become so.

CONSTITUTIONALISM AND THE RULE OF LAW

For as in absolute governments the King is law, so in free countries the law *ought* to be King; and there ought to be no other.
Thomas Paine, *Common Sense*[29]

Freedom, privacy and tolerance are ideals, at first no more than dreams, which in order to be realized (made real) must be embodied in rules, customs and institutions. We have already seen that traditionally liberals have regarded the state as the principal threat to the individual and her freedom. How is this danger to be met?

The first step is to assert, as a matter of fundamental principle, that the power and authority of the state or government is not absolute, but limited. There are two main ways by which this principle is to be established. The first is by making consent the basis of legitimate government. It can be argued, of course, that any government needs a measure of consent from the governed in order to function effectively at all. But the liberal position is not this pragmatic one: it is argued as a matter of principle that since government is for the benefit of society, so it ought to be based on the consent or support of society. Government must be thought of, not as autonomous, but as answerable and accountable for its actions. Consent is normally sought, and accountability enforced, through the device of elections. But whose consent does it need? To whom is it answerable? The commonest rhetorical answer was 'the nation', or 'the people'. But this *was* rhetorical since it was often not clear who exactly was included in these rather vague entities. 'The people' seldom meant all of the people. It seldom meant even all of the male people. The political nation to which the government was answerable was not until quite recently iden-tified with the whole population. Consent was required only from a minority of the propertied classes. Nevertheless, in spite of its limited application, the principle of accountability was in itself a check on government, especially when it was contrasted with the absolute and unlimited authority which some theorists, such as Bodin and Hobbes, had thought the state ought to have, and which some rulers were bold enough to claim and occasionally powerful enough to use.

But there were other methods which, from this point of view, were not less important. The essence of them was the placing of the state or government within a restricting framework of constitutional provisions and fundamental law. The state and its institutions must operate within limits which are either laid down in an explicit, written constitution, or take the form of a rather more vaguely conceived body of 'fundamental' laws and customs. The revolutionary states of the late eighteenth century celebrated their newness with written con-stitutions; but it was also held that England had been a constitutional, and therefore free, state since 1688, although it had no comparable single document to cite.

Among the constitutional provisions of the new United States of America, one of the most important in limiting the power of government was held to be the device of the separation of powers. This represented a challenge not only to absolutism, but also to the theory of sovereignty, which had been used to give intellectual support to absolutism and to the more general principle of the supremacy of the state. Hobbes had argued that the only adequate bulwark against division, civil conflict and chaos within a society was the establishment of a single and indivisible ultimate authority — a sovereign. Sovereignty was indivisible by definition; for if authority was divided, a further authority would be needed to arbitrate between the parties in cases of dispute, and that further authority would therefore be the effective sovereign. Hobbes's argument is irrefutable — so long as one thinks in terms of sovereignty. But first in practice, and later in theory, liberals have moved away from the idea of sovereignty. They have preferred to run the risks of conflict inherent in arrangements whereby state authority is divided. For, unlike Hobbes, their fear of a final and undivided power-cum-authority is greater than their fear of the possible consequences of splitting it up. Hence institutional safeguards against despotism are provided by the separation of powers — the allocation of different portions of the authority of the state to separate institutions, each of which will act as a rival to, and a check on, the others.

The power of the state was to be further circumscribed by the placing of the state within the limits of established law. Government is to be carried on according to 'the rule of law'. This notion, however, is by no means a clear one. Human laws do not, after all emanate directly from God or nature, even if they are thought to be based on divine or natural law. They have to be formulated by someone, even if it is not the king or sovereign. The transference of the law-making function from a king to a parliament or other assembly does not in itself provide any guarantee against unjust or tyrannical laws. However, it was argued that an elected and accountable assembly would find it more difficult to enact laws which were clearly partial or oppressive. And there were other restrictions on their law-making powers. Laws could only be made within the framework of the constitution. Or, if no explicit constitution existed, appeal was made to something like 'the spirit of the laws', to the traditional sense of what was legitimate and what rights it was accepted that people possessed, even if these were not inscribed in any particular document. Finally, the implementation and interpretation of the laws were to be placed in the hands of institutions which would be independent of the government of the day. In these various ways it was hoped that the 'rule of law' could be separated from, and raised above the mere will of the body that did actually make the laws.

But the rule of law meant still more than this. It meant an end to the arbitrariness which was so marked a feature of absolutist rule. It represented an attempt to replace the rule of whim by the rule of rules: '*Freedom of Men under Government* is, to have a standing Rule to live by, common to every one of that society and made by the Legislative Power erected on it.'[30] Part of the meaning of the rule of law was simply a minimum of consistency and impartiality. If something was permitted, then it was permitted to all. If something was an offence, then it was an offence no matter who committed it. The law was supposed to be impartial as between classes, between rich and poor, between the titled aristocrat and the starving beggar who hardly had a name. Of course, in a society of economic inequality this impartiality is not without its ironies, as Anatole France observed: 'The law, in its majestic equality, forbids the rich as well as the poor to sleep under bridges, to beg in the streets, and to steal bread.' Still, it was held to be an essential part of a rational society, and one which offered some security to the individual, that he or she should know where they were in relation to the laws. They should know what they could do with impunity, and what not. They should be able to know what measure of punishment awaited them if they committed an offence of a certain kind. The notion that law was nothing but the will of the sovereign, whoever or whatever that might be, was, in the liberal view, a recipe for uncertainty, insecurity, favouritism and arbitrariness. No man could be safe in possession of either his rights or his property so long as such a principle held sway. Even if he himself took no part in the making of laws, directly or indirectly, it was essential that those laws should have a certain reliability and permanence, and that they should be impartial as between individuals and classes.

Through such principles and devices as these it was hoped that the power of the state could be limited and the rights of the individual made reasonably secure. But there is an ambiguity in the liberal attitude towards both state power and the law. On the one hand there is the liberal view that the state is the chief threat to the individual and his freedom. This is supported by the picture of society as essentially a self-regulating mechanism, so that state or government 'interference' is often regarded as not merely unnecessary but positively disruptive: 'The more perfect civilisation is, the less occasion has it for government, because the more does it regulate its own affairs, and govern itself . . . how often is the natural propensity to society disturbed or destroyed by the operations of government.'[31] Paine looked forward to a steady reduction in the power and activity of the state as society steadily improved.

This tendency in liberalism is reinforced by the stress which many liberals have placed on the supposed antithesis between laws and freedom. Thus Berlin, in reference to both Hobbes and Bentham, says that 'Law is always a "fetter", even if it protects you from being bound in chains that are heavier than those of the law.'[32] All this points in the direction of an anarchist opposition to state, government and laws. Yet the purpose of the liberal apparatus of constitutionalism and the separation of powers is not to dissolve the power of the state but only to curb it. And although law may always be a fetter, liberals readily accept that such fetters are necessary, and have made 'the rule of law' one of their own most conscious slogans.

Imprisonment is the most blatant and basic way in which someone's liberty can be taken away. And from the moment of the fall of the Bastille the prison became a specially potent symbol or epitome of the kind of tyranny against which liberals were fighting.[33] Yet liberals have for the most part accepted prisons and imprisonment as necessary social institutions for the indefinite future. It seems that it is not imprisonment as such to which they object, but its arbitrary use. This is, however, no safeguard against a tyranny which operates through laws, as many contemporary authoritarian regimes in fact do. Such cases ought to make liberals more cautious than they usually are about using 'the rule of law' as a norm and a slogan. Structures of law such as those which enforce racial separation and inequality demonstrate the need for a concept of justice by which laws themselves can be judged.

So there are ambiguities in the liberal commitment to law. They claim to be suspicious of the state and its power, yet accept it as an indefinitely necessary evil. In so doing they accept, too, that there are necessarily limits to the freedom which the individual can expect to enjoy within the context of an 'orderly' society. The commitment to freedom is not quite as absolute as it is sometimes made to appear.

LIBERALISM AND DEMOCRACY

Liberty is more essential than democracy

Title of an article by Salvador de Madariaga, *Indian and Foreign Review*, 1 January 1968

'Liberal democracy' is such a common phrase that it is natural to imagine that the coinage denotes a perfectly harmonious marriage between the two consti-tuent principles. In fact the alliance, like many real-life marriages, has been an affair of compromises and concessions from the start, and of the partners it was liberalism which was always the more reluctant. Liberals wished to replace absolutism by limited government; and limited government was taken to mean government by consent. But whose consent? Once the notion of consent becomes current it is difficult to establish convincing arguments for limiting its application, especially since the arguments in its favour were characteristically couched in a universalist style which tended to contradict any principle of selection or exclusion. The idea of consent tends towards democracy.

Bourgeois liberals were thus increasingly hoist by their own petard. They valued the principle of consent in so far as it applied to themselves, but became fearful when it was taken over by radical spokesmen for the lower classes. Understandably so, since, as C. B. Macpherson has reminded us, democracy was not until very recently something of which everyone was expected to approve. On the contrary:

Democracy used to be a bad word. Everybody who was anybody knew that democracy in its original sense of rule by the people or government in accordance with the will of the bulk of the people, would be a bad thing — fatal to individual freedom and to all the graces of civilized living. [34]

Democracy meant essentially the rule of 'the mob'. Liberals were afraid that the overthrow of the old monarchical or aristocratic autocracies would lead to their replacement, not by the minimal state which most of them wanted, but by a new tyranny still more powerful than the old ones. Its power would derive precisely from its superior claims to legitimacy. Against a government which could claim to be enacting the will of the people, what safeguards could stand firm? Dissident minorities would appear merely as disgruntled and self-interested factions unwilling to accept the elementary democratic principle of majority rule. Dissident individuals would be in an even weaker position. In this way liberals saw the principle of consent, intended by them as a curb on government and as a basis for protecting individual rights, leading to a popular or democratic dictatorship which could offer a more serious threat to liberty than any known before.

Fears of this kind were expressed by some of the American Founding Fathers. 'Give all power to the many, they will oppress the few. Give all power to the few, they will oppress the many', said Hamilton. And Jefferson protested: 'One hundred and seventy three despots would surely be as oppressive as one . . . an *elective despotism* was not the government we fought for.'[35] Many of them despised 'the people', and were openly hostile to the idea of democracy.[36] From these attitudes sprang the carefully devised constitutional arrangements intended to curb the power of the state by dividing it. These anxieties and hostilities remain as a recurring theme in liberal writings of the nineteenth century, even among those who, like Mill, were in principle in favour of the widest popular participation in politics. Lord Acton explicitly distinguished between the liberal and the democrat:

> As to Democracy, it is true that masses of new electors are utterly ignorant, that they are easily deceived by appeals to prejudice and passion, and are consequently unstable, and that the difficulty of explaining economic questions to them, and of linking their interests with those of the State, may become a danger to the public credit, if not to the security of private property. A true Liberal, as distinguished from a Democrat, keeps this peril always before him.[37]

It was not only property which the ignorant masses were held to threaten. Others believed that culture and civilization were also in danger. Matthew Arnold's book of 1869 might have been called 'Culture *versus* Anarchy', since it saw culture, which depends on order and authority, as menaced by working-class demonstrations in favour of parliamentary reform — 'demonstrations perfectly unnecessary in the present course of our affairs'.[38]

But above all, democracy was seen as a potential threat to individual freedom. Whether one thought in terms of majority rule, or the sovereignty of the people, the danger was there. The point is essentially a logical one. Freedom is a matter of the absence of constraints and restrictions which prevent the individual from doing what he wants. Democracy is a matter of how goverments are chosen and to whom they are answerable. There is no necessary connection between the two issues: 'the opposite of liberalism is totalitarianism, while the opposite of democracy is authoritarianism. In consequence, it is at least possible in principle that a democratic government may be totalitarian, and that an authoritarian government may act on liberal principles.'[39] The fact that a government is elected will not in itself prevent it from restricting people's freedom. Quite the contrary, in fact. An 'elective despotism' would be less easily challenged than one the basis of which was patently arbitrary.

The anxiety is exacerbated if democracy is identified not simply with majority rule, but with the more exalted doctrine of popular sovereignty. Liberals are unhappy with the idea of sovereignty in any circumstances. But the concept of popular sovereignty is doubly objectionable because it implies the existence of a recognizable entity which can be called 'the people'. This offends against the liberal doctrine that society is made up of discrete individuals, or at the most, groups, all with their particular and distinct wills and interests. Notions such as 'the general interest' and 'the general will' not only obscure this: they also provide governments with plausible excuses for overriding the concrete interests of particular individuals and groups. According to Bernard Crick it is the essence of what he terms 'politics' to recognize and accept the essential diversity of the various groups and interests which make up society. Therefore 'politics' has to be defended against democracy, for 'The democratic doctrine of the sovereignty of the people threatens . . . the essential perception that all known advanced societies are inherently pluralistic and diverse, which is the seed and the root of politics.'[40]

It might be thought that one way of counteracting such a danger would be to encourage greater popular participation. The involvement of the widest range of groups and individuals might well ensure that particular interests were taken into account, and that decisions were not taken without due contest and debate. But, as we have seen, participation is regarded by many liberals as a *threat* to privacy and freedom. Others go further and see it as a step towards totalitarianism. Thus Rousseau, one of the leading theorists of democracy, has become a favourite target of contemporary liberal polemics. According to J. L. Talmon, who represents himself as a defender of liberal democracy, Rousseau 'demonstrates clearly the close relation between popular sovereignty taken to the extreme, and totalitarianism' precisely because of his insistence on 'the active and ceaseless participation of the people and of every citizen in the affairs of the State'. Talmon concludes 'Liberty is safer in countries where there are numerous levels of non-political private and collective activity, although not so much direct popular democracy, than in countries where politics take everything in their stride, and the people sit in permanent assembly.'[41] Talmon is a conservative rather than a strictly liberal writer, but this is one of many points where liberal and conservative thinking now overlap. Crick makes much the same point when he asserts that the doctrine of popular sovereignty 'if taken too seriously, is an actual step towards totalitarianism. For, quite simply, it allows no refuge and no contradiction, no private apathy even.'[42] Mill made a similar, though perhaps more sophisticated case, when he argued that democracy implies not only a certain style of government but also a certain type of society, in which 'public opinion' will enjoy an unprecedented ascendency. This powerful force, with its intolerance of deviance and non-conformity, will constitute a most serious threat to liberty and diversity. There is one major puzzle about liberalism's portrayal of all these various democratic monsters — the tyranny of the majority, popular participation, and public opinion. All of them assume that the pressure of the mass, the majority, or the public, will be a monolithic force in pushing in a single direction. But if, as liberals ceaselessly reiterate, society is composed of individuals and/or diverse groups and interests, if 'a people doesn't exist except as an abstract conception' (to repeat Dwight Macdonald's words), how is it that diverse individuals nevertheless act in this ominous unified manner when they come together? There is a sharp contradiction here between the liberals' pluralistic and individualistic analysis of society, and the liberal fear of democracy with its accompanying mythology of mobs and monolithic masses.

At worst liberals see democracy, 'taken to the extreme', as a threat to liberty, property and culture. At best it can be a means to liberty, provided the principles of democracy are revised and qualified in a way which provides safeguards against the danger of popular tyranny. It becomes so by being converted into 'liberal democracy', a formulation in which, as Guido de Ruggiero very candidly put it, 'the adjective Liberal has the force of a qualification.'[43] Democracy has increasingly been seen not as an end in itself, but as a means to preserving liberty, individuality and diversity: 'The distinctive features of democratic government, at least as we understand it in the western world, are intended to secure a maximum of liberty for citizens.'[44] The appearance of this bland statement in a representative 'introduction' to political philosophy indicates that this is now the consensus view. Democracy, in its existing limited representative forms, is believed to serve that purpose well. But proposals for extending democracy, or enlarging popular participation are another matter. Liberal democracy is limited democracy. Unlimited democracy is potentially, if not actually, totalitarian, and threatens the liberal values and institutions of personal freedom, private property and the market economy.

These are the fears which have inspired the description of the British political system as one of 'elective dictatorship', and led to revived demands for either a written constitution or a bill of rights in Britain. Attractive as a bill of rights may sound, the clear intention of its contemporary protagonists is to create a constitutional barrier to some of the more radical policies which might be enacted by a left-wing government with strong popular support, and in particular to prevent the enactment of policies which might involve attacks on private property, and private economic power, such as the ownership of newspapers and television companies. These fears are not very different from those aroused by popular political movements and extensions of the franchise in the nineteenth century.

REASON, SCIENCE AND PROGRESS

Reason, which has always been, and still is, a highly prestigious term, is also one of the most complex and elusive in the vocabulary of ideas. We have already noted that it has at least two general meanings, both of which figure prominently in liberal thinking. The narrower and more precise of these identifies reason with the ability to think logically, to make calculations and deductions. The broader conception is not necessarily antithetical to this, but is larger and more positive in its claims. The first conception, strictly interpreted, has no application to ends, only to means. It has nothing to say about ends, except as to whether they are 'realistic' — that is, attainable given the world as it is.

The other conception is not so confined. It has something to say about ends as well as means. Only certain purposes of the individual and of society deserve to be called rational. Tolerance, for example, is a rational policy, because it respects the limits of human knowledge, and makes no claim to certainty or rightness in areas, such as morals and religion, where such assurance cannot rationally be justified. Cruelty and the infliction of suffering, are likewise irrational, since it is evident that in all normal circumstances people try to avoid suffering and unhappiness. Reason is thus not morally neutral. Reason is not compatible with intolerance or dogmatism, or with cruelty and callousness.[45] It was therefore in the name of reason as well as humanity — for the two go together — that the liberals of the Enlightenment campaigned against the power of the Catholic Church and against the judicial use of torture. In this sense of the word reason is 'a normative and not a neutral scientific term', to quote Stuart Hampshire.[46]

Both these conceptions of reason have played a part in liberalism. Hence some of the conflicts and ambiguities within liberalism itself. The larger concept of reason has made many liberals active enemies of religion, or at least of religion in its more dogmatic and superstitious forms. This is the way in which the historian J. B. Bury used the term reason in his *A History of Freedom of Thought* (1913), when he entitled his chapter on Greece and Rome 'Reason free' and that on the Middle Ages 'Reason in prison'. Such hostility to Catholicism now seems rather old-fashioned in Anglo-Saxon countries, though not necessarily in countries such as Italy, Ireland and Portugal where the Roman Catholic Church still retains considerable political and ideological power. Many liberals would still want to insist on a connection between reason and tolerance, and tolerance is still at odds with religious bigotry.

Similarly, reason is often contrasted with tradition, custom and prejudice. The fully rational man will take nothing on trust, nothing on authority. He will think things through for himself, and make up his own mind. A characteristic example is provided by John Maynard Keynes, who wrote retrospectively (and not uncritically) of himself and his Cambridge contemporaries of the early 1900s: 'We repudiated entirely customary morals, conventions, and traditional wisdom. . . . We recognised no moral obligation on us, no inner sanction, to conform or to obey. Before heaven we claimed to be our own judge in our own case.'[47] Such attitudes are incompatible with the hold which habit and prejudice often exert over people's minds and lives. In this respect liberals are at odds with conservatives of the traditional Burkean variety. Nothing in Burke is more significant of his challenge to the Enlightenment than his open defence of prejudice:

> instead of casting away all our old prejudices, we cherish them to a very considerable degree, and, to take more shame to ourselves, we cherish them because they are prejudices. . . . Prejudice renders a man's virtue his habit; and not a series of unconnected acts. Through just prejudice, his duty becomes a part of his nature.[48]

From Burke to W. B. Yeats and Michael Oakeshott, conservatives have consistently expressed their mistrust of reason (or rationalism), and their faith in the virtues of tradition and custom. But the whole tendency of the liberal Enlightenment was in direct conflict with these celebrations of prejudice, custom and habits of thought unthinkingly inherited from the past.

This contraposition of reason to authority and tradition set liberals at odds with conservatives and with the power of established religion. But the definition of reason as calculation created a different kind of problem for liberalism. It raised the question of what value liberalism attaches to feeling; whether liberalism has a theory of imagination and art to rival the place occupied in its philosophy by reason and science. The younger Mill's account of his upbringing is well known: how the process of intellectual 'cramming' led to a complete personal breakdown at the age of twenty, which in turn sent him in quest of 'that culture of the feelings' which had been so totally neglected by Bentham and his father. This experience led Mill to adopt a more critical attitude towards Benthamism, and take an interest in the Anglicized version of German idealism represented by Coleridge and to some extent the young Thomas Carlyle. But it is doubtful whether Mill succeeded in assigning to art and imagination a much larger role that than of providing refreshment to the rational man when he is tired by his intellectual and reforming exertions.

Creative writers of liberal conviction were, naturally enough, particularly disturbed by the priority which calculation so evidently enjoyed over feeling in *laissez-faire* liberalism. This led Shelley, in *A Defence of Poetry*, to attack the prevalent narrow notion of utility, according to which 'the exercise of the imagination is most delightful, but . . . that of reason is more useful.' He argued — and he must have been one of the first to argue — that the accumulation of knowledge and the 'unmitigated exercise of the calculating faculty' had outstripped men's capacity to know how to use this great power to control and exploit nature:

> There is now no want of knowledge respecting what is wisest, and best in morals, government, and political economy, or at least what is wiser and better than what men now practise and endure. But . . . We want the creative faculty to imagine that which we know; we want the generous impulse to act that which we imagine . . . our calculations have outrun conception; we have eaten more than we can digest.' [49]

Shelley, despite his 'Romantic' label, was in no sense an anti-rationalist. On the contrary, he was, through Paine and Godwin, a direct heir of Enlightenment radicalism. But as an artist he was perplexed to know what role there was for him, and for the poet, in the developing industrial capitalist society. And as a radical democrat he saw that the political economy of liberalism was not producing the universal benefits which its proponents had predicted.

But it would be unfair to liberalism not to recognize that anxieties about the relations between rationality and feeling have been a recurring theme within the liberal tradition. In the twentieth century it has been a preoccupation of E. M. Forster and Lionel Trilling, among others, and even Keynes felt the force of D. H. Lawrence's vehement criticisms of the rationalism of the Cambridge—Bloomsbury circles to which he (Keynes) belonged: 'The attribution of rationality to human nature, instead of enriching it, now seems to me to have impoverished it. It ignored certain powerful and valuable springs of feeling. Some of the spontaneous, irrational outbursts of human nature can have a sort of value from which our schematism was cut off.' [50] A sort of value, certainly, but what sort? The claim that is made for imagination by writers from Blake, Wordsworth and Coleridge, through Keats and Shelley to Yeats, is that imagination as well as, if not more than, reason gives men access to truth. Hence Keats's 'Beauty is Truth', and Blake's many exclamations against eighteenth-century rationalism and empiricism: 'All that is Valuable in Knowledge is Superior to Demonstrative Science, such as is Weighed or Measured.'; 'God forbid that Truth should be Confined to Mathematical Demonstration!' [51] Historically and theoretically liberalism has had difficulty in responding sympathetically to such claims and criticisms because of its close association with empiricist and, to a lesser extent, rationalist theories of truth and knowledge. This is one source of that alienation of modern literature from the liberal ideology about which Trilling in particular has written at some length. [52]

But while liberalism has never developed a satisfying theory of art and imagination, it *has* laid claim to a special relationship with science, as we saw earlier. Liberalism is claimed to be the application of the scientific approach to politics and social life. And conversely, or reciprocally, science is held to represent the outstanding expression of the liberals' commitment to reason and empiricism. The interest shown by radical liberals like Paine, Jefferson and Joseph Priestley in inventions and technological developments, at the time of the British industrial revolution, is neither surprising nor coincidental. Material and technological progress was as integral a part of the world-wide advance of reason and enlightenment as was the sweeping away of feudal privileges, superstition and bigotry.

To begin with at least, the liberal conception of progress was of this uncomplicated kind, and apart from isolated figures like Shelley, most doubts about the economic and social effects of industrialization were expressed by radicals and conservatives who stood well outside the liberal mainstream. But misgivings about the supposed benefits of uncontrolled technological change, and about the unlimited exploitation of the planet and its limited resources, are now widespread. And apart from that, the political experience of the twentieth century has made any simple belief in continuous linear progress very hard to sustain. Liberalism has not been immune from the general loss of self-confidence which the capitalist world has experienced in this century. Keynes faithfully recorded the change of mood in the essay already quoted. He described his own generation as having been 'among the last of the Utopians, or meliorists as they are sometimes called, who believe in a continuing moral progress'. By the 1930s he had come to see this belief as mistaken. It ignored the 'insane and irrational springs of wickedness in most men', and it underestimated the extent to which 'civilisation was a thin and precarious crust erected by the personality and the will of a very few, and only maintained by rules and conventions skilfully put across and guilefully preserved.' [53] In the 1940s Cyril Connolly described himself as being one of thousands of 'Liberals without a belief in progress, Democrats who despise their fellow men'. [54] Yet it is significant that those who in recent years have attacked what they call the 'technocratic' character of our society, such as Theodore Roszak, have been denounced by orthodox liberals as 'Luddites' and champions of unreason or irrationalism. Clearly the traditional syndrome which links reason with science, technology and progress is still powerful.

Reason is still regularly invoked as a talisman by liberals, though clearly not always with the same meaning. Reason, for example, is often associated with persuasion and contrasted with force. It is claimed that the quintessential liberal method of going about things is to seek to persuade others, not by what are derogatorily termed 'emotional' appeals, but by rational arguments. Thus Paul Johnson, in a popular history of England, referred to 'the great tripod of the liberal ethic' as being 'the rejection of violence, the reaching of public decisions through free argument and voluntary compromise, and the slow evolution of moral principles tested by experience and stamped with the consensus.'[55] It is one thing to identify these as ideals, or aims, towards which liberals always strive. It is quite another to claim, as Johnson does, that these ideals have actually prevailed in English history, or more generally in the practice of liberalism. Leaving that aside for the moment, it is important to see what the liberals' professed faith in rational persuasion assumes. It assumes that rationality is, in principle, the universal possession of human beings. It also assumes that it is better to persuade than to compel, better that people should do something voluntarily than compulsorily. But what liberalism also assumes is that appeals to rationality can and do work. Or in other words, that rationality not merely can, but does, play a larger part in determining people's decisions and attitudes than their prejudices, feelings and material interests — using 'material' in a broad sense to include people's class-based concern with status, reputation and security as well as more narrowly economic considerations. Liberals constantly hope, or even believe, that people can be persuaded to sacrifice 'selfish' personal, group or class interests for the sake of some seemingly nobler goal, or even in the name of enlightened self-interest. They are equally constantly surprised and disappointed when this does not happen. This sets them apart from conservatives, who take a less optimistic or rationalistic view of human nature, and Marxists, who do not expect ideals or rational arguments to outweigh the commitment of a class and its members to their own interests as they perceive them.

But what happens when appeals to reason and attempts at persuasion fail? What then? Very often we are not told. Thus Talmon declares that as far as 'the final aims of liberal democracy' are concerned, 'the use of force is considered as an evil' — by contrast, of course, with 'totalitarian democracy', which resorts readily to the use of coercion[56] What Talmon does not say is whether the use of force is also considered to be a *necessary* evil. For to suggest that liberalism as a political practice involves, or has involved, the renunciation of force as non-rational, is quite false. It can and has been argued that the liberal belief in reason and liberal respect for the rights and freedom of the individual point logically in the direction of anarchism and pacifism. And liberalism does come close to anarchism at times — in the case of Paine, for example. But liberalism is not anarchism. As we have seen, it may not like prisons, but it has not pulled them down. And although some liberals have been pacifists, they have been a minority. The dominant tradition of liberalism has never renounced either coercion or killing. Whether we think of liberals like Paine and Jefferson, Byron and Garibaldi, fighting in wars of national independence or liberation, or of rebels like the Russian Decembrists, or of the liberal imperialists, or of liberal opponents of fascism and South African racism, or of liberal supporters of the Vietnam War, the conclusion must be the same: most liberals have always been prepared to use force and fight wars when it seems to them that persuasion and argument were no longer effective. Even if the dubious liberal hypothesis of an antithesis between reason and force or violence is accepted, there is still a glaring contrast between the self-image and the reality of liberalism in this respect. Whatever qualms of conscience they may have, liberals generally do not renounce force in politics, and to that extent their own claims to be committed exclusively to the use of reason and persuasion are bogus. [57] I cannot see what other conclusion is possible.

LIBERALISM AND CAPITALISM

There are thus significant discrepancies between the reality of liberalism and its public self-image. Liberals have always been happy to advertise their commitments to freedom, tolerance, reason and the rule of law. Contemporary liberals are willing to endorse 'liberal democracy', though previously not all liberals were prepared to be counted as democrats. I have tried to suggest that these commitments are seldom as unambiguous and as straightforward as they are sometimes made out to be. But the overall picture is further complicated by those commitments which used on occasions to be openly avowed, but have more recently become, for most liberals, sources of embarrassment and unease. So, without ever being generally or openly abandoned, they are relegated to a limbo where they lurk half-concealed like rocks which the liberal steersman wishes to avoid, but which for that very reason cannot be wholly ignored. These half-hidden commitments are mostly to do with the relationship of liberalism to capitalism. In particular they involve the issues of private property, inequality and class.

Liberalism grew up together with Western capitalism, and even today liberal-democratic political systems only flourish in advanced capitalist countries. Attempts to establish such systems in ex-colonial countries of the Third World have collapsed, and even those countries which once looked like exceptions to this general rule, such as Uruguay, Chile and India, have had their electoral systems and civil liberties destroyed or threatened. This can hardly be coincidental. And there are at least two schools of thought which, from opposite angles, would argue strongly that it is not.

On the one hand Marxists argue that capitalism contains, rather than supports, liberal democracy. The state and the political system are not autonomous and sovereign agencies through which the popular will can, if it so wishes, change or abolish capitalism. They are subordinate to the nature and purposes of the capitalist economy. Where there are signs that democracy may lead to a political assault on capitalism, democracy is either distorted — as in Italy, in order to exclude the Communist Party from office — or destroyed — as in Chile in 1973 — to prevent this. Tolerance is only extended to those who do not seriously threaten capitalism. Socialism can only be accommodated in the form of social democracy, which accepts and administers capitalism rather than seeking to abolish it. There are, in other words, quite narrow limits to the freedom and democracy which capitalism can and will allow.

From the opposite political position, there are those economists and politicians, like F. A. Hayek, Milton Friedman, Keith Joseph and Margaret Thatcher, who argue that there can be no liberal democracy, no individual freedom, without capitalism. Socialism and fascism are the alternatives — state-dominated economies which are authoritarian, if not totalitarian, in their power over society as a whole. Not only should our concept of freedom include economic freedom — the freedom to compete in the making of profits — but other kinds of freedom are dependent upon the existence of economic freedom. The existence of economic power in private hands is a safeguard of individual liberties because it limits the power of the state. The position of Hayek, Friedman and their followers is fundamentally that of liberals from Adam Smith to Herbert Spencer. But mainstream liberalism has changed since then, and their position on the British political spectrum now appears as an ultra-conservative one; though it doubtless seems less eccentric in countries such as the USA, Australia and Japan, where the entire spectrum of politics lies further to the right.

It is nearly 60 years since Keynes, the leading liberal economist of the twentieth century, and a supporter of the British Liberal Party, published his historic essay 'The End of Laissez-Faire'. In it Keynes explicitly rejected many of the central tenets of the old creed:

> The world is *not* so governed from above that private and social interest always coincide. It is *not* so managed here below that in practice they coincide. It is *not* a correct deduction from the principles of economics that enlightened self-interest always operates in the public interest. Nor is it true that self-interest generally *is* enlightened . . . .[58]

Rejecting the doctrine of a natural harmony of interests, as well as the slightly more sophisticated argument that the intervention of the state will in the end only make things worse, Keynes went on to suggest what the form and direction of state action should be. He did not attack what he called 'doctrinaire State Socialism' primarily on moral grounds, but for pragmatic reasons: it offered policies which were no longer relevant, remedies for ills which were being abolished in any case by the steady movement of capitalist enterprises away from a competitive obsession with profits towards rationalized monopoly or near monopolies: 'They are, as time goes on, socialising themselves. . . . The battle of Socialism against unlimited private profit is being won in detail hour by hour.' Nevertheless Keynes argues in favour of giving the state a more positive role in managing the economy: 'The important thing for government is not to do things which individuals are doing already, and to do them a little better or a little worse; but to do those things which at present are not done at all.' Keynes was not a socialist economist, and unlike some of his social democratic followers, he was not so confused as to suppose that what he was recommending was a gradualist shift from capitalism to socialism. On the contrary, his explicit intention was to secure adjustments in capitalism which would enable it to survive in a more rational and humane, and therefore more stable, form:

> These reflections have been directed towards possible improvements in the technique of modern capitalism by the agency of collective action. There is nothing in them which is seriously incompatible with what seems to me to be the essential characteristic of capitalism, namely the dependence upon an intense appeal to the money-making and money-loving instincts of individuals as the main motive force of the economic machine. [59]

Keynes did not despise the pursuit of wealth. He played the stock-market himself with considerable success. He regarded the pursuit of wealth as a comparatively harmless employment of energies which might otherwise be deflected into more dangerous channels. But his more serious defence of capitalism was the traditional one. What he called 'individualism', by which he meant scope 'for the exercise of private initiative and responsibility' in the economic field, was in his view 'the best safeguard of personal liberty' and 'of the variety of life'. [60] Capitalism, in Keynes's view, protects and promotes both freedom and variety.

So Keynes, although he shocked many liberals — and social democrats — by the novelty of his proposals, was perfectly candid about his own commitment to capitalism, based as it was upon quintessentially liberal arguments. 'The difficulty is that the capitalist leaders in the City and in Parliament are incapable of distinguishing novel measures for safeguarding capitalism from what they call Bolshevism.' [61] Later liberals have usually been less blunt in their defence of capitalism, and their unease is reflected in the various less provocative euphemisms that are commonly used — 'free enterprise', 'the mixed economy', and so forth. Nevertheless, allowing for some differences of opinion over the extent of desirable state intervention or management, support for capitalism remains the basic liberal position. Hostility to what, like Keynes, they typically refer to as *state* socialism, remains constant.

If pressed, most contemporary liberals, including many social democrats, would probably offer a defence of capitalism along the same lines as Keynes. They might well reject the neo-conservative campaign to rehabilitate *laissez-faire*, but they would agree with Keynes that capitalism does allow and encourage individual enterprise and initiative as socialism supposedly does not. It is not possible (they would argue), and it is not realistic to seek to separate individual economic enterprise from all the other expressions of personal energy and ability. If there is to be scope for individuals to express themselves, this must include the opportunity to 'get on' economically. It is not realistic to think that people will exert themselves if they are to get no material reward from it. There are, of course, other incentives besides purely economic ones, but economic incentives cannot be disregarded. Even the Communists have discovered this, they point out gleefully. Opportunities for the individual must include economic opportunities.

It must follow from this that liberals regard a measure of inequality as not only unavoidable but positively desirable. Keynes was, as usual, quite explicit about this. [62] But it has become ever more difficult for liberals to admit this, since economic inequality is now so widely associated with social injustice. Yet if economic incentives are to operate effectively, and if economic opportunities are to mean anything, individuals must be able to make money and to keep it once they have made it. Of course liberals can hardly afford to renounce altogether the slogan of 'equality'. Like freedom and democracy it is now too prestigious a term to be completely abandoned to one's political opponents. The equality which liberals claim to believe in is equality of opportunity. People should be given an equal 'start' in life, but if energy, ability and merit are to achieve their 'due' reward, they will end up unequally. The principle that such virtues should be rewarded precludes the possibility of a high degree of overall economic and social equality. Liberals subscribe to the classic bourgeois idea of the career open to talent. Merit, not birth or title or privilege, should be rewarded. Hereditary inequality is unacceptable. Inequality which reflects merit or desert is not.

But at this point we encounter yet another contradiction within liberalism. The principle of equality of opportunity, of providing to every one an equal 'start' in life, implies that it should not be possible to transmit wealth, privilege and advantage from one generation to the next. But endowing one's children or heirs with money, a privileged education and other advantages beyond the common lot is precisely what many parents want most of all to do with the money they have acquired. To prevent them from doing this for the sake of equality of opportunity would require 100 per cent death duties and other drastic measures to prevent the passing on of wealth and advantage. This would not only act as a powerful disincentive to individual economic enterprise. It would also be an attack on the rights of property. So if liberals took the principle of equality of opportunity really seriously, they would be obliged to qualify their commitment to two central institutions of capitalism: individual economic incentives, and private property. By and large liberals have not been prepared to do this, any more than they have been prepared to prevent the rich from buying a superior education for their children, with all the social and career advantages that normally accompany it. Clearly in practice liberals assign a higher priority to the freedom to acquire money and use it as you please than they do to equality of opportunity, or to the principle that rewards should accrue to merit alone.

Perhaps this is not surprising. We have already noted that the liberal principle of respect for the individual and his/her rights does not extend to the renunciation of all coercion or killing. The theoretical individualism of the liberals is constantly modified by their acceptance of the legitimacy of more mundane or 'realistic' demands of politics and economics. So it is not out of character that liberalism should be reluctant to interfere with the rights of property and inheritance, even though a consistent regard for the equal rights of all individuals requires such interference. We have already noticed how deeply and how early ideas of possession entered into liberal thought. We are said to *possess* rights, and to *possess* our bodies and their labour, in the same way as we (may) possess material property. But these more metaphysical forms of ownership should not divert our attention from the great importance which liberalism attaches to property in the most elementary material sense of the word.

The self-interest which liberalism generally attributes to the individual is assumed to take, in part, the form of the desire for material possessions. This is neither sordid nor irrational since, as Keynes pointed out, it is through material possessions and money that men and women can enlarge their own lives and a variety of life-styles become possible. But liberals also connect freedom with private property in terms of the independence which property confers on its owners. This is an abiding theme of liberal argument, and it has a variety of implications, not all of them equally attractive. For example, it was contended by Whigs and liberals that the poor and propertyless were, by virtue of their poverty, at the mercy of both the rich and governments. They were susceptible to bribery. They were dependent rather than independent. There was truth in this; and one conclusion might have been that it was desirable to make the poor less poor, and spread property rather more evenly through the nation as a whole. But eighteenth-century Whigs drew a different conclusion. They held that it proved the rightness of restricting the franchise and political participation generally to men who already possessed enough property to make them immune to bribery at its usual level.

To argue that the secure possession of enough to provide a modestly comfortable standard of life forms a basis for personal independence is reasonable. But the logic of this argument points in the direction of what might be called a Rousseauist type of society: a society composed of self-employed artisans owing their own homes and means of production; by implication a society necessarily without extremes of wealth and poverty. That is the level and type of property ownership which confers independence. But property ownership on a larger scale — the ownership of houses in which other people live, and of offices and factories in which other people work — self-evidently places those who are tenants or employees in a position of dependence. Yet liberalism, in its defence of private property as a bulwark of individual freedom, has not discriminated between the small-scale ownership which promotes independence, and the large-scale ownership which generates dependence and exploitation. They have not much concerned themselves with the power of property, nor sought actively to redistribute it on a more equal basis. Nor has there been an effective liberal attack on the inheritance of property. In other words, neither the professed liberal commitment to equality of opportunity and rewards for talent and merit, nor the association of private property with personal independence, has been allowed to interfere with the rights of property as such. When it comes to the choice of priorities, respect for private property, however acquired and on however large a scale, has taken precedence over concern with equality of opportunity and personal independence.

This indicates one of the many limitations which the actual commitments of liberalism place upon its theoretical individualism. The concept of 'the individual' is in essence universal and egalitarian. As individuals we are all equal, of equal worth and with equal rights. The egalitarian character of individualism could quite reasonably be held to require in practice a high degree of economic and social equality. The very least that it requires is equality of opportunity. Yet in practice even this lies beyond liberalism because it requires extensive interference with the rights of property and the accumulation and transmission of wealth. Again, if private property provides a firm foundation for individual freedom, then every individual should share in it; yet liberals have never been happy about expropriation or the compulsory redistribution of property, or indeed about any form of what is tendentiously called 'levelling down'. Property and capitalism do not often figure prominently in the definition of liberalism, or lists of liberal values, which liberals themselves put on display. But I think we are justified in concluding that both play a far more important part in determining the concrete historical character of liberalism than has often been recognized.

This in turn raises the still more awkward question of class. How a class is defined, and on what basis a particular social group maintains its position and privileges, are difficult and much debated questions which cannot be entered into here. It will, however, be generally accepted that the ability to transmit wealth and advantage from one generation to the next is at least one of the means by which a perhaps temporary elite converts itself into an entrenched class. Thus, in so far as liberals are unwilling seriously to obstruct the process of passing on wealth and property from one generation to the next, they are in effect acquiescing in the maintenance of class and class privileges.

But it would not for this reason be true to say that the liberals are consciously and openly committed to the maintenance of a class society. If anything, the opposite is closer to the truth. Historically liberalism has involved a frontal assault on feudal privileges. And conceptually liberal individualism is by nature universalist: it does not think of people as members of classes or other social or national groups, but as individuals, fundamentally alike and equal members of the human species. Phrases like 'regardless of colour, class or creed' are part of the stock-in-trade of liberal political rhetoric. No liberal has ever offered the kind of overt defence of a stable class structure which can be found in conservative writers like Burke, T. S. Eliot, and Yeats. Yet liberals are not levellers in the ordinary sense of the word. They do not share the substantive notions of equality to be found in Rousseau or socialist writers. But they do believe in equality before the law, in equal civil and political rights, and in equality of opportunity.

Once again we encounter a contradiction between the proclaimed principles of liberalism and its actual commitments. And since this contradiction exists *within* liberalism, what it has produced among liberals is a constant evasiveness and uneasiness about the whole question of class. They cannot defend class, but they are unwilling to attack it. So they prefer to pretend that it doesn't exist, or that it is withering away, or that it doesn't really matter anyway. The liberal attitude to class is a classic case of bad faith. There are many good reasons, both historical and conceptual, for regarding liberalism itself, and its priorities, as an essentially middle-class or bourgeois political creed. And many liberals would themselves concede this, without necessarily allowing that this in itself limits the relevance or importance of the liberal values. Yet beyond this they shy away from looking any more closely at the realities of class or at its impact on their own complex of beliefs and attitudes.

Thus although in principle the commitment to the individual and his or her rights stands at the centre of liberal theory, in reality this commitment is constantly diluted by the liberal commitment to other apparently less central principles, or simply by liberal 'realism'. Contemporary liberals attack 'utopians' for their apparent willingness to sacrifice the real, living individuals of today to some distant future goal or harmony or happiness. In practice, however, liberals accept the right of at least liberal-democratic states to conscript young men and send them off to die in wars fought for goals which are often equally uncertain and 'Utopian'. Liberal writers present imprisonment as the absolute antithesis of personal freedom; yet they accept the use of imprisonment by the liberal state for a vast range of offences, not all of which by any stretch of argument could be regarded as infringements of, or threats to, the liberties of others. They are fond of quoting Kant's dictum about treating each individual as an end rather than a means to some further end. Yet they normally accept the legitimacy of using punishments and penalties as deterrents. The concept of 'the individual' is asexual: it makes no distinction between men and women. Yet it is extraordinary how few of the liberal champions of the rights of man have also been champions of the equal rights of woman. John Stuart Mill stands out as an honourably consistent exception to the general rule. Of course this unthinking exclusion of half the human race is not peculiar to liberalism. Socialism, which is supposed to extend radical thought and practice beyond the confines of liberalism, has also been blighted by it. And it is not a question of 'blaming' liberals for this failure, as if they could realistically have been expected to think otherwise. Nevertheless, we must note this as one further way in which liberals have failed to be consistent in their individualism. To be sure, such consistency would have required a degree of penetrating radicalism which is rare at any time and in any creed. But this is only another way of saying that the practice of liberalism has turned out to be a great deal less radical and subversive of established forms of inequality and oppression than one might expect if one looked only at liberal theory, and accepted it at its own valuation.

In the first part of this book I have tried to outline what I take to be the essentials of the liberal world-view, the liberal theory of politics, society and individual and social values. All this assumes that there is some constant hard-core of liberalism, and that the word is not simply over-stretched to cover a variety of disparate and unconnected phenomena. Nevertheless, such an approach runs the danger of presenting too unified and too fixed a picture of something which has taken different shapes at different times, and which also has a history and a development which need to be charted. For liberalism is not reducible to a set of general and abstract propositions. It is a historical movement of ideas and a political and social practice. We misread its character and underestimate its chameleon talents if we abstract too much from its actual history. To complete the picture, and rectify the balance, we must turn now to view liberalism in its historical perspective.

PART II

The Evolution of Liberalism

5

The Beginnings of
Modern Liberalism

Where does the history of liberalism begin? It would obviously be absurd to try to attach too precise a date to the beginning of anything so general as an ideology or movement of ideas. There are few, if any, absolute discontinuities in human history, and historians in pursuit of origins and roots usually find themselves pushing further and further back into the past. They are rightly anxious to avoid the artificiality of tidying history into separate compartments labelled 'medieval' and 'modern', and so forth. Yet such researches can end up by over-emphasizing continuities and playing down novelty, until we are almost persuaded that there is nothing new under the sun, or at least no major development in European thinking since Aquinas, or even Plato.

This historical sketch is done from a more traditional angle. The development of modern liberalism is dated from the Renaissance. For it is not until that period that we find the development on a significant scale of the view of humanity and the world which forms the indispensable philisophical core of modern liberalism. That core is individualism, and an unprecedented perception of the human person as an individual is a central feature of the Renaissance. Equally striking, and equally important to the subsequent development of liberalism, is the humanism of the Renaissance, by which I mean not the recovery of classical literature but humanism in its wider and more ordinary sense: a faith in humankind, and a sense of human dignity and potentialities. This too had not been seen before in such a powerful, enduring and fully developed form.

Certainly neither individualism nor humanism were without ancestry or precedent. The idea of a clean break between the medieval and modern eras is no longer tenable, if indeed it ever was. Awareness of the individual, and the development of individualistic forms of life and art, had evolved, unevenly but unmistakeably, within the context of medieval culture, as Colin Morris, for example, has shown in his study of the so-called twelfth-century Renaissance.[1] Medieval Christianity was not always as collective and institutional as is sometimes supposed. Personalized piety and the highly individual visions of the mystics flourished strongly in the later Middle Ages; while Morris points to a number of phrases common in the twelfth century which were 'suited to express the ideas of self-discovery and self-exploration',[2] and discusses autobiographies and portraits, as well as literary forms such as satire and romance, both of which in different ways reflected a kind of individualism.

Sometimes the genealogy of liberalism has been traced much further back, to classical Greece. Karl Popper, Eric Havelock,[3] and others, have suggested that the conflict between Plato and the Athenian democrats was in essence the same as that between totalitarians and liberals today, and that figures such as Pericles and, in Shapiro's view, even Socrates, should be seen as the real founders of Western liberalism.

There is a good deal of anachronism and romanticizing in all this. It is clearly excessive to describe Athens as 'a full-fledged democracy', as J. B. Bury did,[4] even if, as far as those who came within the pale of the constitution were concerned, it *was* much more democratic than any modern democracy. And to describe Pericles, as Popper does, as 'a great equalitarian individualist' who 'formulated . . . the democratic creed . . . in a manner which has never been surpassed',[5] is equally odd for several fairly evident reasons, among which the existence of slavery and the automatic exclusion of women from citizenship are the most substantial.

Moreover, it was not during the ascendancy of Pericles as first citizen, but after his death that 'something more like true democracy, warts and all, begins to appear.'[6] Professor Peter Green, that great debunker of cherished myths about the ancient Greeks, has shrewdly suggested that the cult of Pericles among modern liberal scholars and commentators derives precisely from the fact that under his leadership Athens was not in fact *too* democratic. Power remained in the hands of a cultivated elite; popular power was kept at bay.

It is true that the Greeks did have a concept of equality between persons, and a concept of the rights of the individual citizen. But equality existed only among citizens. People derived their rights from their membership of the *polis*, which remained the primary entity, individuals being secondary, and dependent upon it. As Hobbes put it: 'The Liberties, whereof there is so frequent, and honourable mention, in the Histories, and Philosophy of the Antient Greeks, and Romans . . . is not the Liberties of Particular men; but the Libertie of the Commonwealth. . . .'[7] This liberty was not extended to non-citizens: women, subjects and slaves. Equality was not universalized. It was not in the classical heyday of the fifth century, but in the Hellenistic period that it was argued that a human being, simply by virtue of being such, possessed rights. And even then it is debatable whether this implied a rejection of slavery.[8] Still, it is the Hellenistic period which is the age of classical individualism, of the cult of privacy and withdrawal, and the search for self-fulfilment outside the context of the *polis*. Yet it is not to this period that those who want to provide liberalism with a classical pedigree normally look. They turn instead to the fifth century and earlier.

No doubt it is possible to find there some of the separate ingredients of modern liberalism. But they form part of a different complex of ideas, of a way of thinking which, as we saw earlier, is in many important respects the diametrical opposite of modern liberalism. Classical Greek liberalism, if it is helpful to use such a word at all in the context of the ancient world, was a qualitatively different phenomenon from the liberalism which has developed in the past five centuries.

If, however, so-called classical liberalism is excluded, should we not pay more attention to the medieval epoch? The old Whig version of English, and even Western, history saw it as a more or less unbroken advance towards freedom. Magna Carta was one of the first signposts on the way, and its goal was the recovery of that legendary Anglo-Saxon liberty which had supposedly been destroyed by the Norman Conquest. One might have thought that this grand illusion belonged only to the nineteenth century. But it lives on, in the work of such historians as Sidney Painter, Walter Ullmann, and even Karl Wittfogel, to say nothing of popularizations like Paul Johnson's *The Offshore Islanders*. Painter and Ullmann see in feudalism, and especially English feudalism, the root and source of all that is best in modern liberal constitutionalism. Feudalism, according to these writers, was a form of government by consent and under the law. Law was the product of 'consultation', 'co-operation' and 'team work' between the king and the feudal barons.[9] Painter goes even further than Ullmann in presenting feudalism as the direct ancestor of liberalism. 'The Feudal system' he wrote, 'fostered individual liberty.'[10] Constitutionalism evolved gradually and painlessly out of feudalism.[11] Both Britain and the USA were the beneficiaries of this continuity: 'the basic feudal idea has remained one of the fundamental political principles of the Anglo-American peoples.'[12] Less fortunate countries, such as France, had to travel the 'bloodstained' road of revolution.

This is really a very weird hypothesis. Exactly the opposite case can be, and has been, argued with at least as much plausibility: that it was in countries where the feudal order lasted longest, such as France and Russia, that revolutions became inevitable. Feudal nobilities were certainly jealous guardians of their own privileges, or liberties — and Painter allows that the latin *liber* meant privileged rather than free. But there is little indication that they were willing to allow these privileges to be extended to other classes — to be converted from class privileges into general rights — except under the pressure of extreme political necessity. Let us leave aside the bizarre claim that *American* constitutionalism is one of the products of feudalism — are we to suppose that feudalism made the Atlantic crossing in the baggage of the Pilgrim Fathers? As far as England is concerned it is clear that the Painter-Ullmann Whig picture of feudalism is an absurd idealization. The virtually uninterrupted succession of baronial revolts, wars, plots, succession disputes and quarrels between king and parliament hardly add up to a pattern of 'co-operation leading to team work'. And the thesis of a gradual evolution from feudalism to liberal constitutionalism depends upon ignoring, or at best whitewashing, the two centuries between the accession of the Tudors and the coup by which James II was bundled off the throne in 1688. Feudal anarchy was ended by the imposition of the Renaissance despotism of the Tudors, while the semi-parliamentary limited monarchy of the eighteenth century was only achieved through a long struggle against Stuart absolutist ambitions, which culminated in the civil war of the 1640s. It is extraordinary how easily that war is overlooked by the Whig-liberals, intoxicated by their own vision of English history as the epitome of peaceful gradualism.

It would be wrong to suggest that there is a complete break between medieval constitutionalism and its modern liberal versions. On the contrary. In the early struggles against absolutism in the Netherlands, France and England, medieval or supposedly medieval precedents were frequently cited. In this way the constitutionalists were able to present their case within a conservative framework, arguing that they were seeking, not innovations, but the restoration of traditional rights. Often they misinterpreted the past and underestimated the novelty of their own proposals. But there is a kind of continuity here, sustained by what they believed about the past rather than by what the past actually was. The Whig history of Ullmann and Painter belongs to the same tradition, although three centuries later it wears a fustian air, and serves only a conservative purpose.

I do not want to overstate the case. The history of modern liberalism would have taken a different shape without the precedents and pointers supplied to it by classical civilization and the medieval experience. Nevertheless, the Renaissance does constitute a turning point in European history, and it is at this turning point that the distinctive world-view of liberalism begins to emerge. From this historical moment onwards it is possible to trace the continuous development of liberalism, conceived of not merely as a movement of ideas, but as a real and substantial social and political force.

'MAN' AT THE CENTRE

The liberal world view is essentially anthropocentric and individualistic, and therefore ultimately secular in character; but during its gestation in the

Renaissance period it is seen as compatible with religious orthodoxy, and even with a revived, more fervent if less dogmatic Catholicism. To begin with there is little that is overtly political in these developments. But the self-consciously archaic forms of Italian, and in particular Florentine, civic humanism, together with the conflicts between republicanism and autocracy within and among the Italian city states do foreshadow the future political shape and struggles of liberalism.

This civic humanism also illustrates the importance, in the early modern period, of examples drawn from classical antiquity, in particular from Rome rather than Greece. For Renaissance dreams of recreating life in the image of an idealized classical past extended beyond literature and the arts. In 1347 in Rome, Cola di Rienzi resurrected the Roman republic for an astonishing seven months; and in the late fourteenth and early fifteenth centuries the Florentine republic was seen by its own leaders and historians as the true heir of the original Roman republic, with the mission of reviving the civic virtues which that classical model was believed to have embodied. Leonardo Bruni, in his *History of the Florentine People*, argued that Rome was at its greatest as a republic. The loss of freedom under the empire was fatal, for freedom and the civic virtues go together. [13]

The word *liberta* — *santissima liberta*, 'a gift to be desired above everything else' [14] — figured prominently in this republican outlook, and was associated both with the independence of the city-state from external domination and with internal self-government. In both cases what is implied, however, is a *collective* freedom, the autonomy of the state and the political community. In this respect the thinking of the Florentine humanists is more classical than modern and individualistic. Nor was internal self-government pushed to any kind of democratic extreme. Even Florence, where the notions of political participation and the citizen's rights were taken most seriously, never moved beyond a participatory oligarchy. It has been estimated that perhaps 3,000 out of a total population of 100,000 were able to take part in the political life of the city. [15] The gap between the generalized language of rights and liberty, and the very restricted reality, is therefore obvious. But this contrast is, as we shall see, a recurring contradiction within the history of liberalism, and so does not deprive the episode of all significance.

Later in the fifteenth century the civic tradition went into retreat as Florence, like most other city states, succombed to the rule of princely despots. And so, when Alamanno Rinucinni turns to the theme of liberty in 1479, he in effect offers a reinterpretation of the term: liberty is to be obtained by withdrawing from political life and cultivating an inner serenity. [16] Pico della Mirandola, in his famous oration, developed the same theme. Liberty ceases to be a public and political possession; instead it becomes a spiritual condition which can be attained by the individual in any situation no matter how hostile. Luther reinterpreted the concept in much the same way. By the time that Machiavelli came to write his *Discourses*, around the years 1513—19, his commendation of classical republicanism looked like an exercise in nostalgia, particularly since he had also produced, in *The Prince*, an incomparable analysis of the characteristic workings of a Renaissance autocracy. Nevertheless, the conflict between constitutionalism and autocracy in Renaissance Italy is the first episode in the conflict between feudal absolutism and a half-traditional constitutionalism through which liberal political ideas first develop. And the revived tradition of classical republicanism, symbolized in the sixteenth century by the independent oligarchy of Venice, makes an important contribution to the evolution of modern liberal constitutionalism, as we shall see.

'Man' at the centre of the world-picture — this conception is the product of the new humanism of this period, a humanism qualitatively different from what had gone before. Within the Christian scheme of things humanity occupied a special place, for it was humanity whom Christ had come down to earth to save. But human beings still existed within a cosmic hierarchy of created beings, supernatural as well as natural. All these beings had their allotted ends and purposes, which they necessarily pursued in so far as they were under God's control.

Whatever they may have intended, the picture of 'man' developed by leading Renaissance thinkers contained an implicit challenge to this teleological view. The philosophy set out, most famously, in Pico's *Oration on the Dignity of Man*, but already developed by his teacher Marsilio Ficino, explicitly excludes 'man' from the Christian-Aristotelian scheme of beings with fixed ends or purposes. Indeed, it is just this absence of a fixed purpose which gives to 'man' his unique dignity and glory. Pico imagines God addressing newly created 'man':

> The nature of all other things is limited and constrained within the bounds of laws prescribed by Us. Thou, constrained by no limits, in accordance with thine own free will . . . shalt ordain for thyself the limits of thy nature. We have set thee at the world's centre that thou mayest from thence more easily observe whatever is in the world. We have made thee neither of heaven nor of earth, neither mortal nor immortal, so that with freedom of choice and with honour, as though the maker and moulder of thyself, thou mayest fashion thyself in whatever shape thou shalt prefer. [17]

'Man's' supreme 'felicity' is that he can 'be whatever he wills'. This celebration of the plasticity of human nature and its apparently limitless potentialities goes well beyond the Christian orthodoxy about free will, with its usual warnings against the misuse of this dangerous gift. Other Renaissance writers, such as the Spanish humanist Vives and the Aristotelian Pompanazzi, also elaborate on this theme.

The sculptural metaphor of creativity which Pico uses in relation to 'man's' power over himself is significant, since it was the Renaissance which first developed the idea of art as creation rather than imitation. This also implied a more exalted notion of human abilities, as expressed in Tasso's near-blasphemous dictum: 'There are two creators, God and the poet.'[18] Thus humanism is linked to the artistic efflorescence of the period.

Architecture reflected the new and more confident view of humankind. Protagoras' proud dictum that 'man is the measure of all things' which the Renaissance revived, had its literal application in the theories of proportion and perspective on which so much building and painting of the age were based. It was a principle of Renaissance neo-classicism that buildings should reflect in their proportions the proportions of the human body, rather than being scaled to the absolute size of human beings as Gothic buildings had been. There are drawings which show how even the groundplan of a church might be envisaged as corresponding to the proportions of the human body. 'Man' was taken as the measure, because, following the principles set out by the rediscovered Roman theorist Vitruvius, it was held that the human body literally incorporated the most fundamental and harmonious forms that could be conceived: the circle and the square. Leonardo's famous drawing of a man whose extended arms and legs reach to the extremities of a square and a circle is only the best known version of a standard Vitruvian diagram. It was not an ingenious trick, but a key to understanding the deep harmony of the world and 'man's' central place within it. 'This simple picture' wrote Rudolf Wittkower 'seemed to reveal a deep and fundamental truth about man and the world, and its importance for Renaissance architects can hardly be overestimated.'[19] Just as a Christianity which stresses humanity's potential rather than our fallen nature focuses on the incarnation rather than the crucifixion, so in Renaissance church design there is a shift away from the cross as a basic ground plan to plans based on the Roman basilica and the circle.

This did not represent a conscious challenge to religion, but rather a shift of emphasis within the context of Christianity. Similarly, the Christian humanism of which Erasmus, Thomas More, John Colet and Lefevre d'Etaples were leading representatives, was intended to promote, not a move away from the church, but a programme for its revival and reform. Nevertheless, in its attitude towards orthodox theology it was perhaps more catholic than Catholic. Erasmus, who admired and learnt from Pico della Mirandola, saw Christianity as a way of life rather than a set of theological truths: 'True theology is possessed by every man who is inspired and guided by the spirit of Christ, be he a digger or a weaver.'[20] Of the New Testament he wrote 'this sort of philosophy is rather a matter of dispositions than of syllogisms, rather of life than of disputation', and he saw no sharp divide between Christian teaching and some forms of pagan philosophy: 'though no one has taught this so absolutely and effectively as Christ, yet also in pagan books much may be found that is in accordance with it.'[21] He it was who formulated the parody prayer 'Sancte Socrates, ora pro nobis'. He was not the first Christian humanist to try to assimilate leading classical thinkers into the Christian tradition: Petrarch had tried to turn Cicero into a Christian saint. Even the reformer Zwingli took a similar view.[22] But Socrates and Cicero could only be incorporated into the Christian tradition by broadening and, in effect, diluting the concept of Christianity itself. The attempt to contain humanism within the framework of orthodox Catholicism was probably destined to fail in the end.

INDIVIDUALISM IN THE ARTS

To anyone who compares the development of Italian painting after Cimabue and Giotto and later Masaccio, with the art that preceded them, the growth in realism is obvious, as it already was to Villani, writing in the mid-fifteenth century. 'Where was the painter's art till Giotto tardily restored it?' he asked rhetorically — 'a caricature of the art of human delineation.'[23] Increasing attention is paid to the visible world, so that we move, in terms of portrayal of the natural world, from 'the landscape of symbol' to 'the landscape of fact', or at least to an idealized version of observable reality.

Most significant of all, from our point of view, is the increasing skill in the depiction of people as individuals rather than as types or symbols. Panofsky has pointed out how Giotto, unlike his Sienese contemporary Duccio, does not paint crowds as groups of anonymous figures, but as 'individuals individually reacting to one another'.[24] Later on comes the development of an art form which, significantly, had never been common in the Middle Ages, although it was not unknown — the individual portrait. Here is the ultimate artistic expression of the new awareness of the human being as an 'individual'. At the same time the painter himself ceases to be an anonymous decorator, and begins to sign his paintings. Van Eyck was one of the first painters in northern Europe to do this consistently.

In Renaissance art two of the principal characteristics of liberal individualism find early expression. There is first its rich celebration of the variety of human beings, which implicitly stresses what differentiates them from each other. Secondly, there is the stress on the individual alone, outside any social context, which is inherent in the very concept of the portrait. But we are here seeing only the beginnings of individualism, and it is natural that neither tendency appears in an unqualified form. Against the individualized images of people we must set the idealized human figure in painting, sculpture and drawing through which the sense of human unity and dignity is expressed. And as well as the individual portrait there were many group portraits, as well as those which portray the person not so much as an individual but rather as a being immersed in his or her social role.

These limitations on individualism reflect the semi-modern character of Renaissance society. It is a society which is not thoroughly atomized, in which the private life still has to compete with the public as a sphere of self-fulfilment, and in which the division of labour — and so of human beings themselves — is not so far advanced as to make the ideal of the complete human being altogether utopian.

This consciousness, both of the dignity of the human species, but also of the variety of men and women as individuals, is expressed also in the literature and historical writing of the age: in the rise of biography, in the keeping of diaries, and in the awareness of the role of individual character among historians. Some humanist writers developed an almost obsessive interest in their own experience. Petrarch in the fourteenth century was a pioneer in this respect. But it is in the essays of Montaigne that we find the fullest development of this exploration of personal experience, and its use to supply the basis of a philosophy of life. And Montaigne's faith in his own experience points towards the philosophies of the seventeenth century, of Descartes and Locke, where this faith receives systematic expression, providing liberal individualism with its permanent philosophical foundation.

Montaigne's fascination with his own experience, and his lack of interest in subsuming that experience into a structure of systematic thought — in a word, his blend of empiricism and scepticism — are expressed in the form in which he chose to write: the essay, or *essai*. And each is indeed a discrete *attempt* to explore and distil a particular subject, idea or kind of experience. But while his empiricism may not be systematic, it is certainly explicit: 'There is no description so hard, nor assuredly so profitable, as is the description of a mans own self' he writes. He is opposed to speculation: 'I would have every man write what he knowes, and no more . . .' He is suspicious of generalization, and convinced of the diversity of things: 'Reason hath so many shapes that wee know not which to take hold of. Experience hath as many. The consequence we seeke to draw from the conference of events is unsure, because they are ever dissemblable. No quality is so universall in this surface of things as variety and diversity . . .' And elsewhere he writes, in relation to travel, that 'Onely varietie and the possession of diversitie doth satisfie me, if at least any thing satisfie mee.' This apprehension of diversity pushed him in the direction of relativism. He declared himself unworried by 'the diversity of fashions betweene one and other Nations'. He believed that 'each custome hath his reason.' Montaigne was liberal, too, in his love of liberty:

No prison did ever receive me, no not so much as for recreation to take in. The very imagination of one maketh the sight of their outside seeme irksome and loathsome to mee. I am so besotted unto liberty that should any man forbid me the accesse unto any one corner of the Indiaes I should in some sort live much discontented. [25]

Montaigne's significance for European liberalism is not exhaus. d simply by the content of his work. His influence on the subsequent development of liberalism was great. Inevitably, despite his own Catholicism, his scepticism and his this-worldliness contributed to a secular, humanist tradition which was already developing and challenging the medieval Christian world view. Descartes took Montaigne as his starting point. [26] To the Enlightenment Montaigne was a hero, a forerunner, an honorary member of the Age of Reason by anticipation. And in the twentieth century, too, he has enjoyed the status of an oracle of the liberal tradition. Best known is E. M. Forster's invocation of him, together with Erasmus, in his credo of 1939, 'What I believe'. But Gide also praised him for similar reasons: 'What Montaigne teaches us especially is what was called at a much later date, *liberalism*, and I think that it is the wisest lesson that can be drawn from him at the present time when political or religious convictions are so miserably dividing all men and opposing them to each other.' [27] He was a hero to Leonard Woolf, who saw his hatred of cruelty as derived from his 'intense awareness of individuality', [28] and he figures prominently in that classic expression of one characteristic mood of latter-day liberalism, still humanist, still individualist, but pessimist and defeatist about politics — Cyril Connolly's *The Unquiet Grave*.

The traditional view of the Renaissance, classically expressed by Burckhardt, stressed its novelty, and the cleanness of the break with the Middle Ages. Much subsequent scholarship has compelled a revision of this interpretation by showing how widespread and persistent was the survival of the medieval and Christian world view. Yet this revisionism can be, and has been, carried too far, particularly, as one might expect, by Christian scholars. Thus E. M. W. Tillyard, in his famous book *The Elizabethan World Picture*, went so far as to suggest that the six 'most eminent' Elizabethan writers, whom he named as Spenser, Sidney, Raleigh, Hooker, Shakespeare and Jonson, were all 'united in holding with earnestness, passion and assurance to the main outlines of the medieval world picture as modified by the Tudor regime, although they all know that the coherence of this picture had been threatened.' [29]

Much could be said in criticism of this assertion. I will make only three points. The first is that there is one very striking omission from this list — the name of Marlowe. And Marlowe was passed over, not, presumably, because he is thought to be less 'eminent' than, say, Sidney or Raleigh, but because he does *not* hold 'with earnestness', etc. to the world view which Tillyard claimed to be a unifying factor among the leading writers of the age. Secondly, Tillyard surely misinterprets Jonson: where, in *Volpone* for example, is such a commitment to traditional values? Thirdly, Tillyard's confidence that he knew what Shakespeare's world view was is surely misplaced. It is a part of Shakespeare's uniquely protean greatness that he evades such summaries. If in some of his tragedies he reaffirms the strength and necessity of the order of nature and society against those who reject it, yet they would not be tragedies if he did not make it plain that the cost of that reaffirmation is often a terrible one. If Shakespeare was as single-minded as Tillyard suggests, his plays would be stripped of their characteristic complexity, which derives in part from the dialectic within them of individuality and order, defiance and compliance, rebellion and harmony.

So it is that in the plays of Marlowe and Shakespeare we find some of the most vivid expressions of of the humanism and individualism of the Renaissance. Whatever Marlowe's attitude towards his heroes may have been — and fascination, if not admiration, was certainly a large part of it — his imaginative understanding of these proud, restless, self-assertive individuals is undeniable. Tamburlaine and Faustus expressed both Renaissance man's eagerness for knowledge of the world, and his confidence in the ability of the human mind to master all the secrets of nature. And it is nature, not God, which

> Doth teach us all to have aspyring minds:
> Our soules, whose faculties can comprehend
> The wondrous Architecture of the world:
> And measure every wandring plannets course:
> Still climing after knowledge infinite,
> And alwaies mooving as the restles Spheares,
> Wils us to weare our selves and never rest,
> Untill we reach the ripest fruit of all,
> That perfect blisse and sole felicitie,
> The sweet fruition of an earthly crowne.
>
> (*I Tamburlaine* II vii)

Both Tamburlaine the conqueror and Faustus the scholar associate knowledge with power, in terms not unlike those later to be used by Francis Bacon:

> O what a world of profite and delight,
> Of power, of honour, and omnipotence,
> Is promised to the Studious Artizan?
> All things that move betweene the quiet Poles
> Shall be at my command: Emperors and Kings,

> Are but obey'd in their severall Provinces:
> Nor can they raise winde, or rende the cloudes:
> But his dominion that exceeds in this,
> Stretchest as farre as doth the mind of man . . .
> (*Faustus*, I.i)

And the power at which both aim is geographical. Faustus looks forward to searching 'all corners of the new-found-world/For pleasant fruites, and Princely delicates' (I.i), and has Mephistopheles bring him grapes in January. Marlowe thus connects the contemporary European exploration and exploitation of the 'new-found-world' with the expansion of human power and knowledge.

Faustus and Tamburlaine represent the extremes of individual self-assertion. Both defy God, as in the consciously irreligious concluding lines of the passage from *Tamburlaine*, where the stress falls naturally on 'the sweet fruition of an *earthly* crowne'; while Tamburlaine also claims control over fate, or *fortuna*, the pagan necessity which in Machiavelli and other writers replaced Christian providence as the embodiment of those forces which man cannot control, and does well not to challenge:

> I hold the Fates bound fast in yron chaines,
> And with my hand turne Fortunes wheel about . . .
> (*I Tamburlaine* I.ii.)

Both Tamburlaine and Faustus are incarnations of a type of person who has not yet been fully delineated — 'man' as he is seen by Thomas Hobbes. Both, like Barabas, the Jew of Malta, serve only themselves. Both are moved only by their own selfish appetites — 'The god thou serv'st is thine owne appetite' (II.i), Faustus tells himself. And Tamburlaine is driven on by exactly the Hobbesian 'restless desire of power after power, which ceaseth only with death'. This theme of restlessness runs through the speech already quoted, and is summed up in the famous words given to Guise in *The Massacre at Paris*: 'That like I best that flyes beyond my reach' (ii).

Perhaps Marlowe can be seen as pointing forward not only to Bacon and Hobbes, but also to Locke. For Faustus asks, in justifying his pact with Lucifer to himself, 'is not thy soule thine owne?' (II.i). It is a piece of property like any other, with which he can therefore do as he likes. Marlowe is well aware of the blasphemy of this; but by Locke's time the metaphor of ownership had become an urbane commonplace.

Marlowe explored some of the most radical implications of Renaissance humanism and individualism, including their potentially anti-religious implications. Renaissance philosophers had rejoiced in man's freedom, his lack of a fixed end. But freedom imposes the necessity of choice; how was the individual to choose his own ends. Marlowe suggested one answer: a man should obey the promptings of his appetites. Indeed, perhaps he could not do otherwise. The idea was to play a central part in liberal thought. [30]

Nor was Marlowe a wholly freakish or isolated figure. In Shakespeare, it is true, the rebellious individualists are often to be numbered among the villains, but not unambiguously so. When Edmund in *King Lear* mocks at his father's superstitious attribution to the stars of the blame for human misfortunes, are we not meant to respect the clear-sightedness of a man who, though thoroughly egoistical and wicked, nevertheless accepts personal responsibility for what he does? And Richard III, who denies all the ordinary ties of love and obligation:

> I have no brother. I am like no brother;
> And this word love, which greybeards call divine,
> Be resident in men like one another,
> And not in me: I am myself alone.

— what are we to think of him? Like Edmund, he is a consciously wicked man, who in a comic yet existentialist manner, accepts responsibility for what he does: 'I am determined to prove a villain.' In the end he must be destroyed, and peace and order must be restored. But it would be strange to set such a villain at the centre of the play if he did not, like Macbeth, possess qualities which give his fall more than a touch of tragedy. The energy and audacity of such a villain, who urges his soldiers at the end to 'march on . . . If not to heaven, then hand in hand to hell', are qualities which are not to be denied either in Richard or, later on, in Milton's Satan. It is this conflict between the old and new values, and world views, which is central to Shakespeare rather than the simple contrast between chaos and order which Tillyard finds there. [31]

But it would be wrong to read too much, retrospectively, into these limited and often cautious developments. The Renaissance was not a period of anti-religious feeling, and humanism was not seen or intended as a secularizing influence. Individualism was widely disapproved of, and the medieval world view maintained a considerable hold on people's mind. The Renaissance had no notion of progress. Its culture hinged on ideas of the recovery and imitation of classical ideals.

It is only when we consider the Renaissance in relation to the other major developments of this period — the Reformation and Protestantism, the rise of modern science and the beginnings of capitalism — that we can see that a conglomeration of different and largely separate developments all unwittingly made their contributions to the emergence of the liberal picture of human beings and the world.

LUTHER, CALVIN AND THE TWO KINGDOMS

There was an old Whig view, still popular in some quarters, which saw the Reformation as leading, in a direct line, to some of the major principles and achievements of liberalism. Protestantism was, surely, the religion of the individual, and therefore led logically, as well as historically, to toleration and freedom of conscience. The secular version of these ideas *was* liberalism. Liberalism, you might say, was basically Protestantism minus God.

This view of the Reformation, and the simple linear approach to history which it exemplifies, were the objects of Herbert Butterfield's justified critique in his famous essay, *The Whig Interpretation of History*. There *is* a path which leads from the Reformation towards liberalism, but it is not the direct and logical development of the Whig historians. Much, though not all, of what is significant for liberalism in the Reformation is to be found, not in the doctrines, and certainly not in the intentions, of the Reformers themselves, but in the subsequent development of the movements they initiated, and above all in the largely unwanted, unexpected outcomes of the conflicts which the emergence of Protestantism provoked.

Neither Luther nor Calvin wanted the revolt against the Papacy to provide a general licence for revolt against the principle of authority as such, especially not in the secular sphere. They gave no encouragement to the spirit of tolerance represented by undogmatic Catholic reformers like Erasmus. When they spoke of 'God's word', or of scripture, it did not seem to them that there could be legitimate disagreement as to what these meant, and both of them expressly condemned the radical Protestants, loosely termed the Anabaptists, who did exalt the judgement of the individual, and denied the authority of all but God in both religion and politics.

Luther did not consider that his doctrine of the priesthood of all believers logically implied a democratically organized church;[32] while in Geneva, Calvin presided over the creation of a harsh and active theocracy for which he himself had provided the blueprint. Both were even more emphatic about the need for order and hierarchy in the secular world, and both insisted strongly on the duty of obedience to 'the powers that be', be they kings or tyrants. Even bad rulers were appointed by God and therefore should be obeyed. 'I would rather suffer a prince doing wrong than a people doing right' was Luther's considered preference. For him disobedience was 'a sin worse than murder, unchastity, theft, dishonesty and all that goes with them'.[33]

Luther urged the suppression of the German peasant revolt of 1525 with a verbal ferocity exceptional even for him.[34] He believed in the necessity of inequality, and defended serfdom, and accused those who demanded its abolition of advocating robbery.[35] Even Christians enslaved to the infidel Turk ought to accept their condition, for the freedom which the Christian valued was a purely inward and spiritual condition, quite compatible with any degree of external political oppression. Luther sharply distinguished between two kingdoms, the kingdom of God and the kingdom of this world. The ethics of the Sermon on the Mount applied only to relations between Christians: they were not guidelines for the exercise of temporal power. 'The world cannot be ruled with a rosary.'[36]

Calvin's views were very similar. He too made a strict separation between the two kingdoms, and held that 'spiritual freedom can perfectly well exist along with civil bondage.'[37] He too enjoined obedience to wicked rulers as well as good ones. But kings do not have a monopoly of secular authority, and Calvin does allow one possibility of resistance to unjust rulers, not to private individuals, but to public bodies or persons 'appointed to restrain the willfullness of kings'.[38] For obedience to men, Calvin reminds his readers in the final sentences of the *Institutes*, must never be allowed to take precedence over obedience to God. These few sentences, placed at the end of his great work, were to be of vast importance in the subsequent history of Protestantism. When Calvinists in France, the Netherlands and elsewhere were confronting a persecuting secular authority, and were forced to choose between compliance and resistance, they took Calvin's words as sanctioning resistance, and their choice had momentous consequences for the growth of political as well as religious freedom in Europe.

But this one loophole apart, there is not, at first sight, much in these teachings which can be connected with liberalism. Indeed, what could be less liberal than their rejection of traditional constitutionalism and of the principle that a legitimate ruler may be distinguished from a tyrant? Yet this refusal to pass judgement on rulers, and the doctrine of the two kingdoms, paradoxically accelerated the secularizing tendencies against which the Reformation was meant to be a protest: 'The gospel . . . does not become involved in the affairs of this world' Luther told the peasants in 1525.[39] We noted in Part I that the liberal cult of privacy tends towards a withdrawal from public and political life. It is striking to find this tendency in evidence at the very birth of Protestantism.

The two kingdoms corresponded to the two worlds of nature and of grace. The natural world had been irretrievably ruined by the fall of 'man'. Luther describes this godless world in dark and vivid terms:

> What is the world if not a perfect hell with nothing but lying, cheating, gluttony, guzzling, lechery, brawling and murder. That is the very Devil himself. There is no kindliness nor honor. No one is sure of another. One must be as distrustful of friends as of enemies, and sometimes more. This is the kingdom of the world where the Devil reigns and rules.[40]

Luther's description is similar to Hobbes's famous account of the state of nature — and he draws from it a similar conclusion about the need for a strong secular authority commanding more or less complete obedience. This separation of the religious from the secular, the spiritual from the material, can be seen as foreshadowing the later separation, characteristic of liberalism, between values and facts — not because Luther withholds judgement upon the fallen natural world, but because he does not think it possible for good to be found in, or injected into, that world.

The divorce between the religious and the secular worlds also helped to create an intellectual climate which encouraged the development of the scientific study of the natural world. For yet another dimension of this divide was the Lutheran separation of faith from reason. This was not Luther's invention. It was a central feature of the nominalist theology associated with the name of William of Occam. But Luther carried this line of thought a stage further when he attacked 'the harlot reason', and asserted that 'whereas by the standard of human reason two and five equal seven, yet if God should declare them to be eight, one must believe against reason and against feeling.'[41]

The obverse of this elevation of God into the sphere of faith beyond reason, was that the natural world was left subject to the rule of reason, free from religious intervention, empty of God. Thus the Spanish humanist Vives wrote in 1531: 'I have grounded all my arguments on Nature and made no appeal to religious authority. I have been scrupulous not to confuse rational enquiry with theology.'[42] The withdrawal of religion from the world is paralleled by the withdrawal of theology from the study of the world. This later becomes the basis of Bacon's bland confidence that the advancement of science can do no harm to the truths of religion, which are immunized from contradiction — or confirmation — by factual evidence.

In Calvinism these developments were taken further. Calvin saw the rational order of the universe as one proof of God's existence: 'this most vast and beautiful system of the universe . . . this skillful ordering of the universe is for us a sort of mirror in which we can contemplate God, who is otherwise invisible.'[43] In this ordered universe nothing happens by chance. What may appear to be an accident is only an event 'of which the reason and cause are secret'. This might appear to reduce God to the status of Newton's watchmaker, but Calvin sees that 'to make God a momentary creator, who once for all finished his work, would be cold and barren', and he asserts that God is an 'everlasting Governor and Preserver' who 'cares for, everything he has made'.[44]

So, if every event has a cause within the context of an ordered universe, why might not reason discover those causes and the pattern of that order? The laws of nature could be seen as the decrees by which God governed the world, and in this way, as S. F. Mason suggested, 'the theological doctrine of predestination' paved the way for 'the philosophy of mechanical determinism'.

By the seventeenth century it was possible for the Puritan preacher John Preston to assert that 'God alters not the laws of nature.'[45] Miracles and haphazard divine intervention were ruled out. God ruled the world as a rational constitutional monarch, abiding by his own laws. God remained the first or final cause, but this need not hinder the study of secondary causes. As Calvin himself had said: 'a godly man will not overlook the secondary causes.'[46] The emergence of this view of the relation between God and the world was attacked by theologians who saw that it did in effect reduce God's active role in the world. 'Men do with God as the Venetians do with their duke' complained Thomas Goodwin in the 1650s.[47] God remained titular lord of the universe, while actual control over it was vested in the laws of nature, which were accessible to scientific study and rational understanding.

This 'handing over of the secular world to its own devices'[48] is also reflected in the Protestant doctrine of the unimportance of works as compared with faith. This doctrine was pushed by the reformers themselves to the point of claiming that *any* action done 'in the faith' could be virtuous. Thus Luther declared that 'if an adultery could be committed in the faith it would no longer be a sin', and William Tyndale that 'to steal, rob and murder are holy, when God commandeth them.' Such teachings were extremely congenial to the development of the capitalist economic order. On the one hand the unbridled pursuit of wealth could be given a gratifying tinge of sanctity, as when a Puritan preacher urged his City of London congregation to 'seek riches not for themselves but for God'.[49] On the other hand the labouring poor could be told that their work, too, was holy if done for God's sake:

> A servant with this clause
>   Makes drudgerie divine:
> Who sweeps a room, as for Thy laws,
>   Makes that and th'action fine.
>
> (George Herbert: *The Elixir*)

It is equally significant, from our point of view, that what Luther and Calvin were preaching was essentially a morality of motives, rather than of specific actions and general moral rules. What matters is not what you do, but the frame of mind in which you do it. This points not only towards Kant, but beyond that towards a subjectivist morality in which it is the *sincerity* of the agent which counts above all. Morality is privatized, both in that people are urged to turn inwards and listen to the voice of God in their consciences, and also because the notion of morality as a set of rules applying to all is weakened. This led to the kind of introspective self-examination epitomized in the Puritan diaries. This is only one of the ways in which the teachings of the reformers exhibit an individualist tendency which goes far beyond anything they themselves intended.

Once the authority of Rome had been undermined, it proved impossible to replace it with any other equally widely effective form of authority. Implicit in Luther's stand against Rome was the claim that he understood better than the hierarchy of the Catholic Church what the word of God really was. But if he could make such a claim, so could others, and they were emboldened in doing so by the Lutheran doctrine of the priesthood of all believers. For as Luther himself had written: 'If we are all priests . . .and all have one faith, one gospel, one sacrament, why should we not also have the power to test and judge what is right and wrong in matters of faith?' It soon turned out that those — and they were many — who claimed to have been directly inspired by the Almighty had received different and even contradictory messages. Protestantism could find no way of resolving these disagreements except through the brute force of persecution.

If the doctrine of the priesthood of all believers was implicitly individualist, it was also explicitly egalitarian: 'If a priest is murdered' wrote Luther, 'the whole country is placed under interdict. Why not when a peasant is murdered? How does this great difference come about between two men who are both Christians?'[50] Luther might want this equality confined to the spiritual realm, but his own example demonstrates the difficulty of separating the two kingdoms. It was not a long step from attacking hierarchy in the church to attacking secular inequalities; and this step was taken by Protestant radicals from the 1520s onwards. The point was certainly not lost on their opponents. The Earl of Hertford observed in 1589 'As they shoot at bishops now, so will they do at the nobility also, if they be suffered'[51] — a point crystallized by James I in his well-known dictum 'No bishop, no king'. This democratic potential in Protestantism was a principal source of liberal and radical political thinking in the early modern period. It was there in Protestant doctrine from the beginning, but, like many other possibilities within the thought of the Reformers, it was left to subsequent generations to develop it.

PROTESTANTISM AND TOLERATION

Neither Luther nor Calvin, nor the leading reformers in general, were advocates of tolerance. To suppose that the arrival of Protestantism heralded an era of religious toleration is more or less the opposite of the truth. It was this period which witnessed the most virulent and sustained of all the outbursts of the persecution of so-called witches. Luther, Calvin and many other Protestants all urged that witches should be burnt. An average of two or three 'witches' were burnt every year in Calvinist Geneva, and it was the Calvinists who introduced the persecution into Scotland.[52] The sixteenth century saw also the appearance and spread of the ghetto, the urban quarter in which all Jews were compelled to live, and of Christian 'services of conversion', which Jews were compelled to attend. And these repressive measures would probably have struck Luther as too lenient, for in his later years he urged that the Jews should be deported from Europe to Palestine, or, failing that, that their synagogues should be burnt and their religion prohibited.[53]

As for heresy, it is true that Luther in his earlier years was emphatic that it was a spiritual condition which could not, therefore, be extirpated by force. But in later years, when heresies arose which threatened the existing social order, or as Professor Chadwick put it, 'when he observed the anarchy that followed religious freedom',[54] his view changed and hardened. By 1536, after the Anabaptist take-over of Münster, Luther was saying that 'the public authority is bound to repress blasphemy, false doctrine and heresy, and to use corporal punishment against those guilty of them.[55] Calvin seems never to have doubted that it was the duty of the Christian ruler to punish heresy; and his principal statement was not just a theoretical document, but a defence of Geneva's action, which he had encouraged, in burning Michael Servetus for heresy in 1553. The first result of the Reformation, therefore, was to produce a revival of religious persecution by all the churches.

There were, however, a small number of the early protestants who adopted both in principle and in practice a more tolerant and less dogmatic position. Many of them were among those radicals of the Reformation who are somewhat loosely termed Anabaptists, and who are still patronized and misrepresented by many orthodox historians of religion.[56] One such was Balthasar Hubmaier, whose tract of 1524, *Concerning Heretics and Those who Burn them*, has been called 'probably the earliest plea for complete toleration penned in Europe'.[57] Hubmaier argued that truth was sure to prevail in the end, and, in the manner of John Stuart Mill more than 300 years later, that the challenge of heresy stimulates and strengthens faith. Christ's precept about letting both wheat and tares grow together until harvest, was adduced in support of a policy of tolerance — and it became a stock scriptural citation. Inevitably, Hubmaier himself was treated as a heretic, and burnt at the stake in Vienna in 1528. Three days later his wife too was punished. She was thrown into the Danube with a heavy stone tied round her neck.

One tradition of tolerance did enjoy considerable prestige. This was the movement of undogmatic Catholicism associated with Desiderius Erasmus, who has since become a hero to many modern liberals. Erasmus and his fellow humanists stood for a kind of anti-theological Christianity which, in terms of church policy, pointed clearly in the direction of an easy-going tolerance of doctrinal differences. His contempt for theologians and theological disputes was almost total, and his view that 'true theology' consisted in being 'inspired and guided by the spirit of Christ' was the kind of sentiment which doubtless helped to ensure that the works of this loyal Catholic were placed on the

Index in 1559, only 23 years after his death.

Erasmus lived and died a Catholic. But as the religious divisions of Europe hardened in the decades after his death in 1536, the Catholic Church retreated into the aggressive dogmatism of the Counter-Reformation. Erasmus and his followers fell under the suspicion of heresy, and it became inevitable that it would be among the Protestants that his influence and his outlook would survive. One who testified to it, in life and in death, was the first martyr to Calvinist intolerance, Michael Servetus.

Servetus was not merely a victim of intolerance: his own doubts about established teaching led him to take up a sceptical and tolerant position towards other dissident individuals and groups. He was even doubtful about the legitimacy of persecuting those whom virtually everyone regarded as indisputably heathen — the Jews and the Moors, groups whose fate touched him closely as a Spaniard. 'No one recognizes his own errors' he said. This spirit of doubt has remained one of the most durable foundations for tolerant attitudes.

Nevertheless, Servetus' execution became a *cause célèbre*. Among those who urged Calvin against persecution was another of its victims, David Joris. Joris had taken refuge under a pseudonym in Basel. And it was in Basel that in the year after Servetus's death there was published *De Haereticis an sint persequendi*, under another pseudonym, Martin Bellius. This concealed the identity of Sebastian Castellio, one of the great champions of rationality and tolerance of that or any other century.

Castellio followed Erasmus in stressing the importance of Christian life rather than Christian dogma. He followed the nominalist division between matters of faith and reason, but he drew from this division conclusions very different from Luther's. So far from abusing the 'harlot reason' as Luther did, he asserted that reason was 'a sort of eternal word of God, much older and surer than letters and ceremonies'. Precisely because religion is a matter of faith rather than knowledge, the possibility of error was so much greater: 'The false cannot be known though it may be believed', he wrote in *De Arte Dubitandi — On the Art of Doubting*, a title which says much about the author's frame of mind.[58]

As we have seen, the strict separation of faith and reason helped to empty the area of natural knowledge of 'spiritual' elements which might obstruct the development of the sciences. In the work of Castellio, and other similar writers, we see the development of the corollary of this: that the realm of faith is also therefore a realm of doubt and uncertainty, in which disagreements are actually more likely and more legitimate than in the realm of certain knowledge. This was not at all what Luther and Calvin had intended, but nevertheless by insisting on the divorce of faith from reason they had inadvertently helped to undermine the basis of their own intolerance.

There is, besides this, in Castellio in particular, a moving concern and horror at the bloodshed for which religion was so evidently responsible. Castellio's pleas to his contemporaries to work for peace and avoid bloodshed — such as his *Conseil à la France Désolée*, written in 1562, when the terrible wars of religion were only just beginning — may have fallen on deaf ears, but this hardly warrants patronizing references to his 'evident sentimentalism'.[59] His indifference to theological disagreements still irritates the clerical historians. But it was only through such indifference that toleration and tolerance gained ground. In this respect, as in others, Castellio is one of the creators of the liberal habit of thought.

It was also to Basel that another dissident Italian, Faustus Socinus (or Sozzini) came in 1574. Five years later he moved to Poland, where he became the *de facto* leader of the Unitarians, who were thereafter known throughout Europe as Socinians. Socinus and the Polish Socinians developed to a more explicit level the agnosticism implicit in some earlier writers. It was not an irreligious agnosticism, but an openness about the varieties of Christian belief. They were willing to accept that the truth could be reached by different ecclesiastical routes. The development of principles of tolerance and liberty in religion is clearly linked to certain versions of theology and religion. From Erasmus onwards there is continuous line of Christian radicals whose concern is primarily with Christianity understood as a way of life. The corollary of this is that the essential theological tenets are reduced to a bare minimum, and there is great stress on the uncertainty which attaches to all but the most fundamental religious convictions. These tendencies — scepticism, doubt, agnosticism — remained fundamental to the liberal case for tolerance and freedom of opinion, long after the terrain of dispute had shifted from the religious to the secular sphere.

There is one other important principle that was put forward in the sixteenth century which deserves mention. That is the idea that there should be a complete separation between religion and the state. This remains a radical notion even today in the context of countries like England, the Irish Republic, Portugal or Iran, where one church or religion enjoys a position of particular privilege in relation to the state. In the early modern period it was advocated only by, not to coin a phrase, tiny minorities on the extremist fringe. Otherwise virtually everyone accepted that the state or the ruler had a right to intervene in religious matters. One group that did not was the Puritan radicals led by Robert Brown, the Brownists. They argued that the state should not interfere in matters of religion, and that churches should be entirely voluntary in their membership.

Few of these ideas made much headway at the time when they were first put forward. Nor was there any steady progress in the direction of toleration of religious liberty. Indeed, many later writings, such as Locke's well known *Letter on Toleration*, are less liberal than the positions taken by the early pioneers. Only in the Netherlands was a bourgeois republic sufficiently firmly established for the principle of religious liberty to flourish in the seventeenth century without too much interruption.

The struggles for religious liberty and tolerance thus continue into the seventeenth and eighteenth centuries, as we shall see, even though the intensity of religious conflicts was gradually reduced. But it is notable how soon so many of the most central arguments in favour of tolerance and liberty emerged in the conflicts and the debate set in motion by the Reformation.

STATE TOLERANCE

The principled advocates of tolerance were, however, few in number, and if they have often been neglected by historians, that is in part because their influence was not great. What *was* more influential in assisting the spread of toleration was the intractable situation which was created by the extraordinarily rapid spread of Protestantism through central and northern Europe. To the religious, of course, this was not so much a problem as a challenge: the heresy or anti-Christ (of Rome or of Geneva) must be rooted out and destroyed. But secular rulers, however pious, were apt to see the situation rather differently. Their primary concern was with order, and although religious dissent was normally seen as a threat to order, a holy war to wipe it out could be a remedy worse than the disease. Politically-minded men and women were quicker to see the virtues of toleration than the fervently devout. Yet, by a characteristic irony of history, Protestantism, which exalted the authority of secular rulers, may have helped them to impose toleration upon the unwilling and unconsenting Protestants themselves.

In any case, the 'heresies' of Luther and the reformers spread so rapidly that it soon became apparent to the more realistic rulers that the rival claims of such strongly entrenched competitors for a monopoly of religion could not always and everywhere be resolved in favour of one party — at least not for the time being — and that there must therefore be some practical recognition of the actual diversity of religious affiliations in Europe. The first acknowledgement of this came in the Peace of Augsburg of 1555. This accepted, within the bounds of the old Holy Roman Empire, the principle of *cuius regio, eius religio*: that each monarch had the right to determine what should be the official religion of his/her state or territory. It made no concessions to any notional right of individual conscience belonging to anyone less important than a ruler. Those who refused to conform to the state religion would have to go elsewhere — or suffer the consequences. The notion of a plurality of beliefs within a single state was still generally unthinkable. The Augsburg agreement was no more than a limited recognition of the fact of religious diversity in Germany — limited in particular because of the exclusion of Calvinism from the terms of the agreement. Nevertheless, it is mainly through such limited, grudging, pragmatic acts that toleration begins to make a little headway in this period.

But one European country consistently followed a peaceable and rational path through the turmoils of the sixteenth century. That was Poland. By the 1550s Lutherans, Calvinists and the Bohemian Brethren were all firmly established in the country. The first two tendencies in particular attracted support among the aristocracy and gentry — the Brethren were too radical, in social as well as religious terms; and the exceptionally strong political position of the Polish aristocracy in relation to the monarchy, which was elective, was probably decisive in producing an accommodation between the various religious groups. Successive rulers resisted pressure from the papacy and other Catholic rulers to persecute 'heretics', i.e. Protestants, and gradually the idea gained currency that the use of force in matters of belief and conscience was wrong as well as futile. As Andrew Modrzewski, Sigismund II Augustus's humanist secretary put it: 'what belongs to the mind and the spirit cannot be forced out of anybody by torture or threats.'[60]

In 1570 the three Protestant groupings came together and formulated the Consensus of Sandomir. The chill wind of the Counter-Reformation was being felt in Poland, and the Protestants were wise enough to see that their survival depended upon their willingness to tolerate each other, and to act in unison in pursuit of guarantees for religious diversity. They were strikingly successful. In the search for a successor to Sigismund, who died in 1572, the Convocation Diet which met to choose his successor agreed on the famous Confederation of Warsaw, by which the signatories bound themselves to 'keep the peace among ourselves on the subject of difference of religion', not to 'shed blood' or 'punish one another' for this reason'.[61] The chosen candidate for the throne, the Catholic Henry of Anjou, was required to take an oath in similar terms, and he and his two successors, continued the policy of peace and toleration.

Poland became 'to the Protestants of the west a symbol of moderation and tolerance', writes J. H. Elliott. But, as he also points out, an appeal from Polish Protestants to their co-religionists elsewhere to follow the example of the Sandomir agreement fell on deaf ears.[62] Elsewhere in Europe the idea of the co-existence of two or more religions within a single state remained virtually unthinkable. Religious unity was seen as a necessary condition of national and social unity and order.

So in the 1560s the formula *une roi, une foi, une loi* (one king, one faith, one law) gained currency as crystallizing the conventional wisdom of the day. Nevertheless, there emerged in France in the 1560s a loose grouping known as the *politiques*, on account of the primacy they gave to political over religious considerations. These men, among whom Michel de l'Hopital was a leading figure, were not committed to tolerance as a principle, but they came to consider that it might be the necessary condition of order and stability, and were prepared

E

to argue for it on those pragmatic grounds. The *politiques* were not generally constitutionalists. It was the partisans of the religious factions in France who developed theories of legitimate resistance, contractual monarchy and popular rights. The *politiques* were generally supporters of absolute monarchy, arguing in a manner later fully developed by Hobbes that only an untrammelled sovereign could offer any insurance for peace and order. The only element which in their arguments which might be considered retrospectively as 'liberal' was their pragmatism, their resignation to the regrettable fact of religious difference — and even this is traditionally a conservative rather than a liberal political attitude.

In France the accession to the throne of the Protestant Henry of Navarre towards the end of the religious wars in 1589 itself dealt a blow to the position of Catholicism as the single religion established in France; and his own acceptance of Catholicism a few years later could not wholly negate the significance of the earlier event. The Edict of Nantes, inevitably denounced by Pope Clement VIII as 'an Edict that permits liberty of conscience, the worst thing in the world', did not in fact go that far, as Lord Acton, the liberal historian of liberalism, was at pains to point out.[63] It granted full civil rights to the Huguenots, and limited rights of public worship in certain specified areas. No such restrictions were placed on Catholicism. The Edict was as much a realistic, *politique* recognition of the continuing strength of the Huguenot party and the impossibility, after more than 30 years of intermittent war, of eliminating it, as it was a declaration of any general principle. But it was through such acts of pragmatism, themselves the products of exhaustion and disillusion as well as sensible statesmanship, that religious toleration made headway. By the beginning of the seventeenth century it was much more common than it had been 50 years before, to acknowledge publicly that persecution did not work. Thus in 1614 James I told the English Parliament that 'no relygeone or heresye was evere exterpated by violense or the swoarde, nor have I ever judged it a way of plantyng truthe.'[64]

Not all of the arguments in favour of toleration were pitched at this level. The commercial advantages of a regime of toleration are not a matter of cynical observation by Marxist, materialist, historians: they were noticed by many contemporaries. The trading republic of Venice was extremely reluctant to introduce the Inquisition, and its eventual decision to do so contributed to the city's commercial decline. William of Orange himself argued that the expulsion from the Netherlands of a 'vast body of Reformers . . . would strip the country of its best workers and chief traders — our country which is "the market of Christendom".' In the seventeenth century the same case was to be put forward in England. Leonard Busher, in a pamphlet called *Religion's Peace*, urged James I in 1614 to remember the 'great benefit and commodity which would redound to your majesty and to all your subjects . . . by the great commerce, in trade and traffic, both of Jews and all people; which now, for want of liberty of conscience, are forced and driven back elsewhere.'[65] Subsequently the link between religious freedom and commercial prosperity became one of the commonplaces of Whig-liberal thinking, and an argument which was made much of by the opponents of absolutism and intolerance in eighteenth century France and elsewhere. It has even been argued that the decline of the great trading and industrial centres of Catholic Europe, such as Antwerp, Augsburg, Milan and Seville, and the contrasting rise of England and the Netherlands to supremacy in world trade, owe much to the enforced emigration from Catholic states of many heretical or Protestant merchants, who found refuge in more tolerant societies.[66]

PROTESTANT POLITICS: FRENCH THEORY AND DUTCH PRACTICE

The French wars of religion in the latter half of the sixteenth century are significant not only for the grudging but important steps towards religious freedom which eventually resulted from the long conflict: the conflicts of allegiances and interests produced some extraordinary developments in political thought.

To begin with, in the 1560s, both Huguenots and Catholics could persuade themselves that they were not challenging royal authority as such. They were, according to the traditional formula, seeking to rescue the king from his bad advisers. But after the Massacre of St Bartholemew in August 1572, it was no longer possible for the Huguenots to sustain this position. This savage pogrom sent a wave of horror through Protestant Europe, while Pope Gregory XIII celebrated the event with a *Te Deum* and a commemorative medal. The massacre was so clearly instigated by the king, the queen mother and the court, that the French Calvinists were forced into a position of open opposition to the crown, as were the Catholics of the League in the 1580s, when faced with the prospect of a Protestant king succeeding to the throne. This position had to be justified.

One of the first Huguenot tracts to appear after the Massacre was Francois Hotman's *Francogallia*. It was actually written about five years before the Massacre, and takes the shape of a piece of historical research into the origins and early history of the French monarchy and system of government. What Hotman was principally concerned to show, by means of a vast array of historical references and quotations from classical authors, is that the French monarchy was originally elective and limited, not hereditary and absolute. And in this shape it respected, and indeed embodied, the traditional freedom of the French people. Even before the Roman conquest of Gaul the kings of the various tribes did not possess 'an unlimited free and uncontrolled authority', and their positions were more like 'permanent magistracies'.[67] In the polemics that followed the appearance of the book, Hotman strongly denied that he was suggesting that France could or should revert to an elective monarchy. These denials must be taken with a pinch of salt. *Francogallia* is clearly not a work of pure history. It is in fact one of the first works in a genre which was very common in early modern Europe — the radical critique presented in the form of antiquarian research. *Francogallia* is one of the first and most elaborated versions of the myth of primitive freedom, which provided so many of the opponents of absolutism with a quasi-historical justification for their demands.

But the book is conservative in a more substantial way, in that the notion of a monarchy limited by law and by accountability to an assembly of the people or estates, is the traditional feudal one. As in other writings of the time, references to 'the people' (*populus*) are not to be taken in too democratic a sense. Hotman made it clear by his amendments to the first edition of the book, that by 'the people' he means 'the estates' or 'the people in their assemblies'. As so often, it was taken for granted that 'the people' or 'the nation' meant the politically recognized sections of the population — although, as we shall see, it was open to radicals to interpret these terms more generously. And such observations as 'there may be a people without a king . . . But the idea of a king without a people is as inconceivable as a pastor without a flock' could be interpreted in a decidedly subversive way.[68]

The *Vindiciae contra Tyrannos*, which appeared in 1579, is addressed more directly than *Francogallia* to the central issues of disobedience and resistance. Like Hotman, the author of the *Vindiciae* (claims to the authorship are still disputed) stresses the accountability of kings to the people, as well as the subordination of kings to God, 'the King of Kings', whose vassals they are. But the author is still more careful than Hotman to specify whom he means by 'the people':

> When we speak of all the people, we understand by that, only those who hold their authority from the people, to wit, the magistrates, who are inferior to the king, and whom the people have substituted, or established, as it were, consorts in the empire, and with a kind of tribunitial authority, to retrain the encroachments of sovereignty, and to represent the whole body of the people. We understand also the assembly of the estates, which is nothing else but an epitome, or brief collection of the kingdom. . . .[69]

He is specifically concerned to reassure his readers that he is not allowing a right of restraint or resistance to 'a whole people, that beast of many heads' to 'run in a mutinous disorder, to order the business of the commonwealth', and later he warns Christians against the danger of following false prophets into the catastrophe of another Münster.[70] This fear of 'the mob' or 'the many-headed monster' is expressed in most theories of resistance and rebellion, whether they are aristocratic or bourgeois in origin, and is insisted on precisely because their advocates perceive the danger of their own theories providing the 'lower orders' as well with a licence for revolt.

So the general argument of the *Vindiciae* is that the right of resistance to tyrants or unjust rulers belongs, not to the people as a whole, but to those bodies and institutions which are deemed to represent the people. No right of resistance exists for 'private and particular persons considered by one by one' (p. 100). Yet towards the end of the book the question is asked whether God 'cannot . . . when He pleases stir up particular and private persons, to ruin a mighty and powerful tyranny? . . . cannot He also even from the meanest multitude raise a liberator?' (p. 211). And the author allows that when a ruler is not merely a tyrant 'by practice' but is also 'without title', and is therefore without any basis in popular assent, 'it is indifferently permitted to all to oppose and depose them' (p. 213).

The *Vindiciae* was once described as 'Whig', and by Lord Acton as 'the beginning of the literature of revolution'.[71] These judgements exaggerate its novelty. The arguments of the book are to a large extent extensions of the traditional medieval and feudal view of kingship as contractual and limited by law.

Nevertheless, there is novelty in the thoroughness and determination with which the *Vindiciae* elaborates a theory of legitimate resistance and rebellion, and in the repeated insistence on the primacy and supremacy of the people over the king. In this work, as in Hotman's, the origins of kingship emerge as human rather than divine. The point is again made that a people can exist without a king, but not vice versa. And we find in the *Vindiciae* an early version of what is to become part of the stock-in-trade of liberal political theory: the schema whereby human beings only renounce their original, natural liberty and place themselves under government because of the greater benefits that will accrue to them from this transition:

> . . . every one consents, that men by nature loving liberty, and hating servitude, born rather to command, than obey, have not willingly admitted to be governed by another, and renounced as it were the privilege of nature, by submitting themselves to the commands of others, but for some special and great profit that they expected from it. (p. 139)

A third contribution to this remarkable Calvinist literature of constitutionalism and resistance appeared in the same year as the *Vindiciae* — George Buchanan's *De Jure Regni apud Scotos*. Here, too, there is the emphasis on monarchy as an institution created by the people for their own benefit: 'kings are not ordained for themselves, but for the People',[72] and therefore bound by law and answerable to the people. There is the customary stress on the lawfulness of tyrannicide. Once again the spectre of the 'mob' is evoked, and once again the author hastens to assure his questioner that it is not to the people *en masse*, but to a council or parliament, that the king must answer. But there is a more democratic strand in Buchanan's thinking, and he asserts that 'a multitude for the most part doth better judge of all things, than single persons apart.' By contrast, the personal fallibility of kings is cited as one reason for denying them 'an Arbitrary Power over all things. . . . For I remember, that he is not only a King, but also a Man.' Finally, Buchanan enlarges on the theme of the liberty of the state of nature: 'the time hath been, when men did dwell in cottages, yea and in Caves, and as strangers did wander to and fro without Laws.' But, interestingly, he rejects the suggestion that 'utility was the first and main cause of the association of Men' on the grounds that 'if every one would have a regard to his own private advantage, then surely that very utility would rather dissolve than unite human society together.'[73] He argues, instead, that 'man' is a naturally social creature, rather than a purely egoistic calculator of advantages. This passage can be taken as an implied critique, not only of Hobbes, but of the whole ensuing liberal tradition which wrestles, more or less unconvincingly, with problem of reconciling its conception of the individual as naturally selfish with the creation or existence of society and social life.

It is natural for the historian of political ideas to connect these writers with later developments in liberal constitutionalism, and in particular with Locke's version of the right of rebellion. But this can obscure the fact that these writings represent a unique and in some ways isolated moment in European history. It is the moment when the crisis precipitated by the Reformation interlocks with the crisis of the feudal order, which can no longer take its classical form, but has not yet in most countries attained its modernized form of absolutism. Because the nobility had not yet reconciled themselves to absolutism as the price for their own survival, they were willing to join with other social groups in resistance to the growing power of the crown. It was a shared religious commitment which made these trans-class alliances possible. Even so, the alliances were never less than uneasy. For example, when it came to considering whether the Calvinist peasantry should be urged not to pay tithes to the Catholic Church, the French Huguenot nobility put 'order' and class interest first, and declared at Nîmes in 1562 that tithes should be paid. Those who urged that they should be withheld were denounced as 'sowers of sedition'.[74]

It was in the Netherlands, however, that Huguenot ideas of resistance had their most effective application, and it was there that principles of toleration and constitutionalism could be realized on a basis that was uniquely secure in Europe at that time — the basis of an essentially bourgeois and mercantile society. This was the outcome of that extraordinary, confused, yet undeniably heroic struggle known as the revolt of the Netherlands — the most striking thing about it being, not that it was protracted, confused and only partially successful, but that it succeeded as far and as permanently as it did.

As in so many subsequent wars of national independence, the harshness with which the imperial power reacted to the first stirrings of protest only intensified the resistance and compelled diverse social groups to sink at least some of their mutual suspicions in a unified struggle. There was at first no thought of national independence, and it was not until the end of the 1570s that the leaders of the revolt finally acknowledged that they were indeed engaged in a revolt against their legal sovereign, Philip II of Spain. At the start, William of Orange and the other aristocratic leaders took their stand on the king's obligation to respect traditional rights and liberties. But a decade or so later a Calvinist pamphleteer was arguing that 'it is unreasonable in turbulent times to stand so much on privileges, old traditions and persons',[75] and Orange himself, who despite his Lutheran parentage had been brought up as a Catholic and a favoured protege of Charles V, had identified himself with the reformed religion and with the cause of freedom of conscience.

In the famous Edict whereby the States General of the Netherlands finally renounced their allegiance to the king of Spain in 1581, the constitutionalist arguments of *Francogallia* and the *Vindiciae* are invoked by way of justification at the very opening of the document:

> It is common knowledge . . . that the subjects are not created by God for the benefit of the prince, to submit to all that he decrees, whether godly or ungodly, just or unjust, and to serve him as slaves. On the contrary, the prince is created for the subjects (without whom he cannot be a prince) to govern them according to right and reason and defend and love them as a father does his children. . . . [76]

But the document also contains many references to the 'ancient freedom' and rights which the king had not respected, and much effort went into constructing a history and genealogy in support of this contention.

The establishment of conditions of true tolerance in religious matters was of equal political importance. There was nothing inevitable about this. The militant Calvinists who played such an important part, militarily as well as ideologically, in sustaining the struggle against Spain were not fighting for religious 'licence'. They were promoting the ascendancy and exclusive claims of their own brand of Protestantism. But against them the weight of political, economic and class interests proved to be decisive. Political realists like Orange himself saw clearly that mutual toleration between Catholics and Calvinists was the only basis on which the national war could be continued with any chance of success. Undogmatic Christians like him were genuinely appalled by the cruelties of the Inquisition, and had no wish to see it replaced by the kind of theocracy which Calvin had set up in Geneva. Besides, militant Calvinism was all too clearly a popular creed: as in other parts of Europe, including France and England, the majority of those burnt for heresy were of plebeian background. [77] The nobility and bourgeoisie were naturally anxious to forestall the danger of a popularly-based religious dictatorship, which might bring in its train revolutionary social change as well.

Finally, from an early stage in the conflict the merchants and industrialists had perceived the economic advantages of religious openness. A pamphlet published in 1566 claimed that as a result of religious persecution 'trades which belong specially to the Low Countries have been driven into the hands of the English, French and other nations. And I do not mention innumerable other decent and experienced craftsmen who have sought shelter in foreign countries in order to enjoy freedom of conscience.' It was a point which did not escape even the Spanish Governor of the Netherlands, who wrote to Philip II in 1577 that 'the Prince of Orange has always insisted on impressing on the people that freedom of conscience is essential to commercial prosperity.' [78]

This is not to say that those who advocated toleration, or tolerance, considered only its material advantages. On the contrary, the principled case for toleration was pushed further forward in the Netherlands, both in theory and practice, than in most other parts of Europe. Dirck Coornhert was perhaps the best known of those who argued, not so much that the state should *allow* two or more religions within its borders, as that the state had no right to prohibit any religion, since 'God alone is entitled to authority over men's souls and consciences.' [79]

Nevertheless, it is doubtful whether such arguments would have carried much weight in practice, had they not coincided with the real needs of the economy of the Netherlands, which centred on trade and industry. And indeed, the new state of the United Provinces benefited hugely and rapidly from its chosen policies of constitutionalism and toleration. To them came refugees from religious persecution not only from other parts of Europe, but also from the southern Netherlands, which remained under Spanish rule; and as the once great port of Antwerp declined, so did the northern capital of Amsterdam grow and thrive. Other centres of toleration in Europe benefited in a similar way.

Tolerance and trade: here was a recipe for prosperity which could give liberal ideas of liberty an irresistible appeal to unsentimental merchants and manufacturers. It would be anachronistic to describe the Dutch Republic as 'liberal'. Nevertheless, in the difficult, piecemeal, haphazard process of the establishment of liberal principles in Europe, this middle-class republic represents their first secure foothold in modern history. And its national struggle against Spain rightly became a potent symbol for liberals in later times. The plays and music of Goethe and Schiller, Beethoven and Verdi, are the noble salutes of liberal posterity to the heroic struggle against Spanish absolutism.

The intellectual and cultural life of the Netherlands also benefited from the establishment of a climate of tolerance and openness. Even those who were not actually forced into exile by the pressures of Catholic absolutism found its offer of comparative liberty attractive. Among them was René Descartes, who, despite being an orthodox Catholic in religion, lived by choice for 30 years in Holland, and whose role as one of the creators of the philosophical basis of liberal individualism is what we must now consider.

6

The Philosophical Foundations
of Liberalism

Most accounts of philosophy divide the seventeenth- and eighteenth- century philosophers into two groups, the rationalists and the empiricists. Descartes, Spinoza and Leibniz are dubbed rationalists, while Bacon, Hobbes, Locke and later Hume, are the creators and sustainers of the chiefly British empirical tradition. In the Anglo-Saxon world it is still the empiricists who are studied and revered, while the rationalists, especially Spinoza, are comparatively neglected. This academic bias towards empiricism is itself part of the history of liberalism. And the differences between the two tendencies also have their significance for liberalism. For our present purposes, however, these differences are less important than what the two traditions have in common: that is, a stress on the experience of the individual as the basis for knowledge and certainty. Individual sense-experience as the basis of knowledge — this is the core of Locke's empiricism. Descartes, with a thoroughness and clarity which Locke never achieved, also started with the individual, though not with his/her sense-experience.

DESCARTES

Descartes was not the first person to engage in systematic doubt 'in order to discover the true way of gaining knowledge'. He had been anticipated by Francois Sanchez in 1581, as Butterfield pointed out.[1] But it required a philosopher of genius to move from this sceptical position to the systematic construction of a new philosophy. So, employing his method of systematic doubt, not, as he pointed out, for the sake of scepticism, but in order to achieve certainty, Descartes concluded that the one thing he could not doubt was the existence of the person, or mind, that doubted. Whether or not that conclusion is justified has been much debated, but that is not our concern. It is the significance of Descartes' argument and its structure that concern us. The primary, bedrock certainty for Descartes is that of his own existence as a thinking or doubting being. No more than that. This being has no temporal or spatial dimensions. It is not a body. For a body implies the existence of space and a material, three-dimensional world, and of the existence of such a world Descartes, at this stage of his argument, is not convinced.

So Descartes' conviction, or certainty, of his own existence as a thinking being, does not lead him directly to a similar conviction that the external world exists. Such a conviction is only reached via a logically prior conviction that God exists: 'I think I have discovered the road which will lead us from the contemplation of the true God . . . to the knowledge of everything else.'[2] I do not think it is fanciful to suggest that this pattern of argument has had an enduring influence. For what happens when God is removed from the argument; when the Cartesian *cogito* is retained in the context of an atheistical world view, as in the case of Sartre? It clearly becomes more difficult to move from a conviction of one's own existence to a conviction of the existence of the external world, unless other arguments replace the link supplied by God in the Cartesian argument. Hence the danger of solipsism, of anomic isolation from the world, which is always present in this argument, is greatly enhanced. (It was Turgot who suggested, in the middle of the eighteenth century, that the reason Descartes did not push his philosophical radicalism further than he did, was his own fear of isolation: 'One might say that he was frightened by the solitude in which he had put himself, and that he was unable to endure it.'[3])

Such latter-day despair is a characteristic of liberalism in retreat, not of Descartes' energetic and purposeful style of thinking. Nevertheless, the element of stoic acceptance and resignation in the face of an apparently intractable world in his outlook has perhaps been insufficiently noticed. Since 'there is nothing that lies wholly within our power save our thoughts', it is better 'to try to alter my desires rather than the course of the world'. We should be content with our present lot: 'we should no more desire to be well, when we are ill, or to be free, when we are in prison, than we now wish we had bodies as incorruptible as diamonds, or long for wings with which to fly like birds.' Fatalism of this kind can have more than one basis, but there is clearly a link in Descartes between the belief that only our own thoughts are wholly within our power, and the gulf that he sets between his primary conviction, of himself existing as a thinking being, and his secondary (or tertiary) conviction of the existence of the external world. Here may be one of the philosophical roots of the tendency within liberalism towards withdrawal from public action into the private world of meditation and resignation.

Thinking, for Descartes, is and should be a solitary business. I am not merely thinking of the man himself, sitting alone in his stove-heated room. But in that very passage Descartes tells us that one of his first thoughts was that 'there is often less perfection in what has been put together bit by bit, and by different masters, than in the work of a single hand.' He was thinking primarily of the accumulation of ideas from the past, which he regarded as an inchoate jumble. So this individualistic affirmation is associated by Descartes with the rejection of tradition. But it is not intended only as a justification for Descartes' own philosophical project: he believes that every individual possesses equally the faculty of reason, the capacity to think for oneself: 'the power of judging rightly, and of separating what is true from what is false (which is generally called good sense or reason), is equal by nature in all men.' even if this potential is not always realized. The specifically human faculty of reason is something which all possess: 'Reason itself, or good sense, inasmuch as it alone makes us men, and marks us off from the beasts, I must believe is found whole and entire in each man.' The ideal is that every man should be a philosopher, and Descartes believes this is a practicable aim. Indeed, the simple man of sense may come nearer to realizing it than he who is weighed down by a great burden of opinions derived from books: 'what we learn from books . . . is further from the truth than the simple reasonings of a man of good sense with regard to what he observes or encounters.' This essentially democratic and egalitarian faith in the universal possession of reason is one of the most important positive convictions in liberal politics. Descartes demonstrated his own commitment to this belief by writing in the vernacular, instead of Latin, the language of the learned, in the hope that 'those who make use of their own pure and natural reason will be better judges of my opinions than those who believe only in ancient texts.'[4] In his faith in the rationality of the independent individual, and his corresponding lack of faith in tradition, Descartes is the exact opposite of a thoroughly conservative thinker like Burke, whose faith in tradition is reinforced by his fear of putting men 'to live and trade each on his own private stock of reason; because we suspect that this stock in each man is small' and they do better to rely on prejudice.

This faith in the rationality of the individual, together with the philosophical emphasis on the primacy of the individual's own experience, help to explain the autobiographical form of the *Discourse on Method*, and why he first intended to give it the pre-Wordsworthian title 'A History of my Mind'. As Christopher Hill has remarked: 'Montaigne and Descartes turned philosophy into autobiography, a style it long retained.'[5]

Despite the element of fatalism noted above, Descartes affirmed the links between thought and action, and knowledge and power. He claims that the new philosophy, unlike the 'speculative philosophy' of the medieval tradition, is 'a practical one' which will provide a knowledge 'of all the physical things that surround us', so that 'we can apply them . . . to all the uses for which they are fit, and thus make ourselves, as it were, the lords and masters of nature.' There is, at this stage in European thought, no divide between philosophy and science, and Descartes quite naturally associates his philosophical work with the progress in knowledge of the natural world then being made by contemporary scientists.

Descartes shared their mechanistic picture of the natural order. He looked on the human body as a machine of an exceptionally sophisticated kind 'which, as it comes from the hands of God, is far better ordered, with a far more wonderful movement, than any machine that man can invent.'[6] And elsewhere he declared that

> The only difference I can see between machines and natural objects is that the workings of machines are mostly carried out by apparatus large enough to be readily perceptible by the senses . . . whereas natural processes almost always depend on parts so small that they utterly elude our senses.[7]

Marx, in a footnote to *Capital*, Volume I, remarked that 'Descartes, in defining animals as mere machines, saw with the eyes of the period of manufacture. The medieval view, on the other hand, was that animals were assistants to man.'[8]

One of the things that distinguished Descartes the rationalist from the empiricists was his stress on the extent to which the senses are fallible and unreliable as sources of information about the world. Reason plays an essential part in the acquiring of true knowledge, and this stress on the positive character of reason is one factor that separates the rationalists from the empiricists, and sets up a tension which becomes a permanent feature of the liberal tradition.

The empiricists characteristically dwell on the particularity of things, and hence the artificiality of generalizations, categories and universal names. Descartes, on the other hand, stressed the generalizing character of science: 'it does not do to be over-curious about discovering the details of a subject: the important thing is to make general surveys of the most common things.'[9] He accepted that universals are not things, but categories of thought; but it is characteristic of him that he was, according to S. F. Mason, the first to use consistently 'both the concept and the term, "the laws of nature"'.[10] The world was not simply a jumble of individual things. It possessed a logical, even mathematical order, accessible to the human intellect, provided that it was approached in the right rational and philosophical spirit.

It has been conventional for some time now to criticize rationalism, and to associate Descartes as well as Bacon with a 'dissociation of sensibility', a damaging divorce between reason and feeling which is supposed to have taken place in the seventeenth century. It is therefore worth pointing out that it was the rationalist influence of Descartes which was credited by the Christian

Thomasius in 1701 with having dealt a fatal blow to the European witch-craze, while it was the representative of empirical and conservative wisdom, Jean Bodin, who in 1580 'wrote the book which, more than any other, reanimated the witch-fires throughout Europe'.[11] The achievements of the supposedly 'arid' spirit of science and rationalism in humanizing European life are not to be derided or discounted. Leading figures in the eighteenth-century Enlightenment understood this very well, as is clear from the generous tribute which d'Alembert paid to him in his *Discourse preliminaire* to the great project of the Encyclopaedia: 'Descartes at least dared to show advanced minds how to shake off the yoke of scholasticism, of opinion, of authority, in a word of prejudices and barbarism. By this revolt, whose fruits we today gather, he rendered to philosophy a service more essential perhaps than all those it owes to his well-known successors.'[12]

BACON

Meanwhile the empiricist tradition was already being created, and Francis Bacon, whose work antedates that of Descartes, stands somewhere near the beginning of that tradition — although it would be a mistake to regard him as a wholly isolated pioneer. Many of the ideas he incorporated into his work were already current in scientific circles.[13] Bacon's empiricism makes his revolt against Aristotle and the post-medieval schoolmen even more radical than Descartes', in that he is sceptical of the value of *any* intellectual activity that is not closely tied to the study and observation of brute facts. There is even something anti-intellectual in his deep mistrust of logic and reasoning: 'The understanding, left to itself, ought always to be suspected . . . . Logic . . . by no means reaches the subtilty of nature.' If 'the wit and mind of man' is allowed to 'work upon itself, as the spider worketh his web, then it is endless, and brings forth indeed cobwebs of learning, admirable for the fineness of thread and work, but of no substance or profit.' If, on the other hand 'it work upon matter' it will be 'limited thereby', and the inherent tendency of the intellect to ingenious but futile invention will be kept in check. 'Those, therefore, who determine not to conjecture and guess, but to find out and know . . . must consult only things themselves.'[14] This phrase echoes William Gilbert, who dedicated *De Magnete* (1600) to those 'who look for knowledge not in books but in things themselves'.[15]

This world of matter or things, is composed of discrete individual entities: 'nothing exists in nature except individual bodies, exhibiting clear individual effects, according to particular laws.'[16] All knowledge begins with these particulars, and must not depart too quickly from them either. Bacon deplores the habit of flying 'from the sense and particulars to the most general axioms'. The correct scientific, empirical method makes 'a grand and unbroken ascent' from particular facts, 'so that it arrives at the most general axioms last of all.'[17]

Marie Hall has written of Bacon that 'never before had anyone argued that the best way to arrive at truth was through the fallible, readily confused senses.'[18] But it is not altogether clear how much reliance Bacon did place on immediate sense perceptions. Thus in *The Great Instauration* he asserts that 'it is a grand error to assert that sense is the measure of things', and that, therefore 'we . . . lay no great stress upon the immediate and natural perceptions of the senses.'[19] On the other hand, elsewhere he declares that 'all knowledge' comes from but two sources: 'either from divine inspiration or external sense'; and expresses scepticism about what the mind is apt to do to the evidence that it takes in from the senses:

> The evidence of the sense, helped and guarded by a certain process of correction, I retain. But the mental operation which follows the act of sense I for the most part reject; and instead of it I open and lay out a new and certain path for the mind to proceed in, starting directly from the simple sensuous perception.[20]

Thus Bacon seems to have conceded something to the traditional view which regarded the senses as fallible, yet at the same time he regards them as the only source of knowledge about the natural world, and as more to be trusted than the over-active, over-inventive mind. He is, however, in less doubt that Descartes about the possibility of knowledge of the external world. There is a natural consonance between the human mind and the natural world: 'God has framed the mind like a glass, capable of the image of the universe, and desirous to receive it as the eye to receive the light.'[21]

Bacon accepts and systematizes the separation between faith and knowledge which, as we have already seen, is conspicuous in early Protestant thought. There is, in his view, absolutely no common ground between scientific knowledge and religious or divine truth. 'Sacred theology must be drawn from the word and oracles of God, not from the light of nature, or the dictates of reason.' And he goes so far as to suggest, in an echo of the medieval view, that 'the more absurd and incredible any divine mystery is', so much the greater is 'the victory of faith.'[22] However, despite Bacon's apparent glorying in the absurdities of faith, Christianity itself was increasingly submitted to the tests of reasonableness, and there was a growing pressure to bring religion into conformity with the criteria of science, even while religion was still trying to subordinate science to its notions of truth. 'Bacon put an End to Faith' wrote William Blake in the margin of the *Essays*.[23]

Bacon is not so much a scientist as a philosopher and propagandist of science, and, unlike many pure scientists, he is as much concerned with the usefulness of science as with its truth. Intellectual work of 'no substance or profit' — the economic overtones are not accidental — did not interest him. Taking 'all knowledge to be my province' he hoped to 'bring in industrous observations, grounded conclusions, and profitable inventions and discoveries; the best state of that province.'[24] There is a constant stress in his writings on scientific knowledge as the basis of extended human power: 'The truth and lawful goal of the sciences is none other than this, that human life be endowed with new inventions and powers.' The confidence with which he dismisses the past is more than equalled by his hopes for the future. And, as with Descartes, there is a democratic note in Bacon's conviction that his scientific method is not a recipe for geniuses only, but is readily available to all: 'My way of discovering sciences goes far to level men's wits; and leaves but little to individual excellence, because it performs everything by the surest rules and demonstrations.'[25] He even suggests that through the sciences man may regain that 'dominion over created things' which was lost in the Fall, and which will free him to some degree at least from the curse of labour which fell upon him at that time. He thought it worthwhile to conjecture what an ideal society might be like, even though *The New Atlantis* was left unfinished. Bacon's utopianism was partly fanciful, but it was also partly inspired by the sense of vast possibilities which science and technology were generating. This sense of hope, and even confidence, in the future is one of the characteristics which distinguishes evolving liberalism from liberalism in decline.

Bacon is one of those intellectual figures whose name is much more familiar than his actual writings. But this should not be allowed to obscure the great impact he made upon European thought. Bacon and Descartes were regarded by subsequent generations as the two great liberators — the champions who had emancipated philosophy from the cramping confines of scholasticism, Aristotelianism, and theology, and who had inaugurated a new era of intellectual progress. Abraham Cowley, in his 'Ode for the Royal Society', compared Bacon to Moses, who led us out of the wilderness of 'Errors', and pointed out the promised land.[26] The Enlightenment revered him, Voltaire called him 'the father of experimental philosophy', and Macaulay 'the greatest of English philosophers' because of the importance he attached to the notions of utility and progress. It was only with the emergence of radical romanticism that there was a reaction against Bacon, pioneered, as so many ideas were, by the genius of Blake. 'Good Advice for Satans Kingdom' was Blake's verdict on Bacon's *Essays*.[27]

HOBBES

Bacon embodies empiricism, and subscribes to ontological individualism. But for a really thorough and systematic exposition of both we must turn to a far more formidable thinker, Thomas Hobbes.

The one thing which everyone knows about Hobbes is the conclusion to his argument in *Leviathan*: that to establish human society on a basis of lasting security, it is necessary to place 'an Absolute and Arbitrary Legislative Power'[28] in the hands of a single sovereign. Divided authority, or divided sovereignty (if that is not a contradiction in terms) is a recipe for insecurity and conflict. It is this conclusion which has led to Hobbes being associated with theorists of absolutism, like Bodin, and to his being charged, rather vaguely, with 'authoritarianism'.

But what is chiefly interesting and significant about *Leviathan* is not so much the conclusions, as the process and arguments through which they are reached. And these are so radical, so untraditional, that it is not surprising that, despite his apparently reassuring conclusions, Hobbes was mistrusted and condemned by contemporary monarchists. Sir Robert Filmer, who attacked him from that angle, commented 'It may seem strange that I should praise his building but mislike his foundations — but so it is.'[29] It was not strange at all. Hobbes's arguments have nothing in common with those of the divine right theorists. The structure of his case does not rely upon the quotation of authorities or the citing of precedents. His method is to start from what he takes to be empirical premises — factual truths about human nature — and arrive at his conclusions by deductive arguments based upon these premises: 'For I ground the Civill Right of Soveraigns, and both the Duty and Liberty of Subjects, upon the known naturall Inclinations of Mankind, and upon the Articles of the Law of Nature' (pp. 725). He wished to construct a science of politics, or a civil philosophy, analogous to what was currently being achieved in natural science.

To realize this scientific ambition, it was necessary to see human beings themselves as parts of nature, subject to the same fundamental laws as all other natural beings. Hobbes does this by applying to human motivation and action Galileo's law of inertia — the proposition that 'When a Body is once in motion, it moveth (unless something els hinder it) eternally' (p. 88). The types of motion which animate human behaviour are gathered by Hobbes under the two headings of 'appetite or desire' and 'aversion' (p. 119), and these forms of movement, either towards or away from things and beings, are not merely occasional urges or impulses: they are the springs of all human behaviour: 'to have no Desire, is to be Dead' (p. 139) — Hobbes repeatedly makes this point. Restlessness, of the same kind as Marlowe attributed to the endlessly ambitious Tamburlaine, is the essence of all human life. There is no point of rest on this side of the grave: 'For there is no such thing as perpetuall Tranquillity of mind, while we live here; because Life it selfe is but Motion, and can never be without Desire, nor without Feare, no more than without Sense' (pp. 129—130). As soon as one desire, or appetite, is gratified, we move on in search of a further satisfaction: 'So that in the first place, I put for a generall inclination of all mankind, a perpetuall and restlesse desire of power after power, that ceaseth onely in Death.' (p. 161)

With the possible exception of Bentham, no writer brings out more clearly than Hobbes the central role played by desires in the liberal theory of human nature. It is they which animate and dominate our actions. In relation to them reason and thought are purely instrumental: 'the Thoughts, are to the Desires, as Scouts, and Spies, to range abroad, and find the way to the things Desired' (p. 139). Hobbes, whose capacity for clear and logical thought most of us can only envy, yet believed with Hume that reason was the 'slave of the passions', and that reason meant little more than 'reckoning', a fundamentally calculating ability of the mind (see pp. 110—11). And not only reason, but also ethics, are subordinated to the desires. For it is Hobbes's view that 'good' and 'evil' are simply the names we give to the objects of our particular individual appetites and aversions. There cannot be 'any common Rule of Good and Evill, to be taken from the nature of the objects themselves; but from the Person of the man' who uses the terms (p. 120). As with Bentham, the good is simply the desired.

Hobbes's ethical reductivism derives in part from his nominalism. For him, words are names, and the naming quality of language is linked in turn to his ontological individualism. Common or general names, as opposed to proper names, do not refer to single objects, despite their singular form, but to many individual objects grouped under a single heading or name. These 'universals' have, therefore, no real existence — 'there being nothing in the world Universall but Names; for the things named, are every one of them Individuall and Singular' (p. 102).

This ontological individualism, which Hobbes shares with Bacon, Locke and the other liberal empiricists, provides the general philosophical foundation for his individualistic conception of human beings. For the natural world is composed of unique and discrete individual bodies, and human beings conform to this principle. Each of them is a self-contained, self-moving, and totally self-orientated being. There is nothing naturally social about Hobbesian man: 'We do not . . . by nature seek society for its own sake, but that we may receive some honour or profit from it; those we desire primarily, that secondarily.' [30] Hobbes explicitly distinguishes human beings from such naturally social creatures as bees and ants, and further denies that there is in human affairs the same coincidence of the common good with private interests as there is in the worlds of these insects. 'Every man is presumed to do all things in order to his own benefit' (p. 213), and this egoism leads directly to competition, rivalry, perpetual insecurity and, at worst, to unrestrained physical conflict. This is one of those several points at which Hobbes is in conflict with later and more optimistic versions of liberal theory. Hobbes, like Sade, does not make the bland assumption that all humankind's desires are directed towards ends which are in themselves rational, civilized and moderate. Nor does he postulate a hidden hand which ensures that individuals pursuing their own interests automatically further the general good at the same time.

But what is the basis of Hobbes's presumption of universal self-interest? Here Hobbes follows the method adopted by Montaigne and Descartes: 'know thyself', or '*Read thy self*' (p. 82). It is possible to generalize from observation of oneself and others, because people are much the same, despite the varieties of time and place. Hobbes gives to this 'sameness' a democratic or egalitarian dimension by claiming that, taking one thing with another, men are about equal in their natural endowments: 'Nature hath made men so equall, in the faculties of body, and mind; as that . . . when all is reckoned together, the difference between man, and man, is not so considerable, as that one man can thereupon claim to himselfe any benefit, to which another may not pretend, as well as he' (p. 183). Indeed, Hobbes like Descartes suggests that just because 'the Common-peoples minds' are not 'scribbled over with the opinions of their Doctors' (meaning the traditionalist university teachers) they may be more receptive to new ideas (pp. 378—9). But just at this point Hobbes once again undercuts later liberal optimism, which interpreted the 'blank sheet' or *tabula rasa* theory of the mind as the basis for a faith in the transforming potential of education, by pointing out that those whose minds are like 'clean paper' are also 'fit to receive whatsoever by Publique Authority shall be imprinted in them' (p. 379). It is an opportunity for manipulation and indoctrination as much as for education.

Hobbes's conception of human nature illustrates the change in the concept of nature itself which took place in this period. From being a moral category, which signified the divinely appointed ends or purposes which each natural being was supposed to fulfil, it has been changed into the concept of an irreducible, amoral and even anti-social bedrock of urges and passions which any realistic social and political theory and prescriptions must, however regretfully, take account of. [31] It followed from this conception of human nature that the supposed 'state of nature' is simply a condition of unrestrained competition, of what Hobbes calls 'warre . . . of every man,' against every man' (p. 185), though he is careful to point out that by this he means not necessarily open conflict, but that condition of insecurity which is always apt to break out in war.

There are, however, some distinctive aspects to Hobbes's version of this myth which, as so often with Hobbes, expose some of the most problematic assumptions of liberal theory. Hobbes adopts the view which the authorial protagonist in Buchanan's dialogue *De Jure Regno* explicitly rejected — namely, that the creation of society and government is inspired purely by considerations of self-centred utility. Buchanan's argument was that such a motive tends to dissolve rather than unite society, and it tells powerfully against Hobbes, as it does against Bentham. But there is a sense in which Hobbes, like Bentham, sidesteps this criticism by postulating a society which remains little more than a collection of self-seeking atoms, and therefore never achieves the coherence which Buchanan and other more traditional theorists saw as essential to the very concept of society.

Alasdair MacIntyre is therefore wrong to suggest that it is a 'confusion' on Hobbes's part 'to make political authority . . . constitutive of, social life'.[32] This, on the contrary, is the logical consequence of his thorough-going individualism. Only an all-powerful sovereign can prevent these jostling atoms from destroying each other. Hence Hobbes's absolutism is the necessary response to his individualism, and reflects a tendency within liberal thought to negate itself by pushing individualism to the point where authoritarianism seems to be the only possible political answer. But Hobbes is consistent in both his absolutism and his individualism. On the one hand he denies to the individual the right to follow his conscience, since this might then imply a right of resistance or opposition to the sovereign. Similarly there can be no question of the sovereign being limited by a pre-existing constitution or set of laws, since this makes the constitution or the laws the actual sovereign. For Hobbes, law is what the sovereign decrees, and justice is synonymous with law. All this is decidedly anti-liberal.

On the other hand, since the purpose of each individual in joining the compact to establish the sovereign is to further his (or her) own self-preservation, it follows that the individual does retain the right to defend his own life (see p. 199, and pp. 268—9). Hobbes therefore allows the right of resistance to 'private and particular men', the very thing that earlier and more traditional theorists, such as the author of the *Vindiciae*, ruled out. In this he exemplifies a more modern and individualistic kind of political thought — although the individual right he allows would, of course, be of little practical use against the might of Leviathan. Hobbes is equally consistent in allowing that it is no crime for a starving person to steal food, 'because no Law can oblige a man to abandon his own preservation' (pp. 345—6). Hobbes, unlike Locke, was not so attached to the institution of property as to allow its protection to distort his central argument.

I have dwelt here on what I see as Hobbes's radical and drastic individualism — although several recent writers have been concerned to emphasize the more traditional elements in his thought. It is not at all surprising that his thinking incorporated 'feudal' as well as 'bourgeois' elements, and I think that Keith Thomas, perhaps following Leo Strauss, was right to point to Hobbes's stress on honour, glory and reputation as reflecting an aristocratic rather than a bourgeois scale of values.[33] It is notable, too, that Hobbes does not altogether adopt the harsh attitude towards the unemployed which was to become the orthodoxy among liberal thinkers. Those who, by no fault of their own, 'by accident unevitable' find themselves 'unable to maintain themselves by their labour', ought not to be left to the uncertain fortunes of 'the Charity of private persons', but should be 'provided for (as farforth as the necessities of Nature require) by the Lawes of the Commonwealth' (p. 387).

There are, however, two further elements in Hobbes's contribution to developing liberal thought which must be mentioned. The first is his philosophical empiricism: that is, the stress on sense-experience as the source of knowledge: 'For there is no conception in a mans mind, which hath not at first, totally, or by parts, been begotten upon the organs of Sense' (p. 85). Hobbes extends this analysis of mental activity to cover imagination, which he describes as 'nothing but *decaying sense*', the fading image of what has already been experienced. '*Imagination* and *Memory* are but one thing' for Hobbes (pp. 88—9). Blake, who attacked Bacon and Locke, would also have attacked this downgrading of the creative and perceptive activity of the imagination, had he known of it, for in his view 'Imagination has nothing to do with Memory.'[34]

Secondly, Hobbes offers what is to become a classic statement of the liberal conception of liberty, or freedom, to be quoted with approval by leading liberals even in our own time.[35] Hobbes's first definition is 'the absence of externall Impediments' (p. 189), and when he returns to the subject he elaborates on this. An internal impediment, that is to say something that is 'in the constitution of the thing it selfe' does not imply a want of liberty, but of power. It is quite consistent with this definition that Hobbes should assert that 'Feare and liberty are consistent', because a person who throws his goods overboard to prevent the ship he is on from sinking, or pays a debt in order to avoid going to prison, *can* act otherwise. His action is therefore that 'of a man at *liberty*' (pp. 262—3).

That Hobbes should provide such examples, which expose the narrowness, (some would say strictness) of his notion of freedom, is typical of his honesty and precision as a thinker. Hobbes's thoroughness makes him an especially revealing, and so especially valuable writer for the student of political ideas.

JOHN LOCKE

Today John Locke, or perhaps rather his reputation as a major philosopher, presents a puzzle. His influence in the eighteenth century is well-attested. He enjoyed extraordinary prestige as one of the liberators of the human mind, and one of those who, in Hume's words, 'began to put the science of man on a new footing'. What is more, modern commentators seem agreed on his centrality to the liberal tradition. Bertrand Russell described him as 'the founder of empiricism', and Trevor-Roper has called him 'the greatest of liberal philosophers'.[36] Yet in what, precisely, does this greatness consist?

Many modern critics have pointed out that he is confused and inconsistent, and that he often fails to pursue his line of thought back to first principles. As we have seen, at one crux of his argument about the reliability of the senses as sources of knowledge, he falls back on bluff common-sense assertions in the manner of Dr Johnson. It may well be, as Berlin has suggested, that 'Locke may almost be said to have invented the notion of common sense'[37] but one function of philosophy is to penetrate into and behind common sense, and this Locke often damagingly fails to do. Locke lacks the rigour and probing thoroughness of the very greatest philosophers. And his political philosophy lacks the systematic constructiveness of Hobbes, or Bentham. Locke is, as Macpherson aptly put it, 'the confused man's Hobbes'.[38]

Confusion and inconsistency, so far from being obstacles to influence and popularity, may be aids to them, especially if they reflect the interests and pre-judices of the literate, or the dominant class. On the whole that class in eighteenth-century Western Europe found Locke very much to their taste, while the remorselessly logical reasonings of Hobbes made them distinctly un-comfortable — if they ever encountered them. But it is not only Locke in his role as the ideologist of the Whig settlement of 1688—89 who is important to liberalism. It is by virtue of his empiricist philosophy of knowledge that he takes his place among the principal philosophers of liberalism.

Locke was the first to work out a whole theory of knowledge based on the empiricist principle — the contention that such knowledge as we have, or can have, of the external world, can only come from sense-experience. The theory against which he argued was that there were certain ideas innate or inherent in the mind, 'which the Soul receives in its very first Being, and brings into the World with it.'[39] Locke thought that this was a quite unnecessary hypothesis: 'Men, barely by the Use of their natural Faculties, may attain to all the Knowledge they have, without the help of any innate Impressions' (p. 48). Instead, Locke proposed a picture of the mind as an empty room, or a blank sheet of 'white Paper void of all Characters, without any *Ideas*' (p. 104). How does this empty room come 'to be furnished'?

> To this I answer, in one word, from *Experience*: In that all our Knowledge is founded; and from that it ultimately derives it self. Our observation, employ'd either about *external sensible Objects; or about the internal Operations of our Minds, perceived and reflected on by ourselves, is that, which supplies our Understandings with all the materials of thinking.* (p. 104)

Noam Chomsky's view that certain common features of human language indicate something akin to innate ideas in human minds or thought processes, and the vehement reactions to that view, suggest that this philosophical issue is by no means settled. But whatever opinions may be held on the subject today, Locke's attack on innate ideas was a liberating step at that moment in history.

It cut away the ground from those who claimed that certain traditional ideas, beliefs and dogmas were beyond test or question because they were part of the permanent furniture of the mind, placed there by God. The dangers of Locke's theory were very quickly spotted by his religious contemporaries, one of whom, William Sherlock, wrote: 'if all the knowledge we have of God, and of good and evil, be made by ourselves, atheists will easily conclude that it is only the effect of education and superstitious fears.'[40] At the same time the notion of the mind as a blank sheet or empty room became the ground for a (sometimes boundless) optimism about the potentialities of education. Yet it was a further consequence of this blank sheet theory that the idea of the personality as a stable centre of the individual tends to dissolve, and is eventually replaced by Hume's disturbing picture of the human being as nothing more integrated or continuous than a 'bundle of sensations'. At this point liberal atomism succeeds in dissolving the very notion of personality.

Locke insists upon the passivity of the mind in its role as a receiver of 'simple ideas'. It cannot control the flow of information into it from the sense, any more than a mirror can refuse to reflect what stands before it: 'for the Objects of our Senses do, many of them, obtrude their particular *Ideas* upon our minds whether we will or no' (p. 118). This, too, was encouraging. Today we are all familiar with the notion of selective perception. Psychologists with ambiguous pictures and diagrams can demonstrate how the 'same' object looks quite different to different people. We see what we want to see, or, more depressingly, what we have been conditioned to see. But in Locke's view the reality of the external world forces itself upon our minds through our senses. The very passivity of the mind, far from being a negative notion, provides the strongest grounds for believing that we are not deceived by our senses — as we might be were they more active and selective, more capable of manipulating the impressions they receive.

Similarly, when Locke emphatically denies the capacity of 'the most exalted Wit or enlarged Understanding . . . *to invent or frame one new simple* Idea in the mind, not taken in by the ways before mentioned (p. 119) — this denial, which to the Romantics and post-Kantian idealists would seem like a denial of the creative roles of mind and imagination, was intended to reinforce the empiricist case. For just as a factory can only make its products out of the raw materials of the natural world, so the mind can only manufacture ideas in the same way. At both levels there is a necessary dependence of humankind upon nature.

But there is a major peculiarity in Locke's account of the sources of knowledge. Besides experience mediated through the senses, he sets a second source: the 'observation' of the mind's own operations, or 'reflection'. And although Locke clearly means by 'reflection' the *activity* of thought, yet the mirror sense of the term is also part of what is meant, since Locke suggests that 'reflection' is also a kind of perception, or 'internal sense'. This notion of the mind watching itself is certainly interesting, but it is hard to see how it can be a source of knowledge comparable to sense-experience. And this was a point taken up by some of Locke's Enlightenment admirers, such as Condillac, who suggested that although Locke named two sources for our ideas, 'It would be more exact to recognize only one, either because reflection is in its origin only sensation itself, or because it is less the source of ideas than the channel through which they flow from the senses.'[41] Nor is it clear how this mental activity is to be reconciled with the notion of the open, passive, receiving mind. It is however characteristic that Locke should present the mind's own activities as in the first place another form of perception. The conception of the rational man, and in particular the scientist, as a detached observer, or a camera, which is so central to liberal ideas of rationality and rational knowledge, has its philosophical roots in Lockean empiricism with its stress on passive perception.

Locke believes that each of us can be quite certain of the validity of our own experience. Other people's reports may be fabrication, but our senses cannot, in the last analysis, seriously mislead us. Trust your own experience above all, rather than any kind of report, authority, tradition or established belief. Many people had already begun to do this in matters of religion. Locke provided a ground for doing so in every aspect of life.

The world of which our senses provide us with knowledge is individualistic, too. Just as sensations, or sense-experiences, are particular and unique, so the world itself is made up of things which are also separate, individual and unique — 'All Things, that exist, being Particulars' (p. 409). It is true that language is not made up of the names of particular things and beings, but of general names. But it is a mistake to confuse the pattern of language with that of reality. For although 'words are general', 'universality belongs not to things themselves, which are all of them particular in their Existence' (p. 144).

The implication is that the world is a chaos of individual entities, while the order implied in the general names and categories which human beings use is something 'in the mind', invented and imposed on the world from outside. This atomizing approach was to be extended by David Hume in his celebrated analysis of causation. We never actually perceive a causal connection, he argued. We perceive only conjunctions of events or things, and from regular conjunctions we *infer* a chain of causes and effects: 'all our distinct perceptions are distinct existences, and . . . the mind never perceives any real connexion among distinct existences.' Thus 'all events seem entirely loose and separate.'[42] There is a gap between the order upon which the mind insists, and the disorder of reality itself. In the age of Newton it seems odd to find this, especially since Locke's name was so often coupled with Newton's. But in some respects empiricism, although often associated with science, shares less of the scientific outlook of the seventeenth century than does rationalism, which argues that there must be some congruence between the rationality of the human mind and the rationality of nature, if any true understanding of the world is to be possible. In this respect Spinoza, the supposed metaphysician, is closer to the scientific project than the empiricists Locke and Hume.

Locke was interpreted by the eighteenth century as providing a foundation for a general optimism about the potentialities of both science and education. Retrospectively, this looks like a misinterpretation, because Locke himself did not see the area of actual or potential human knowledge as all that wide. He claims that reason must evaluate the claims of faith and revelation, and that nothing in faith should be contrary to reason. This is the predictable encroachment on the domain of faith which was, sooner or later, bound to follow from the Baconian separation of the two territories. But he is anything but dogmatic about matters of religious belief, and strongly aware of the vast areas in which opinion rather than knowledge must prevail. His arguments for toleration are classically liberal, in so far as they are based at the most fundamental level upon scepticism about the possibility of resolving disputes over religious beliefs.

So, at a stage when confidence in the possibilities of knowledge and rationality is still growing, Locke strikes a slightly discordant note. In some ways he represents, in philosophy as well as politics, a limited and tentative liberalism rather than the wholehearted optimism which we might expect at this stage in its development. Some contemporary liberals would retort that it is recisely this cautious, undogmatic approach which makes Locke rather than, say, Spinoza or Condorcet, a true liberal.[43] But this is a judgement which reflects the outlook of the retreating liberalism of our century. My point is that we do not necessarily expect to find such attitudes in the philosopher who is taken as central to liberalism when it was still a developing and dynamic ideology.

SPINOZA

In some ways the supposedly more marginal figure of Benedict Spinoza embodies the confidence and dynamism of developing liberalism more truly than Locke. But at the same time Spinoza, like Hobbes, can only be partially incorporated into the liberal tradition.

All things come within the domain of reason. That other realm of mysteries penetrable only by faith, still part of the philosophy of Locke, has no place in the world view of the rationalist Spinoza. The natural world is not merely a chain of causes and effects: it is linked by logical necessity. Nothing is accidental or fortuitous; everything is as it must be. There is nothing contingent in nature. The world itself is rational and logical: 'Things could not have been produced by God in any other manner or order than that in which they were produced.'[44]

The uncontrolled and random sense-perceptions which Locke identifies as the primary source of our knowledge of the world, Spinoza regards as fundamentally untrustworthy. They yield only 'confused and mutilated knowledge', because in such cases the mind 'is determined externally, that is, by fortuitous cirucmstances'.[45] A true understanding of the world depends upon applying to it the connecting and logical powers of the mind, not upon immediate and unsystematic sense-impressions. Leibniz questioned Lockean empiricism even more directly than Spinoza. In his *New Essays on the Human Understanding*, he asked: 'why is it necessary that everything should be acquired by us through the perceptions of external things, and that nothing can be unearthed in ourselves? Is our soul, then, such a blank that, besides the images borrowed from without, it is nothing?[46] Leibniz believed that this was too simple a picture to account for the activity and fertility of the mind, and in particular he argued that because 'the senses never give anything except examples, that is to say, particular or individual truths', we cannot, on the basis of sense-experience alone, arrive at any truths which are universally and necessarily true. And it is this kind of knowledge, 'the knowledge of necessary and eternal truths', which, in Leibniz's view, is 'what distinguishes us from mere animals, and furnishes us with reason and the sciences, raising us to a knowledge of ourselves and of God. This is what we call the rational soul or spirit in us.'[47]

Spinoza and Leibniz thus do not share the liberal-empiricist faith in 'experience'. Experience is unreliable if not guided and corrected by reason, and by reason they do not mean the mere calculating faculty of Hobbes or Hume. So far from being the slave of the passions or appetites, reason is the faculty which can liberate us from the ordinary condition of thralldom to passion and appetite, and raise us to the level on which our actions take on a pattern of purpose and consistency, rather than being determined by each passing gust of fancy or feeling. Spinoza's ideal is Hamlet's:

> . . . blest are those
> Whose blood and judgement are so well commingled,
> That they are not a pipe for fortune's finger
> To sound what stop she please. Give me that man
> That is not passion's slave. . . .
> (Act III, 2)

This positive, normative conception of reason also has its part to play in the history of liberalism, and Spinoza is the first modern philosopher to give it sustained expression.

For Spinoza, rationality and freedom are connected: no one can be truly free in whom reason does not hold sway over emotion and desire, for they are among the forces which obstruct self-direction. And self-direction is the essence of freedom: 'That thing is said to be FREE which exists by the mere necessity of its own nature and is determined in its actions by itself alone.' To act freely is not to act arbitrarily. The one being that is absolutely free is God. But God 'does not act from freedom of will', but in accordance with the necessity of his own nature. If freedom is not actually equated with the recognition of necessity, it certainly involves that recognition: 'In so far as the mind understands all things as necessary it has more power over the emotions or is less passive to them.'

The ontological basis of Spinoza's commitment to freedom, and to the ideal of the autonomous, self-moving person, is his belief that every being in nature is animated by a will or urge to survive and flourish as a distinct individual: 'The endeavour wherewith a thing endeavours to persist in its being is nothing else than the actual essence of that being.' And this endeavour is directed towards activity: 'The more perfection anything has, the more active and the less passive it is.' Spinoza interprets this as a principle of being applicable throughout the natural world. And hence nature has its own purposes, and is not to be regarded only as a realm to be dominated, a means to human ends: 'the perfection of things is estimated solely from their nature and power; nor are things more or less perfect according as they delight or disgust human senses, or according as they arc useful or useless to man.'[48] Thus Spinoza goes beyond the Baconian-utilitarian attitude to nature, and stresses the 'otherness' and autonomy of nature and its beings. Human beings have it in common with other natural beings that they wish to 'persist in their being', and freedom is the necessary condition of their being able to do so. But this freedom is not just the absence of external impediments, but also the autonomy of the rational will. Happiness, or fulfilment, is linked to freedom because we find happiness in our own self-moving activity: it cannot be found when a being is impelled and directed from outside itself.

By connecting the ideas of reason and freedom, Spinoza moves well beyond orthodox liberal ideas as we find them in Hobbes, or Locke, or Bentham. He can therefore be interpreted as a potential critic of liberalism. Yet his positive conception of reason links him to the heroic age of science and is shared by the liberals of the Enlightenment. After the French Revolution similar links between freedom, self-direction and reason are made by Hegel and by the late nineteenth-century English liberals led by T. H. Green. Hegel, Green, L. T. Hobhouse, and others in this tradition, all have their affinities with socialism, but none of them are socialists. And one way of seeing them would be to place them, with Spinoza, in an uneven, discontinuous line of thinkers who attempt repeatedly to extend and deepen the liberal philosophy of freedom and of the personality — but without success. They tried in vain to shift liberalism's centre of gravity.

Spinoza is an individualist without being an atomist. He does not see autonomy as the natural, primal condition of the individual, as so many liberals do. Autonomy is not the starting point, but the goal or ideal. And the realization of this ideal will not produce a potentially chaotic collection of discrete atoms. A being is most free when it is most rational, and to be rational is to act in accordance with nature and necessity — to accept one's place in the cosmic order. So in Spinoza's world view individualism and order are harmonized by reason, whereas in Hobbes the jarring atoms are only kept in check by sheer power, and in later liberal writings by the hopeful supposition of the hidden hand or the laws of the market.

I have not, in this chapter, discussed at length the political ideas of the great seventeenth-century philosophers. Something will be said of them in the following chapters. I have been concerned here to uncover what I take to be the philosophical foundations of liberal individualism. They take a variety of philosophical forms, ranging from Locke's faith in personal experience and Hobbes's atomism, to Leibniz's theory of self-contained 'windowless' monads and Spinoza's ideal of self-directing autonomy. But they all share an element of individualism which was, broadly speaking, a novelty of post-Renaissance philosophy. And it was noticed at the time. It is worth quoting once more Donne's famous lines from *The First Anniversary*, not so much because of his reference to the 'doubt' engendered by what he terms the 'new philosophy', but because he associates the collapse of traditional hierarchical relationships, which he laments in terms similar to Gloucester in *King Lear*, with the new conviction of uniqueness on the part of each individual:

> 'Tis all in pieces, all coherence gone;
> All just supply, and all relation:
> Prince, subject, father, son, are things forgot,
> For every man alone thinks he hath got
> To be a phoenix, and that then can be
> None of that kind, of which he is, but he.

Donne's reference to the new 'philosophy', when he is as much concerned with new views of the solar system and the universe as with what we would understand by philosophy, illustrates the point that at this stage in European thought, no great gulf is placed between philosophy and the natural sciences. I have suggested that in some ways it was the rationalists rather than the empiricists who were closest in spirit to the enterprise of science; but there is no doubt that the continuing spread of a scientific outlook is tied up with the development of liberalism in this period. Thomas Sprat, the first historian of the post-Restoration Royal Society, suggested that there was a parallel between the Society and the Church of England, in that both operated by 'passing by the corrupt copies, and referring themselves to the perfect Originals for their instruction; the one to the Scripture, the other to the huge Volume of Creatures.'[49] Thus the connection between Protestantism and science is not simply the hypothesis of modern historians; it was thought to exist even in the seventeenth century. Sprat's emphasis on the study of things rather than words (copies) is of a piece with Bacon's and Locke's faith in individual observation and experience. It was this faith in personal experience to which religious traditionalists so strongly objected. The rationalist and empiricist philosophers of the seventeenth century provided this faith in personal experience, and this individualism, with a deeply laid and thoroughly elaborated philosophical foundation.

7

Early Bourgeois Liberalism: Holland and England

The great French historian Marc Bloch once gave a necessary reminder about those neat, symmetrical divisions which humanity has imposed upon time — years, decades, centuries — and the absurdity of supposing that these are likely to correspond in any way to the real turning points of history. Yet we still strain to find the supposed common characteristics of the year, decade or century.

From our perspective the year 1600 does not mark any kind of turning point. The developments and conflicts set in motion by the Renaissance and the Reformation continued to work themselves out in the first 50 or 60 years of the seventeenth Christian century. 'The eighteenth century', the epoch of relatively stable absolutism and rational enlightenment, begins in most of Europe around 1660, and ends, in most of Western and Central Europe, in the years after 1789. By 1660 early liberal and constitutionalist developments had been decisively checked and widely defeated throughout most of Europe. Only the United Provinces of the Netherlands was firmly established as a bourgeois republic. England was an ambiguous case: Stuart absolutist ambitions were finally defeated in 1688, but republicanism had also suffered its defeat in 1659—60. Elsewhere in Europe feudal absolutism was firmly established as the modernized political form through which the landed aristocracy continued to dominate political, social and economic life. This was the unpropitious context in which the liberals of the Enlightenment fought their battles.

At the opening of the seventeenth century, however, things looked very different. There was a confusion of beliefs, and there was widespread social unrest. Some people lamented (as some have continued to do ever since) the disappearance of a stable, hierarchical social order. Social and political instability reached a climax in the years around 1648, when there were rebellions in France, England, Catalonia, Andalucia, Naples, Sicily and Moscow. But these were more of an end than a beginning. Within a few years, the old order, which had seemed so near to dissolution, was restored with a new lease of life.

In the apparent confusion of these decades we can find two important general tendencies. On the one hand there was the gradual formation of the essentially bourgeois social philosophy which was to become the middle-class orthodoxy of the eighteenth century. On the other hand, these ideas were challenged from a more democratic and popular standpoint by the short-lived popular movements of the period. This popular ideology often goes well beyond liberalism, and illuminates it by exposing some of its limitations. This conflict between incipient Whiggery and popular radicalism was particularly clear and sharp in England during the revolutionary turmoil of the 1640s. But at the opening of the century, it was the Dutch Netherlands which embodied the hopes of both militant Protestants and the constitutionalist opponents of absolutism.

THE DUTCH REPUBLIC: TRADE AND TOLERATION

The prolonged resistance of the Dutch to the Spanish empire — a struggle finally resolved only by the peace treaties which ended the Thirty Years War in 1648 — continued to command the admiration of Protestant Europe. Despite the natural reluctance of rulers like Elizabeth of England to support open revolt against a fellow monarch, England was drawn into the struggle, while militant Protestants proved their commitment by providing a steady stream of volunteers for the Dutch armies. Comparison with the impact of the Spanish Civil War on the European Left in the 1930s is entirely apt.[1] Constitutionalists were also impressed by the fact that the Dutch had succeeded in creating what had often been said to be an impossibility — a state without a head. Having renounced Philip II of Spain, the Dutch offered the vacant post of sovereign to a number of candidates who turned out to be unsuitable, after which they reconciled themselves to being a republic. Holland provided a working example of a headless commonwealth. It was also noticeably less hierarchical and rigidly stratified than other European societies. For example, the great commanders of the Dutch navy of the seventeenth century were, many of them, lifelong sailors who rose to the top through sheer ability. And having risen, they often retained much of the style and appearance of the ordinary sailor, which must have made it easier for them to command the loyalty of those they commanded.[2]

From the last quarter of the sixteenth century, the Dutch Netherlands, along with some of the Protestant cities of Germany, attracted a great flood of religious refugees from many parts of Catholic Europe, but above all from the war-torn Spanish Netherlands and the great trading and industrial city of Antwerp. It was the promise of toleration, of being free from inquisition into their beliefs, of being able to practise as much or as little of their religion as they chose, and (for intellectuals) being able to publish what they wrote, that drew them to this tiny new state in North-Western Europe.

Toleration was not complete in the Dutch Republic, nor was it won without a struggle. But although freedom of worship was not officially conceded, it was tolerated in practice. Not for nothing did Pierre Bayle describe the country as 'the great arc of the refugees'. Holland had by far the freeest press in Europe in the seventeenth century, and Bayle's own *Dictionnaire* was published in Rotterdam rather than in France.

Of the philosophers considered in the last chapter, Descartes decided, out of prudence, to settle in Holland and lived there for 20 years; Locke took refuge there with his employer the Earl of Shaftesbury during the reign of James II, and there wrote and published his *Letter on Toleration*. Spinoza was a native of Amsterdam, but his family were Portuguese Jews who had been part of the great emigration of Jews from Iberia in the late sixteenth century. It is unlikely that Spinoza's works could have been published anywhere else in Europe. And Hobbes, when his works were banned in England in 1666, continued to publish in Amsterdam.

The Dutch Republic appeared to many observers to embody an obviously winning combination of qualities: it had discarded monarchy, it was relatively free and tolerant, and it was overwhelmingly busy and prosperous. The attractiveness of liberality was enhanced by the fact that it was evidently profitable. Spinoza himself observed that

> The city of Amsterdam reaps the fruit of this freedom in its own great prosperity and in the admiration of all other people. For in this most flourishing state, and most splendid city, men of every nation and religion live together in the greatest harmony, and ask no questions before trusting their goods to a fellow-citizen, save whether he be rich or poor, and whether he generally acts honestly, or the reverse.

A French visitor, St Evremond commented more cynically that if the Hollanders 'love the Republick, 'tis for the Benefit of their Trade; more than for any Satisfaction they find in being Free.'[3]

This prosperity was significant for liberalism in more than one respect. It is interesting to find that the Dutch commitment to trade pushed them in the direction of a foreign policy based on what one historian has called 'an empirical, largely self-interested and qualified pacifism'.[4] A comparable syndrome of attitudes is to be found among British liberal advocates of free trade in the nineteenth century. Here, if anywhere, we find the material basis for middle-class liberal internationalism.

Secondly, this trading society produced an individualistic ethos, striking to observers in its novelty. Descartes described Amsterdam as a city where 'apart from myself there dwells no one who is not engaged in trade; everyone is so much out for his own advantage that I should be able to live my whole life here without ever meeting a mortal being.'[5] To Descartes, capitalist Amsterdam seemed something like Hobbes's state of nature. By the end of the century the Dutch, according to Daniel Defoe, had become a by-word for avarice.[6]

It was not only in Holland, but throughout Western Europe, that the decline of the Catholic-feudal social order produced a new response to the old problem of poverty. According to the traditional Christian ethic, poverty was certainly no sin, and might even be a sign of virtue; but in the world of emerging capitalism it was increasingly seen as a sign of failure. And in a period of social unrest the poor, and especially the vagrant poor, were seen as a threat by the prosperous. The early modern period is a time of edicts against begging in many parts of Europe.

But a prohibition against begging is also a prohibition of charity. What was to take the place of charity? The answer was: institutions. The poor were, as far as possible, tidied away into hospitals and homes. The bleak cruelty of the new poor house, which is often more associated with the nineteenth century, is already there at this time, as we can see in Frans Hals's chilling picture of the guardians of the old people's home in which he himself ended his days. The harsh and punitive treatment of poverty and the poor is, from this time on, part and parcel of the rise of the liberal capitalist economy and social order.

Finally, we should note that the Dutch Republic's reputation as a model of 'democracy' was much exaggerated. Popular Calvinism was a force which the House of Orange was ready to exploit in its power struggles with the merchant aristocracy, but it was a force which was not allowed to get 'out of hand', as it had done so frighteningly (to the propertied) in the 1560s and 1570s. Power remained firmly in the hands of the rich merchant oligarchies of the states and cities. And these oligarchies got smaller. By the end of the seventeenth century, Amsterdam was effectively dominated by a mere three families.[7] As Sir William Temple, the English ambassador observed, the Republic was not a democracy, but 'a sort of oligarchy and very different from a popular government'.[8] No doubt the border between an extensive oligarchy and what was then thought of as democracy was a shadowy one. Nevertheless the Dutch Republic is the first example of the natural equation which the bourgeoisie makes between a 'free commonwealth' and one in which they themselves hold power.

Or perhaps not quite the first. If the Dutch were one source of inspiration in the seventeenth century, another was the much older self-governing city of Venice. La Serenissima, the most serene republic of Venice, was in the early modern period the object of a cult. It was seen by many, not only as the pattern of a mixed polity, judiciously blending the best of monarchy, aristocracy and democracy, but also as a link with the world of classical republicanism. Those who were struggling against the growth of absolutism took encouragement from the fact that the Venetians had so successfully contained the power of their titular head, the doge.

F

In 1644 some of the English parliamentary leaders asked the Venetian ambassador to let them have a description of the Venetian constitution, and less than two months before Charles I was executed, an ill-informed royalist agent reported that the Independent leaders were intending to make the king 'a Duke of Venice which I hear is the hard condition they intend to impose on him.' Milton, in his last pamphleteering effort to prevent the restoration of the monarchy in 1660, cited the example of Venice, while James Harrington described the Venetian system as 'the most Democratical or Popular of all others'.[9] Once more, the distinction between oligarchy and democracy is disregarded — though not by all observers. Marchamont Nedham, for example, said accurately enough 'Tis rather a Junta than a Commonwealth.'[10] But the myth of Venice persisted until the very end in 1802, when Wordsworth, in a famous sonnet, described the city as 'the eldest Child of Liberty'.

LIBERTY AND PROPERTY

At the heart of the political conflicts and arguments of the seventeenth century lies a hard issue which is central to liberalism: the question of the relation between freedom and property. It was increasingly asserted and accepted that a man may do what he will with his own, or in the words of the House of Commons in 1628: 'every free subject of this realm hath a fundamental property in his goods and a fundamental liberty of his person.'[11] But who counted as a free subject? This was the subject of much dispute, yet in the end it was the property-owners who triumphed. It was accepted that they had the right, not only to do as they pleased with 'their own', but also to control the state itself. Property became the essential qualification for holding political rights and freedoms.

The notion that individual self-interest and an eye to the main chance were no sin, but plain common sense, can be found quite early in this period; in, for example, Thomas Wilson's *A Discourse upon Usury* of 1572: 'What man is so madde to deliver his moneye out of his owne possession for naughte? or whoe is he that will not make of his owne the best he can?' When in 1604 a Commons committee wished to complain about monopolies and exclusive franchises in trade, it argued that just as 'all free subjects are born inheritable, as to their land', the same was also true of 'the free exercise of their industry, in those trades whereto they apply themselves and whereby they are to live.' It concluded that it was 'against the natural right and liberty of the subjects of England' to confine trade 'into the hands of some few'.[12] Thus freedom in trade and industry was seen as logical extension of personal liberty and the right to property.

But how was this 'sensible' concentration on one's own interests to be reconciled with the good of the whole community? This was a question which troubled many, and there were those, such as the Digger, Winstanley, who concluded that the competitive scramble for wealth would produce a large crop of casualties, and set all against all: 'pleading for property and single interest divides the people of a land and the whole world into parties, and is the cause of all wars and bloodshed and contention everywhere.'[13]

This was, however, a deviant view, at once too old-fashioned and too advanced to be much noticed. More 'realistic' writers soon concluded that there was really no problem. If the individual merchant or manufacturer worked hard for his own benefit, he would at the same time add to the sum of society's prosperity. This was the message of Thomas Mun in *England's Treasure by Forraign Trade*, written in the 1620s, in which he urges his son to fulfil his 'vocation' as a merchant, 'that so the private gain may ever accompany the public good.'[14] By the 1650s the argument had been carried a stage further. John Hall, in *Of Government and Obedience* (1654), scoffs at the notion that a society can survive on the basis of altruism or dedication to the common good. In the manner later popularized by Mandeville and theorized by Adam Smith, he argues that altruism is damaging and the pursuit of self-interest a social necessity:

> to dream of public-spirited persons or public souls (meaning such as have no private interest) is not only untrue, but could it be, it would instead of benefit, be the ruin of that whole state. For through the distracted endeavours of so many voluntary public undertakers, the whole would perish by degrees, and while each particular failed for want of due self-regard, the whole would fail by consequence.[15]

Nor was there any necessary conflict between serving God and Mammon, as had once been supposed. 'Do not tradesmen in following their vocations aim at their own advantage, do none of them glorify God thereby?' asked the Reverend Joseph Lee, rhetorically.[16]

At the same time as the right to property was being so strongly asserted, the common land rights of the poor were beginning to be whittled away, in the interests of the propertied classes. The first English Enclosure Act was passed by Parliament in 1608, a year after widespread anti-enclosure riots in the Midlands. Other acts and actions to facilitate enclosures followed. It was not only property-owners who favoured enclosure: it was supported by intellectual reformers such as Samuel Hartlib, who believe that 'There are fewest poor where there are fewest commons.'[17]

It was axiomatic that the poor were not part of the political nation. As Sir Thomas Smith put it in 1565, 'the poorer and meaner people . . . have no interest in the commonweal but the use of breath.'[18] It is a matter of considerable dispute who precisely was included in the category of free-born or free subjects. Quite apart from the entire female sex, it certainly did not include all men. It seems to have been generally accepted that servants and apprentices could not be counted as free, since they were too dependent upon their masters. Whether 'servants' included all wage labourers, as has been argued by C. B. Macpherson, is in my opinion doubtful; but it is not in doubt that many people saw wage labour as involving a loss of freedom, and as a degradation for those who thought of themselves as free-born.[19] Thus at the same time that many people were being forced into a situation of greater poverty and dependence, the argument was being developed that it was precisely this dependence which disqualified them from participating in politics. It was argued that property was the indispensable foundation of personal independence. Only those who were in this sense their own masters could be relied on to speak and act independently. Hence a franchise based upon property qualifications safeguarded freedom as well as property.

This was the philosophy for which Harrington provided what he intended to be a scientific exposition, in *The Commonwealth of Oceana*. Harrington, like Hobbes, to whose works he referred with admiration, was less interested in prescription than analysis. It was his view that the stability of any system of government depended upon whether it reflected the actual distribution of property (economic power) in society. It was essential that property-owners should also have political power; but the durability of a political system was best ensured by devices to prevent property being concentrated in too few hands. Hence his objections to the system of primogeniture: it was more desirable that inherited property should be shared out among the eligible children. Harrington recommended, in effect, a commonwealth ruled by a property-owning oligarchy — something which, with various pragmatic modifications, came into being after 1688. What was the alternative? One of the group of Harringtonian MPs, Captain Adam Baynes, made the position clear in 1659: 'We must either lay the foundation in property, or else it will not stand. Property, generally, is now with the people; the government therefore must be there. . . . All government is built upon property, else the poor must rule it.'[20] For Harrington as well as Captain Baynes, 'the people' were not the same group as 'the poor'.

THE ENGLISH REVOLUTION

This, then, was the dominant movement of liberal ideas in the seventeenth century: towards the establishment of the rights and political power of private property, and towards the habitual connection of freedom with both property and prosperity. But in the revolutionary upheaval which shook England in the 1640s, a wider range of positions and arguments found expression. Some of them can be seen as representing more radical tendencies within liberalism itself; others challenge liberal thinking from outside.

Whether or not there was a 'revolution' in England in the mid-seventeenth century is still debated by historians; and this in itself indicates that the revolution, if it occurred, was at best incomplete and limited. But what is not in doubt is that, whatever the outcome of the turmoil, the 1640s in particular bore many of the characteristic marks of a revolutionary epoch. Hence, among other things, the amazing flood of pamphlets, books and newspapers written and published in this period: 2,000 pamphlets in 1642 alone, 15,000 at least between 1640 and 1660.[21] Hence the intensity and quality of the political debate of the period, which included not only the pamphlet controversies and the army debates, but also the major works of Hobbes, Harrington and Winstanley, as well as Milton's political tracts and the Leveller manifestos.

Hence, too, the utopianism of the period. 'All sorts of people dreamed of an Utopia and infinite liberty, especially in matters of religion' wrote a royalist pamphleteer in 1648.[22] It was a utopianism which was rarely completely secular. The good society was envisaged in terms of bringing about God's kingdom on earth, or of undoing the damage done by the Fall of Man. In the 1640s expectations of the imminent second-coming of Christ jostle with practical schemes for better education, technological progress and greater toleration. Liberalism is now so generally interpreted as a cautious empirical and often explicitly anti-utopian creed that it is hard to realize that, in its period of dynamic growth, utopianism was a quite natural expression of liberal confidence in the future and in the power of liberal ideas. In the English Revolution utopianism and liberalism overlap and are combined.

JOHN MILTON

A number of these developments come together in the career and work of John Milton. Milton seems to have shared in millenarian hopes from an early age, to judge from his poem *At a Solemn Musick*, composed around 1632, when the poet was twenty-four. Milton expresses through musical metaphor the hope

> That we on Earth with undiscording voice
> May rightly answer that melodious noise;
> As once we did, till disproportion'd sin
> Jarr'd against natures chime . . .

— in other words that the harmonious prelapsarian order may be restored on earth, something which Milton did not think beyond possibility, as the last lines make clear: 'O may we soon again renew that Song, And keep in tune with Heav'n. . . .' — paradise regained.

Milton's reasons for preferring a commonwealth to monarchy are interesting. Both in *The Tenure of Kings and Magistrates*, written in 1649 to defend the execution of Charles I, and later in *Paradise Lost*, Milton emphasizes the natural, original equality and freedom of men: 'No man who knows ought, can be so stupid to deny that all men naturally were borne free, being the image and resemblance of God himself, and were by privilege above all the creatures, born to command and not to obey: and that they liv'd so.' Adam restates this view in Book XII of *Paradise Lost*:

> He gave us onely over Beast, Fish, Fowl
> Dominion absolute; that right we hold
> By his donation: but Man over men
> He made not Lord; such title to himself
> Reserving, human left from human free.
> (lines 67—71)

It was the Fall that made government necessary. But even then it was human beings acting together for their common safety who set up kings and magistrates as authorities over them. So far Milton's account of the origins of government is strikingly like Hobbes's. But unlike Hobbes, Milton insists that ultimate authority remains in the hands of the people. Kings and magistrates are set up 'Not to be thir Lords and Maisters . . . but, to be thir Deputies and Commissioners, to execute, by vertue of thir instrusted power, that justice which else every man by the bond of nature and of Cov'nant must have executed for himself, and for one another.'[23] Otherwise there can, says Milton, be no explanation why 'free Persons' — Milton quite often avoids using the masculine mode — should subordinate themselves to the authority of a single person.

Government then being a human creation, it follows that human beings have the right to change it when they want to. Hence Milton argues, not just that society has the traditional right to resist and depose a tyrant, but that it has the more fundamental right to remove any king or ruler who displeases it: 'then may the people as oft as they shall judge it for the best, either chose him or reject him, retaine him or depose him though no Tyrant, meerly by the liberty and right of free born Men, to be govern'd as seems to them best.'[24] By 1660, and probably earlier, Milton was clear that monarchy was a form of government hard to reconcile with the proper dignity of free citizens. Monarchy, he said in *The Readie and Easie Way*, may make the people rich, but only in order to fleece them, while at the same time it encourages servility and conformity. It makes the people 'servilest, easiest to be kept under; and not only in fleece, but in minde also sheepishest'. On the other hand, 'of all governments a Commonwealth aims to make the people flourishing, vertuous, noble and high spirited.'[25] Milton sees freedom, not simply as a condition in which certain things are allowed, but as a condition which positively encourages independence of mind. Allowing for his evident deep antipathy to Milton, Samuel Johnson was right to say that Milton's republicanism was 'founded in', among other things, 'a sullen desire of independence . . . and pride disdainful of superiority'.[26] Milton did have a strong sense of what was appropriate to the dignity and rationality of men — and even of women; and he counted it as one of the virtues of a 'free commonwealth' that those who govern in it are also 'perpetual servants and drudges to the public', who 'are not elevated above their brethren', but 'walk the streets as other men', and do not need to be deferred to.[27]

Milton was not generally sympathetic to paternalism. In his most famous pamphlet, *Areopagitica* (1644), he argues that to control and censor what is written and published is to treat people like children, beings not capable of using their own reason to make their own choices. But 'God uses not to captivat [man] under a perpetuall childhood of prescription, but trusts him with the gift of reason to be his own chooser.' Everyone is endowed with reason, and hence with ability to make choices: Milton says of Adam that 'when God gave him reason, he gave him freedom to choose, for reason is but choosing.' Censorship displays a lack of trust in 'the common people', and this, to Milton in 1644, smacked of a popish authoritarianism.[28]

Milton reinforced his argument by holding that only freely chosen actions and commitments can truly be called virtuous: there is no credit in apparently good actions done under compulsion. This is a point which recurs again and again in *Paradise Lost*. God argues in Book III (lines 98—134) that angels as well as humans were created free, so that they — and God — might have the satisfaction of serving God freely. And Raphael confirms this, when he tells Adam in Book V that 'freely we serve / Because wee freely love' (538—9). This is the basis on which Milton expressed his contempt, in *Areopagitica* for 'a fugitive and cloister'd virtue, unexercis'd & unbreath'd, that never sallies out and sees her adversary, but slinks out of the race, where that immortall garland is to be run for, not without dust and heat.'[29] Virtue involves choice, and to evade choice by withdrawal is as bad as using censorship and control to deprive people of the opportunity of choice.

It has been conventional to connect Milton's hatred of conformity and respect for independence of mind with John Stuart Mill's similar sentiments in *On Liberty*. Milton expressed a similar faith that truth will emerge through the processes of debate — 'who ever knew Truth put to the wors, in a free and open encounter' — and a similar fear that censorship and prohibition will impede truth itself: 'consider this, that if it come to prohibiting, there is not ought more likely to be prohibited than truth it self; whose first appearance to our eyes blear'd and dimm'd with prejudice and custom, is more unsightly and unplausible then many errors.' That truth may be unfamiliar, and likely to be in conflict with conventional beliefs, became a liberal commonplace. Milton, before Mill, recognized that accepted truths degenerate into dead dogmas. Of truth he said: 'if her water flow not in a perpetuall progression, they sick'n into a muddy pool of conformity and tradition.'[30] Nor was custom in itself deserving of respect: 'custom without truth is but agedness of error.'[31] But it is also striking that Milton should share with Mill a certain intellectual elitism and contempt for the 'rude multitude', and that both should have toyed with elaborate electoral systems through which the weight of popular opinion could be diminished.

One other point may be made, if only to counter any tendency to idealize Milton's thought. To some extent he shared the increasingly commercial mentality of the age. Thus in *The Readie and Easie Way* he reiterates the view that a republic rather than a monarchy was good for trade: 'trade flourishes no where more then in the free Commonwealths of *Italie, Germanie*, and the Low-Countries.' But even more revealing are the passages in *Areopagitica* where he refers to truth as 'our richest Marchandize', and argues that censorship implies that the censors hold a monopoly of truth: 'We must not think to make a staple commodity of all the knowledge in the land, to mark and licence it like our broad cloath, and our wooll packs.'[32] It is agreeable to find the bourgeois merchants' hostility to monopolies brought so neatly into harmony with the liberal intellectual's opposition to censorship and thought control.

THE RIGHTS OF PEOPLE AND THE RIGHTS OF PROPERTY:
DEBATE WITH THE LEVELLERS

Conservatives often exaggerate the fragility of the social order and the dangers of change, but those among both the royalists and parliamentarians who feared that the conflict between King and Parliament would inevitably lead to an eruption of the rumbling discontents of the 'lower orders', for once prophesied correctly. 'We know not what advantage the meaner sort also may take to divide the spoils of the rich and noble amongst them, who begin already to allege that all being of one mould there is no reason that some should have so much and others so little', reflected Sir Simonds D'Ewes anxiously in 1642. And in the same year Charles I warned Parliament that 'at last the common people' might 'set up for themselves, call parity and independence liberty' and 'destroy all rights and properties, all distinctions of families and merit.'[33]

But how real was the threat to property? The Levellers, for instance, were so called by their enemies, who wanted it to be thought that this group was in favour of abolishing all distinctions of rank and property. This was, of course, sheer scaremongering. It angered not only the Levellers, who repeatedly proclaimed their commitment to the institution of private property, but also those such as the Diggers who did attack property as an institution, and who therefore claimed to be the 'True Levellers'. Writing from the Tower of London in April 1649, William Walwyn and some of the other Leveller leaders protested: 'We profess therefore that we never had it in our thoughts to Level mens estates, it being the utmost of our aime that the Common-wealth be reduced to such a passe that every man may with as much security as may be enjoy his propriety.'[34] This was true. The Levellers' Humble Petition of the previous September had actually included the demand that Parliament should bind itself 'and all future Parliaments from abolishing propriety, levelling mens Estats, or making all things common.'[35]

But while they supported the principle of private property, its actual distribution was another matter. They opposed monopolies and tithes, and demanded the restoration to the people of common lands which had been enclosed. Walwyn was reported as saying that it was 'unconscionable' to 'the poorer sort of people' that one man should have £10,000, while another more useful citizen should not be worth twopence.[36] They objected to the unequal distribution of property and the poverty which resulted from this, and they objected in particular to the correspondingly unequal distribution of political rights and privileges. This was the central issue in the famous debates of October-November 1647 at Putney church, in which the Levellers and their supporters in the army confronted the army leaders, notably Cromwell and Ireton.

Professor C. B. Macpherson has argued, partly on the basis of Petty's remarks during the Putney debates, that the Levellers did not envisage manhood suffrage, as has often been supposed, or anything near it, since in excluding 'servants' from the franchise, they were in fact excluding 'anyone who worked for an employer for wages', which meant in effect nearly three-quarters of the male population.[37] In his interpretation the Levellers turn out to be a great deal less radical than is generally supposed. They should, he suggests, be looked on rather as 'radical liberals than radical democrats', and therefore as precursors of Whiggery, who 'paved the way, unwittingly, for Locke and the Whig tradition'.[38]

Both as an interpretation of the Putney debates, and of the Leveller movement as a whole, I find this forced and unconvincing. A number of historians, including Keith Thomas, J. C. Davis and A. L. Morton have made compelling criticisms of Macpherson's 'revisionism', of which one particularly important point is that the extensive definition of 'servants' to include all wage earners is certainly not the only way in which that term was used in the seventeenth century. Keith Thomas claims that 'there is an overwhelming volume of evidence to suggest that in the mid-seventeenth century the term "servant" normally had a more restricted meaning.'[39]

If we now return to the debates at Putney, Macpherson's interpretation, apart from leaning very heavily upon a single, not unambiguous statement by the comparatively unimportant figure of Petty, does create a puzzle. For, as A. L. Morton has pointed out, if the Levellers were proposing only a limited extension of the franchise, then it is hard to see why the whole debate was so passionate and protracted; for both Ireton and Colonel Rich agreed at an early stage in the argument that they too were prepared to contemplate *some* extension of the franchise.

Macpherson wants to present the Putney debates as an argument within the Whig-liberal tradition, between two groups both of whom 'equated freedom with proprietorship'.[40] But the Levellers were not as thoroughly bourgeois as this suggests. Rainborough's famous affirmation — 'For really I think that the poorest he that is in England hath a life to live, as the greatest he' — is not mere rhetoric, for he goes on to assert the general principle of consent as following from this basic right:

> and therefore truly, sir, I think it's clear, that every man that is to live under a government ought first by his own consent to put himself under that government; and I do think that the poorest man in England is not at all bound in a strict sense to that government that he hath not had a voice to put himself under.[41]

This was a theme to which John Wildman returned later in the debate (see p. 66), and is implied too in what Sexby said.

It was to these general principles that Cromwell, Rich and, most explicitly, Ireton, took strong exception. Cromwell was clearly scandalized by any suggestion that 'men that have no interest but the interest of breathing' (p. 59) might have a voice in government. But it was Ireton who made the substantive case against Rainborough and the Levellers. His view was that political power, including the power to vote, should rest exclusively with property-owners:

> I think that no person hath a right to an interest or share in the disposing of the affairs of the kingdom, and in determining or choosing those that shall determine what laws we shall be ruled by here — no person hath a right to this, that hath not a permanent fixed interest in this kingdom, and those persons together are properly the represented of this kingdom . . . that is, the persons in whom all land lies, and those in corporations in whom all trading lies. (p. 54)

Rainborough argued that 'the chief end of this government is to preserve persons as well as estates' (p. 67), but Ireton was clear that an extension of the franchise was a potential threat to property: 'liberty cannot be provided for in a general sense, if property be preserved' (pp. 73, 63).

Property came first. Talk of natural rights and government by consent was dangerous, because it menaced the security of property, which depended, in Ireton's view, not on natural right but on man-made law: 'Constitution founds property' (p. 69). The Levellers' assertion of natural and individual rights had awkward egalitarian implications, as Ireton perceived, but this assertion entitles them to be placed, along with later popular radicals such as Tom Paine, on the radical edges of liberalism, not in the incipient Whig tradition.

Although they did not reject property as an institution, they wished to see it widely distributed. Their ideal world was one 'of owner-occupiers on the land, plus self-employed craftsmen and independent traders'.[42] In this sense, they can be described as petty-bourgeois. But they were also advocates of individual rights and the sovereignty of the people (not Parliament), with many proposals for political reform, some of which still appear radical today. They produced a draft written constitution. They asserted the sovereignty of the electors over Members of Parliament, whom Overton described as 'our Agents'. They wanted to establish the supremacy of the House of Commons over the Lords and the monarchy, and it was even suggested that the right of peers to sit in Parliament should be abolished. Some of them wanted to see mayors, sheriffs, justices of the peace and other officials elected. They were champions of freedom of conscience, but they also demanded prison reform, hospitals for 'aged, sick and lame persons', and the general provision of free schooling.[43] There is no evidence that they, or anyone else, demanded votes for women, but one of the Leveller pamphlets, a *Petition of Women,* and others for the release of the imprisoned Leveller leaders in May 1649, raised the issue of equality:

> . . . since we are assured of our creation in the image of God, and of an interest in Christ equal unto men. . . . Have we not an equal interest with the men of this nation in those liberties and securities contained in the Petition of Right, and other the good laws of the land? . . . And must we keep at home in our houses, as if our lives and liberties and all were not concerned?[44]

Yet, despite their evident concern for the plight and right of the poor and propertyless, it can still be said that their concentration on political and constitutional change was characteristically liberal, and that they did not fully grasp that the reforms and changes which the mass of the people needed and looked for were social and economic rather than political. Nevertheless, it was the Leveller author of *The mournfull Cryes of many thousand poor tradesmen* (January 1648) who asked bitterly 'Is not all the Controversy whose Slaves the poor shall be?'[45]

However, the needs of the poor were better understood by the Digger writer and spokesperson, Gerrard Winstanley. Like every writer of the time, Winstanley uses the language of freedom and bondage; but he gives to these familiar terms a specifically economic and social content: 'And this is the bondage that the poor complain of, that they are kept poor by their brethren in a land where there is so much plenty for everyone.' For the poor, the freedom that mattered most was the chance to escape from poverty, and this necessarily involved a challenge to property and the propertied: 'Take notice that England is not a free people till the poor that have no land have a free allowance to dig and labour the commons, and so live as comfortably as the landlords that live in their enclosures.'[46] From Winstanley's point of view — and that of the many still discontented poor and landless — the revolution was, at the end of the 1640s, still incomplete. But it was already too late. The Levellers were decisively crushed by Cromwell and Fairfax at Burford in May 1649, and the radical development of the revolution came to a firm halt.

The principles that triumphed were those represented by Ireton at Putney. However much the Commonwealth leaders might be execrated after the Restoration, there was a fundamental accord on the issue of the rights of property, as the author of *A Discourse for a King and Parliament* (1660) makes plain:

> This island . . . is . . . governed by the influence of a sort of people that live plentifully and at ease upon their rents, extracted from the toil of their tenants and servants . . . each of whom within the bounds of his own estate acts the prince; he is purely absolute; his servants and labourers are in the nature of his vassals; his tenants indeed are free, but in the nature of subjects. . . .
> Now . . . this sort of people have by influence and in effect the command of this nation. . . .[47]

It was still property in land that counted for most, and it was for the rights and power of this type of property above all that John Locke provides the ideological justification. But it was not until after 1688 that the sovereignty of property was finally assured in England. Locke is part of the history of triumphant Whiggery.

Nevertheless, at this moment in the history of Europe, it would have been a brave person who predicted the future triumph of liberal, or even Whig, principles. By 1660 the old feudal assemblies had nearly everywhere died out or been abolished. In France the States General met for the last time before 1789 in 1614, and the *Parlement* of Paris in the 1660s. Similar bodies came to an end in the Spanish Netherlands in 1632, in Naples ten years later, in Castile in 1665, in Russia in 1653, and in Prussia in 1663. As Henry Kamen remarked: 'Landlord and absolutism had triumphed in the west by 1660, in the east serfdom was firmly entrenched by the same date.'[48] Absolutism was the price which the propertied were willing to pay for their security, for an end to the threat of social revolution which had haunted them for a hundred years after the Reformation. Everywhere the popular revolutionary movements had been crushed — and not always by the forces of outright reaction. It was William of Orange, not the Spanish, who put an end to the popular Calvinist dictatorship of Ghent, just as it was Cromwell, not Charles I, who destroyed the Levellers and presided over the suppression of the Diggers. This was the unpropitious political and social climate in which liberal ideas and movements had to struggle for growth after the defeats of the mid-seventeenth century.

8

The Eighteenth Century: Whiggery Triumphant

Eighteenth-century liberalism takes two forms: in England, that of Whiggery, established and complacent; elsewhere, the reforming and often militant liberalism of the Enlightenment and the *philosophes*. These two forms can be contrasted, but the relationship between them is a complex and dialectical one. Some doyens of the Enlightenment, such as Voltaire and Montesquieu, saw in contemporary England a model of constitutionalism, liberty and prosperity which they hoped would be adopted throughout Europe. Whig England did not, however, always return the compliment. In 1763 a seventy year-old schoolmaster, Peter Annet, was put in the stocks and imprisoned partly for the 'crime' of translating Voltaire into English.[1] It was easy for those who battled against arbitrariness and absolutism to exaggerate the degree of liberty which existed in Whig Britain. And indeed, when we look closely at Whiggery, we are likely to find something a great deal less attractive than the image of benign and tranquil constitutionalism which was created and sustained by the Whig historians themselves, and is still not extinct. It is right to begin our examination with its first and most celebrated theorist and ideologist, John Locke.

LOCKE AND PROPERTY

Locke's name is so closely associated with the intellectual history of the eighteenth century, and with the political settlement of 1688 and after, that it can be something of a shock to realize that he was involved in politics for more than 20 years before William III was brought to the English throne, principally as a member of the household of Anthony Ashley Cooper, the first Earl of Shaftesbury, and effective leader of the Whig aristocratic opposition to Charles II.

Locke's Latin epitaph for his great patron described him as a 'vigorous and indefatigable champion of civil and ecclesiastical liberty',[2] and there is good reason to think that the two men thought alike on major political issues.[3] It now seems clear that Locke's *Two Treatises of Government* were first drafted during the Exclusion crisis, even though they were not published until 1690, with a preface in which the (anonymous) author offered them specifically as a justification of the 'Revolution' of 1688—89. Thus Locke was closer to being a professional political propagandist, like Milton, than a scholarly recluse like Hobbes or Spinoza. His biographer, Maurice Cranston, has even asserted that 'the whole of Locke's political philosophy was called into being by the exigencies of the times he lived through and the circumstances of his being in the household of the opposition leader.[4] Locke deploys general arguments, not for academic purposes, but to provide a theoretical basis for specific policies and actions. It is these practical pressures which provide one clue to his notorious confusions and inconsistencies.

Central to the political thought of this 'greatest of liberal philosophers', is the concept of property, which, as Locke immodestly said, 'I have nowhere found more clearly explained, than in a book entitled, Two Treatises of Government.'[5] In the *Second Treatise* Locke argues that the reason that men set up government, and therefore the purpose for which governments exist, is '*the Preservation of their Property*' (p. 395). Exactly what Locke means by property is a complex matter. In so far as he means land and goods, he devoted an important chapter to discussing what gives an individual (a man) the right to claim sole ownership of a piece of land. This is a problem, for Locke begins by accepting the traditional biblical view that God gave the world 'to Mankind in common' (p. 327). He then argues that the right to self-preservation, and the implied need to consume or use the fruits of the earth, lead inevitably to individual ownership. He even argues that cultivation and use necessarily depend upon individual possession, as if common ownership was synonymous with neglect — a view taken, not surprisingly, by many advocates of enclosure: 'God gave the World to Men in Common; but . . . it cannot be supposed he meant it should always remain common and uncultivated. He gave it to the use of the Industrious and Rational, (and *Labour* was to be *his Title* to it)' (p. 333). Self-preservation, the need to consume, and finally labour, are what create the right to property. A man who works his patch of earth is thereby entitled to its product. A man owns his labour, because 'every Man has a *Property* in his own *Person*', and so 'The *Labour* of his Body, and the *Work* of his Hands, we may say, are properly his' (p. 328—9).

The right to property derived from labour implies, however, a corresponding limitation: a man may not own more than he can cultivate (pp. 334—5). This limitation is reinforced by a second and similar one: we may not own anything that we let go to waste, for 'Nothing was made by God for Man to spoil or destroy' (pp. 332). Finally, the equal right of all to self-preservation implies that there must be 'enough, and as good left in common for others' (p. 329). Such a justificatory theory of ownership is strongly egalitarian in principle, and the assertion that labour in itself confers a right to ownership is particularly radical in its implications.

But Locke immediately shies away from these radical implications of what he has written. The limitations on property ownership which he has set out, he then negates, principally by the device of money: 'the *Invention of Money* . . . introduced (by Consent) larger Possessions, and a Right to them' (p. 335). For money enables an owner to sell off such products as he cannot himself consume; in this way he evades (or fulfils) the limitations imposed by the criteria of use and non-spoilage. Money does not spoil, and is always useful. As for the labour limitation, it vanishes almost as soon as it is introduced. In the second of the paragraphs in which Locke discusses the rights conferred by labour, he makes it embarrassingly clear that he does not really mean what he says: 'Thus the Grass my horse has bit; the Turfs my Servant has cut; and the Ore I have digg'd in any place where I have a right to them in common with others, become my *Property*, without the assignation or consent of any body' (p. 330). Apart from the oddity of assuming the existence of servants in what is supposed to be the 'state of nature', Locke assumes, naturally and without feeling any need to argue the point, that a servant does not own the fruits of his/her labour: their employer does. Just because I 'own' my labour, I can sell it, and its product, to another. The 'right' goes with the property (labour), not with the person who labours.

The third requirement, that there should be 'enough, and as good' left for others, imposes no restraint on accumulation, since the increased productivity of privately-owned or 'inclosed' land is of greater benefit to mankind than if it were left 'lyeing wast in common' (p. 336). Locke assumed a natural identity between individual profit and the general welfare. It turns out, too, that unequal property ownership, like government itself, developed by consent. For since money only has value by consent, 'it is plain, that Men have agreed to disproportionate and unequal Possession of the Earth' (p. 344). In this way, in the course of a few paragraphs, Locke moves from egalitarian premises to anti-egalitarian conclusions. Later on, he takes a further step away from his original individualistic analysis by adding a further right that 'Every Man is born with': '*A Right*, before any other Man, to *inherit*, with his brethren, his Fathers Goods' (p. 441).

Clearly, if Locke was to produce a defence of existing property and property rights, his conclusions were necessary. But why then does he choose such an obviously contradictory starting point, and proceed by such unconvincing routes? Here, it seems to me, we find the conflict between Locke the theorist, anxious to explore fundamentals, and Locke the ideologist. But it is also a conflict between his concern with universal, individual rights, which is an inheritance from the time of the Levellers, and his need to endorse Whig orthodoxy, which defended property regardless of the gross inequality of its distribution.

Locke's treatment of the notion of 'consent' is very similar. Consciously or not, he follows Hobbes in arguing that the legitimacy of government derives from the fact that it is set up by agreement among persons who voluntarily divest themselves of their natural liberty. But Locke undermines the principle of *individual* consent by suggesting that government can be set up by the consent of a *majority* (p. 377). Further dilutions follow. In response to the criticism that few societies are actually created in this manner, and that men are in fact '*born under Government*', Locke replies that '*the Consent of Free-men*' is given by each individually as he comes of age, which is why it goès unnoticed (p. 391). A child, he is bound logically to admit, '*is born a Subject of no Country or Government*' (p. 391—2).

But Locke knows very well that few societies require a formal or explicit declaration of consent or allegiance: he therefore introduces the notion of *tacit* consent, which is judged to be given by a person's mere presence in a particular state: 'in Effect, it reaches as far as the very being of any one within the Territories of that Government' (p. 392). Thus the fundamental requirement of individual consent turns out to mean very little in practice. Even by 'travelling freely on the Highway' a man 'doth thereby give his *tacit Consent*' (p. 392). It is disturbing to find a key democratic idea like consent so diluted and distorted so early in the evolution of liberal thought.

Returning now to Locke's use of the term 'property', we find that it is given two meanings, one broad and one narrow. The narrow and conventional one we have already discussed. But at other points in the *Second Treatise* Locke suggests that by property he means 'Lives, Liberties and Estates' (p. 395). However, it is by no means as certain, as Laslett suggests (p. 115), that the term is usually to be read in this latter sense. Section 138 (pp. 406—7) is one of the clearest examples of the term being used ambiguously. In it, Locke repeats his view that 'the preservation of Property' is 'the end of Government, and that for which Men enter into Society', but this time without specifying the wider meaning. He then goes on to speak of property synonymously with 'Estates'. In this section he also makes the point that if men enter into society to preserve their property, this implies that they have some property to preserve. Now if Locke here is speaking of estates alone, rather than life and liberty as well, then the inference is that the state exists for property-owners rather than for all. Locke's meaning is unclear, and it is therefore quite fair for Macpherson to argue that 'men without estate or goods, that is, without property in the ordinary sense, are rightfully both in and not in civil society',[6] since the ambiguity is there, in Locke himself. It is in any case indicative of his thoroughly bourgeois frame of mind that he should think of life, liberty and labour as essentially *possessions*, and subsume them under the single heading of 'property'. It says much about liberalism that the philosopher who is often said to be its 'founder' or 'father' should have placed property, even as a metaphor, at the heart of his philosophy of government and human rights.

The relation between freedom and laws (or restrictions) is another major issue on which Locke again tries to have it both (or all) ways. On this issue Hobbes, as we saw, is absolutely clear: freedom consists in the absence of external restraints or impediments, in 'the silence of the law'. Locke's account, by comparison, is totally confused. On the one hand he values the Hobbesian type of liberty: 'A Liberty to follow my own Will in all things, where the Rule prescribes not.' Yet in the same sentence he suggests that the rule of law is itself a form of freedom: '*Freedom of Men under Government*, is, to have a standing Rule to live by, common to every one of that Society and made by the Legislative Power erected in it' (p. 324). Later he extends this line of argument by suggesting that law itself is not really a restriction: 'that ill deserves the Name of Confinement which hedges us in only from Bogs and Precipices' (p. 348). There is a good case to be made for saying that law and liberty are not inherently in conflict, but it is not made by Locke, since he wishes also to argue that a concern for liberty requires that laws should be kept to a minimum.

The confusions and ambiguities in the *Second Treatise* over property, labour rights, consent and freedom, are confusions and ambiguities at the heart of liberalism. For they reveal simultaneously both the democratic, egalitarian and even anarchist potentialities in the liberal idea of individual rights, together with the bourgeois liberal's anxious recoil from those alarming tendencies. In the 1660s, when his political views were more authoritarian, Locke had written of the maxim *vox populi, vox dei*, 'Surely we have been taught by a most unhappy lesson how doubtful, how fallacious is this maxim.'[7] By 1680 the threat of what Marchamont Nedham had called 'popular tyrannie' had long receded, and it was hardly necessary to say that by 'the people' was meant only the political nation of already enfranchised property owners. In case it was, Locke's friend James Tyrell spelt it out: 'when I make use of the word people, I do not mean the vulgar or mixed multitude, but in the state of nature the whole body of free-men and women, especially the fathers and masters of families; and in the civil state all degrees of men, as well the nobility and clergy as the common people.'[8]

Cranston has referred to Locke's 'revolutionary liberalism',[9] but this is only appropriate if taken as a reference to Locke's identification with the events of 1688—89. Most of Locke's opinions were not notably radical by the standards of his time. His *Letter on Toleration* is conventional and restricted in its recommendations. Locke rules out toleration for Catholics, on the ground that they owe their allegiance to 'another prince' (i.e. the pope), and for atheists, since 'promises, covenants, and oaths, which are the bonds of human society' supposedly have no hold on them. Nor should anyone be allowed to preach with impunity 'things which manifestly undermine the foundations of society'.[10] What such doctrines might be, Locke does not say, but such a limitation could be interpreted in a very restrictive manner. Locke's *Letter*, wrote a recent historian of toleration, was 'neither as original nor as liberal' as several earlier defences.[11]

Even the momentous events of 1688—89, Locke is concerned to stress, were not so much a revolution as the preservation of the 'Just and Natural Rights' of 'the People of England', which 'saved the Nation when it was on the very brink of Slavery and Ruine'.[12] It was James II who had threatened innovation, while the Whigs had successfully defended the traditional rights of the people. But this had involved resistance, and Locke in common with all the Whigs was torn between the need to offer a theory of legitimate resistance to 'tyranny', while ensuring that such a theory gave no encouragement to any further popular uprisings, like those of the 1640s, and that of Monmouth in 1685. Caution and compromise were the keynotes of Lockean liberalism. Even Lord Acton, who worked in the grand tradition of Whig history, and who regarded 'the Revolution of 1688' as 'the greatest thing done by the English nation', could not muster much enthusiasm for Locke and his party: 'The very essence of the new Party was compromise. . . . They were a little disappointing, a little too fond of the half-way house. Their philosophy, or rather their philosopher, John Locke, is always reasonable and sensible, but diluted and pedestrian and poor.'[13] It was a sign of this poverty of spirit that Locke should have thought that the ability to play a musical instrument was a waste 'of a young man's time' — although it was a good enough pastime for women — and believed that if children showed a taste for poetry it should be 'stifled and suppressed as much as may be'.[14] William Blake was right to see Locke as an enemy of the imagination.

THE TRIUMPH OF PROPERTY

The 'Glorious Revolution' of 1688 came to be seen as the central and greatest achievement of the Whigs. The protracted political conflicts of the century had finally been resolved in a gratifyingly 'moderate' manner: the tendency towards absolutism and Catholicism had been decisively checked, while the equally frightening prospect of popular republicanism had also been averted, once Monmouth's rising with its alarming echoes of the Levellers, had been defeated and savagely punished. The way was clear for a century of more or less undisputed dominance by the landed aristocracy and gentry.

The process by which this occurred was not particularly glorious, nor did it amount to a revolution. It was more like a nearly bloodless *coup d'état*, engineered by a united ruling class, against the final Stuart bid for absolutism. But by calling this coup a revolution, the prestige of radicalism was appropriated for an essentially conservative achievement, and radicalism itself was partially disarmed. Nor did the Whigs wish to set any kind of precedent. As Burke rightly said, a century later, 'the great men who influenced the conduct of affairs at that great event' were anxious 'to make the Revolution a parent of settlement, and not a nursery of future revolutions.'[15] The majority of the Whigs were from the beginning determined to minimize the radical implications of what they had done. They shrank from any outright assertion of popular or even parliamentary sovereignty. Therefore the fiction was maintained that James II had not been deposed, but had abdicated, leaving the throne vacant and needing to be filled. It was only the radicals, who in this case included Locke, who wished to defend the displacement of James on such general grounds as the ultimate sovereignty of the people, or the right of resistance to tyranny. And not even they wished to revive Milton's argument that the people had the right to change their government or form of government whenever they chose.

So for nearly a quarter of a century after 1688 the 'Glorious Revolution' was as much a source of weakness as of strength to the Whigs. They had constantly to rebuff Tory accusations that what they had done, or claimed to have done, provided not just the political nation but also the 'lower orders' with a licence for disaffection and rebellion. Hence a Whig pamphlet of 1696 argued that

> A revolution so brought about carries in it no precedent against the security of government, or the peace of mankind. That which an absolute necessity enforced at one time can be no warrant for irregular proceedings at any other time, unless it be where the like necessity shall require the like remedies.[16]

So even Locke's limited and qualified arguments were too radical for the ascendant Whig oligarchy. From the very moment of their triumph in 1689 there began a withdrawal from the principles commonly associated with the term 'Whig', until with Walpole's ascendancy in the 1720s and 1730s, nothing remained but an appetite for power, office and their many advantages. The Whigs ceased to be the party of the more modest and stable wealth of the landed gentry, and the old idea that it was property *in land* which formed the basic qualification for political participation was more or less openly abandoned. It was left to the outsider, Jonathan Swift, to restate the traditional principle: 'Law, in a free Country, is, or ought to be, the Determination of the Majority of those who have Property in Land.'[17]

Thus, contrary to the Whig interpretation of their own history,[18] neither the

Whig triumph in 1689 nor the establishment of their ascendancy after 1715, led to any further political progress. In fact their success resulted in political reaction. For example, the tendency in the first half of the seventeenth century to resolve electoral disputes in favour of a wider rather than a narrower franchise was not sustained after the Restoration, and was decisively reversed after 1688. At the same time a considerable number of boroughs with tiny franchises were created, while Plumb notes that 'after 1689, borough after borough diminishes the number of freeman voters or forgets to admit any at all.'[19] Attempts were made in 1696 and 1729 to freeze electorates; but the most blatant Whig attack on the still very limited right to vote was the City Elections Act of 1725, whereby at a stroke 3,000 freemen of the City of London were deprived of their voting rights, thus greatly enhancing the power of the rich City aldermen.

Meanwhile, the Septennial Act of 1716 had extended the length of each parliament, including the one that passed the Act, from three to seven years; and in 1721 Walpole favoured a Bill to reintroduce parliaments with no limit on their duration, although Lord Molesworth, an 'old' Whig who was, significantly, the translator of Hotman's *Francogallia*, had pronounced 'frequent parliaments' to be an absolutely 'fundamental part of the constitution'.[20]

The logic of these tendencies, together with the government's extensive methods for the control and management of parliament and elections, was that an increasing number of parliamentary seats went uncontested, particularly the county seats.[21] It was Walpole's achievement to turn the country into what was effectively a one-party state, in which the opposition could not hope to match the government's vast powers of manipulation and patronage.[22]

Meanwhile admiring foreigners and self-congratulatory natives praised the extent of British freedom and toleration. But both these had their limits, which the Whigs did nothing to extend. The Whigs were supposed to be committed to the principle of toleration for dissenters. Yet Walpole evaded every pressure from dissenters to remove some of the civic disabilities from which they continued to suffer. And it was Walpole who, to prevent satirical attacks upon himself, introduced in 1737 the system of censorship over the theatre by the Lord Chamberlain which was then not finally abolished until 230 years later.

It may perhaps be asked what this dismal record of political stagnation has to do with the principles of liberalism. Surely, it might be said, what is illustrated here is the abandonment of Whig principles by those who called themselves Whigs — a phenomenon with many political parallels, and no more to be laid at the door of liberalism than, say, the crimes of Stalin are to be imputed to socialism or Marxism, *per se*. Two considerations weigh against this argument. The first is that in exploring and evaluating an ideology, we have always to consider not only its *professed* values and principles, but also those which its adherents exemplify in their lives and actions. The second is that practice affects principles, particularly in the case of a movement of ideas with a long history and a complex evolution. Thus, for example, the fears and doubts about democracy expressed by so many nineteenth- and twentieth-century liberals reflect, at least in part, their inheritance from eighteenth-century Whiggery. The hatred and contempt for the mass of the people expressed by the Whig journalist Addison in the early eighteenth century: 'Nothing can be more contemptible than the scum of the people, when they are instigated against a king who is supported by the two branches of the legislature. A mob may pull down a meeting house, but will never be able to overturn a government.'[23] has its muted echo in the fears expressed by George Eliot and Matthew Arnold on the eve of the Second Reform Bill, and even in contemporary arguments that too much popular participation would threaten the stability of our political system.

Above all, there is continuity in relation to the issue of property. And where property is concerned, Whig practice is as important, and revealing, as Whig theory. Not that there was a great disjunction between them. For while the Whigs might seem to Swift and the Tories to have abandoned the old principle that those who own land should govern, they did not neglect to extend the rights of landowners. Their alliance with the money men simply reflected their recognition that the forms of property and wealth were changing, and that land was no longer the only form of property or source of wealth and power. As Marx observed: 'the new landed aristocracy was the natural ally of the new bankocracy of newly-hatched high finance, and of the large manufacturers, at that time dependent on protective duties.'[24] It was the Tories who identified themselves with landed property, while the more flexible Whigs emerged as the defenders of property in all its forms, commercial and financial as well as landed.

The Whig hegemony inaugurates a golden age of property rights. Back in the days of the Commonwealth, Thurloe had referred to 'elective parliaments' as 'the bulwark of property'.[25] That is what they became after the Restoration. A great battery of new laws were passed which extended the rights of the propertied at the expense, directly or indirectly, of the traditional rights and customs of the poor majority of the people. The most striking demonstration of this was the great increase in the number of offences for which the prescribed penalty was death. These are estimated to have increased from about 50 in 1688, to over 200 by 1820, and almost all of them were offences against property:[26] 'A man was hanged for stealing one shilling, a boy of sixteen for stealing 3s.6d. and a penknife, a girl for a handkerchief. A boy of eleven was hanged for setting his master's house on fire. Many more were sentenced to transportation.'[27] The ferocity of the British laws became a by-word, and Kenyon describes capital punishment in eighteenth-century England as 'not so much a way of government as a way of life, enforcing by fear an increasingly stratified class system.'[28]

Just as significant was the extension of the rights of property-owners into areas where such exclusiveness was a novelty. The Game Laws of 1670 made it an offence for all but the very rich to kill birds and animals even on their own land, the basic qualification being an income of £100 a year from freehold property, fifty times greater than the property qualification needed to vote in a county election. The same set of laws gave to *gamekeepers* the right to search people's houses and confiscate weapons. *Wild* birds and animals, which had not been thought to 'belong' to anyone, and which had provided meat for the rural poor, were now declared to be the property of the large landowners. In this way some of the traditional rights of the poor were 'simply redefined as crimes: poaching, wood-theft, trespass'. [29]

Even many aspects of what 'rational' economists and economic historians have always interpreted as 'improvement', such as the large-scale reclamation of the fens, were no gain to the poor and landless, who lost food resources as a result — as Thomas Fuller noted at the time. And this was generally true of enclosure. Enlightened bourgeois opinion was unanimous in lauding the merits of enclosure. Daniel Defoe and the late seventeenth-century economist, Sir William Petty, were among those who urged that the whole process should be speeded up by the passing of general acts for enclosure. [30] This was not to happen until 1801, but Parliament was never reluctant to pass legislation for specific enclosures: 2,000 such acts were passed between 1750 and 1800, and another 900 in the following decade. Under these acts between six and seven million acres were enclosed, about a fifth of the whole land, and a quarter of all cultivated land. Two-thirds of that total was *not* waste, as writers like Locke implied, but land which was already cultivated and used under the old open-field system. [31] Legislation was needed for enclosure because landowners were usually unable to get villagers to agree voluntarily to the loss of their traditional common lands. It was little more than legalized robbery:

> The advance made by the eighteenth century shows itself in this, that the law itself now becomes the instrument by which the people's land is stolen. . . . The Parliamentary form of the robbery is that of 'Bills for Inclosure of Commons', in other words decrees by which the landowners grant themselves the people's land as private property, decrees of expropriation of the people [32]

Enclosure was not a new phenomenon, of course. It had provoked much protest in the sixteenth and early seventeenth centuries. But the last parliamentary bid to restrain the process was made, unsuccessfully, in 1656. After that Parliament reflected only the interests and ideology of the substantial property-owners.

The speed with which the process of enclosure went ahead after about 1760 reflects not only the power of property, but also the growing ascendancy of a new kind of economic rationality. It was economic in a very pure sense, in that it was only economic gains and losses which were taken into account: social gains and losses, being less measurable, were left out of the account. Modern economic historians, imbued with the same kind of rationality, have endorsed the view that enclosure was beneficial. Thus G. E. Mingay has written:

> The conclusion must be, then, that enclosure, and hence the landlord, stand acquitted of most of the charges brought against them . . . enclosure greatly helped in the increase of output, so necessary in an age of growing population, and the expansion of cultivation and wider use of improved techniques helped to absorb the rising labour force. [33]

Such complacent conclusions make it hard to see what all the fuss was about. Yet the economic gains were long-term at best, and must be weighed against the social misery it caused, and against the permanent loss of rights and independence on the part of the villagers, whose conversion into a landless rural proletariat was completed by this process. This was noticed even at the time. Thus the Reverend David Davies wrote in 1795: 'for a dubious economic benefit, an amazing number of people have been reduced from a comfortable state of partial independence to the precarious condition of mere hirelings, who when out of work immediately come on the parish.' [34] And even Arthur Young, for long a fervent advocate of enclosure, and promoter of the first general Enclosure Act of 1801, came to doubt in the end whether all the sufferings involved had been justified: 'I had rather that all the commons were sunk in the sea than that the poor should in future be treated on enclosing as they have generally been hitherto. . . . By 19 out of 20 enclosure bills, the poor are injured, and some grossly injured.' [35]

The Highland clearances of the late eighteenth and nineteenth centuries, and the consequent enforced emigration of thousands of the Highlanders to Canada and elsewhere, was no doubt a special case of enclosure, with an important political purpose. But they too, were applauded by the liberal economists. Nassau Senior described the particularly brutal clearances on the vast estates of the Duke of Sutherland, in which people were more than once burnt out of their homes, as 'one of the most beneficent clearings since the memory of man'. [36] Beneficent to whom?

From the generally accepted axiom that those who had property should govern, it was not a long step to arguing that the function of government was the protection of property. Defoe argued this way in 1706:

> . . . here all the governments in the world began: the right of possession always had the right of government, which is the band and guard of that possession. Reason, thus finding itself possessed of property, dictated government for its regulation and security, and this is a right whose divinity cannot be disputed. [37]

The theoretical justification for this was that property alone gave a man the material basis of independence necessary if he was to act as a free person. Those without property were necessarily dependent, and could not therefore be relied on to vote freely. They were easily bribed with promises of money, food, or employment, by unscrupulous political adventurers or radical agitators. Hence the poor constituted a threat to freedom as well as to property. An abiding fear and mistrust of the poor was the corollary of the dominant commitment to property.

PROPERTY VERSUS POVERTY

It is easy to be confused about the relationship between liberalism and poverty. This is partly due to the American interpretation of the word 'liberal', according to which a liberal is something like a social democrat, one who favours a regulated rather than a free market economy, as well as welfare measures to relieve poverty and hardship, More generally, too, the term is associated with humane and compassionate attitudes. But, considered historically, liberalism has always been linked to attitudes and policies of harshness towards the poor. This harshness is in part a legacy from early Protestantism, but it was given 'scientific' justification by classical liberal economics.

As the new 'science' developed, the poor came to be thought of simply as 'labour' or 'hands' — that being the only part of their bodies of any interest to their potential employers. 'The hands of men employed are true riches', wrote Thomas Sprat. It was increasingly recognized that it was labour which created wealth. 'Labour is the Father and active principle of Wealth, as Lands are the Mother' wrote Sir William Petty, the author of *Political Arithmetick*. So the idleness of the poor was a threat to the wealth of the rich. How was this idleness to be eradicated?

The answer, to the progressive bourgeois mind, lay in two different, but not incompatible forms of compulsion. The general and fundamental compulsion was simply the pressure of necessity, of want and hunger. This became the basis of all policies towards the poor, according to which if their wages allowed them anything more than a bare subsistence, they would cease to work altogether. Petty argued that a law which regulated wages 'should allow the labourer but just wherewithall to live'.[38] Arthur Young put it colloquially: 'every one but an idiot knows that the lower classes must be kept poor, or they will never be industrious.' In 1785 the Reverend Joseph Townsend argued that 'it is only hunger which can spur and goad them on to labour', and that in fact hunger was an incentive which was vastly preferable to 'legal constraint'. For the latter 'is attended with much trouble, violence and noise', and so 'creates ill will', whereas the advantage of hunger is that it is a 'peaceable, silent, unremitting pressure' and is 'the most natural motive to industry and labour'.[39] Thus, by the late eighteenth century, many people understood how the workings of the capitalist market could themselves serve to discipline the labouring classes, without any need for overt compulsion by employers or the state. But it was at least prudent to supplement the pressures of the market with punitive measures directed against the supposedly idle or 'workshy'. In practice this meant above all workhouses.

Thus the economic role of the poor was readily recognized. Bernard Mandeville, author of the celebrated *The Fable of the Bees*, put it with his customary edge of irony: 'it is manifest, that in a Free Nation where Slaves are not allow'd of, the surest wealth consists in a multitude of Laborious Poor.'[40] And if the full value of their labour was to be realized, it was necessary to get them to work as early as possible. It was logical, therefore, for the rational economic liberal to favour the employment of children. And so we find Locke recommending in a report for the Board of Trade in 1697 that children over three 'should be taught to earn their living at working schools for spinning and knitting', while Defoe, on his travels through England, took the employment of young children as a reliable index of prosperity. 'Hardly any thing above four years old but its hands are sufficient to itself', was the admiring comment on Halifax of this predecessor of Samuel Smiles.[41]

What particularly irked these hard-headed economists was the misplaced charity of providing education for the poor. Therefore the charity schools were made a special target of derision and attack. Mandeville set out the bourgeois case against charity schools with a somewhat embarrassing bluntness in an essay appended to *The Fable of the Bees*: 'To make the Society Happy and People Easy under the meanest Circumstances, it is requisite that great numbers of them should be Ignorant as well as Poor.' This was also economically advantageous, since 'By bringing them up in Ignorance' you keep 'Labour cheap', and as a result 'we must infallibly out-sell our Neighbours'.[42]

But what particularly scandalized his contemporaries was Mandeville's argument that if a society wished to be wealthy it would have to give up any commitment to old-fashioned virtues like thrift, frugality and selflessness, and recognize that production is only stimulated by luxury and extravagance among consumers, and by greed and avarice among producers. In other words, he drew attention to the conflict between the dynamics of a capitalist economy and some of the traditional Christian virtues. The paradox in which he summed up his argument — 'Private Vices, Publick Benefits' — belongs squarely to the developing tradition of market liberalism, which postulates an identity between the individual pursuit of self-interest and the general good of society. But Mandeville's very candour exposes a double standard at the heart of his argument. For while the high incomes and lavish spending of the rich will stimulate production, similar practices by the 'multitude of Laborious Poor' are by no means to be encouraged. Society is to consist of an elite of consumers supported by a great mass of producers. Basil Willey said of Mandeville that but for his ' "cynical" view of human nature' he would be 'an eighteenth-century *laissez-faire* liberal'.[43] It is part of the argument of this book that those two elements are more closely integrated than Willey supposed.

Mandeville concealed his real position, or lack of one, behind the masks of irony and satire. It was left to Swift, a Tory and a supposed misanthrope, to produce a committed assault on this kind of economic thinking. In *A Modest Proposal for Preventing the Children of Ireland from being a Burden to their Parents or Country*, published in 1729, Swift exactly mimics not merely the language but also the arguments of the pioneers of 'political arithmetic'. No one who looks into the contemporary writings on the treatment of the poor, and then turns to Swift's brief essay, can fail to be struck by the chilling similarities:

> Some Persons of a desponding Spirit are in great concern about that vast Number of poor People who are Aged, Diseased, or Maimed. . . . But I am not in the least Pain upon that matter, because it is very well known, that they are every Day dying, and rotting, by cold and famine, and filth, and vermin, as fast as can be reasonably expected. And as to the younger Labourers, they are now in almost as hopeful a Condition.[44]

As a Tory and an Irish patriot, he found himself out of tune with the complacent, commercial Whiggery of his day.

Another famous pamphleteer of that time, Daniel Defoe, may fairly be taken as an articulate representative of that Whiggery. The notion that God originally gave the earth to men in common, which still made a vestigial appearance in Locke, has now disappeared entirely. The 'naturalness' of private property is firmly established:

> Subjects honestly labouring, honestly possessing, ought to be left quietly, enjoying what they are Masters of; and this is the Foundation of what we call Law, Liberty, and Property. . . . this is the End of Parliaments, Constitutions, Government and Obedience; and this is the true Foundation of Order in the World. . . .

But Defoe is nothing if not bourgeois, and it is trade rather than land which excites his interest, and which he sees as the real source of England's prosperity: 'an *Estate's a pond*, but *a Trade's a spring*', and it is the springs which supply the ponds. 'As to the wealth of the nation, that undoubtedly lies chiefly among the trading part of the people.' Defoe has no time for the superstition that it is pedigree that makes a gentleman. He knows that, within a generation or two, wealth acquires the necessary social status, and that titles can be bought as well as estates. A self-made man himself, he naturally praised and exaggerated the possibilities of social mobility which England afforded:

> Wealth, howsoever got, in *England* makes
> Lords, of Mechanicks, Gentlemen of Rakes.
> Antiquity and Birth are needless here;
> 'Tis Impudence and Money makes a Peer.

It was to be expected that Defoe should be an enthusiast for Britain's imperial expansion. *Robinson Crusoe* reflects this, and in *The History of the Pyrates* he speaks of 'the Interest I take in every Thing, which may tend to the enriching or extending the Dominions of our glorious *Britain*, my dearly loved Country.'[45] Once again it was a Tory, Samuel Johnson, who drew attention to the darker side of this expansion. 'I do not much wish well to discoveries', said Johnson, 'for I am always afraid they will end in conquest or robbery.' Defoe's Crusoe thinks nothing of misusing and selling a black slave, but Johnson's hatred of slavery was deep and passionate. He described Jamaica as 'a place of great wealth and dreadful wickedness, a den of tyrants and a dungeon of slaves', and once proposed a toast to 'the next insurrection of the negroes in the West Indies'.[46]

Those who, like Butterfield, praised the Whig tradition of 'gradual, ordered progress', contrasting it with rash and destructive revolutionism, not only forget what price is paid in human suffering for progress that is called gradual, and is therefore slow; they also overlook those ways in which Whiggery was not progressive at all. Just because Whiggery still enjoys a reputation for benevolence, enlightenment and progress, I have, at the risk of being unfair, stressed in this chapter the extent to which it ought also to be associated with political stagnation and reaction, and with an ideology and policies of extreme harshness towards the poor and unfortunate and towards non-Europeans. These were some of the grimmer consequences of an ideology which placed the ownership of property at the centre of both its theory and practice.

9

The Eighteenth Century:
the Enlightenment

It is at least a pleasing coincidence — it may be more — that two of the founding fathers of the Enlightenment, Voltaire and Montesquieu, should have visited England within a year or two of each other. Voltaire's stay lasted from 1726 to 1729, and Montesquieu followed him in 1730—31. For both of them it was a significant experience. Both of them found much to admire in the English way of life and political system. Both of them contrasted it favourably with the condition of France. The limitations of the Whig settlement and the reactionary aspects of Walpole's ascendancy, on which I dwelt in the last chapter, were no more apparent to them than they were to most contemporary commentators. But Voltaire's praise of the English social system in the *Lettres Philosophiques*, published in 1733—34, is lavish even by eighteenth-century standards.

'You are my friend, you love liberty, you have a thinking soul; therefore England must please you', he wrote to a friend visiting England in 1732.[1] For, as he put it in a letter from England, 'Reason is free here and walks her own way'. Voltaire was impressed, not only by the fact that England was the land of Bacon — 'the father of experimental philosophy' — and Locke — 'Perhaps there has never been a wiser, more orderly mind, or a logician more exact, than Mr Locke' — and Newton; but also by the esteem and respect in which these pioneering heroes of science and rationality were apparently held. Voltaire attended Newton's funeral in Westminster Abbey in March 1727, and wrote of it in the *Lettres* that 'he was buried like a king who had benefited his subjects.'[2]

He was, if anything, even more impressed by the fact that a mere actress, Mrs Anne Oldfield, should also have been buried in the Abbey, while in France the Catholic Church denied both last rites and Christian burial to Voltaire's actress friend, Adrienne Lecouvreur.[3] It was not only reason which was honoured, but talent of all kinds. Voltaire saw England as an open and mobile society in which 'Such is the respect that this people has for talent, that a man of merit there always makes his fortune.'[4] And just as talent without title was honoured and rewarded, so it was not thought dishonourable for the titled to be involved in trade and industry. Voltaire contrasted this lively respect for profitable activity with the deference shown to mere empty titles in his own less enlightened country. It was a further merit of the English system that no one was exempted from taxation on account of his rank, and that tax was paid, so Voltaire believed, according to income.

Voltaire endorsed the widespread view that England's commercial success, like that of Holland, owed much to the country's freedom, in particular its freedom in matters of religion. He noted that 'Where there is not liberty of conscience, there is seldom liberty of trade, the same tyranny encroaching upon the commerce as upon Religion.'[5] And just as freedom promoted trade, so trade promoted freedom. Voltaire was enthusiastic about the religious tolerance shown on London's Royal Exchange: 'There the Jew, the Mahometan, and the Christian deal with one another as if they were of the same religion, and reserve the name of infidel for those who go bankrupt.'

As for the English political system, Voltaire found that in it the three traditional modes of monarchy, aristocracy and democracy were happily 'mixed' in such a way as to counterbalance and restrain each other. But unlike the more complacent English celebrants of this triumph of political moderation, Voltaire did not forget that this 'balance' was the outcome of a long struggle against monarchical power, including the civil war of 80 years before when: 'the idol of arbitrary power was drowned in seas of blood.' He expressed no word of condemnation even of the execution of Charles I, while on the other hand he mocks the myth, already current, that English liberty had been kept alive by Magna Carta and medieval parliaments.[6] His realism about the English struggle for liberty raises implicitly one of the central questions that the Enlightenment had to grapple with: how were comparable benefits to be won in other parts of Europe?

The *Lettres Philosophiques* had not long been circulating in Paris before the government ordered Voltaire's imprisonment, and the *parlement* of Paris ordered that the book should be publicly burnt. This did not prevent the book from being read or being influential, however. Montesquieu's *The Spirit of the Laws* was perhaps even more successful in propagating the political example of England. For not only did the book enjoy a great success on its publication in 1748, but it was used, both by the American founding fathers, and by the drafters of constitutions during the French Revolution. Montesquieu has been called 'the most influential foreign champion that England ever had'.[7]

Like Voltaire, the Baron de Montesquieu admired the English combination of trade, tolerance and freedom. And he saw, correctly, that this sprang from the principle of not allowing politics to interfere with the interests of commerce.

And like Voltaire, he believed that in England it was merit, rather than servility, which found its due reward. But it was the division of power within the English state that Montesquieu was particularly interested in, and particularly admired, since in his view this structure was designed to create and safeguard 'political liberty'.[8] He argued that for liberty to be secure, there must be a separation between three aspects of political authority: the legislative, the executive, and the judiciary. The separation of the legislative and executive powers is especially necessary. Without it, there is no institutional bulwark against despotism. He believed that in the English system executive power was in the hands of the king, while Parliament held the legislative power — failing, in fact, to recognize how far, even in the eighteenth century, executive and legislature overlapped and were integrated within the parliamentary system. In this way Montesquieu restated a myth of balance through separation within the English constitution which the propagandists of Whiggery were happy to carry back into English political ideology. Thus Sir William Blackstone — Old Mother Blackstone, as Bentham called him — consciously borrowed from Montesquieu in his celebrated *Commentary on the Laws of England*, published in 1765:

> And herein consists the excellence of the English government, that all parts of it form a mutual check upon each other. In the legislative, the people are a check upon the nobility, the nobility a check upon the people . . . while the King is a check upon both, which preserves the executive power from encroachments.[9]

But the reinforcement of British complacency was not the purpose of these writers. They wished to use the example of British constitutionalism as a weapon in their own war against arbitrary power and as a spur to reform in France and the rest of Europe. England was 'a republic disguised as a monarchy'. It was a modern incarnation of the old republican tradition, which in the seventeenth century had been represented symbolically by Venice, and more concretely by the United Provinces of the Netherlands. Holland still had its part to play, as Montesquieu well knew, since his first book, *Les Lettres Persanes*, was published there, anonymously, in 1721; but it was not the dynamic power it once had been. The surviving Italian city-republics, like Genoa, still kept the republican tradition alive, but only on the margins of history, as it were. In terms of power, they offered no serious challenge to European absolutism.[10]

England alone did that. Her enormous commercial success, and her proven ability to check militarily the expansionism of Louis XIV, provided the strongest evidence that the English political and social system actually worked; that the old republican tradition of 'mixed' government, religious toleration and a degree of individual liberty was not an anachronism in the world of absolutism. It was the example of England which first suggested to the liberals of the

Enlightenment that they were not fighting a losing battle, but that, on the contrary, it was they who were on the side of the future.

SCIENCE AND EMPIRICISM

England was also, of course, the land of Bacon, Locke and Newton, and of many of the important developments in seventeenth-century science. And although, ironically, English science was beginning to stagnate when the French *philosophes* came to write about it, its past glories earned for it their enduring respect. Newton above all commanded unstinting admiration. For the Enlightenment it was Newton who represented the pure spirit of scientific empiricism, of a commitment to nature and facts uncomplicated by any hankering after the neatness of a unified theory or system. In a letter to Oldenburg, Newton expounded this approach:

> the best and safest method of philosophizing seems to be, first, to inquire diligently into the properties of things and to establish those properties by experiments, and to proceed later to hypotheses for the explanation of things themselves. For hypotheses ought to be applied only in the explanation of the properties of things, and not made use of in determining them. [11]

Hypotheses non fingo. I do not construct hypotheses. This claim of Newton's deeply impressed the *philosophes*. They distinguished between the *esprit systématique* and the *esprit de système*. A systematic approach was essential to science, but the temptation to construct systems should be avoided. Voltaire's advice to a friend who was thinking of making a serious 'study of nature' was that 'you must begin by making no system . . . examine, weigh, calculate, and measure, but never conjecture. M. Newton never made a system: he saw, and he made people see.' [12] Descartes, for all his success in sweeping away old errors, had been one of those who were 'led astray by that spirit of system which blinds the greatest of men'. [13] D'Alembert expressed a similar view in the *Preliminary Discourse* for the *Encyclopedia*.

The *philosophes*, in other words, were empiricist rather than rationalist. They mistrusted grand, all-embracing systems, and anything else that smacked of metaphysics. They took over the sensationalist, empiricist theory of the origins of knowledge from Locke virtually without reservation. Abstract ideas, as Condillac said, 'are only ideas formed from the common elements of several particular ideas'. They have their uses, in setting 'our knowledge in order', but they do not themselves lead to knowledge. It is all too easy, he suggests, to invent hypotheses, but 'it is not so easy to consult experience properly and to gather facts discriminatingly.' [14]

Not everyone endorsed this interpretation of scientific method. Turgot, for example, put forward a view which is closer to the modern understanding of the relation between facts and theory in science: 'The natural philosopher erects hypotheses . . . and brings them to bear upon the enigma of nature. He tries them out, so to speak, on the facts.'[15] But this represented a departure from empiricist orthodoxy. And it was a corollary of that orthodoxy, as it had been with Locke, to devalue poetry.[16] The notion of imagination as a way of access to truth lay beyond the bounds of this kind of empiricism.

Philosophical empiricism was the basis of the coherent world view which the *philosophes* set out to construct, and their starting point in this respect was Locke. But while in Locke empiricism had tended to coexist with political liberalism rather than being fully integrated with it, in the Enlightenment the two are brought together. It brought out, as never before, the political and ideological meaning of empiricism.

The first step was to identify empiricism as the essence of science. Fact-gathering, not the formulation of theories, is the business of the scientist. Truth is particular, because the world is composed of particular things. As d'Alembert put it: 'We cannot repeat too often that nature is composed merely of individual things which are the primary object of our sensations and direct perceptions.' It would not be quite true to say that any concept of totality, any attempt to grasp reality as a whole, had been abandoned. The ideal of a unified knowledge persisted. To quote d'Alembert again: 'The universe, if we may be permitted to say so, would only be one fact and one great truth for whoever knew how to embrace it from a single point of view.' The project of producing an encyclopedia in itself expressed this aspiration: for d'Alembert its aim was 'to encompass the infinitely varied brands of human knowledge in a truly unified system'.[17] But the organizing principle of an encyclopedia is collection rather than unification. Unified knowledge remained the ideal for some, but it was an ideal which atomizing empiricism rendered suspect.

The Enlightenment has often been accused of hubris, of claiming too much for human reason. I think it can be argued that the opposite is true: that in rejecting theory and system they were too modest in their view of the scope of human understanding. Their optimism was rather an optimism of the will: 'I know very well and I feel even more clearly' wrote Voltaire, 'that the mind of man is very limited, but it is for this very reason that we must try to extend the frontiers of this little empire by fighting against the laziness and the natural ignorance with which we are born.'[18] It was Hume who gave classical expression to the modest and sceptical view of the limits of human knowledge:

And tho' we must endeavour to render all our principles as universal as possible, by tracing up our experiments to the utmost, and explaining all effects from the simplest and fewest causes, 'tis still certain we cannot go beyond experience; and any hypothesis, that pretends to discover the ultimate original qualities of human nature, ought at first to be rejected as presumptuous and chimerical. [19]

We should aim at unified, or 'universal' knowledge, but 'we cannot go beyond experience.' In this stress on the test of experience, and the particularity of things, we have the root of the obdurately blinkered 'modesty' of later liberalism, which refuses to speculate or generalize or look beyond the immediate and apparent.

THE ATTACK ON RELIGION

But in the Enlightenment itself this is only a subsidiary theme. The main purpose is not to stress the limitations of the human mind but to press the claims of the empirical, scientific approach in every field, and, in the name of reason, to do battle with superstition, credulity and religious bigotry. *Sapere aude!* Dare to know, or 'have the courage to use your own reason' — this was the motto which Kant chose for the Enlightenment. [20] Using your own reason necessarily implies a certain disrespect for authority in matters of thought and belief, a refusal to take things on trust, to accept them because they are conventional, or because someone, usually a priest, tells you that they are true. This is, said Kant, 'the age of criticism, and to criticism everything must submit.'

To say 'everything' was to deny the distinction which earlier apostles of reason like Bacon, and even Locke, had accepted between matters of faith and matters of reason. The Enlightenment broke down that barrier, and after that it was inevitable that some thinkers would push beyond the deism of Voltaire and the scepticism of Hume to reach a position of outright disbelief. Such a thinker was the notorious atheist, the Baron d'Holbach, who simply dismissed theology as 'nothing but ignorance of natural causes reduced to a system'. [21]

The Enlightenment's frontal assault on religion remains an embarrassment to today's far less militant liberals. But it was central to their whole campaign. Institutionalized religion, and in particular the Catholic Church, was the chief enemy of freedom of thought and discussion in Europe at that time. The *Index* of books technically prohibited by Rome may not have prevented books from being published or read, but it was an effective way of making it clear to the mass of the faithful which books were unorthodox and dangerous, and it provided a handy justification for secular authorities who wished to proscribe or destroy particular publications. Nearly every major work of philosophy and speculation in the seventeenth and eighteenth centuries was placed on the *Index*. Hence it was inevitable that the *philosophes* would come into conflict with the Catholic Church.

They for their part were more than ready to do battle. For the Catholic Church not only opposed free thought; it was also the embodiment of fanaticism and sanctified cruelty. The liberals of the Enlightenment were living in the aftermath of more than a century of religious wars. Even in the 1760s it was possible for Protestants to be tortured and executed simply for being Protestants. It was to fighting cases of this kind that Voltaire in his seventies devoted so much energy and passion. In the twentieth century liberals have tended to equate any kind of strong conviction with fanaticism, but in the eighteenth century fanaticism had a more specific meaning. It meant the readiness to torment and burn those whose religious views differed from your own. The principles of toleration and tolerance were comparatively new, and still needed to be fought for — with conviction. Not surprisingly, therefore, Voltaire regarded fanaticism as more dangerous than atheism: 'for atheism does not inspire bloody passions, but fanaticism does; atheism does not discountenance crime, but fanaticism causes crimes to be committed.' [22]

Thus the *philosophes* opposed reason to fanaticism, and sought constantly to reduce the power of organized religion to impose beliefs and punish heterodoxy. Their influence helped to secure the abolition of judicial torture in several European countries, and if today the principle of pluralism in matters of belief and even politics is quite widely accepted, that is something which we owe in part to the Enlightenment and its 'irreligion'. Contemporary liberals can afford to be beningly indifferent towards organized religion in most countries only because their eighteenth-century forebears were not.

Religion was not the only enemy of reason, knowledge and the scientific spirit. The Enlightenment believed that the secular forms of arbitrary power throve equally on the basis of promoting and sustaining ignorance. An American preacher, Jonathan Mayhew, expressed the common view: 'Tyranny brings *ignorance* and *brutality* along with it. It degrades men from their just rank into the class of brutes . . . There can be nothing great and good, where its influence reaches.' [23] This was really only the converse of the lessons which were very readily drawn from the examples of Britain and Holland. It was not a coincidence that in lands of limited government and religious toleration science should flourish and human knowledge steadily advance. Hume's claim on England's behalf, that 'however other nations may rival us in poetry, and excel us in some other agreeable arts, the improvements in reason and philosophy can only be owing to a land of toleration and of liberty', [24] was widely accepted. The progress of reason required freedom.

THE VIRTUES OF TRADE AND INDUSTRY

If religion and arbitrary power were the chief enemies of reason and knowledge, their allies were tolerance, trade and technology. 'Commerce' Montesquieu believed, 'is a cure for the most destructive prejudices.' Trade in goods is also a trade in knowledge, for commerce diffuses 'a knowledge of the manners of all nations'. [25] One of the less well-known figures of the Scottish Enlightenment, John Millar, argued in like vein that the spread of trade and industry reduces the extent to which 'persons of inferior rank' are 'dependent upon their superiors'. And 'as the lower people, in general, become thereby more independent in their circumstances, they begin to exert those sentiments of liberty which are natural to the mind of man.' [26] Industrialization, by destroying feudal dependence, tends naturally to encourage independence of mind. That was why Hume could describe the 'middling rank of men' as 'the best and firmest basis of public liberty'. Such people 'submit not to slavery, like the peasants' but 'covet equal laws, which may preserve their property'. [27]

If industry encouraged independence, it was also held that trade promoted international peace. Montesquieu believed that 'peace is the natural effect of trade', since through it nations develop a mutual interdependence which draws them together. Kant believed that 'the spirit of commerce' was 'incompatible with war', [28] and Voltaire too believed that trade would bring nations together rather than set them at odds. The wars of the eighteenth century, which to the modern historian appear essentially commercial, were interpreted by the Enlightenment as the consequences of the competitive pursuit of glory and power by the European monarchies. [29]

The effect of trade on the individual trader was, however, another matter. Commerce may unite nations, but 'it does not in the same manner unite individuals', said Montesquieu. Millar was even clearer about the atomizing effects of commerce upon society. In a commercial society 'there occur innumerable competitions and rivalships, which contract the heart, and set mankind at variance. In proportion as every man is attentive to his own advancement, he is . . . prompted to regard his competitors with envy, resentment, and other malignant passions.' [30] At this stage in the development of capitalism, even those who generally welcomed it were able to see what was being lost as well as gained.

Kant, however, was among those who took a harsher view. In one of his essays on the history of humankind, he argues that it is through competition between individuals that human capacities are developed. This is what he calls 'the unsocial sociability of men', and it is through these 'unamiable characteristics' that progress is achieved: 'Thanks be to Nature, then . . . for heartless competitive vanity, for the insatiable desire to possess and to rule! Without them, all the excellent natural capacities of humanity would forever sleep, undeveloped.' [31] It is perhaps surprising, and certainly significant, to find the great 'idealist' philosopher writing in the style of Mandeville, and adding his voice to those who celebrate selfishness and competitiveness as social virtues.

There was one form of trade, then in the most flourishing condition, of which the *philosophes* did not in general approve. That was, of course, the slave trade. Montesquieu, it is true, is somewhat half-hearted in his condemnations of slavery in Book XV of *The Spirit of the Laws*. But Montesquieu belongs anyway to the conservative wing of the movement — hence his popularity with modern liberals. Other *philosophes* spoke out more strongly. Diderot and Condorcet condemned slavery. Voltaire called Spartacus's war against slavery 'the most just war in history, perhaps the only just war', and was more topically savage about slavery in *Candide*. In Surinam Candide and his companion meet a negro whose left leg and right hand have been cut off. The negro explains to them: 'When we work in the sugar mills and the grindstone catches our fingers, they cut off the hand; when we try to run away, they cut off a leg. Both things happened to me. This is the price paid for the sugar you eat in Europe.'[32]

That such figures as Montesquieu, d'Holbach and Condorcet were aristocrats has sometimes been held to falsify the view that the Enlightenment was an essentially bourgeois movement. But what is relevant is the content of their thought, not their social origins; and generally speaking the Enlightenment saw in the commercial, technical and professional middle class their natural audience and supporters.[33] As in the British eighteenth-century novel the middle class was seen as the repository of all the key virtues, of moral discipline and seriousness and social dynamism.

UTILITY

Usefulness, or utility, was a central theme. The *Encyclopedia* itself was described by d'Alembert as a 'Reasoned Dictionary of the Sciences, Arts, and Trades', and he concluded his *Preliminary Discourse* by suggesting that 'Too much has been written on the sciences; not enough has been written well on the mechanical arts.' It was appropriate that he should have quoted Thomas Sprat, first historian of the Royal Society, on the purpose of science being to make everything 'serviceable to the quiet and peace and plenty of Man's life'.[34] Science was not merely truth; it was useful truth, as opposed to the supposed truths of theology, which, even if true, added nothing to human progress or welfare.

Enlightenment liberalism endorsed unhesitatingly the exploitative approach to nature which had been earlier spelt out by Bacon. This approach was taken, not only to inanimate nature, but also to animals, as Kant made unambiguously clear. Speculating on the beginnings of human history, Kant suggested that once man 'came to understand, however obscurely, that he is the true end of nature, and that nothing that lives on earth can compete with him in this regard', he was 'raised . . . altogether above community with animals . . . And from then on he looked upon them, no longer as fellow creatures, but as mere means and tools to whatever ends he pleased.'[35] This explicit statement is the more striking in that Kant deliberately contrasts it with a version of his famous dictum that a man (or human being?) should be treated as 'an end in himself . . . a being which no one might treat as a mere means to ulterior ends.' The alienation of humanity from the rest of the natural world implicit in the concept of 'man' as the dominator of nature has rarely been exposed with such clarity.

But Kant's explicit contrast between treating animals as means and human beings as ends, prompts a further question: might not those who treat animals merely as means come to see at least some human beings in the same way? Another leading figure of the Enlightenment, Cesare Beccaria, seems to have envisaged this possibility: 'There is no liberty whenever the laws permit that, in some circumstances, a man can cease to be a *person* and become a thing.'[36]

Another strand within the Enlightenment was also likely to produce problems for the Kantian rule. This was the development of the human and social sciences, with their inherent tendency to treat human beings as the *objects* of study and analysis. The clue here was the concept of nature. If the human race is part of nature, as well as its master, subject to natural laws, then it is presumably susceptible to the same kind of scientific study and understanding. At this point 'Reason . . . becomes knowledge, technique, and the individual is the object, rather than the subject, of its exercise.'[37] From *seeing* men and women as objects within the social sciences, it is not a long step to *treating* them as the objects of (supposedly) scientific social and economic policies. This was what happened in the practice of liberal political economy.

HAPPINESS

But what was the concept of utility which science and the command of nature were intended to promote? For the Enlightenment, something was useful in so far as it increased human happiness or pleasure, or diminished human pain and misery: 'The VIRTUOUS MAN is him whose actions tend constantly to the well-being and happiness of his fellow creatures; the VICIOUS MAN is him whose conduct tends to the misery and unhappiness of those with whom he lives, from whence his own peculiar misery must most commonly result.' The idea of earthly human happiness was at the centre of Enlightenment thought, and this represented the culmination of the secularization of moral and political thought which had begun with Renaissance humanism. 'There is only one duty, it is to be happy' wrote Diderot. 'Since my natural, unconquerable and inalienable bent is to be happy, it is the one and only source of my true duties, and the only basis of all good legislation.'[38]

'Happiness is a new idea in Europe' said the Jacobin Saint-Just. He was right. Such an idea is commonplace now, but the Enlightenment had to champion it against more traditional and less humanist principles. Thus Beccaria, in his influential essay *On Crimes and Punishments*, used happiness as the criterion to which laws and the administration of justice should conform. His actual phrase, *la massima felicitá divisa nel maggior numero* (the greatest happiness divided among the greatest number), was one of the things that Bentham borrowed from him, although both Bentham and Beccaria derived the *principle* of utility from Helvetius. Beccaria argued that since punishment involves pain or unhappiness by definition, it should be kept to the minimum level at which it could be effective. 'For a punishment to attain its end, the evil which it inflicts has only to exceed the advantage derivable from the crime. . . . All beyond this is superfluous and for that reason tyrannical.' If the implications of Beccaria's approach were humane and humanizing, it is the rationality of his approach which is perhaps most striking: 'it is evident that the purpose of punishment is neither to torment and afflict a sensitive being, nor to undo a crime already committed . . . . The purpose can only be to prevent the criminal from inflicting new injuries on [the] citizens and to deter others from similar acts.' He argues that torture is unlikely to produce either truth or justice, since the pain is so overwhelming that 'filling the entire sensory capacity of the tortured person, it leaves him free only to choose what for the moment is the shortest way of escape from pain.' [39] The tortured are likely to say whatever is expected of them. In these times of much more sophisticated modes of torture, and what is euphemistically called 'in-depth interrogation', Beccaria's arguments have lost none of their relevance. D'Alembert even argued that the sharpness of pain is such that philosophers might well have limited 'their definition of the sovereign good of the present life to the exemption from pain' [40] — thus anticipating by 200 years the modest, revised liberalism of Karl Popper, who has similarly suggested that the reduction of pain and suffering may be a more 'realistic' and less 'utopian' goal than the realization of happiness.

What emerges with particular clarity from Beccaria's discussion of punishment and torture is his reliance on the empiricist-sensationalist account of experience and the personality. The horror of torture is that a person's whole being is filled with the sensation of pain, when the natural direction of human nature is to seek pleasure and avoid pain. Pain and pleasure stand at either end of the spectrum of sensations., '*Bonheur*, or happiness, was the logical objective of sensationalist psychology.' [41]

Thus the connection between an empiricist psychology and an ethic of happiness is not accidental. Nor is the tendency to consider happiness, not in terms of self-realization or individual fulfilment, but in terms of a sum of discrete experiences or sensations of pleasure. For there is a clear tendency within the empiricist account of experience to dissolve the notion of personality entirely, as we saw above. Hume exemplifies this tendency at its strongest: 'What we call a *mind*, is nothing but a heap or collection of different perceptions, united by certain relations, and suppos'd, tho' falsely, to be endow'd with a perfect simplicity and identity.'[42] This has political consequences, in that a concern for happiness, defined in terms of sensations of pleasure, need not imply any respect for the rights or autonomy of the individual person — an implication which Bentham, for one, fully accepted.

Other problems with the idea of happiness were exposed by the permanently embarrassing figure of de Sade. Many people believed that the individual's pursuit of happiness was at least harmless, and at best naturally coincided with the furtherance of the general happiness, as d'Holbach had implied. But what if the pleasure sought was sexual, and what if it involved the exploitation, humiliation or even suffering of others, as de Sade made plain could well be the case? As we noted in Part I, it is de Sade who more than anyone else brings out the tendency within individualistic utilitarianism for each individual pleasure-seeker to treat other persons, not as ends, but as means to his/her own satisfaction. Nor does de Sade qualify his hedonist psychology with any notion of personality. His characters simply live for each moment of sexual pleasure, each physical sensation. In other words, they conform to the eighteenth-century model: they pursue happiness, and they equate it with sensations of pleasure — and in so doing they cast off, or disregard all conventional moral or social inhibitions. De Sade's logic had been anticipated, more abstractly, by La Mettrie:

> it is perfectly clear that, from the point of view of happiness, good and evil are things quite indifferent in themselves, and he who obtains greater satisfaction from doing evil will be happier than the man who obtains less satisfaction from going good . . . there is a kind of individual felicity which is to be found, not merely without virtue, but even in crime itself.[43]

The scandal which has surrounded de Sade's explicit sexual fantasies has almost always obscured the profoundly subversive implications of his interpretation of the individual pursuit of happiness.

REASON AND EDUCATION

If all our ideas are derived from sense-experience, then widespread agreement on matters of truth was clearly possible. For much sense-experience is the common property of humankind. As d'Alembert put it: 'All our knowledge is ultimately reduced to sensations that are approximately the same in all men.'[44] Clear away the clutter of old prejudices and superstitions. Persuade people to put their trust in their own experiences of the world, and then the way is open for consensus of all rational persons.

But how were people's minds to be emptied of all the accumulated lumber of the past ages of ignorance and credulity? Here too sensationalist theory had an answer: the picture of the mind as a blank sheet or *tabula rasa*, void of ideas until experience began to fill the vacuum. If there were no innate ideas — and this idea was firmly rejected — then beliefs and attitudes could only be the product of education and upbringing. So what the extirpation of prejudice and superstition required was the universal adoption of rational and enlightened forms of education and nurture. 'I imagine the minds of children', said Locke, 'as easily turned, this or that way, as water itself.' The optimists of the age dwelt enthusiastically on the vistas of improvement which such a theory of the mind opened up: 'If error and ignorance have forged the chains of the peoples, if prejudice perpetuates them, science, reason, truth will one day break them. The human mind, benumbed for a long succession of centuries by superstition and cruelty, has at last reawakened.'[45] Nor was it only the philosophers in their studies who attached such importance to education. The rational reformers of the age shared this view — the Spanish reformer Jovellanos, for example, who wrote 'Numerous are the streams that lead to social prosperity, but all spring from the same source, and that source is public education.'[46]

This picture of the mind and of the sources of knowledge has obvious egalitarian and democratic implications. No one was born with a special stock of ideas or understanding. All had the capacity to understand, and truth was accessible to all: it was not a metaphysical mystery, unveiled only to the specially gifted, or comprehensible only to the very learned. Yet these egalitarian implications were only partially grasped. Thus there was no reason, apart from traditional prejudice, to think that women were inherently less capable of rationality than men; yet it was only the most radical among the *philosophes*, such as d'Holbach and Condorcet, who recognized that women's abilities were being stunted and suppressed by the trivial and patronizing education then thought suitable for 'young ladies'.

PROPERTY VERSUS DEMOCRACY

Despite the universalism of much Enlightenment theory, in practical and political terms their thinking was often conventionally class-bound. Thus Voltaire once told d'Alembert that education was unsuitable for the children of labourers: it would 'spoil them for the plough' — exactly the view that Mandeville and others had taken of charity schools. He went on: 'It is not the labourer who should be taught, but the good bourgeois, the townsman.'[47] But he became more radical in this respect, as in others, as he got older, and his own practice, as an employer and landowner was more enlightened. At Ferney he had a free school for workers' children.

Politically, though, Voltaire shared with many of his bourgeois contemporaries the standard fear of the lower class 'mob', or the *canaille*, to use his own term. Diderot took a similarly disdainful attitude towards 'l'homme peuple', the man of the people,[48] and d'Holbach was explicit about who was and was not included in his conception of 'the people':

> By the word people I do not mean the stupid populace which, being deprived of enlightenment and good sense, may at any moment become the instrument and accomplice of turbulent demagogues who wish to disturb society. Every man who can live respectably from the income of his property and every head of a family who owns land ought to be regarded as a citizen.[49]

D'Holbach's view is that of the Old Whigs of the early eighteenth century: he even thought that the merchant was not entitled to full citizenship until he had acquired land. Diderot argued similarly in the *Encyclopedia* that 'It is property that makes the citizen . . . it is by reason of his possessions that . . . he acquires the right of having himself represented.'[50] And when it came to defining the purposes of government, d'Holbach again sounds like a Whig, albeit a utilitarian one: 'Laws, to be just, must have as their invariable end the general interest of society, that is to say, to ensure to the greatest number of citizens the advantages for which they are associated together. These advantages are liberty, property and security.' Helvetius, similarly, described 'the preservation of private property' as 'the moral god of the state'.[51] These were typical sentiments, since property was for the Enlightenment as central an institution as it had been for Locke.

Rousseau was one of the few among the *philosophes* to question radically the social function and effects of private property, and in this respect as in many others, this most original thinker of the Enlightenment pushes beyond the bounds of conventional liberalism towards socialism. It certainly troubled the *philosophes* that their world was still so full of poverty, ignorance and suffering, but because they were unable to see what might be done about this, they tended towards fatalism, while putting their faith in the long run in the gradual spread of enlightenment. Kant regarded inequality as inevitable, and in any case productive of much good as well as evil.[52] Voltaire in a single sentence balanced reforming passion with fatalism: 'It is inevitable that the majority should be poor, but it is not necessary that it should be wretched.'[53]

The *philosophes* were not economic levellers: the equality they believed in was equality before the law, and sometimes political equality as well. They were the enemies of traditional aristocratic privileges. They believed in opportunities for men (and perhaps women) of talent and merit. They were constitutionalists and usually republicans. They believed firmly in the rule of law or laws, as opposed to the arbitrary exercise of monarchical will. In all this they were thoroughly bourgeois and typically liberal. Contrary to the claim of de Tocqueville, it was not their aim 'to demolish the entire social and political structure of the kingdom'. [54] Almost all of them were reformers rather than revolutionaries, who, as Peter Gay has put it, 'much as they wished to change it, were at home in their world'.

Nevertheless they had to wrestle constantly with a simple, but seemingly insoluble problem: *how* were the changes they wished to see going to be brought about? Where could they find the political forces capable of implementing their reforms and ideals?

THE PROBLEM OF POLITICAL AGENCY

It is in relation to this problem that we have to understand the apparent paradox of these militant liberal reformers looking to some of the most despotic of the absolutist rulers of their age to carry out their plans. The *philosophes* represented a will for bourgeois reforms which required a strong and militant bourgeoisie to put them into effect. It was the absence of such a class to support, if not initiate, reforms which blighted the efforts at reform by genuinely enlightened politicians in Spain and by Joseph II in Austria. But this same absence prompted some of the *philosophes* to look to the so-called 'Enlightened Despots' for hope of change, while others, less able to believe in the possibility of reform from above, contented themselves with sketching out imaginary utopias — a form which is often as much an expression of despair about the present, as of hope for the future.

Frederick the Great of Prussia, Catherine II of Russia, Joseph II of Austria, and a number of lesser potentates, all, at one time or another, aroused the hopes of some leading figures of the Enlightenment; and all, with the possible exception of Joseph II, disappointed these hopes. The story of Voltaire's un-productive and disillusioniong stay at the court of Frederick in Potsdam is well known. Catherine II was similarly anxious to give her regime a veneer of enlightenment. But it amounted to little more, as both Diderot and Bentham found out. Diderot was flattered by Catherine's generosity to him, and we may assume that she hoped he was impressed by the *Nakaz*, or statement of general legislative principles which she herself drew up in the 1760s. It owed much to the writings of Montesquieu and Beccaria. But Catherine's power was not in any way restricted by it, and she continued to pursue policies which had little relation to the elevated principles set out in the *Nakaz*. Diderot's one visit to Russia in 1773 did nothing to reassure him. [55]

Bentham had a similar experience a decade later. He once announced that he was happy 'that I write in the age of Catherine, of Joseph, of Frederic, of Gustavus, and of Leopold', and he told his brother, who was then working in Russia, that 'I could bring more of my ideas to bear there in a month than here in my whole life.'[56] He therefore made the journey to Russia in 1785 in an optimistic mood. But he was deeply dismayed by the backward and barbarous nature of Russian society, and did not even bother to seek an audience with the Empress. So he returned to England with the greatest practical question for utilitarianism still unsolved: how and where were his schemes for reform to be put into practice, or even tried out?

The great disappointment which finally dashed many Enlightenment hopes of reform and progress 'from above' was the failure of Turgot's reforming ministry in France itself in 1776. Turgot appeared to be the very model of an Enlightenment statesman. He was an intellectual and a reformer, committed to the economic ideas of the physiocrats, and as Controller-General between 1774 and 1776, he made a genuine effort to modernize the tax system and ease the burden on the rural poor by introducing free trade in grain. These and other measures alienated the aristocracy, and the new king, Louis XVI was not, in the end, willing or perhaps able to support Turgot's reforms against the forces massed in opposition to them.

The fall of Turgot destroyed the hopes that some, including Voltaire, had placed in the arrival of a new monarch on the French throne. Voltaire was deeply depressed by the event, and did not live long enough to find a way out of the dilemma. But it turned Diderot's mind in the direction of more radical solutions. The year 1776 was, after all, remarkable for its events, of which the most striking was the Americans' final decision to break with Britain. Such an event was welcome to the French, as Britain's traditional European rivals, but it was also welcome to the *philosophes* for other, less chauvinist reasons. Diderot saw the American struggle as a fight for freedom, and saw that the Americans had the opportunity to set a pioneering example by founding a new society and government on the basis of reason.[57] Not everyone was as enthusiastic as Thomas Paine, the Englishman who had identified himself with the American cause, and wrote in 1776 that 'We have it in our power to begin the world over again. . . . The birth-day of a new world is at hand.'[58] But there was a widespread sense of new possibilities, of hope revived. However, *the* event which was to transform the situation globally, and make it possible for the dreams and plans of the Enlightenment to be translated into practicable political programmes — that event still lay 13 years ahead. By that time most of the leading figures of the Enlightenment, with some conspicuous exceptions such as Kant, Condorcet and Bentham, were dead. Whether they would have welcomed the French Revolution, or, having welcomed it, would have continued to support it, can only be a matter for speculation. What *is* clear is that a revolution with global impact was necessary if the liberal principles of the Enlightenment were ever to be translated into reality.

VOLTAIRE

But we cannot leave the Enlightenment without taking a further look at perhaps its most famous figure — one who personifies in a remarkably vigorous form many of the strengths and some of the limitations of classic liberalism. Voltaire's life has a remarkable unity: with him it was not possible to believe in a principle and yet not act upon it. It is therefore right that he is remembered, honoured and written about, not so much as an apologist for liberal principles of tolerance, freedom and humanity, but as an active fighter on their behalf. Rousseau, he said, rather unfairly, writes for the sake of writing, but 'moi, j'écris pour agir' (I write in order to act).[59] For those who believe that art can only endure by transcending the moment and aiming at timelessness, Voltaire is an embarrassment. For while his 'high art', his classical dramas and elegant epic poems, much admired in their day, have become museum pieces, his squibs and polemics and angry outbursts still communicate their original vitality.

When Voltaire died in 1778 he was eighty-three. His fame had for long been enormous, and his long and active life had turned him into a European as well as a French giant. But this eminence was not easily attained. He spent the last few months of his life in Paris, where he was greeted and feted as a hero; but this was his first visit in 28 years, and his exile at Ferney on the French—Swiss border was only partly voluntary. It is true that he enjoyed literary success in his twenties, but this gave him no immunity from legal harassment by the state and the aristocracy. He was in fact imprisoned three times, twice in the Bastille, and exiled twice. This was a common fate for literary men in France. During the reigns of Louis XIV and Louis XV more than a thousand authors and booksellers were imprisoned in the Bastille alone. Diderot spent four weeks in solitary confinement in Vincennes, and might have been so confined much longer but for the efforts of influential friends on his behalf. The effects of imprisonment should not be underrated. It helped to produce a climate of fear and caution, in which people thought twice before publishing anything likely to offend the authorities. As we have seen, it was common for possibly 'subversive' works to be published in the more liberal climate of Holland.

Voltaire, then, knew what it was to be harassed by the powerful, and he saw his books condemned and burnt in Paris, Berlin and Geneva. Such experiences helped to shape his firm belief in the rule of law as the only acceptable alternative to arbitrariness. 'Let law govern, and not caprice' — this was a precept which he repeated and elaborated on a hundred times.[60]

Nor did his prudence get the better of his principles. He was always a campaigning writer, and he grew more militant as he grew older. He was in his late sixties when he took up the infamous case of Jean Calas, the Protestant from Toulouse who was executed for the alleged murder of his own son, in order, it was said, to prevent him becoming a Catholic.

There were several aspects of this case which aroused Voltaire's creative anger. The verdict against Calas was not based on compelling evidence against him, but on the popular belief that Huguenots were obliged by their faith to murder their children if they abandoned their religion. In these circumstances the prosecutors had to rely on extracting a confession of guilt from Calas by torture. This they failed to do, and despite being stretched on the rack and having his bones broken on the wheel, Jean Calas died protesting his innocence. The use of torture, and of a particularly cruel and protracted method of execution, made the case a prototype of the legalized barbarity, based on religious superstition, to which the Enlightenment opposed its own ideas of humanity and rationality.

Nor was the case by any means an isolated one. Less than three weeks before Calas' execution in March 1762 a Protestant pastor, Francois Rochette, was hanged in Toulouse for the 'crime' of performing an illegal baptism. Three Protestants who had tried to rescue him from jail were beheaded at the same time. If these were the last Protestants to die for their faith alone in France, that was certainly due in some measure to the furore generated by Voltaire over the Calas case.

The Calas case was only the first and best known of a number of cases of injustice and fanaticism in which Voltaire worked tirelessly and shrewdly to secure redress. The cases of the Calas and Sirven families, and of the young Chevalier de la Barre, who was tortured and executed for blasphemy in 1766 (with a copy of Voltaire's *Dictionnaire Philosophique* being burnt along with his body), were all cases in which the injustice was the product of Catholic bigotry and intolerance. Others, such as those of Martin, Montbailli and General Lally, were cases of innocent men being wrongly executed, and Voltaire waged energetic campaigns to have them posthumously vindicated. The energy and persistence of his campaigning can be gauged from a single figure: during the seven years it took to win justice for the Sirven family Voltaire wrote some 2,000 letters in that cause alone.[61]

The Enlightenment has often been accused of 'facile optimism' — although very often the implication is that any kind of optimism is by definition facile. Voltaire's optimism was anything but facile. Not only in *Candide* but in many other places he assailed with a passionate ridicule the claim that the world as it is is 'the best of all possible worlds'. 'Just show me . . . why so many men slit each other's throats in the best of all possible worlds, and I shall be greatly obliged to you', he wrote in 1744, and he called optimism 'a cruel philosophy under a consoling name'.[62] He drew a crucial distinction, in his poem on the

Lisbon earthquake of 1755, between the, to him cruel and ludicrous, belief that all is already well, and the *hope* that one day that happy state might come about. The two beliefs are antithetical. It is precisely the perception that the world is *not* as it should be that inspires the determination to improve it. The only optimism required is the belief that improvement is possible — and that, certainly, Voltaire and his allies never doubted. For him the convenient consolations of other-worldliness were not available. He mistrusted any suggestion that the miseries and injustices of this world could be made up for in the next. Notwithstanding his deism, he represents the secular, this-worldly character of liberalism in its purest and strongest form, in which form it supplies the basis for a militant reformism.

He had a great deal of compassion for the great masses of the poor and hungry. [63] But it was natural that he, a wealthy and successful bourgeois, should also be wary and afraid of that great mass of untamed, uncivilized humanity. Voltaire was nothing of a democrat, and although he deplored a social order which left the poor to starve, he did not for a moment believe that the poor should obtain equality as well as food and work. He was typically bourgeois too in his mistrust of 'indiscriminate' charity, and his preference for useful work as a remedy for distress.

One of his arguments against capital punishment was that it deprived society of potential forced labour: 'A hanged man is good for nothing, but a man condemned to public works still serves his country and is a living lesson.' Peter Gay rightly calls this a 'chilly, commercial kind of humanity . . . characteristic of bourgeois liberalism in the eighteenth century'. [64] It demonstrates the affinity between Enlightenment liberalism and the 'political arithmetic' of the economists. We find the same calculating style of would-be benevolence in the prison plans of Bentham and others. [65] In his *Chinese Catechism* of 1764 Voltaire advises a ruler on how to help the poor while developing the economy: 'you will feed the poor, by employing them on useful works, and not by rewarding idleness; you will beautify the highways; you will dig canals; you will raise public buildings; you will encourage all the arts, you will reward merit of every kind.' [66] The stress on usefulness is characteristic. Voltaire approved the construction of canals and road, but not pyramids. Egypt's most famous structures were he pointed out, 'the monuments of a nation of slaves'. [67]

In his passionate concern for justice, his hatred of cruelty, and his unremitting opposition to fanaticism and intolerance. Voltaire personifies the liberal humanism of the Enlightenment at its courageous and crusading best. He was a great and committed man who left the world a measurably better place than he found it. If the boundaries of his understanding and sympathies were those of his class, it must also be said that in his virtues, Voltaire represented that class at its combative best, waging its historic war against religious obscurantism and feudal arbitrariness.

10

America: The Rights of Man and the Rights of Property

'We can no longer say there is nothing new under the sun. For this whole chapter in the history of man is new' wrote Thomas Jefferson to his old friend, the radical scientist Joseph Priestley in 1801.[1] Jefferson, at that time President of the new nation whose Declaration of Independence he had drafted 25 years before, had as much right as anyone to rejoice in the magnitude and novelty of what had been achieved by the Americans. Their successful struggle for independence may not have produced a social and economic revolution, but it was a revolutionary *political* step, which contemporaries rightly interpreted as a triumphant challenge to the old order of the old world.

'The birth-day of a new world is at hand', proclaimed Paine. The discontinuity was not as great as Paine and Jefferson supposed, but it was striking enough. Here was a new nation building up a new order, on the basis, not of old customs and prejudices, or of empirical muddling through, but of clearly articulated rational principles — principles which were shared by enlightened liberals throughout Europe. To them it was a clear victory for enlightenment, reason and freedom, and an equally clear defeat for tyranny — the apparently absolutist leanings of George III — and the old order.

It was noteworthy, however, that Englishmen such as Burke were able to support the American cause on quite the opposite grounds: that the Americans were, at least before 1776, demanding only the traditional rights accorded to British citizens, no break with precedent or history being implied. Nevertheless it was not wrong to place a liberal interpretation on the American Revolution. We do not need to join in the debate on the precise sources of the ideas of the rebel leaders, nor speculate on whether Jefferson had read or was much influenced by Locke, to see that many of the ideas of the American founding fathers as they were embodied in the institutions of the new state do belong firmly within the developing tradition of liberal thought and practice.

It was a still evolving tradition, however, and, as in the French Revolution, the revolutionaries drew heavily on the older tradition of classical or neo-classical republicanism. It was from this tradition that they derived the belief that the ideal model of government was both mixed and balanced. From this tradition, too, and in particular from the influential theorizing of Harrington, they borrowed the notion that political institutions and power should reflect the distribution of economic power and property, or, as the English authors of *Cato's Letters* had put it: 'the first Principle of all Power is Property; and every Man will have his Share of it in proportion as he enjoys Property'[2] — a teaching which John Jay boiled down to the blunt maxim: 'The people who own the country ought to govern it.'[3]

The justification for this proposition was the familiar one that property alone guarantees independence of judgement and action. The poor, by virtue of their poverty, are at the mercy of the rich. Their votes can .be bought. 'Give the votes to people who have no property', said Gouverneur Morris, 'and they will sell them to the rich, who will be able to buy them.'[4] The conservative conclusion, which was widely drawn, was that political power should be confined to the existing property-owners. Although property-ownership was far more widespread than in Europe, this did mean that there was actually some reduction in the extent of political rights under the new state constitutions, in that women, who had in some places enjoyed limited political rights in the colonial era, lost them after 1776.[5]

But some, including Jefferson, were anxious that measures should be taken to extend property-ownership in order to draw more people into the franchise. For Virginia he proposed distributing 50 acres of land to 'every person of full age'. Like Harrington, he opposed the principle of primogeniture, and recommended that inherited property be divided among all the children, male and female: 'legislators cannot invent too many devices for subdividing property.' He looked back nostalgically to the Roman ideal of a republic of farmers. It was they, he believed, who represented incorruptible independence at its best. 'Those who labour in the earth are the chosen people of God, if ever he had a chosen people' he wrote in his *Notes on the State of Virginia*. 'Corruption of morals in the mass of cultivators is a phenomenon of which no age nor nation has furnished an example.' Manufacturing, on the other hand, implies dependence on sales and customers, and 'Dependance begets subservience and venality, suffocates the germ of virtue and prepares fit tools for the designs of ambition.' Thirty years later, Jefferson had been compelled to change his mind: 'experience has taught me that manufacturers are now as necessary to our independence as to our comfort.'[6] But it was not a change he relished.

At this early stage in the development of capitalism, a liberal belief in free trade did not necessarily imply a belief in the virtue of traders. Benjamin Franklin, who in his *Principles of Trade* (1774) quotes with approval the saying *Laissez-nous faire*, and claims that free trade is mutually beneficial to all nations, nevertheless also refers to '*commerce*, which is generally *cheating*'. As with Adam Smith, there is a vein of candour and clear-sightedness in these writers which is lost in the later development of liberal political economy. Franklin was also worried that the general interest might be lost sight of in the new world of atomized individuals pursuing each his or her own interest: 'Naturally one would imagine, that the interests of a few individuals should give way to general interest; but individuals manage their affairs with so much more application, industry and address, than the public do theirs, that general interest most commonly gives way to particular.'[7]

Jefferson believed that to interfere with the inequalities of wealth and property which derived from the unequal exercise of 'industry and skill' would 'violate arbitrarily the first principle of association, "the *guarantee* to everyone a free exercise of his industry and the fruits acquired by it"'.[8] But he did not therefore believe that the rich were entitled to special political privileges. He was opposed to the idea of a second chamber of the legislature composed of representatives of the wealthy, and had no high opinion of their qualities: 'my observations do not enable me to say I think integrity the characteristic of wealth. In general I believe the decisions of the people, in a body, will be more honest and more disinterested than those of wealthy men.' That was his view in 1776, and 40 years later it had not changed: 'I am not among those who fear the people. They, and not the rich, are our dependence for continued freedom.'[9]

But Jefferson's relative faith in 'the people' was not generally shared by the leaders of the American revolution. They identified themselves much more wholeheartedly with the interests of property, and they saw these interests as threatened by popular demands for democracy. As Carl Becker put it long ago, 'the doctrine of self-government . . . was a two-edged sword.'[10] If it was in the name of self-government that the war of independence was fought, how could the same right be denied when it was demanded by the lower orders? The issue of home rule raised also, as has been said, the issue of who should rule at home. This problem was exacerbated by the fact that popular agitation played a large part in the campaign of opposition to Britain that had preceded the war; while the war itself, like most wars in which there is wide popular participation, gave the participants a sense of their own worth which they wanted to see reflected in the laws and institutions of the newly independent states.

Inevitably, therefore, when it came to devising the new state constitutions, the demand for democracy and for popular sovereignty was raised. The Massachusetts author of *The People the Best Governors* argued, as Bentham was to do later, that the people themselves 'best know their wants and necessities and therefore are best able to govern themselves.' It was in this spirit that the delegates from Mecklenburg County to the North Carolina Congress of 1776 were instructed: 'that the Government be a simple Democracy or as near it as possible . . . In fixing the fundamental principles of Government you shall oppose everything that leans to aristocracy or power in the hands of the rich and chief men exercised to the oppression of the poor.'[11]

Apart from the demand for a wide franchise — which, however, even the most democratically inclined accepted should not include servants, nor women or slaves — the idea of a 'simple democracy' was embodied in the form of a single chamber or unicameral legislature, popularly elected. And it was around this issue that so much argument revolved. For those who feared the people saw a 'balanced' political structure as, in effect, the best means of containing and neutralizing the popular will. In particular they favoured bicameral legislatures with the second chamber not subject to popular election. Various ways of choosing it were proposed; but broadly speaking what was wanted was a body which would restrain the democratically-elected chamber and represent, either explicitly or implicitly, the interests of wealth, property and social stability. John Adams objected to Paine's proposals in *Common Sense* as being 'so democratical, without any restraint or even an Attempt at any Equilibrium or Counterpoise, that it must produce Confusion and every Evil work.'[12]

Fears about 'mob rule' were voiced from an early stage in the crisis. Gouverneur Morris commented apprehensively: 'The mob begin to think and reason . . . I see and I see it with fear and trembling; we will be under the worst of all possible dominions . . . a riotous mob.'[13] These fears grew when three states, most notably Pennsylvania, whose constitution had many democratic features clearly reflecting Paine's influence, opted to set up single-chamber legislatures.[14] Popular discontent continued when the war was over and the poorer sections found themselves encumbered with heavy debts, and the Shays rebellion in New England in 1786 provided the property-minded Whig leaders with the final proof that property was not secure under existing federal arrangements. General Knox reported that the rebellion had 'alarmed every man of principle and property in New England', and he told Washington that 'our government must be braced, changed, or altered to secure our lives and property.' It led to the devising of a Constitution which was specifically intended to provide for 'strong government', by incorporating all the devices by which the popular will could be held in check: the division of powers and a bicameral legislature. As John Adams put it in his *Defence of the Constitution etc*: 'The rich ought to have an effectual barrier in the constitution against being robbed, plundered, and murdered, as well as the poor; and this can never be without an independent senate.'[15] James Madison argued in similar vein.

Even Jefferson's declared faith in the people was not as unqualified as he sometimes suggested. Like Mill and other later liberals, he believed in what he called 'a natural aristocracy' based on 'virtue and talents'; and he thought the best political system was one by which this natural aristocracy was chosen to govern. The Senate which he envisaged for his state of Virginia would, he hoped, be filled with 'the wisest men', chosen, not by the people themselves — 'I have ever observed that a choice by the people themselves is not generally distinguished for its wisdom' — but by the lower house of Representatives. Once chosen, they ought to be 'perfectly independent', that is, non-accountable to the people. A unicameral legislature he regarded not as the expression of democracy, but as an 'elective despotism': '173 despots would surely be as oppressive as one.'

Thus in the debates which took place in America in the 1770s and 1780s, and especially those which revolved around the Constitution of 1787, two related themes clearly emerge which are to be dominant in nineteenth-century liberalism: a concern to structure the political system in such a way as to protect property, and an abiding fear and anxiety about democracy. But the fear of democracy and the opposition to a single sovereign body were inspired by more than the concern to safeguard property. As Jefferson and the other leaders saw it, it was against despotism — that of George III — that the fight for independence was waged. It followed, therefore, that the newly-independent states should devise constitutions which would prevent any other form of despotism replacing that of Britain. Hence the concern to divide state authority among a number of institutions which would reciprocally check any despotic tendencies that any one of them might display. Hence Jefferson's objection to Virginia's original constitution, under which 'all the powers of government, legislative, executive, and judiciary, result to the legislative body.'[16]

Jefferson, like most liberals, was less concerned with *who* governed than with limiting the powers of government as such, even if, in a democratic context, this meant curbing the popular will. It is in this context that we find the Founding Fathers voicing their fears that democracy will produce a new and more powerful kind of despotism — popular despotism. 'Give all power to the many, they will oppress the few' said Alexander Hamilton. 'Give all power to the few, they will oppress the many.'[17] This democratic despotism could pose a threat, not only to property, but also to the rights of minorities and the right to dissent, unless some limits were set to the power of the majority.

We can also see, in the thinking behind the division of powers, the germ of a different conception of democracy from that which identified it with the sovereignty of the popular will. This is the pluralist conception of society as a collection of diverse and conflicting interests, all of which are legitimate and ought therefore to be represented politically, but not to the exclusion of others. It was, of course, the particular interest of property-owners for which a guaranteed place was being sought — and this tells us something about the function and appeal of this, as yet undeveloped, pluralist theory. It was, of course, capable of extension and elaboration, and has now become central to the Western World's specifically liberal version of democracy.

Despite the fear of democracy which the leaders of the Revolution so freely expressed, the principles they proclaimed did amount to more than a mere rationalization of class interest, and were capable of being given a more generous and radical interpretation than they themselves envisaged. It was because the struggle was seen as a fight for fundamental human rights that it generated such widespread enthusiasm and support. And the rights which the Americans claimed were not, despite Burke, simply their historical rights as British citizens, but their natural rights, the rights of man. Even relatively conservative Whigs like Hamilton and Dickinson shared this view. Hamilton claimed that these rights 'are not to be rummaged for among old parchments and musty records. They are written, as with a sunbeam, in the whole *volume* of human nature, by the hand of divinity itself, and can never be erased or obscured by mortal power.'[18]

Following Locke, the standard definition of these rights was 'life, liberty, and property'. The Virginia Bill of Rights enumerated 'the enjoyment of life and liberty, with the means of acquiring and possessing property, and pursuing and obtaining happiness and safety.' It is indicative, not only of Jefferson's largeness of mind, but also of the exalted mood of 1776, that in the Declaration of Independence 'the pursuit of happiness' replaced the conventional narrower reference to property. It is also indicative of the universalizing tendency in the liberal ideology.

The Americans, then, proclaimed the natural rights of man. But to whom, precisely, did these rights belong? It is at this point that we encounter the perennial contradiction between the universalism of liberal principles and the relative selectivity of liberal practice. The rights of man were the rights of men. Women were not seriously considered for inclusion in the new arrangements, despite some precedents in the colonial era. Except for the famous letters which the resourceful Abigail Adams wrote to her husband John at the time of the Continental Congress in 1776, there appears to be little evidence that the question of women's rights was even raised at this time. In one letter, Abigail Adams asked that 'in the new code of laws which I suppose it will be necessary for you to make, I desire you would remember the ladies and be more generous and favorable to them than your ancestors'; and in another she observed sardonically that 'whilst you are proclaiming peace and good-will to men, emancipating all nations, you insist upon retaining an absolute power over wives.' John Adams' initial response was not to take his wife's request seriously ('I cannot but laugh', he wrote), but his second thoughts showed that he was alarmed by the airing of such notions: 'New claims will arise; women will demand a vote . . . and every man who has not a farthing, will demand an equal vote with any other, in all acts of state.'[19]

The issue of slavery was more obviously embarrassing. For the American polemicists had used the term 'slavery' freely when referring to the relationship between Britain and America, or to the dangers inherent in a British victory. Samuel Johnson, in his anti-American pamphlet of 1775, *Taxation no Tyranny*, made effective play with this. Noting the American claim that 'when they are taxed, we shall be enslaved', he went on to ask 'If slavery be thus fatally contagious, how is it that we hear the loudest yelps for liberty among the drivers of negroes?' Another Tory, John Wesley, made the same point: 'The Negroes in America are slaves, the Whites enjoy liberty. Is not then all this outcry about Liberty and Slavery mere rant, and playing upon words?'[20] The British authorities were able to exploit the issue by promising slaves their liberty if they would fight with Britain against the American 'rebels', and many blacks responded to this call.

The democrats on the American side saw the contradiction and drew the necessary conclusion. William Gordon argued that slavery was incompatible with the Declaration of Independence, if the preamble represented 'our genuine sentiments'.[21] And Richard Wells asked how it was possible to 'reconcile the exercise of SLAVERY with our *professions of freedom*'.[22] But Jefferson's passage saddling George III with the responsibility for perpetuating the slave-trade was cut from the final version of the Declaration, and the Constitution also contains no mention of slaves or slavery.

There can be no doubt that Jefferson regarded slavery as wrong, and that he hoped and looked for its eventual abolition — although he was himself a slave-owner. In 1774 he wrote 'The abolition of domestic slavery is the great object of desire in those colonies where it was unhappily introduced in their infant state.' In his *Notes on the State of Virginia* he commented on the evil influence which slavery had on both slaves and slave-owners, and expressed the hope that 'total emancipation' would come, 'with the consent of the masters, rather than by their extirpation'. But this was more of a pious hope than a policy, and it was qualified by the fact that Jefferson did not believe that blacks and whites could exist peaceably in the same state, and was inclined to think that blacks were 'inferior to the whites in the endowments both of body and mind'.[23] It is the judgement of one recent historian, Staughton Lynd, that 'almost without exception the Fathers felt that slavery was wrong and almost without exception they failed to act decisively to end it.'[24]

As with the extension of the franchise, and the issue of democracy, so it was with slavery: concern and respect for private property prevented the Founding Fathers from pursuing the radical logic of the universal rights which they themselves proclaimed. As the French revolutionaries were also to discover, the rights of man and the rights of property were not as naturally compatible as many Whigs had hitherto supposed.

11

The Moment of the French Revolution: the Climax of Liberalism

Many historical turning points have passed unnoticed by their contemporaries. The outbreak of the French Revolution was not one of them. From the moment of the capture of the Bastille by the Parisian crowd on 14 July 1789, it was widely recognized that an upheaval was taking place which had few, if any, precedents in history. Only a fortnight later the English Whig leader, Charles James Fox, exclaimed: 'How much the greatest event it is that ever happened in the world, and how much the best',[1] while Sir Samuel Romilly greeted it as 'the most glorious event, and the happiest for mankind, that has ever taken place since human affairs have been recorded.'[2]

Much of this enthusiasm was soon to fade, but years later Wordsworth could still recall the experience of his visits to France in 1790 and 1792:

> . . . 'Twas a time when Europe was rejoiced,
> France standing on the top of golden hours,
> And human nature seeming born again.[3]

The rebirth of human nature: that indeed was the scale of the potential change as it appeared to many people, and that, according to de Tocqueville, was what the Revolution aimed at, and why it inspired such extraordinary excitement: 'No previous political upheaval, however violent, had aroused such passionate enthusiasm, for the ideal the French Revolution set before it was not merely a change in the French social system but nothing short of a regeneration of the whole human race.'[4] A vast range of new and undreamt-of possibilities had suddenly been opened up. It was, in Paine's words, 'an age of Revolutions, in which everything may be looked for'.[5]

Opponents of the Revolution, such as Burke, agreed on its significance: 'It looks to me as if I were in a great crisis, not of the affairs of France alone, but of all Europe, perhaps of more than Europe. All circumstances taken together, the French revolution is the most astonishing that has hitherto happened in the world.'[6] Thus from the beginning the term 'revolution' was habitually used to describe the events of 1789 and after.

The American and French Revolutions transformed the historical power and prospects of liberalism. Without the French Revolution the liberal and radical ideas of the Enlightenment would have remained essentially ideas, circulating among the progressive intelligentsia, but without any substantial influence on political life. Hopes of converting some of the rulers of Europe to the principles of the Enlightenment had been repeatedly disappointed, and the inability of a genuine would-be reformer like Joseph II to carry through his programme, suggested that the path of reform from above was irreparably blocked.

If the ancien regime was impervious to attempts at reform from above, the Revolution showed that it could be destroyed by revolt from below. In August 1789 the feudal order and its privileges were legally abolished in France, while within a few years, one of the oldest and seemingly most powerful monarchies in Europe had been swept away, and the Catholic Church had been firmly subordinated to a secular state. To those who had so long railed and fought against the tyranny of kings and the bigotry of priests, this was a dream come true, and many people in the early 1790s shared Paine's confidence that other revolutions would follow the French, and the feudal order would soon come tumbling down all over Europe. Within a few short years the French Revolution translated liberal ideas of legal equality and individual rights into political realities, and it showed *how* such a transformation could take place — through popular revolution based among the great masses of those who had always been politically excluded. It was the French Revolution which made the freedom of nations and the freedom of individuals into real and central issues in the politics not only of Europe, but of a wider world. And it was the Revolution which ensured that political democracy also became a major issue. These changes were directly reflected in the changing vocabulary of politics: 'It was not until the French Revolution that *democracy* ceased to be a mere literary word, and became part of the political vocabulary.'[7] Within 20 years of the Revolution the word 'liberal' itself acquired its modern political meaning.

The French Revolution was thus the 'moment' when, and the means by which, liberalism was transformed from a dream and an aspiration, the goal of much arduous campaigning, into a dominant, dynamic political force. It was the decisive victory which opened the way for the great liberal achievements of the nineteenth century. It was also the moment at which the ideals of liberalism inspired some of the greatest achievements in European art — Mozart's *Magic Flute*, Beethoven's *Fidelio* and many other works, plays by Goethe and Schiller, poetry by Shelley, Byron, Pushkin, and Heine, and the political art of David, Delacroix, Géricault and, above all, Goya. The

Revolution inspired radical women to demand the same political and legal rights that were being demanded for men, and it inspired black people to claim the same rights and dignity as whites. Its impact was at once world-wide and profound.

But — such is the dialectic of history — the Revolution marked not only the decisive victory of liberalism; it also initiated a fundamental crisis for and within liberalism — a crisis which persisted throughout its subsequent development. At that time liberalism, particularly in alliance with nationalism, was in many contexts an ideology of revolution — revolution made in the name of the rights of men and nations against feudalism and arbitrariness. Yet most liberals, like their Whig predecessors, were not natural revolutionaries. They normally believed in gradualism and constitutionalism, and were unhappy that it should require rebellion and violence to establish these peaceable principles. And they were greatly alarmed by the extent of popular participation in these upheavals. It was no part of their plans to see political power placed in the hands of the 'vulgar mob'. What they looked for was a share, preferably the lion's share, in political power for themselves, the enlightened bourgeoisie. They had grave misgivings about the principles of democracy and the rights of man (let alone woman), in so far as these implied a political equality not qualified by respect for the rights of property. In less than five years after 1789, dangerously egalitarian currents gathered strength, and 'rights' interpreted in the manner of the *sans culottes*, or their British artisan equivalents, seemed to threaten the very foundations of order and respect in society.

It is not surprising, therefore, that the issue of the Revolution itself divided liberals; nor that the issues of equality, democracy and nationalism, which it placed permanently on the agenda of modern politics, should have continued to divide liberals ever since. A microcosm of this crisis is provided by the break-up of the English Whig party under the pressures of the 1790s. This decade pushed political changes to the very borders of what bourgeois liberalism could encompass, and inspired a whole range of developments in political thought which moved beyond those limits. Paine's *Rights of Man* points beyond even radical liberalism in the direction of both anarchism and social democracy, while within a year or two, William Godwin had produced in his *Enquiry Concerning Political Justice* a well-developed theory of anarchism, and another of that same circle of English radicals, Mary Wollstonecraft, had published the first classic of modern feminism, *Vindication of the Rights of Woman*. Babeuf's Conspiracy of Equals is often identified as the first truly socialist political movement, while Burke's *Reflections* has rightly become a foundation text of modern conservatism. Two decades later, at the very moment when the word 'liberal' takes on in Spain its modern political meaning, Robert Owen was setting out the first thoroughly socialist critique of the new industrial capitalism which had developed in Britain. Thus the Revolution, which assured the future of liberalism, also inspired a range of political developments and movements situated outside and beyond liberalism, all of which were to grow up to challenge liberalism's brief hegemony.

THE REVOLUTION IN FRANCE

Today liberals are more likely to be counter-revolutionaries than revolutionaries, or even sympathizers with revolution. Liberalism has moved closer to conservatism, and shares the traditionally conservative mistrust of political doctrines and principles. Seen from this angle, 1789 might appear the political equivalent of the Fall of Man — the point in history when the politics of 'realism' and compromise begin to be replaced by the politics of holistic dogmas, and the world embarked on the fatal journey towards totalitarianism.

That is not, however, the way it seemed to liberals at the time. Everywhere, people of liberal outlook welcomed the outbreak of the Revolution. News of the fall of the Bastille is reputed to be one of the only two occasions — the other was his reading of Rousseau's *Emile* — on which Immanuel Kant varied his daily routine in Königsburg; while in Tübingen, the young Hegel joined with Holderlin and Schelling to plant a tree of liberty and dance round it singing revoutionary songs. [8]

In its beginnings, the French Revolution, like other revolutions, tried to establish its continuity with the past. It is 'precisely in such epochs of revolutionary crisis', Marx noticed, that men 'timidly conjure up the spirits of the past to help them'. And so it was that 'the Revolution of 1789—1814 draped itself alternately as the Roman Republic and the Roman Empire.' [9] A revival of the classical republican tradition, to which liberals had often turned in their struggles against despotism, formed part of the ideological preparations for 1789. It found striking visual expression in the paintings of Jacques-Louis David, who became the designer and stage-manager of great revolutionary ceremonies, but before the Revolution played a leading part in reviving classical themes and styles in painting. One picture more than any other, the *Oath of the Horatii*, exhibited by David in 1785, expressed the dedication and stern moral seriousness of the developing revolutionary opposition, which regarded the ancient regime as corrupt and decadent as well as tyrannical. This image of civic virtue made an overwhelming impact at that crucial historical moment. [10]

The classical republican tradition continued to exert an influence in the years of the Revolution itself. It was quite common to identify the king as a tyrant by calling him Tarquin or Caligula. The red bonnet worn as a sign of commitment by the *sans culottes* was a re-creation of the Phrygian cap, symbol of liberty in antiquity. Madame Roland claimed that it was reading Plutarch's *Lives* that made her a republican. In America too the new polity had consciously modelled itself on classical precedents, as the very terms republic, capitol, senate, etc. indicate, and Jefferson had sought to embody this revival of the classical republican tradition in the use of the classical style for public buildings — something which later became an empty commonplace, but had a real political meaning at this time.

It was not only in public symbolism that the old civic ideal was kept alive. The Revolution asserted the rights of the (male) individual. Yet some of the leading champions of those rights were also uneasy about the atomizing potential of modern individualism; and it was to counteract this that they stressed the unity of the nation and the sovereignty of the people as a whole, or the general will. The Abbé Sieyès wrestles with this problem in the final chapter of his famous pamphlet of 1789, *What is the Third Estate?*

On the one hand he contends, in classic individualist fashion, that 'the will of a nation . . . is the resultant of the individual wills, just as the nation is the aggregate of the individuals that compose it.' On the other hand, he recognizes, as did Benjamin Franklin, that this very individualism threatens the formation of a common will: 'At a time when public morals are in decay, when everybody seems actuated by self-interest, it is necessary . . . that . . . the assembly of a nation should be so constituted as to insulate each personal interest it contains, and ensure that the will of its majority is always consistent with the general good.' Like Rousseau, he mistrusts organized sectional interests; guilds, he suggests, should be prohibited: 'In this and in no other way can the common interest be made to dominate private interests.'[11]

The whole passage, with its echoes, conscious or unconscious, of Rousseau's *Du Contrat Social*, shows that French liberals had not yet succumbed to the illusion of a natural harmony of individual interests, but still recognized the need for that public spirit which they saw as being embodied in classical republicanism. Hence, to counterbalance the rights of the individual, Sieyès, and the Revolution itself, proclaimed the sovereignty of the nation. And hence too the fact that the famous *Declaration* is of the rights of man *and citizen*. The sense of individuals as being members of a community has not yet been entirely lost.

This same delicate balance, or tension, is present in the politics and thought of Robespierre. Robespierre — the bloodstained fanatic of popular conservative mythology — was in fact from the beginning of the Revolution an outspoken advocate of individual rights. As a member of the Assembly in 1789 he demanded that civil rights be extended to such hitherto excluded groups as Protestants, actors, and Jews: 'How can you blame the Jews for the persecutions they have suffered in certain countries? These are, on the contrary, national crimes that we must expiate by restoring to them the imprescriptible rights of man of which no human authority can deprive them.' He also opposed the restriction of the franchise and other political rights to property-holders, and affirmed his belief that 'all men *born* and *domiciled* in France are members of the body politic termed the French nation; that is to say, they are French citizens.'[12] Such demands need to be remembered when we are told that Robespierre was one of the anti-individualist fathers of modern totalitarianism.

On the other hand, there is his belief in the virtue and sovereignty of the people as a body, even to the point of suggesting that 'the morality which has disappeared among most individuals will only be rediscovered in the mass of the people and in the general interest.'[13] Like Rousseau, whose *Du Contrat Social* he knew so well, he tried to reconcile individual liberty with popular sovereignty, safeguards against tyrannical government with the need for a single national will. It is no surprise to discover that he knew ancient history, and that 'his imagination had, from an early age, been fired by the republican virtues of Brutus and the Gracchi.'[14]

But the French Revolution was perhaps the last occasion when revolutionaries felt so strongly the need to disguise the novelty of their ideas and demands by looking to antiquity for precedents — and even then the disguise is a thin one. The novelty of such slogans as 'equality' and the 'rights of man' was plain to all. It was the turning-point of modern history, and this Janus-like character, one face looking to past precedents, the other welcoming the advent of a new world and the rebirth of human nature, was typical of this transitional moment.

Along with the attempt to recreate the virtues of the classical republics went a decisive rejection of what, taking their cue from the Enlightenment, the revolutionaries regarded as 'feudal barbarism'.[15] It is true that the Revolution itself was prefaced by the last of the aristocratic revolts against absolutism, and the summoning of the Estates General for the first time since 1614 was seen as a return to the medieval constitutionalist tradition. But it was too late. The Third Estate could not accept their menial position within this antiquarian framework. Hence Sieyès' pamphlet answered his own question by asserting that the Third Estate, having been for so long *nothing* in the political order, in fact was and should be *everything*.

The actual policies of the Revolution towards feudalism and the nobility were a good deal less intransigent than such ringing declarations might suggest, just as the universalism of its concern with rights was in some ways more apparent than real. In its ambiguities and limitations the Revolution revealed the substantive concerns of the class that identified itself with the political principles of liberalism. Thus Sieyès' assertion that the rights of citizens 'belong to all' does not quite mean what it says. 'In all countries, the law prescribes certain qualifications without which one can be neither an elector nor eligible for election.' Women, for example, are 'rightly or wrongly . . . everywhere excluded' from being potential representatives. Tramps, beggars, servants, and non-naturalized foreigners are also rightly excluded. Tenants of the nobility and clergy are too dependent to be trusted with the vote. Sieyès is, in fact, blandly confident that the people as whole can be represented by that minority of the Third Estate who are rich enough to have had a 'liberal education'. Like J. S. Mill, he has great confidence in the enlightenment of the educated section of his own class.

Sieyès also advanced another, less elevated argument on behalf of the Third Estate. That was the quintessentially bourgeois claim that forms of wealth other than land were equally entitled to representation: 'do not manufactures and the arts create new riches, new taxes and a new population just as much as territory does?' Here Sieyès speaks, not for humanity, but for his class, as he does, too, when the vexed issues of property and equality are in question. He stressed that it was equality of citizenship that was being affirmed, and that this was entirely compatible with 'inequalities of wealth or ability'. Nor does a concern with the common interest 'prevent anyone, according to his natural or acquired abilities, according to more or less favourable accidents, from increasing his property with all that a prosperous fortune or a more productive labour can add to it.'[16] The rights of man are entirely compatible with the rights of property and the workings of a 'free' market.

This is equally clear in the *Declaration*, which names property as one of the four 'natural and imprescriptible rights of man', and declares it, in the final article, to be 'an inviolable and sacred right'. The original draft of Article IV was a forthright assertion of the right of every citizen to use his industry and capital as he judged to be beneficial and useful to himself, but this was replaced in the final version by a more restrained statement of the general right to liberty. Similarly, Sièyes, in his draft, wished to make explicit the distinction between equality of rights, which was acceptable, and equality of means, which was not. As Georges Lefebvre wrote, 'economic liberty, though not mentioned, is very much in its spirit.'[17]

The question of property was from the start of the Revolution in July—August 1789 to the fall of Robespierre five years later, a central problem of the greatest difficulty. The bourgeois leaders of the Revolution wanted to prosecute their campaign against feudalism. However, they did not want an attack on feudal property to turn into an attack on all property, nor the abolition of feudal privileges to lead to criticism of other forms of inequality. At the same time they needed the support of 'the people', both in the cities and the countryside. So, as Cobban has pointed out, although the distinction between feudal and non-feudal property 'was an almost impossible distinction to make', it was also absolutely necessary. The *principle* of private property had to be upheld, while at the same time popular discontents had to be assuaged.

Nevertheless, peasant discontent continued throughout the revolutionary years, and one reason for that is clear: not all of their grievances were directed against the old feudal order. They were equally resentful, and perhaps equally exploited by, the capitalist farmers, and they suffered, as did the rural poor in England at this time, from the capitalization of the countryside — from enclosures. Nor did they find that the substitution of money taxes for the old labour requirements (the *corvée*) was a great improvement. They had nothing to gain from that economists' nostrum, free trade in grain, which was introduced in 1789, and wanted rather a return to the old regulated economy. The leaders of the Revolution were incapable of responding to these discontents, not so much because they had no experience of the peasant condition as because they were fundamentally committed to the market principles of economic liberalism.[18]

Much the same problems beset them in their relations with the urban revolutionaries and the masses who supported them. The revolution which the revolutionary leaders always envisaged was thoroughly liberal in that it was committed to *economic* as well as political liberty, and to the limited measure of social equality implied by the abolition of privileges based on birth and inheritance. They believed in the great bourgeois principle of the career open to talents. By the same token they were necessarily opposed to economic equality (equality of means) and to interference with the operations of the market.

The concerns of the *sans culottes* and the mass of the people were not the same at all. The people demanded that the revolution should meet their basic needs — for cheap food, and some relief from abysmal poverty. They therefore demanded price-control of basic commodities, above all of grain and bread. This interference with the market was something to which even the Jacobins, including Robespierre, were in principle opposed. Saint-Just said in 1792: 'People are asking for a law about food supplies. Positive legislation on that subject is never wise.'[19] Robespierre too remained committed to the principle of *laissez-faire*, besides taking the typically high-minded line that popular action should be directed to political ends not 'mere' material gains. Nevertheless, he came reluctantly to recognize that there was a right to subsistence, and that society had a responsibility to see that people did not starve. He justified interference with the market by distinguishing between the necessities of life and other non-essential commodities. The latter, he thought, 'may be left to unlimited commercial speculation . . . generally, it may be assumed that the unrestricted freedom of this trade will redound to the greater profit of both the State and the individual.' But he maintained that 'Food that is necessary for man's existence is as sacred as life itself. Everything that is indispensable for its preservation is the common property of society as a whole. It is only the surplus that is private property and can be safely left to individual commercial enterprise.'[20] It was not until five months after this speech that the first *loi maximum*, controlling the price of bread, was introduced in response to further intense popular pressure. At the most radical point of the Revolution, the Jacobins were reluctantly pushed beyond orthodox liberalism, in that they agreed to what was seen as a limited and temporary measure of control. Their reluctance, as well as the speed with which, after the fall of Robespierre, the *maximums* were abolished, bear eloquent witness to the dominance of economic liberalism within the Revolution.

Although all groups, from the Jacobins to the *sans culottes* and even the small group of the so-called *enragés*, who came closer than any other to representing the attitudes of the Parisian poor, were agreed that property as an institution was not to be challenged,[21] the radicals amongst them were demanding some very substantial limitations on the right to property.

First, there was the insistence that property carried with it social obligations, and that no one should be allowed to use wealth or property to the detriment of the general good. Or, as Robespierre put it, 'freedom of trade is necessary up to the point where homicidal greed begins to misuse it.'[22] Secondly, there was a strong resentment of the rich among the poor, which had a class character even though it was not always expressed in class terms. Thus Jacques Roux said in June 1793: 'It is the rich who, for four years have made a profit out of the Revolution, it is the merchant aristocracy, more terrible than the aristocracy of nobles, by whom we are oppressed.' This was linked to a general popular belief that the inequalities of wealth that actually existed were too great, and that there therefore ought to be some redistribution of wealth. Despite the fact that a decree of March 1793 prescribed the death penalty for anyone advocating a *loi agraire* (i.e. equalization of wealth), popular demands for a maximum limit on individual fortunes continued, and two leading Jacobins, Saint-Just and Billaud-Varennes, contemplated schemes for the break-up and redistribution of large estates.[23] Robespierre asserted that 'equality of possessions is fundamentally impossible in civil society', yet he too believed that 'extreme disparities of wealth lie at the root of many ills and crimes.'[24] Among the radicals a Rousseauist egalitarianism hovered uneasily between the liberal commitment to property and its rights, and an emerging socialist awareness of the interrelations of wealth and poverty, property, power and exploitation.

Thus the French Revolution, which placed liberal notions of rights and freedoms at the centre of the political stage, also looked backward and forward beyond capitalism, and in a few brief, hectic, unforgettable years exposed some of the dilemmas and difficulties inherent in liberal thought: problems pivoted on the crucial issues of property, equality and rights. Were the 'rights of man' political and legal only, or were they to be given a social and economic content as well?

THE INTERNATIONAL IMPACT OF THE REVOLUTION

If the epoch of the Revolution, which in some respect lasts until 1848, is properly seen as the 'moment' of liberalism's most powerful and positive impact, this is in part because in this period liberal ideas transcend the conventional limits of 'politics' and dominate the imaginative culture of Europe. In the next two sections we shall consider briefly a few of the many political and cultural forms which liberalism took at this central point in its development.

By a striking irony, it was partly through the revolutionary and Napoleonic wars that the liberal principles of the Revolution were to spread. For although the satellite republics and puppet monarchies of Napoleon's Europe crumbled into dust, many of the changes they introduced proved to be irreversible. Some old states, such as the fragile republics of Venice and Genoa, and many of the petty principalities of the Rhineland, finally disappeared, along with that shadowy relic, the Holy Roman Empire. The ghettos to which Jews had been confined in such cities as Bonn, Rome, and Venice were closed down, and equal legal rights were accorded to the Jews, and, in the Netherlands, to Catholics. Slaves were set free, and feudal dues and serfdom, where they still existed in Germany and Switzerland, were abolished. Church lands were confiscated and put on the market. [25]

Another state which disappeared at this time was Poland, which Russia, Prussia and Austria carved up between them in 1795, in direct response to the attempted revolution led by Kosciuszko in 1794. Like so many other uprisings of the age, it had both a nationalist and a revolutionary character. Directed against the Russian occupation and domination which resulted from the earlier partition of the country in 1791, it also took inspiration from the French example, and the universal symbols of revolution — the caps of liberty, civic hymns and patriotic altars — were in evidence. Most significant, perhaps, was the proclamation of freedom for the serfs issued by Kosciuszko on 7 May 1794: 'Against this horde of frightened slaves we must set the imposing mass of free men. Victory, we may be sure, will go to those who fight in their own cause.' [26] But the liberal revolutionaries were too few to withstand the pressure of the landowners, and even when Poland was incorporated into the Napoleonic empire, serfdom was not successfully abolished.

'Jacobin' conspiracies in Austria and Hungary were repressed without so much difficulty. But such agitations testified that there were few corners of Europe which remained wholly immune to the infection of revolutionary ideas. In Russia A. N. Radischev published his *Journey from St Petersburg to Moscow* together with his *Ode to Liberty* in 1790. The book contained a fierce attack on serfdom, which he compared to slavery. Catherine II saw to it that he was sentenced to death for this, although this sentence was commuted to exile in Siberia. The Spanish Government responded to the Revolution in like manner. For three years from 1789 to 1792 it did all it could to prevent even news of events in France being printed in the press, and the successive French invasions of Spain provoked a strongly nationalist reaction of a largely traditional character. Despite all this, some Spanish intellectuals and administrators responded positively to the Revolution. In 1792 José Marchena published a tract attacking the Inquisition, and urging the Spanish to make their own revolution. His denunciation of superstition reads like a commentary on Goya's famous etching, *The Sleep of Reason produces Monsters*: 'Nature did not intend man to be the slave of man; superstition may put a people to sleep for an instant in the chains of slavery; but if reason awakes it, beware, hypocrites and oppressors.' Like would-be revolutionaries elsewhere in Europe, Marchena looked on the French armies not as invaders but as liberators: 'Peace and war the French carry with them, peace toward men and war on the tyrant kings.'[27] Various reformers of the 1790s were also anxious to import some of the economic ideas of Adam Smith. It was out of the ferment generated in Spain by the Napoleonic wars that there eventually appeared the first political group to be given the title of *liberals* or *liberales* — the devisers of the Spanish Constitution of 1812, which Raymond Carr has described as 'the classic liberal constitution of Latin Europe in the early nineteenth century'.[28]

In Germany, Rhineland cities such as Wurms and Mainz opened their gates to the revolutionary armies in 1792, and even the later imposition of the *Code Napoléon* was welcomed. 'Where the Code Napoleon comes there begins a new age, a new world, a new state', declared the Bavarian lawyer, Anselm von Feuerbach. The Bavarian Constitution of 1808 incorporated many of the reforms for which the Enlightenment had campaigned and the Revolution had finally made possible. It abolished both serfdom and the special privileges of the nobility, and was intended to establish the great bourgeois principles of equality before the law and equality of opportunity. The words of the chief minister, Montgelas, summarize the contents of this very liberal document: 'The law guarantees to all citizens the safety of person and property, freedom of conscience and of the press, as defined by law, equal access to all offices, ranks and benefices, a civil and criminal code that is the same for all.'[29]

Everywhere the French Revolution gave a fresh impulse to national feelings and to the desire for national autonomy, and the development of strong nationalist movements, with support from both the middle class and 'the people' may be dated from this time. The 1790s certainly marked a new chapter in the Irish national struggle. At this stage the fatal divide between the Protestant and industrialized north-eastern corner of the island and the Catholic rural mass of the population had not opened up, and the agitation for independence centred at first on Belfast, and found its outstanding leader in Theobald Wolfe Tone, a Protestant lawyer. Tone said that the Revolution 'changed in an instant the politics of Ireland . . . the French Revolution became the test of every man's political creed.'[30] But it was not so much the Revolution itself, as Paine's *Rights of Man*, which inspired a renewal and a radicalization of the struggle for Catholic emancipation and for independence. When, as in other parts of Britain after the war with France began, the radical organizations were outlawed and the

H

hope of constitutional progress faded, the United Irishmen looked to France for support in their struggle, not in vain, although all ended in disaster in the 'year of liberty', 1798. The Irish nationalists, and even Burke, had seen in the American struggle against Britain in the 1770s a cause very similar to their own, and Tone said at his trial: 'I have pursued the path chalked out by Washington in America and Kosciuszko in Poland. Like the latter I have failed to emancipate my country; and unlike both I have forfeited my life.'[31]

Some of the most striking and, in the longer term, some of the most significant responses to the Revolution, and the wars that followed, took place outside Europe altogether — above all in Latin America and the Caribbean. The flight of the Portuguese royal family to Brazil in 1807 was the event which led to Brazil gaining its independence 14 years later, and the simultaneous collapse of Spanish authority produced a similar response in the Spanish dominions in Latin America. As so often, the national movements did not originally envisage anything so radical as complete independence, but were driven towards it by the logic of events. The weakness of Spain, the interest that other powers, including Britain and the USA had in seeing the end of the Spanish empire, and in particular the end of the Spanish monopoly of trade with her colonies, combined with the dynamic leadership and military ability of José San Martin and Simon Bolivar to ensure that the liberation of Latin America was virtually complete by 1830. Bolivar himself was thoroughly read in the major philosophers of the Enlightenment — Rousseau, Voltaire, Montesquieu and Locke — and regarded Napoleon as 'the bright star of glory, the genius of liberty', until he had himself crowned emperor. It was while in Europe as a young man that he committed himself to the liberation of his native Peru.[32]

Still more remarkable was the success of the first black slave revolt against white rule in the French colony of Haiti. At that time the island of San Domingo was France's single most important colony, supplying, according to C. L. R. James, £11 million worth of France's total of £17 million worth of exports. It was, says James, 'the most profitable colony the world had ever known'.[33] And its economy was founded on the slave labour of half a million negroes.

As with other such upheavals, the black revolt against slavery began with the support of the revolutionary leaders in France, and the subsequent history of the struggle mirrors the history of France from revolutionary internationalism to Napoleonic nationalism. In February 1794 a delegation from San Domingo consisting of a black, a mulatto and a white was received with enthusiasm by the Convention in Paris, and slavery was declared abolished. The black leader, Toussaint l'Ouverture, recognized that the hopes of his people were dependent on the support and protection of France: 'It is under its flag that we are truly free and equal.' And conversely, the French came to rely on Toussaint for support against the royalists in the colony and against the British in the Caribbean, who were anxious to restore the old regime, and with it slavery. Even when, having defeated and driven out the British occupying force, Toussaint found himself finally facing Bonaparte's expedition to reconquer San Domingo for France, the black leader was unwilling to contemplate a complete break with France. But 'I took up arms for the freedom of my colour, which France alone proclaimed, but which she has no right to nullify. Our liberty is no longer in her hands: it is in our own. We will defend it or perish.'[34] Toussaint himself perished in a French prison in April 1803. Napoleon was meanwhile planning the restoration of slavery in San Domingo and the other colonies. But by the end of 1803, the blacks had finally beaten the French and obtained the independence of Haiti. Not many years later, Pietion, then ruler of Haiti, was able to offer valuable support to Bolivar.

The successful struggle of the blacks in Haiti for independence was one of the most remarkable consequences of the Revolution, and it shows, perhaps more clearly than any other single development, that the liberal ideals of individual rights and personal freedom possessed at that time a revolutionary potential which no processes of retraction or stabilization in France itself could stifle or destroy. Wordsworth was right:

> . . . Thou hast left behind
> Powers that will work for thee; air, earth, and skies;
> There's not a breathing of the common wind
> That will forget thee; thou hast great allies;
> Thy friends are exultations, agonies,
> And love, and man's unconquerable mind.
>
> (To Toussaint l'Ouverture)

REVOLUTIONARY CULTURE AND LIBERAL NATIONALISM

It is not to diminish the emancipatory achievements of the Revolution and of the movements it helped to inspire, to say that today the essence of the great revolutionary liberal dream of freedom and human brotherhood can be most directly and powerfully experienced in some of the music of Beethoven; above all, perhaps, his one opera, *Fidelio*, with its story of release from imprisonment and of injustice defeated by a woman's resolute heroism.

It is a subsidiary purpose of this book to show how politics and culture constantly interact, to the extent that it makes no sense to talk about a culture without politics, or a politics in which culture plays no part. This point was made, suitably enough, in the preface to the first issue of *The Liberal*, the magazine brought out in 1822 by Byron, Shelley, and Leigh and John Hunt: 'The object of our work is not political, except inasmuch as all writing now-a-days must involve something to that effect, the connexion between politics and all other subjects of interest to mankind having been discovered, never again to be done away.'[35] At no point is this more clearly true than in the revolutionary epoch between the 1780s and 1848. This is the moment at which the grand ideas of liberalism seize hold of the European imagination, but are also seized by the imagination, and developed into some of their most powerful, enduring and exalted forms.

Let us start with the image of the prison, for this is at the very centre of the liberal imagination. The prison is the symbol and essence of the oppression which militant liberalism seeks to destroy, and the prisoner is the clearest, most incontrovertible example of the person whose freedom has been denied or taken away. The Bastille may not have contained many prisoners in July 1789, but it stood for a whole system of cruel and arbitrary oppression, and it was entirely apt that the age of liberal triumphs should have begun with the capture and destruction of a prison and the release of its inmates. As Trilling noted, when discussing this theme: 'the prison is an actuality before it is ever a symbol.'

The prison, both as reality and as metaphor for a wider oppression, is what inspires some of Goya's most powerful drawings and etchings, while it provides the entire setting for *Fidelio*. This story of a wife who disguises herself as a man in order to rescue her unjustly imprisoned husband is based on a French libretto of the 1790s, which was in turn based on an actual episode during the Terror, which the librettist J. N. Bouilly had witnessed. This is not the opera's only link with the French Revolution. *Fidelio* is a version of the genre of rescue-from-prison operas which had become particularly popular with French audiences in the 1790s, of which Cherubini, a composer whom Beethoven particularly admired, was a leading exponent. Indeed Bouilly had already provided Cherubini with the libretto for an opera with a very similar story, *Les Deux Journées*. Nor is it without significance that the hero of the story is a woman, and that the full title of the original libretto was *Léonore, ou l'Amour Conjugal*.

What Beethoven produced is not only a drama of *individual* heroism, but also of collective oppression and liberation. Act I ends with the prisoners stumbling out of their dark cells into daylight and fresh air, and singing longingly of freedom, 'the forbidden word', before the governor of the prison sends them back into darkness once again. The opening of Act II evokes that darkness in its deepest form, the secret cell where Florestan, Leonora/Fidelio's husband is held in solitary confinement and where he is to be secretly murdered — in fact to 'disappear'. The murder plan is thwarted by Leonora armed with a gun, and by the arrival of the minister, signalled by the famous trumpet call which also occurs at the climax of the Leonora No. 3 Overture — a call which, as Trilling wrote, 'sounds through the century, the signal for the opening of gates, for a general deliverance'.[36] In the final scene, darkness gives way to a blaze of C major light. It is Leonora who removes Florestan's shackles, and all rejoice in the triumph of justice and conjugal love.

To some sophisticated latter-day liberals, used to seeing nothing in life but shades of grey, Beethoven's plain contrasts between justice and injustice, liberty and oppression, darkness and light, no doubt seem simplistic — at any rate outside the theatre. But it is this passionate identification with great and fundamental issues which allows us to see Beethoven, in his music, as the very essence of the heroic, emancipatory spirit of the revolution. As Hugh Ottaway wrote: 'to us Beethoven *is* the Revolution.'[37] The same spirit is to be found in the *Egmont* Overture, written for Goethe's play about the sixteenth-century struggle for freedom in the Netherlands, and in the Ninth Symphony, with its setting of the poem which Schiller had originally called an *Ode to Freedom*, before censorship made a less dangerous title necessary — and which was sung to the tune of the Marseillaise by German radicals in the 1790s. The Third Symphony, the *Eroica*, was to have been dedicated to Napoleon, but Beethoven like Bolivar was disillusioned by Bonaparte's decision to make himself an emperor. Beethoven had expressed his fundamental political beliefs in some lines he wrote in 1792:

> To help wherever one can.
> Love liberty above all things.
> Never deny the truth
> Even at the foot of the throne.[38]

The 'withdrawal' of the composer's last years was not, as some would like to suggest, a purely 'spiritual' affair: Beethoven was in fact withdrawing from the real anti-liberal world of reaction after the final defeat of Napoleon and the revolutionary process at Waterloo.[39]

The Enlightenment imagery of darkness and light is found elsewhere in music, in, for example, Mozart's *Magic Flute* and Haydn's *Creation*, both works of the 1790s. *The Magic Flute*, composed in 1791, is full of the symbolism associated with freemasonry, which was at that time an organized expression of Enlightenment ideology. It celebrates, in music of sublime clarity, human brotherhood, and the triumph of the light of reason over the darkness of superstition and error. But nowhere does the central image of light find a more dazzling expression than at the opening of *The Creation*, where, after a graphic orchestral evocation of chaos and darkness, God utters the decree 'let there be light', and the chorus dispels at a stroke every hint of uncertainty with a sustained C major shout on the single word 'light'.

Lux et Tenebris was the title of a drawing in which Goya celebrated the liberal revolution of 1820 in Spain. The contrast between the darkness of cruelty, bigotry and superstition, and the light of rationality, which, as John Berger has said, he connected with 'dignity, grace and pleasure',[40] dominates much of his graphic work from his personal crisis of the 1790s onwards. Inevitably in the Spanish context his particular targets were clerical obscurantism and superstition, and the ignorance and credulity which they so relentlessly exploited.

If the *Disasters of War* are the most powerful expression of his humane horror at cruelty and barbarism, the *Caprichos*, which owe something to the ideas of the reformer Jovellanos, contain much of his scorn and hatred for superstition. *The Sleep of Reason . . .* was originally intended as a frontispiece for the *Caprichos*. Above all, perhaps, there are the unpublished drawings done after 1814, which, as Gwyn Williams says, 'are explicitly, indeed harshly, *liberal*; their anti-clericalism is ferocious.'[41] Goya returns in these drawings to the theme of victims of the Inquisition, but also includes a remarkable series of drawings of prisoners, followed by some in which the liberal revolution of 1820 and the arrival of liberty — *divina liberdad* — are depicted and celebrated. Goya's achievement is the more extraordinary in that, being born in 1746, he had reached maturity as a man and artist well before the Revolution, and, had he died in 1790, would have been considered a quintessentially eighteenth-century painter in a normally elegant vein. As it was, he responded to history and continued to work produc-tively until well into his seventies. And, as one of these late drawings shows, he knew what the price of being a liberal then could be.

The dynamic of revolutionary liberalism was not exhausted in a single generation. In literature, the cause was upheld in the period after Waterloo — and later — by poets such as Shelley and Byron, Pushkin and Heine, and the great essayist William Hazlitt. In painting, Delacroix and Géricault both responded powerfully, in more romantic modes than David, to such events as the Greek struggle for independence, the French Revolution of 1830, and the horrors of the continuing traffic in slaves between Africa and the Caribbean.[42] Berlioz commemorated the 1830 Revolution in his *Symphonie Funèbre et Triomphale*, while Chopin, Liszt, and above all, Verdi were three of many composers who in their music expressed their identification with the liberal nationalism of the mid-nineteenth century.

The Napoleonic period, and even more the period after his defeat, were difficult times for liberals. For while no democrat or egalitarian could fail to see that Bonaparte had in many respects abandoned or betrayed the principles of the Revolution, they could also see that those who triumphed over him in 1815 were of a far more reactionary character. It was exactly these ambivalent feelings that Shelley expressed in his sonnet 'Feelings of a Republican on the Fall of Bonaparte'. Hazlitt, who actually wrote a biography of Napoleon, gave way to a feeling of despondency:

For my part, I started in life with the French Revolution, and I have lived, alas! to see the end of it. But I did not foresee this result. My sun arose with the first dawn of liberty, and I did not think how soon both must set. . . .I little dreamed that long before mine was set, the sun of liberty would turn to blood, or set once more in the night of despotism. Since then, I confess, I have no longer felt myself young, for with that my hopes fell.

('On the Feeling of Immortality in Youth')

There were, however, still concrete grounds for hope, not least in the struggles for national independence in Italy and Greece. Byron, Shelley's friend and fellow exile in Italy, was involved with both. Ever since Hazlitt wrote dismissively in *The Spirit of the Age* of Byron's 'preposterous *liberalism*', and contrasted his professed politics with his 'genius', which was 'haughty and aristocratic', it has been the custom to be patronizing about Byron's politics, and to over-emphasize his aristocratic attitudes. Certainly he was not free from patrician disdain, as evidenced by his characterization of democracy as 'an Aristocracy of Blackguards',[43] and his view that popular radicals like Cobbett and Henry ('Orator') Hunt were 'infamous Scoundrels . . . no better than Jack Cade, or Wat Tyler — and to be dealt with accordingly'.[44] Against this must be set his sturdy defence of the Luddites, or framebreakers of his home county of Nottingham, in his maiden speech to the House of Lords in February 1812, when he challenged the very attitude which stigmatized such people as a 'mob':

You call these men a mob. . . . [but] It is the mob that labour in your fields and serve in your houses — that man your navy, and recruit your army — that have enabled you to defy all the world, and can also defy you when neglect and calamity have driven them to despair! You may call the people a mob; but do not forget that a mob too often speaks the sentiments of the people.[45]

From his schooldays, when he had a bust of Napoleon in his rooms, to the last years of his life, when he named his boat the *Bolivar*, he was consistently on the liberal side, and if his attitude towards democracy and the people was ambiguous and spiced with *hauteur*, that was not uncharacteristic of many liberals, bourgeois as well as aristocratic. Few liberals of later generations showed as much open sympathy for 'the mob' as Byron had done in 1812.

In Ravenna in 1821 he was much involved with the *Carbonari*, the secret society of Italian nationalists which waged a sporadic guerilla war against the occupying Austrians in the early 1820s, and helped launch insurrections in Naples in 1820 and Piedmont in 1821:

. . . my lower apartments are full of their bayonets, fusils, cartridges, and what not. I suppose that they consider me as a depot, to be sacrificed in case of accidents. It is no great matter, supposing that Italy could be liberated, who or what is sacrificed. It is a grand object — the very *poetry* of politics. Only think — a free Italy!!!⁴⁶

His final, fatal involvement was with the Greek struggle for independence against the Turkish empire, and it was in Greece that he spent the last nine months of his life. However mixed his motives for involvement may have been — and most of us do not expose our motives so clearly as Byron — the seriousness of his commitment can hardly be doubted. He did not romanticize the Greeks. He had ample experience of their weaknesses and lack of unity. He was realistic: 'We must not look always too closely at the men who are to benefit by our exertions in a good cause, or God knows we shall seldom do much good in this world.'⁴⁷ His mission was to channel and organize aid, some of it from his own resources, some from the Greek Committee in London, to the Greeks, and, if possible, to unite their quarrelsome factions. It was a difficult task, but his disinterested patriotism — 'I did not come here to join a faction but a nation'⁴⁸ and his death in April 1824, did help to unite the Greeks and focus their energies on the struggle for liberation.

That struggle had much in common with other national independence movements of the time. It first emerged in the 1790s, when one of its early heroes, Velestinlis Rigas, published in Vienna in 1797 his revolutionary manifesto for Greece. It contained a declaration of the rights of man which followed closely the French prototype. Similarly, his projected constitution was modelled on the French constitutions of 1793 and 1795, just as the constitution actually drawn up by the Greeks in 1822 was also based on the French one of 1795. Finally Rigas had composed a martial hymn, a kind of Greek *Marseillaise*, which became widely popular in the years that followed.

Initially the Greeks looked to the French for support. In the end it was the British Government which, for power-political reasons of its own, was to play the more decisive role in the crucial decade of the 1820s. But at the time when Byron went to Greece, actual support came, not from the British Government, but from the liberal and utilitarian Philhellenes in Britain who had set up the London Greek Committee. This committee was an expression of the general liberal support for nationalism which was so characteristic of the age. Liberals then regarded personal and national freedom as indivisible parts of a single struggle for liberty. And they recognized that national independence would usually have to be fought for. Therefore they bent their energies to providing the money and supplies necessary to wage a war of liberation.

A little later in the century the liberal response to Italian nationalism was comparably enthusiastic, and in this instance we find a full and memorable fusion of art with liberal politics in the work of Italy's greatest composer, Verdi. Verdi was himself a passionate patriot, and even allowed himself to serve briefly as a deputy in the newly independent Italy's Parliament in the early 1860s. But his real commitment, and his liberalism, were expressed in his music and his choice of subjects.[49] His deep response to collective oppression and suffering is articulated in famous choruses, like that of the Hebrews exiled in Babylon in *Nabucco* (Va Pensiero), and that of the Scottish exiles in *Macbeth* (Patria Oppressa), but also in the scene in *Don Carlo* in which Posa denounces Philip II to his face for the devastation his armies are bringing to the Netherlands, and urges the king to allow that country its freedom. Both Schiller's play and Verdi's adaptation of it testify to the symbolic importance which the Dutch struggle for independence possessed for a later liberalism. It was not accidental that Verdi's choruses of oppression were interpreted by Italian audiences as comments on their own situation under continuing Austrian rule.

Verdi was much excited by the events of 1848 in Italy, when the Milanese rose against the Austrians and drove them out of the city for a while, and the King of Piedmont expelled the Austrians from Venice. He wrote a patriotic song which he sent to Mazzini, but his more profound response was another opera, *La Battaglia di Legnano*. This referred to the battle of 1176 in which the Lombard league of northern Italian cities led by Milan had defeated the German emperor, Frederick Barbarossa. The opera is full of patriotic choruses, oaths of dedication to the national cause, and a particularly powerful scene in which the Milanese leaders appeal, in vain, to the people of Como to sink old civic rivalries in the common national cause — a theme which recurs in the great council chamber scene in *Simon Boccanegra*. The opera is far from being merely a piece of ephemeral tub-thumping, and contains much fine music.

The other major liberal theme in Verdi's work is his detestation of clerical intolerance and cruelty. This is particularly clear in two operas in which public themes are central — *Don Carlo* and *Aida*. In the former it is the Grand Inquisitor who is given the most chilling music in the score, and who uses the power of the church to prevent either humanitarianism or family feeling from diluting Philip's commitment to stamping out 'heresy'. Similarly in *Aida* it is the priests who throughout the opera call for harshness, punishment and vengeance, and here too the music as well as the words convey this meaning.

It is illuminating to contrast Verdi's handling of such political situations with that of his best-known successor, Puccini. Two at least of Puccini's operas handle situations with clear political dimensions — *Madama Butterfly* and *Tosca*. Puccini makes little or nothing of them. *Tosca* is set in Rome in 1800, just after a counter-revolution based partly on British naval intervention had destroyed the Roman republic, and Scarpia, the chief of police, had instituted a reign of terror against the republicans. The opera hinges on Scarpia's determination to hunt down the former consul of the republic, Angelotti. It is not hard to imagine what Verdi would have made of the themes of oppression, freedom and patriotism implicit in such a situation. With the dramatist Sardou, and following him, Puccini, the story becomes an ugly melodrama of sadism, lust and revenge. There is a significant contraction of scope: the public is reduced to the private. But this is everywhere the trend in the later nineteenth century. In the 1860s and 1870s Verdi's heroic liberalism and political awareness are already almost an anachronism.

As a final illustration of the extent of the liberal permeation of European culture in the first half of the century, I will briefly consider two more poets, Pushkin and Heine. The comparison between Pushkin and Byron has become so much a commonplace that it is almost instinctively resisted by those who know most about either poet, or both. Nevertheless, it has some validity. There are many similarities in character and lifestyle. Byron died at thirty-six, Pushkin at thirty-eight, and both had by then come to feel old and weary beyond their years. Byron's death could not match the futility of Pushkin's death in a duel, but that in itself is a reflection of the backwardness of Russian society at that time. Pushkin had a considerable, though qualified, admiration for the older poet, whom he first read with great excitement in 1820, and his poem 'Farewell to the Sea' commemorates the deaths of two heroes, Napoleon and Byron. Like Byron, Pushkin was in some ways a child of the Enlightenment, and he was much influenced by the satirical and blasphemous poetry of Voltaire.

Pushkin developed liberal opinions at an early age, and because he was uninhibited in expressing them, the whole pattern of his life as a writer was shaped by the repressive response of the Tsarist police and censors. Much of his work could not be published in his lifetime, nor, indeed, for many years after. By the age of twenty-one his outspoken views had earned him a period of exile which lasted from 1820 to 1824, and was followed by a further two years of exile under stricter surveillance. During this period he was in contact with the Decembrists, the secret societies of army officers who staged the rising against the autocracy in December 1825. Several of these officers, questioned afterwards about the sources of their liberal ideas, mentioned Pushkin, and but for his absence from St Petersburg at the time, he would probably have been convicted along with them. He identified himself with the exiled and imprisoned rebels, and sent them a poem beginning 'Deep in Siberia's mines, let naught / Subdue your proud and patient spirit', to which Prince Alexander Odoevsky replied:

> Our grievous toil will not be lost,
> The spark will quicken into flame;
> Our people, blindfolded no more,
> A new allegiance will proclaim.

'And, in a cruel Age, I sang of Liberty' wrote Pushkin towards the end of his life, but in Pushkin's own manuscript this line read 'And, like Radischev, sang of liberty'. Pushkin knew to which tradition be belonged. [50]

Heinrich Heine, born a little over a year before Pushkin, began by sharing with him many of the common radical liberal responses: admiration for Napoleon, and an intoxication with the idea of freedom. He looked forward to emancipation on a global scale: 'Not merely that of the Irish, the Greeks, the Jews of Frankfurt, the blacks of the West Indies and suchlike oppressed people, but the emancipation of the whole world, particularly of Europe, which has now come of age.' Freedom, he said, is the 'religion of our age'; the French are its 'chosen people', for 'it is in their language that the first gospels and dogmas have been recorded'; and 'Paris is the new Jerusalem.' [51]

It was in the new Jerusalem that Heine spent most of his life after 1830, and his social experience, therefore, was not that of a backward feudal autocracy, but of a rapidly industrializing society in which new forms of class conflict were becoming central. He saw that it was the people who played the leading part in the revolutionary upheavals of the day, but that in effect they were fighting not for themselves but for the bourgeoisie who, in 1830 as before, reaped the major benefits. He was convinced that this could not last: 'But make no mistake about it, when the tocsin sounds again and the people run to arms, this time they will be fighting for themselves and will demand their well-deserved reward.'

This was a prospect which aroused in Heine very mixed and complex feelings. On the one hand he felt and understood the sufferings of the working class, and could identify with them, as in his *Ballad of the Silesian Weavers*. He accepted that justice demanded that in the coming 'great duel between the dispossessed and the aristocracy of property', the dispossessed ought to triumph. He also dreaded such a triumph, writing on one occasion to a friend: 'I am very afraid of the horrors of proletarian rule, and I confess to you that fear has made me conservative.' He had the bourgeois artist's distaste for popular crudity and philistinism: 'I intend it not at all figuratively, I mean it literally, when I say that if my hand is shaken by the people I will wash it afterwards.' [52] Heine was generally regarded as a wild revolutionary — an impression which was probably strengthened by his friendship with Marx in the 1840s — but in reality he was a radical liberal, who articulated with exceptional sensitivity and clarity the classical ambivalence of the cultured radical liberal towards the rise of the working class. In this respect Heine lived in his own life the change in the ethos of liberalism, from the liberating enthusiasm of the early part of the century to the more cautious and anxious mood of the mid-century, when it became clear that, in the hands of the working class, the grand ideas of the Revolution, rights, liberation and equality, would be extended in the direction of socialism and a challenge to the hegemony of the bourgeoisie. But this is to anticipate the themes of a later chapter.

12

The Moment of the French Revolution: Crisis and Division

In the last chapter I discussed the largely positive developments of liberalism in the period following the French Revolution; there were, however, at the same time, other developments of a more ambiguous and even negative character. First there was the fragmentation of the liberal political tradition, of which the Revolution itself was the catalyst. Secondly, there was the rise to dominance of liberal political economy.

The essence of the crisis within liberalism after 1789 can be tersely summarized: the Revolution had created a situation in which liberal changes were now possible, but it was only popular, or 'mob', action which had achieved this. The experience of other societies proved to be much the same as that of France. The middle class were seldom strong enough to win liberal reforms on their own. They needed to enlist popular support. But once enlisted, or stirred up, the 'lower orders' usually turned out to have aspirations that ran well beyond liberal reforms. What then was to be the liberal attitude towards 'the people', or towards popular rule, that is, democracy? As we have seen, these were not new issues, but after 1789 popular political activity and the emergence of the urban working class gave them an entirely new urgency, and they were to be the cause of quite fundamental divisions within the liberal tradition.

One early and positive response was simply forthright faith in the people. Bentham, perhaps surprisingly, was an example of this. The Revolution made Bentham a democrat, and in 1790 he wrote: 'I have not the horror of the people. I do not see in them that savage monster which their detractors dream of.'[1] Much of Wordsworth's earlier poetry is imbued with a similar democratic faith. Thirty years later this faith was being kept alive by Hazlitt: '*Vox populi vox Dei*, is the rule of all good Government: for in that voice, truly collected and freely expressed (not when it is made the servile echo of a corrupt Court, or a designing Minister) we have all the sincerity and all the wisdom of the community.'[2] Charles James Fox was removed from the Privy Council for proposing the toast of 'our sovereign, the people' at a dinner, and it was the Whigs who set up the Association of the Friends of the People in 1792, although these Friends kept their distance from more popularly-based organizations, and would have preferred that they, the Friends, should act *for* the people rather than that the people should act for themselves.[3] Besides, it was unclear, as usual, who was included in 'the people', and who was not. Nevertheless, increasingly a rift grew between those who were democrats because, in the last resort, they trusted popular judgement, or accepted it, and those who were not because they did not. The rift was reflected in the splits and divisions within the Whig party in the 1790s, and in the public debate over the Revolution and political principles between Burke and his critics, notably Paine, Mary Wollstonecraft and Sir James Mackintosh.

BURKE AND THE WHIGS

In the process of fragmentation Edmund Burke played a central part. That Burke *was* a Whig can easily be overlooked, so fully appropriated has he been into the Conservative tradition. All too many subsequent British conservative writers have done little more than paraphrase Burke in rather less sonorous prose; and his dominance has been such that even a proclaimed democratic socialist like Richard Crossman once called him 'not the philosopher of British conservatism, but of British political life from Right to Left'.[4] But it is precisely the ease with which Burke could move from a relatively liberal Whiggism to a fiercely counter-revolutionary conservatism that is so significant, not only in his own case, but also in the subsequent history of liberalism.

In his earlier political career Burke had argued the necessity of party in politics, he had defended the American cause in the years leading up to the break with Britain, and had argued that the break had to be accepted. He ¹ erefore had opposed the attempt to regain the American colonies through war. He supported the cause of equal rights and emancipation for Catholics in his native Ireland, and also the abolition of the slave trade. On one occasion he incurred considerable odium by opposing the execution of two men convicted of homosexual practices.

But although Burke had a reputation for liberalism, he had never been a believer in universal principles or rights, but in the preservation of whatever rights and customs had already been established. It took Burke only a short time to be convinced that the French Revolution involved, not the extension or renewal of existing traditions and institutions, but their destruction in the name of new and universal principles — not the rights of Frenchmen, but the rights of man.

It appeared to him, even by October 1789, that in France 'the Elements which compose Human Society seem all to be dissolved, and a world of Monsters to be produced in the place of it.' He was most alarmed, however, by the prediction of Paine (in a letter to him in January 1790) that 'the Revolution in France is certainly a Forerunner to other Revolutions in Europe.'[5] It was the possibility of this contagion spreading to Britain, through the medium of radical agitators like Paine and Richard Price, and with the perhaps unwitting connivance of Whigs like Fox, that appalled him, and led to the writing and publication of the *Reflections on the Revolution in France* in 1790. Sir James Mackintosh called it, accurately enough, 'the manifesto of a counter-revolution'.[6]

A book, even one so powerfully written as the *Reflections*, and so well received by conservative opinion, would not necessarily have had great political consequences. But Burke was a politician, and his book was only one ingredient in the campaign which he waged consistently in the early 1790s to get the Whigs to support the Pitt Government's anti-French policies abroad and repressive measures at home, and to persuade the Government to commit itself to a war to destroy the Revolution. Burke was committed to counter-revolution, and he could not therefore tolerate Fox's ambivalent attitude towards the Revolution. The famous clash of views between these two old friends and political colleagues, which came during a parliamentary debate in May 1791, was bound to have come at some stage, given their deep differences; but it was Burke who insisted that it must mean also the end of their friendship. In due course there followed the defection of the more conservative Whigs to make up a coalition with Pitt's Tories, leaving Fox at the head of the rump of the more loyal and more radical Whigs.

Fox has had at best a grudging press from the historians, while Burke's 'far-sightedness' and other qualities, have received lavish praise.[7] But Fox is a crucial figure in British political history. He refused to be seduced by the now all-too-familiar appeals for national unity in a time of crisis. He saw that the Revolution and the war that followed would be used as the pretext for an attack on political liberties at home; so he believed that the duty of the Whigs was to remain in opposition and defend civil and political freedom as far as they could. Neither he nor his followers were democrats, let alone Jacobins. Fox was only lukewarm even about the reform of Parliament. The Foxites were mainly aristocrats who kept their distance from the plebeian radicals. Nevertheless their stand in the 1790s renewed the old association of the Whigs with the principle of liberty, and so began the transformation of Whiggery into nineteenth-century liberalism. As early as 1792, Lord Holland, Fox's nephew, was rejecting the idea that the mere membership of one of the old Whig families (such as his own) was sufficient qualification to make you a Whig. Principle was what counted now.[8]

But this does not mean that Burke and his allies should be written out of the liberal genealogy. For one thing Burke was extravagantly venerated by many nineteenth-century British liberals, who clearly did not regard him as simply a conservative. In fact what Burke did was to articulate, for the first time, many of the anti-revolutionary and anti-radical sentiments, which then became the stock-in-trade of respectable liberalism as much as of conservatism in the century that followed. Challenged by the Revolution and the reviving radicalism of the 1780s and 1790s, Burke made an uncompromising defence of property. It is in the nature of property to be unequal. The right to inherit property is that aspect of it which 'tends the most to the perpetuation of society itself'.[9] The dominance of 'large proprietors' in politics was wise and justified. The idea that each man or person should count equally in politics Burke dismisses scornfully as mere 'arithmetic' (p. 141). Burke was so concerned to protect property that he was entirely opposed to parliamentary reform, and might even have preferred to see the electorate *reduced* in size.[10] He viewed with horror the appearance in the French Assembly of large numbers of ordinary lawyers: 'the inferior, unlearned, mechanical, merely instrumental members of the profession', along with 'country clowns' and 'traders' who 'had never known any thing beyond their counting-house' (pp. 130—1). Along with the American Founding Fathers, Burke was one of the first to put forward the idea of democracy as tyranny: 'I hate tyranny, at least I think so; but I hate it most where most are concerned in it. The tyranny of a multitude is but a multiplied tyranny.'[11] This theme was to be most strongly developed by liberal writers like de Tocqueville and the younger Mill.

Burke was not generally a reactionary, nor was his response to revolution wholly negative. Against the revolutionary project of wholesale change he sets the idea of piecemeal reform within the context of established traditions and institutions — 'At once to preserve and reform' (p. 280). Reform is 'a direct application of a remedy to the grievance complained of'. This may be regarded as the quintessence of conservative flexibility, but it came to be adopted by liberals as well, as an alternative to the revolutionary or radical perspective.

Burke wrote scornfully of 'the homicide philanthropy of France', and suggested that the supposedly benign revolutionaries were in fact sacrificing the real benefits of real people in the present, for the sake of 'the *future and uncertain* benefit of persons who *only exist in idea*.'[12] This, he believed, was the outcome of the doctrinaire, abstract, theoretical approach to politics which the revolutionaries had learnt from the Enlightenment. This hostility to 'abstract' principles and grand designs has become part of the common currency of conservatism. But these conservative elements are also absorbed into an increasingly anti-revolutionary liberal outlook in the later nineteenth century and after.

It is true that Burke's defence of prejudice and superstition, and his lack of faith in individual reason mark him out as a conservative rather than a liberal. But it should be noted that, for all his apparent espousal of an ordered, stable community based on land-ownership, Burke was equally strongly committed to the new political economy of Adam Smith, and to the harsh treatment of poverty and need that it was taken to imply. If labour is a commodity, as Burke asserted it was, then 'the impossibility of the subsistence of a man, who carries his labour to a market, is totally beside the question. . . . The only question is, what is it worth to the buyer?' He denied that governments could help to relieve poverty, for that would be to interfere with 'the laws of commerce, which are the laws of nature and consequently the laws of God'. [13] There is not much sign of conservative paternalism here.

RADICAL LIBERALISM FROM PAINE TO SHELLEY

Paine's relationship to the central liberal tradition is one of exceptional historical interest. On the one hand in many respects we can 'place' him as a radical who does not finally move beyond a liberal outlook. On the other, in his militant 'levelling' egalitarianism, his concern for the economic condition of the people, and the welfare measures he proposes in Part II of the *Rights of Man*, he points towards a radicalism which is specifically working-class and even socialist. These were the elements which made a particularly powerful appeal to his vast popular readership. This ambivalence locates Paine at the very margin of the liberal tradition.

Despite this, Paine can be seen as essentially liberal and bourgeois, in so far as his radicalism is political rather than economic, and anti-feudal rather than anti-capitalist. His targets are kings, priests and aristocrats, and the system of hereditary privilege, bolstered by superstition and ignorance, which they sustained. War, he firmly believed, was the product of the old system of government, of dynastic rivalries: 'Man is not the enemy of man, but through the medium of a false system of Government.' [14] Commercial rivalries did not come into it. On the contrary, Paine believed, as did Adam Smith, that free, unrestricted trade between nations could only be mutually beneficial:

> In all my publications, where the matter would admit, I have been an advocate for commerce, because I am a friend to its effects. It is a pacific system, operating to cordialize mankind, by rendering nations, as well as individuals, useful to each other. . . . If commerce were permitted to act to the universal extent it is capable, it would extirpate the system of war. (p. 234)

Paine was also an 'advocate for commerce' because he made no class division between the capitalist, merchant or property-owner and the landless labourer or proletarian. To him they all belonged to the useful productive part of society, which could unite against the old order (see p. 148). Paine hated hereditary privilege because it offended against the principle that rewards should be earned by merit and hard work; and he accepted the consequence of this — that a high degree of *economic* equality was not possible:

> That property will ever be unequal is certain. Industry, superiority of talents, dexterity of management, extreme frugality, fortunate opportunities, or the opposite, or the means of those things, will ever produce that effect, without having recourse to the harsh, ill-sounding names of avarice and oppression. . . . All that is required with respect to property is to obtain it honestly, and not to employ it criminally. [15]

This was a view which was widely shared among radicals at that time. A Leeds broadside of 1793, for example, explicitly demanded 'Equality of Rights, not an Equality of Property', and *An Explanation of the Word Equality*, published by the Manchester Constitutional Society, the year before, spelt out this distinction with great care and emphasis. No threat to property as such was intended. [16]

For Paine, taxation was one of the most obnoxious aspects of the old order, and it was 'the enormous expense of governments' which was driving people into opposition and revolt (p. 140). Good government should be cheap. He shared the *laissez-faire* liberal belief in minimal government, because he also shared the conviction that society was essentially a self-regulating mechanism which functioned best when least interfered with. The whole of the first chapter of Part II of the *Rights of Man* is in fact a restatement of the liberal view that, as he puts it in *Common Sense*, government is at best 'but a necessary evil', [17] and that men in pursuit of their own interests automatically promote the general good. Paine saw a 'nation' as being 'composed of distinct, unconnected individuals, following various trades, employments and pursuits', haphazardly interacting with each other, [18] yet in such a way as to produce social harmony: 'But how often is the natural propensity to society disturbed or destroyed by the operations of government!' (p. 187). Paine stands midway between *laissez-faire* liberalism, with its belief in minimal government, and anarchism, with its belief in the malevolent effects of government. It is only a short step from Paine to Godwin, whose *Enquiry concerning Political Justice* was in part a response to *Rights of Man*.

If Paine's thought is liberal in so many respects, it would nevertheless be wrong to underestimate his radicalism. For Paine was a thorough revolutionary. 'A share in two revolutions is living to some purpose' he wrote to Washington, when the French Revolution broke out. He believed that revolutions were necessary to establish the rights of man, and at a dinner held by the Revolution Society in London in 1791 he proposed a toast to 'The Revolution of the World'. He identified himself unhesitatingly with the people and the rights of the people, and while he defended property as an institution, he was explicit that political rights attached not to property but to persons (or, at least, men). If there is 'equality of rights', Paine believed that 'property is secure in consequence.'[19]

Finally, and most fascinatingly, in the influential second part of the *Rights of Man* he put forward a series of proposals for welfare benefits for the poor, for children, for education and old age, which amount to a remarkably comprehensive scheme of state support for need. Paine is much concerned to show that these proposals will actually cost *less* than the old, expensive system of government, but nevertheless he here by implication contradicts his own belief in minimal government, and he is driven to do so by his commitment to the relief of popular distress. Whether, had he lived longer, or later, he would have evolved a theory of intervention to justify this, we cannot know. But this may be the first appearance of that contradiction between an anti-interventionist theory and an increasingly interventionist practice, which was to be one hallmark of nineteenth-century legislative history. Paine stands at the very point where the divide between radical democrats and the more cautious and conservative liberals begins. He helps to create the radical democratic tradition, but retains in his thinking much of bourgeois liberalism, which associated taxation with tyranny, and freedom with free trade.

Shelley was a direct inheritor of that radical democratic tradition from Paine, and from Godwin and Wollstonecraft, the parents of his second wife. He also represents that fusion of art with politics so typical of liberalism at its apogee. Shelley's political analysis, even more than Paine's, is a conflation of Enlightenment rationalism and liberalism with an emerging socialist class-consciousness. Shelley shares to the full the Enlightenment's hatred of kings, priests and organized religion, as can be seen, for example, in his *Ode to Liberty*, written in 1820 in response to the revolutions in Spain and Naples. And when, at the age of twenty, he went to Ireland to campaign for Irish independence in 1812, he used virtually the same words as Paine when he declared that 'Government is an evil' and 'Society is produced by the wants' but 'government by the wickedness...of man'.

Even at this early date Shelley was concerned not only with political and religious freedom, but also with 'the miseries of the Irish poor' and with economic inequality: 'Nature never intended that there should be such a thing as a poor man or a rich one.'[20] And when we come to the political poems of 1819, we find that while the old enemies remain in view, Shelley has moved beyond the liberal definitions of 'slavery' and 'freedom' to more materialist conceptions. Of freedom he writes in *The Mask of Anarchy*:

> For the labourer thou art bread,
> And a comely table spread
> From his daily labour come
> In a neat and happy home.

Thou art clothes, and fire, and food
For the trampled multitude —
No — in countries that are free
Such starvation cannot be
As in England now we see.

while slavery is defined conversely in terms of hunger and poverty, the exploitation of labour and the 'mind-forg'd manacles' of which Blake had written years before. The *Song to the Men of England* is based on a clear concept of exploitation, and of a class conflict between those who produce wealth and those who appropriate and use it: 'The seed ye sow, another reaps / The wealth ye find another keeps . . .' Mary Shelley's comment on the poems of 1819 was that 'He believed that a clash between the two classes of society was inevitable, and he eagerly ranged himself on the people's side.'[21] Significantly, however, it was the early *Queen Mab*, a work much more in the tradition of eighteenth-century radicalism, with its denunciations of 'Kings, priests, and statesmen' which became 'the Chartists' Bible'; although in Part V, with its accompanying prose notes, Shelley makes a powerful attack on the dominance of the market, the reduction of work to mechanical repetition, and the conversion even of human beings into commodities — Shelley appends a note on prostitution and its connection with indissoluble marriage. And there is more than one hostile reference to Adam Smith: 'The harmony and happiness of man / Yields to the wealth of nations. . . ' (lines 79—80).

His attack on political economy can be connected with his better known critique in *A Defence of Poetry* of 'the calculating faculty', and of narrow conceptions of utility and knowledge which leaves no place for the imagination or for poetry. It may be said that this famous essay belongs to the history of romantic responses to industrial capitalism, but liberalism's tendency to identify itself with both free-market capitalism, and with reason and science, gives Shelley's essay its relevance to our theme. It is one of the classic reference points for any discussion of the difficult relationship between liberalism and imagination.

THE FIRST MANIFESTO OF FEMINISM

It is justice, not charity that is wanting in the world![22] Although one of Paine's first published works had been a protest against the subordination of women, it is nevertheless unclear from the *Rights of Man* whether women were included under that heading. And it was probably in part as a response to this neglect of women's rights even by male *radicals* that Mary Wollstonecraft wrote the *Vindication of the Rights of Woman*, which appeared almost simultaneously with the second part of the *Rights of Man* early in 1792. The issue has a uniquely ironic relation to liberalism. Liberalism, which takes as its focus the individual and the rights and freedom of the individual, ought logically to make no distinction between persons on the ground of sex, any more than of nationality, race or status. And it has been precisely the refusal to allow such differences to count against the claims of persons to be treated as persons which has been the inspiration of many liberal campaigns. It might therefore be thought that the oppression of women, like racial oppression, would be particularly obnoxious to liberals. Yet liberals who championed women's rights, such as John Stuart Mill and his godson Bertrand Russell, stand out by virtue of their isolation. Their consistency was seen at the time as eccentricity.

In some respects Wollstonecraft's thinking about women, as about other issues, moved beyond liberalism. She was emphatic, for example, that she was demanding more than equality of opportunity for talented women. 'let it be remembered that for a small number of distinguished women I do not ask a place' (p. 119) and this should be related to her more general objection to the meritocratic principle: 'It is not for the benefit of society that a few brilliant men should be brought forward at the expense of the multitude.' (pp. 278—9). She did not welcome the 'aristocracy of wealth' which she saw emerging in post-revolutionary France, and, in terms which recall Adam Smith but possess a more radical nuance, she deplored 'the division of labour, solely to enrich the proprietor, [which] renders the mind entirely inactive.' Nor did she share the liberal and even Paineite radical respect for property as an institution: 'From the respect paid to property flow, as from a poisoned fountain, most of the evils and vices which render this world such a dreary scene to the contemplative mind' (p. 252). And she mocked Burke, in her reply to the *Reflections*, for identifying liberty with property: 'Security of property! Behold, in a few words, the definition of English liberty.'[23]

But the core of her feminist argument derives directly from the orthodoxy of the Enlightenment. She accepts the *tabula rasa* picture of the mind, and the consequent stress on the formative, determining power of education and upbringing, then goes on to argue that it is in these terms that the existing characteristics, or 'nature', of women has to be understood: they are the products, not of their own wills or abilities, but of their conditioning. This was certainly to hoist the male radicals with their own petard. And she does indeed argue that if reason is the possession of each and every individual, as she firmly believes (p. 142), then it must be the possession of women as well as men. What then becomes of some of the traditional arguments for male supremacy? 'Who made man the exclusive judge, if woman partake with him of the gift of reason?' (p. 87). And it is in the same vein of rationalist radicalism that she attacks what she dubs the '*divine right* of husbands' (p. 127).

Yet it seems to me that her analysis of women's behaviour as the product of their conditioning — still relevant after nearly 200 years — in fact pushes beyond the conventions of the time, because it challenges the basic liberal assumption that people's expressed desires and preferences are to be taken as authentic and unquestionable. She is offering an essentially sociological account of the formation of women's preferences which does question their authenticity, just as Mill questioned the authenticity of people's preferences when they are the product of unthinking, habitual conformity.

The feminist argument was not wholly lost sight of after her early death in 1797. Her future son-in-law Shelley was to take up the cause in at least some of his writings. By and large, though, the *Vindication* stands alone — an application of liberal principles to the situation of women, and thereby, ironically a challenge to liberalism itself.

FRENCH RESPONSES: CONSTANT AND CONDORCET

Two notable French figures, the Marquis de Condorcet and Benjamin Constant, represent two contrasting styles of liberalism, rather in the manner of Paine and Burke. But Constant's mixed response to the Revolution makes him a more representatively liberal figure than is Burke in his extreme anti-Jacobinism.

Benjamin Constant read Burke's *Reflections* as soon as they appeared, and disagreed with them. It was not that he had much sympathy with the revolutionary process — 'what we are witnessing is fundamentally knavery and fury' — but it was a choice of evils. The regime that suited him best was the Directory. This was neither the radical 'fury' of the Jacobins, nor the despotism of Napoleon, which he also consistently opposed, noting at the same time, in a letter to Sir James Mackintosh, that the anti-Napoleonic powers were making 'attempts . . . to establish their own despotism'. The Directory respected the right of property — that was crucial. The inviolability of property was an essential part of freedom, in Constant's view. And landed property-owners were entitled to political dominance: 'all citizens have civil rights, but only those who possess landed property have political privileges.'[24] The stress on *landed* property seems anachronistic, particularly in view of the fact that Constant, as one would expect, is wholly committed to *laissez-faire* economic principles. There must, he says, be 'unlimited freedom' for people to do what they like with their property. This is 'the inherent right, the essential requirement of all those who own property'.[25] His companion, Madam de Staël, another courageous opponent of Napoleon, stated as a general principle: 'One must not therefore place government in opposition to this natural order of things; governments must protect property instead of rivalling it.'[26] Nor should there be any interference with production or prices. There must be no intervention 'whether to save individuals from their own mistakes (they must learn by experience) or else to secure for the public the best objects of consumption (their experience must guide their choices).' Cruickshank comments, mildly enough, that 'there is little about poverty or social welfare in Constant's writings.'[27]

Constant was a thorough-going individualist outside the economic sphere as well. Freedom for him meant the maintenance of the rights of the individual, not only against despotism from above, but also against the power of the people: 'the masses which claim the right to enslave the minority to the majority'. Like many later liberals, he saw freedom as threatened by democracy, and he explicitly demanded that 'individual freedom must always take precedence over the sovereignty of the people.' One reason for attaching such a high value to individual freedom was the fact that by contrast with the ancient world, 'almost all modern man's pleasures are related to his private life.'[28] Again, like Mill and later liberals, he attached great importance to variety: 'Variety is life; uniformity is death'; and therefore, again like Mill, he was opposed to the state provision of education, as likely to encourage uniformity.

It is not hard to see why Constant should appeal so strongly to latter-day liberals, uneasy about both democracy and state power. Constant found in himself a 'strange mania which enables me to see the opposite sides of a thing one after the other.' Modern liberals have made a virtue of this 'mania'. Discreetly overlooking, or underplaying, Constant's firm commitment to property power and a wholly unregulated market, they find Constant in every other respect a sympathetic figure.[29]

Condorcet, on the other hand, is either neglected or actively disliked. The modern conservative liberal sees in Condorcet a rigid, schematic, utopian, rationalistic figure whose thought is suffused with a dangerous dogmatic self-confidence and facile optimism. It may only be another way of putting this from another angle to say that Condorcet does indeed reflect the tenor of liberalism at its peak, before it lost its ambition and hope of transforming the world.

Having played a conspicuous part in the intellectual activities and campaigns of the *philosophes*, Condorcet survived to identify himself enthusiastically with the Revolution. He embodies the connection between these two phases in the development of European liberalism. As a man of the Enlightenment, Condorcet believed that science and reason, progress and freedom, were all bound up with each other. In so far as human society was directed by reason, it would be civilized and humane. Superstition, and the misuse of intellectual skills to deceive and dominate the ignorant, were what obstructed science and progress.[30]

How was progress to be achieved? The *philosophes* did not suppose that their efforts alone were sufficient. 'To do good one must have at least as much power as goodwill', wrote Condorcet to Turgot, and it was on Turgot that Condorcet placed his hopes for reform in the 1770s. Turgot's failure was a great dis-appointment to him, as it was to Voltaire; but while he rejoiced in the American Revolution, as far as Europe was concerned, he continued in the 1780s to sing the praises of the enlightened despots, and to place his faith in reform, or revolution, from above. [31]

Even after 1789 Condorcet was not easily reconciled to the principle of democracy. For while he stressed the potential rationality of every human being, he also believed that the 'masses' were easily manipulated, and that 'every society which is not enlightened by *philosophes* is deceived by charlatans.' [32] So the people must be educated to make them fit to exercise political power. Condorcet's mixed feelings about popular politics may have been intensified by his firm belief in the rights of property, which he listed among the fundamental rights of man, and by the limits of his egalitarianism. For while he believed that education should seek to reduce natural inequalities (*Sketch* p. 184), he also wrote in 1791 that 'it is impossible for instruction, even when equal, not to increase the superiority of those whom nature has endowed more favourably', and that egalitarianism should not lead to attempts to eliminate intellectual differences altogether. [33]

His economic philosophy is that of Adam Smith: 'How . . . is it that, by a universal moral law, the efforts made by each individual on his behalf minister to the welfare of all, and that the interests of society demand that everyone should understand where his own interests lie, and should be able to follow them without hindrance?' (p. 130). It followed that 'men, therefore, should be able to use their faculties, dispose of their wealth and provide for their needs in complete freedom.' The common interest, so far from requiring interference with the market, actually forbids it (pp. 130—1). By a similar logic Condorcet believed that wealth, left to itself, 'has a natural tendency to equality', and that it is only misguided laws which tend to produce gross inequalities (p. 180). His belief in free trade and its beneficial effects led him to attack European imperialism, and the establishment of settlements and monopolies. And it is at this point that his economic liberalism and his political radicalism come together. For Condorcet's condemnation of imperialism is not purely economic. He is outraged by 'the insolence of our usurpations' and 'our murderous contempt for men of another colour or creed' (p. 175), and above all by the institution of slavery — 'this odious remnant of the barbarous politics of the sixteenth century'. It was his one major criticism of the newly-independent Americans that they had not abolished slavery, although he was confident that they would soon do so. [34] Moreover there was a domestic danger in such overseas oppression: 'Nations will learn that they cannot conquer other nations without losing their own liberty' (p. 194).

Unlike many more 'moderate' liberals, Condorcet was consistent in his respect for the rights of the individual. He was scathing about those who 'disdained to consider' black people 'as members of the human race' (p. 141). And he explicitly recognized that 'the individual' was not invariably male. He noted in 1790 how even those most concerned with human rights nevertheless 'violated the principle of the equality of rights in calmly depriving half the human race of the right of taking part in the formation of laws.' In this same pamphlet, *On the Admission of Women to the Rights of Citizenship*, he called on his opponents to 'show me a natural difference between men and women which may legitimately serve as foundation for the deprivation of a right.'[35] He returned to this when he came to write the *Sketch* (see p. 193).

Condorcet's *Sketch* argues that history has already demonstrated the human capacity for progress, and that the future is likely to see this advance carried much further. The discredit into which the idea of progress has fallen in this century should not blind us to the fact that many of the developments which Condorcet predicted have in fact taken place. Nor did he believe that progress was either easy or steady. It was an uneven process, marked by struggles, costs and losses as well as advance (see p. 24). But his overall optimism, his faith in the beneficial character of the free market, and his consistent advocacy of the rights of persons of both sexes and all races — all these reflect the confidence not only of Enlightenment liberalism, but also of liberalism's great moment of triumph, the French Revolution. Stuart Hampshire was surely right to call the *Sketch* 'one of the few really great monuments of liberal thought' (p. ix).

It is one of the most illuminating ironies in the history of liberalism that it was in response to the optimism of Condorcet and Godwin that Thomas Malthus wrote *An Essay on the Principle of Population*, a work which stands squarely within the tradition of liberal political economy, and which was to have immense influence on the practical politics of nineteenth-century liberalism. It is to that tradition that we must now turn our attention.

13

Liberal Political Economy: Theory

If some recent writers were to be believed, the traditional conception of classical liberal economics as, by and large, a doctrine of the free market, or *laissez-faire*, is a total *mis*conception, in relation to both theory and practice. One writer tells us that 'most serious commentators' regard it as a 'myth' to think that Adam Smith preached 'a simple doctrine of the harmony of egoisms through *laissez-faire* market behaviour.'[1] According to another, the attitude of the classical economists 'towards *laissez-faire* was of a very relativist and conditional kind'.[2] It is the same with actual policies. *Laissez-faire* is a 'myth' which 'never prevailed in Great Britain or any other modern state'. Kitson Clark believed that the conception of a 'period of *laissez-faire*' was not 'helpful', while T. S. Ashton went even further and asserted that 'the whole practice of coining phrases and attaching them to particular periods of time has tended to cloud rather than illumine, our vision of the past.'[3] In the light of such claims the reader begins to wonder whether there actually *was* a tradition of liberal economics to discuss. Or is the whole notion an anachronism?

I think not. Ashton's obviously rather extreme statement in fact exposes the underlying tendency of this whole approach: it carries empiricism to the point of 'historical nihilism', as Arthur J. Taylor rightly said, the point at which every generalization is suspect because exceptions to it, or some contrary evidence, can always be found. But this is a methodological confusion. Such generalizations, or models, are not intended to conform to reality in every detail. Their function is to provide a rough map or guide to an area of knowledge. The notion of an 'age of *laissez-faire*' is not discredited by a handful of exceptions; nor is the 'model' of classical political economy undermined by the fact that no particular economist conforms to it in every respect. The question is whether these general conceptions still provide useful guidance in understanding both the theory and practice of classical liberal economics. I believe that they do, and that the 'revisionist' historians of economic thought have not succeeded in displacing them, although they have certainly modified and qualified them in important ways. We will consider first the development of liberal economic theory, and then look at aspects of the practice which was, in part at least, derived from the theory.

The overall pattern of the development of classical liberal economics shows a rapid and striking shift from the relative confidence and optimism of Adam Smith to the fatalism and pessimism which were injected into economics by Ricardo and, above all, Malthus. This shift was reflected in changing popular attitudes: the belief that all would automatically benefit from the operations of the 'free market' gave way to less sanguine expectations. Everyone would benefit, but only in the long run; or, even if the market did not produce universal benefits, what was the alternative? Intervention would only make matters worse. A confident outlook was replaced by a grimmer, more defensive one. This was one indication of the gradual decline and retreat of liberalism after the supreme moment of the Enlightenment and the Revolution.

It has become fashionable to stress the eighteenth-century character of Adam Smith's thought, as well as its philosophical and moral dimensions, and to suggest that these aspects of his work stand in opposition to his interpretation as a 'liberal capitalist' theorist.[4] This is, I think, a false antithesis. Whether or not the various ingredients in Smith's work are mutually compatible has long been debated; but, rather than trying to iron out the contradictions or tensions in his thought, a more historical awareness will see them as signs of Smith's specific historical position, poised uneasily between the securities of the pre-industrial world and the glittering prospects of apparently unlimited growth which industrialization opened up.

With whatever moral misgivings, Smith in the *Wealth of Nations* (published in that epoch-making year 1776), accepts that human beings are in fact motivated by the desire for self-preservation and, beyond that, by a more thorough-going self-interest. In this respect he follows in the steps of Hobbes and Spinoza.[5] But whereas for Hobbes it is this self-centredness which makes government and authority so necessary, Smith sees in this drive the root and source of the progress of human society and, in particular, of economic growth:

> The uniform, constant, and uninterrupted effort of every man to better his condition, the principle from which public and national, as well as private opulence is originally derived, is frequently powerful enough to maintain the natural progress of things toward improvement, in spite both of the extravagance of government and of the greatest errors of administration.[6]

Perhaps he had Hobbes in mind when he described competitive trade as 'a species of warfare' (II, p. 241), but it was a warfare from which the consumer could only benefit.

Smith was clearly impressed by Mandeville's famous paradox of private vices producing public benefits, yet as a moralist he was also unhappy about it. His only answer, however, is to suggest, in effect, that Mandeville artificially sharpens the conflict, and that if selfish action not only does not harm others, but actually benefits them, then it does not necessarily deserve the name of vice.[7] Apart from this Smith endorses Mandeville's analysis, and enlarges upon it. He points out how 'the most childish vanity' of the great landowners, and the greed of merchants 'in pursuit of their own pedlar principle of turning a penny wherever a penny was to be got' (I, p. 369), both quite unwittingly promote 'a revolution of the greatest importance to the public happiness' — that is, the rise of a market economy.

But Smith goes further, and shows how, in the context of a free market economy, the pursuit of one's own interests can *only* be successful in so far as one at the same time serves the interests of others:

Every individual is continually exerting himself to find out the most advantageous employment for whatever capital he can command. It is his own advantage, indeed, and not that of the society, which he has in view. But the study of his own advantage naturally, or rather necessarily, leads him to prefer that employment which is most advantageous to the society. (I, p. 398)

This system of mutual benefits provided in spite of the intentions of the individual participants operates at every level of the economy: 'It is not from the benevolence of the butcher, the brewer, or the baker that we expect our dinner, but from their regard to their own interest. We address ourselves, not to their humanity but to their self-love' (I, p. 13). Nor is this morally undesirable. For under such a system each person, or family, is independent and responsible for its own welfare. This is clearly preferable to the degrading dependence fostered among the 'lower orders' by the feudal order of society, in which many thousands of families were directly maintained by large land-owners, and so made dependent on them. In the market society the expenditure of the rich provides employment and a living for the poor without establishing direct ties of dependence. In such a society 'Nobody but a beggar chooses to depend chiefly upon the benevolence of his fellow-citizens' (I, p. 13). Smith was a moral as well as an analytical individualist.

The operations of self-interest within the market are generally far more reliable in promoting the general good than the good intentions of individuals — 'I have never known much good done by those who affected to trade for the public good' (I, p. 400) — let alone the actions of central government. Even when it comes to those public works which cannot be left to the market to supply, it is preferable, where possible that they be undertaken and financed by local bodies, those with the closest personal interest in them: 'Were the streets of London to be lighted and paved at the expense of the treasury, is there any probability that they would be so well lighted and paved as they are at present, or even at so small an expense?' (II, p. 218). Smith was writing before the days of the rate support grant.

Thus the supposed 'myth' of 'the harmony of egoisms through *laissez-faire* market behaviour', as Winch calls it, still appears to be central to his argument. The market, which allows, indeed encourages, each individual to be as selfish and greedy as he/she pleases, by a remarkable paradox also ensures the welfare of all and a steady increase in general prosperity.[8] The regulatory character of the market leads Smith to argue against governmental interference and regulation of such elements as the supply of labour and the level of wages. Such interference may be well-intentioned, but it will almost certainly harm the consumer, and therefore the producer too; it is therefore self-defeating. 'Whenever the law has attempted to regulate the wages of workmen, it has always been rather to lower them than to raise them' (I, p. 119). What is put in the place of regulations is what Smith calls 'the obvious and simple system of natural liberty', according to which: 'Every man, as long as he does not violate the laws of justice, is left perfectly free to pursue his own interest his own way, and to bring both his industry and capital into competition with those of any other man, or order of men' (II, p. 180).

This does not mean that Smith has no reservations about the system he is advocating, or that he allocates no positive role to government. Indeed, having outlined his system of 'natural liberty', Smith goes on immediately to discuss the functions which government must continue to play in relation to such a system (II, pp. 180—1). These fall under the three general headings of external defence; internal order, security and justice; and thirdly, 'certain public works and certain public institutions' which the individual pursuit of profit will not supply. Under this third heading he has in mind projects such as roads and canals. Those who wish to stress the scope for government intervention which Smith's rubric allows can argue with some plausibility that his principles do not actually rule out extensive public works. Nevertheless his scepticism about both the capabilities and intentions of government, together with his faith in the beneficial effects of the market, do suggest that this is not a provision which should be stretched indefinitely.

As to the other two headings, little needs to be said, except to note that a market economy does not imply a state that is weak and inactive in respect of public order — as Margaret Thatcher has recently reminded us. Smith recognizes that in a society composed of self-interested individuals there must be some authority capable of preventing unfairness and resolving conflicts between them: 'In the race for wealth, for honours, and preferments [every man] may run as hard as he can, and strain every nerve and every muscle, in order to outstrip all his competitors. But if he should jostle, or throw down any of them, the indulgence of the spectators is entirely at an end.'[9] Not all conflicts or potential conflicts, of interests are ineluctably ironed out by the market mechanism.

As to what makes justice, and government itself necessary, Smith is remarkably clear and candid: it is the existence of private property unequally distributed within society (II, p. 199), because big property attracts the resentment of the poor, and will not be safe from their attacks without the protection of the state: 'Law and government, too, seems to propose no other object but this; they secure the individual who has enlarged his property, that he may peaceably enjoy the fruits of it.' So, in these same lectures, Smith came to the conclusion that 'Law and government may be considered in this, and indeed, in every case, as a combination of the rich to oppress the poor, and preserve to themselves the inequality of goods which would otherwise be destroyed by the attacks of the poor'[10] — a point which is restated, in a slightly qualified form, in the *Wealth of Nations* (II, p. 203). Smith's bluntness sets him apart from the more evasive apologists for capitalism, who later were to take up many of his ideas.

Smith's association of government with property is one of those points at which he is close to Locke, though without Locke's equivocations. The other important connection is that he, like Locke, takes labour and a person's property in labour, as his starting point. Smith follows the traditional pattern in speculating on what was supposedly the original state of human life. In this 'original state of things . . . the labourer enjoyed the whole produce of his own labour' (I, p. 57). This situation could not survive the introduction of the private ownership of land and capital. Yet Smith holds to the view that labour is the basic justification and source of property, and that 'the property which every man has in his own labour . . . is the most sacred and inviolable' of all forms of ownership (I, p. 110). So far as I can see, he makes no attempt to reconcile this principle with his observation that 'Wherever there is great property there is great inequality. For one very rich man there must be at least five hundred poor, and the affluence of the few supposes the indigence of the many (II, p. 199). But Smith's candour is perhaps preferable to Locke's tortuous attempts to reconcile the irreconcilable.

Smith's moral uneasiness, his awareness that material progress has been achieved at some cost in terms of justice and virtue, comes out most clearly in his characterization of merchants and businessmen. He welcomes the results of their activities, but deplores the spirit which inspires them. He condemns roundly 'the mean rapacity, the monopolizing spirit of merchants and

manufacturers, who neither are, nor ought to be, the rulers of mankind'
(I, p. 436). What is more, these groups cannot be trusted to respect the market
principle of competition. Their interest lies in creating price rings and
monopolies: 'To widen the market and to narrow the competition, is always
the interest of the dealers' (I, pp. 231—2) and therefore their interest 'is always
in some respects different from, and even opposite to, that of the public' (I,
p. 231). 'Combinations', that is, in effect, trade unions, among workmen are,
he points out, widely noticed and generally deplored — by non-workmen —
if not outlawed. But in fact employers combine quite as readily, and much
more easily because there are fewer of them, even though this is seldom publicly
noticed, and their combinations are the more effective (I, pp. 59—60 and 129).
Politically, too, merchants are not to be trusted, because a merchant 'is not
necessarily the citizen of any particular country' (I, p. 373), but will shift his
activities and his capital from place to place according to the prospect of profit,
whereas 'The proprietor of land is necessarily a citizen of the particular country
in which his estate lies.'[11] This is the basis on which Burke, economically a
follower of Smith, based his argument for large landowners retaining their
dominant position within the political system.

There is a similar ambiguity in Smith's attitude to the division of labour.
On the one hand it is the key to economic growth. On the other, the elementary
nature of the work done fosters stupidity and ignorance (II, pp. 263—4 and
I, p. 115). This is dangerous, for 'an instructed and intelligent people . . . are
always more decent and orderly than an ignorant and stupid one', and therefore
less likely 'to be misled into any wanton or unnecessary opposition to the
measures of government' (II, p. 269). Smith does not therefore share
Mandeville's hostility to charity schools, and is anxious to see local provision
for popular education.

It can thus be said with reason that Smith is not an apologist for the capitalist
or middle class. Unlike, say, James Mill or Richard Cobden, he has no belief
in the special virtues of the bourgeoisie. Neither is he an uncritical enthusiast
for the competitive market system which nevertheless forms the core of his
economic recommendations. He does not regard poverty as a necessary and
permanent feature of society: 'No society can surely be flourishing and happy,
of which the greater part of the members are poor and miserable' (I, p. 70).
He believes that high wages are a stimulus to good work (I, p. 73), and unlike
Malthus he regards the 'multiplication of the human species' as an indication
of 'public prosperity' (I, pp. 71—2). The market system, when operating
properly, and not interfered with by monopolizing merchants or busybody
governments, is seen as bringing real benefits to society as a whole, not simply
to the rich. Thus his conception of the capitalist market is of a mechanism which
is genuinely benign, and his outlook is, broadly speaking, optimistic and
confident. Smith, working within the tradition of liberal individualism,

provides classical political economy with an honest, humane and confident send-off.

THOMAS MALTHUS: A LICENCE FOR HARSHNESS

Smith's extraordinary understanding is evidenced by the fact that he was writing at, or just before, the moment of industrial 'take-off'. Yet it was also this anticipatory juncture which allowed him to be comparatively optimistic. Those who witnessed the actual impact of early industrial capitalism, when not blinded by wealth or ideological enthusiasm, found it more difficult to share his confidence. Whether or not the living standards of the mass of the people rose or fell in real terms, the sheer visibility and extent of urban poverty and squalor (as opposed to the dispersed, concealed character of its rural counterpart), and the acute contrast between the wealth of the few manufacturers and owners and the misery of the mass of their employees, made a deep impression on observers from a wide range of political angles.

Faced with this experience, the liberal faith in the market mechanism begins to turn into fatalism. It is futile to try to interfere with the 'laws' of economics. Indeed, such intervention, however well-meaning, may only make matters worse. The first and most damagingly influential element of pessimism was injected into classical economics by Thomas Robert Malthus, whose name is universally and rightly associated with the idea that population, if unchecked, always grows faster than food supplies, with predictably disastrous consequences.

It may be hard to see, at first sight, what this idea has to do with either economics or liberalism. But economics was less narrowly conceived then than it is now. And it was not only Malthus's 'scientific' achievement in uncovering some of the 'laws' that govern human society that gave him his place in the tradition of political economy, but also the fact that, as he was himself eager to make clear, there were important practical policy conclusions to be drawn from his theory. As to his place in the liberal tradition, not only did Nassau Senior hail him as 'a benefactor to mankind, on a level with Adam Smith',[12] but the younger Mill, too, was a consistent defender of Malthus against his many critics. In the twentieth century, Keynes paid warm tribute to him as 'profoundly in the English tradition of humane science' — a tradition he associated with 'the names of Locke, Hume, Adam Smith, Paley, Bentham, Darwin, and Mill', a predominantly liberal list.[13] Thus liberals have been happy to claim Malthus as one of their own.

The shift in liberal thought which Malthus represents is indicated by the contrast between his own relatively pessimistic outlook and that of his father, who was an admirer and even disciple of Rousseau. Still more explicit is the fact that the *Essay*, as its title page indicated, was written as a response and a rebuke to the expectations of future progress which had been expressed in the 1790s by Condorcet and Godwin.

In its first version Malthus's argument was presented in a simple and memorable mathematical formula: population, if unchecked, increases geometrically, while food supplies can at best increase only arithmetically. If humankind does not control its own reproductive capacity, then nature intervenes to restore the balance through the devastation of famine and disease. This disparity, and the process by which it is rectified, 'form the great difficulty that to me appears insurmountable in the way to the perfectibility of society. . . . I see no way by which man can escape from the weight of this law which pervades all animated nature.' [14] Malthus was consciously attacking 'utopianism' and what he took to be unrealizable ideals. He even attacked the setting up of ideal models, which 'by wasting our strength of mind and body, in a direction in which it is impossible to proceed, and by the frequent distress which we must necessarily occasion by our repeated failures, we shall evidently impede that degree of improvement in society, which is really attainable' (p. 176). In fact he went further, and suggested that 'any very marked and striking change for the better, in the form and structure of general society; by which I mean any great and decided amelioration of the condition of the lower classes of mankind' (p. 172) was ruled out by his principles. It is true that in the second edition of the *Essay* (1803), which was in fact five times as long as the first, Malthus was at pains to stress that he was not preaching a doctrine of total defeatism, but one which allowed for limited rather than unlimited improvements in the human condition. [15] But Malthus was among the first who, from within the liberal tradition, developed an explicitly anti-utopian position which recommended limited, piecemeal reform as a 'realistic' alternative.

It has often been claimed by Malthus's defenders that the mathematical precision with which he first stated his basic thesis is not essential to the argument: 'every candid reader knows', wrote Mill tendentiously, 'that Mr Malthus laid no stress on this unlucky attempt to give numerical precision to things which do not admit of it, and every person capable of reasoning must see that it is wholly superfluous to his argument.' [16] It is certainly true that Malthus himself moved away from the mathematical style of his first formulation. But some doubts may remain, even among candid readers and persons capable of reasoning. The most important concerns the weight to be attached to the qualification 'if unchecked'. Malthus himself admits that population growth is only rarely unchecked. He also admitted that his first claim, that all such checks could be subsumed under the heading of 'misery and vice' was too sweeping. 'Moral restraint' was added to the list. [17] But the more qualifications are added to the argument, the more it tends to become self-confirming.

Population does *not* grow at a geometrical rate, therefore checks *must* be operating. If this can happen, then the Malthusian scenario loses much of its horrendous character, as Hazlitt pointed out.[18] If, in addition, Malthus underestimated the rate at which food supplies can be increased, then his argument is weakened still further, and so are the practical political conclusions which he and others deduced from it.[19]

Such considerations did little if anything to diminish the fundamentally negative impact of Malthus's case, in which the mathematical formula certainly played its part. As Mark Blaug put it: 'The contrast that Malthus drew between the two kinds of mathematical progression carried the hypnotic persuasive power of an advertising slogan.'[20] A small minority of secularist radicals drew a rational conclusion from the Malthusian argument and campaigned in favour of birth control — something which Malthus, as an Anglican clergyman, disapproved. Among them was the seventeen year-old John Stuart Mill, who said of the younger utilitarians in his *Autobiography* that 'Malthus's population principle was quite as much a banner, and point of union among us, as any opinion specially belonging to Bentham.'[21]

Malthus himself, and the great majority of those who so readily and rapidly accepted his thesis, drew a very different practical conclusion. This was, in essence, that nothing should be done which might encourage the poor to 'breed', and that everything possible should be done to discourage it. No message could have been more welcome to the propertied classes. As Marx noted, his message 'was greeted jubilantly by the English oligarchy as the great destroyer of all hankerings after a progressive development of humanity.'[22] If the 'laws' of economics demonstrated the counter-productiveness of charity or benevolence towards the poor, there was an end of the matter. There could be no argument with 'science', and, as Hazlitt noted, Malthus was 'one of those rare and fortunate writers who have attained a *scientific* reputation in questions of moral and political philosophy.'[23]

The essence of Malthus's case is that anything that improves the condition of the poor will encourage them to have children, thus creating more poor, but not creating more wealth. Therefore the poor will get poorer as they get more numerous (p 97) He went on to argue that the poor who produced children without having the means to support them (i.e. those on low wages or without work) ought to be punished for their irresponsibility and lack of sexual restraint. A law should be made declaring that no child born from future marriages should be eligible for poor relief. After that, 'if any man choose to marry, without a prospect of being able to support a family, he should have the most perfect liberty to do so.' But he (and she) would also have to take the consequences, for Malthus denies that the poor have any *right* to support. And so 'To the punishment therefore of nature he should be left, the punishment of want . . . He should be taught to know that the laws of nature, which are the laws of God, had doomed him and his family to suffer for disobeying their repeated admonitions.' The punishment, conveniently enough, is inflicted by nature, not by society or government, despite the law which would bring this state of affairs into being. As for illegitimate or abandoned children, 'If the parents desert their child, they ought to be made answerable for the crime. The infant is, comparatively speaking, of little value to society, as others will immediately supply its place.'[24]

After reading passages like this, it is hard to understand how Keynes could have described the *Essay* as being 'profoundly in the English tradition of humane science'. This judgement is the stranger in that Keynes himself quotes another, equally non-humane passage, in which Malthus effectively denies the right of existence to those born into poverty:

> A man who is born into a world already possessed, if he cannot get subsistence from his parents on whom he has a just demand, and if the society do not want his labour, has no claim of *right* to the smallest portion of food, and, in fact, has no business to be where he is. At nature's mighty feast there is no vacant cover [i.e. place] for him. She tells him to be gone, and will execute her own orders. . . .[25]

Malthus does not for one moment concede a basic right to the necessities of life. There is simply not enough to go round. 'All cannot share alike the bounties of nature' (p. 134). Those who already possess the world — the metaphor of ownership is all too apt — have the right to these bounties, and if they are so misguided as to show compassion to the hungry poor, they will soon be shown the error of their ways. So, whereas Adam Smith could not accept that a nation could be said to be wealthy when the majority of people were poor and miserable, Malthus finds this perfectly acceptable. England itself was an example: 'The increasing wealth of the nation has had little or no tendency to better the condition of the labouring poor' (p. 186).

Satire, and especially Dickens' brand of it, is often supposed to be a matter of exaggeration, but it is clear that he was scarcely exaggerating in *The Chimes* when he put these Malthusian sentiments into the mouth of Mr Filer, horrified by the plan of two young and evidently poor people to get married:

> 'A man may live to be as old as Methusaleh', said Mr Filer, 'and may labour all his life for the benefit of such people as those; and may heap up facts on figures, facts on figures, facts on figures, mountains high and dry; and he can no more hope to persuade 'em that they have no right or business to be married, than he can hope to persuade 'em that they have no earthly right or business to be born. And *that* we know they haven't. We reduced it to a mathematical certainty long ago.'

The middle-class critical response to *The Chimes* when it was published in 1844 showed that Dickens had hit his target.[26]

Malthus's defenders regard this kind of attack as grossly unfair. As a man Malthus was kindly and well-liked, not at all 'the cruel and vicious monster of pamphleteering controversy'.[27] This may well be true, but it is beside the point. The anger and hatred that Malthus evoked were directed not against his private personality but against his public pronouncements and policy recommendations. Malthus was not an innocent theoretician who should be exonerated of any responsibility for the policies carried out in his name. He played an active part in the contemporary debate over the treatment of poverty, and put forward his own scheme for the gradual abolition of the Poor Law. He believed that the Poor Laws encouraged early marriage, and so 'may be said to create the poor which they maintain'. Appearing before the Commons Committee on Emigration in 1827, Malthus recommended that parishes should cease to pay the rent of paupers, and urged that taxation should be used to discourage the building of new cottages. Landlords who pulled down empty cottages were commended. The Committee's report included Malthus's testimony as well as several of his policy recommendations.[28] In view of the consistent harshness of the policies he himself advocated, it is hard not to agree with Marx that 'The hatred of the English working class against Malthus . . . is therefore entirely justified.'[29] Malthus did more than any single individual to push English middle-class liberalism towards attitudes of defeatism and harshness where mass poverty and misery were concerned. It was the poor who paid the price.

There is one footnote to be added to the story of Malthus's influence. It concerns the impact of his ideas on Darwin and the theory of evolution. In *The Origin of Species*, Darwin suggests that what he calls the 'struggle for existence', 'inevitably follows from the high rate at which all organic beings tend to increase', and since in the case of animals there can be 'no artificial increase of food, and no prudential restraint from marraige . . . the doctrine of Malthus [can be] applied with manifold force to the whole animal and vegetable kingdoms.'[30] Darwin read, 'for amusement', Malthus in 1838, while he was working on the theory of natural selection:

> and being well prepared to appreciate the struggle for existence which everywhere goes on from long-continued observation of the habits of animals and plants, it at once struck me that under these circumstances favourable variations would tend to be preserved, and unfavourable ones to be destroyed. The result of this would be the formation of new species. Here, then, I had at last got a theory by which to work. . . .[31]

Not only Darwin, but also Alfred Wallace and, in a different way, Herbert Spencer, arrived at conclusions about the evolutionary significance of the struggle for existence after reading Malthus.[32] But, as Burrow points out, whereas Malthus's was an *equilibrium* theory, of nature restoring the balance between population and resources, the theorists of evolution gave the idea a more optimistic direction: out of this struggle new species emerged; or what occurred, in Spencer's phrase, was 'the survival of the fittest'. Spencer, but not Darwin, applied this idea to the struggle for existence within the human species. It is a doctrine of progress, but of progress through struggle and conflict, in which some must be the losers. Thus Malthus is one of the links between classical political economy and the 'Social Darwinist' theory of competition which proved to be so influential in the late nineteenth century.[33] And if Malthus's doctrine had been regarded as 'scientific', the apparent application of his ideas to the non-human world made the harsh decrees of social Darwinism appear even more so — and both Marx and Engels saw Darwin as providing a scientific basis for the doctrine of the class struggle.

RICARDO

David Ricardo's father was a Jewish stockbroker who migrated from Amsterdam to London around 1760. The Ricardos were originally Portuguese Jews, who like Spinoza's family, had fled from the Inquisition to the more tolerant atmosphere of Amsterdam in the seventeenth century. Ricardo was himself educated in Amsterdam. He first met Malthus in 1811, and from then until Ricardo's early death at the age of fifty-one in 1823, they were constantly in touch, discussing and debating some of the central issues of political economy.

They did not agree on all issues, but Ricardo accepted Malthus's theory of population, and paid fulsome tribute to it in his own *Principles of Political Economy and Taxation*: 'The assaults of the opponents of this great work have only served to prove its strength', he wrote.[34] Ricardo's contention that there was a 'natural' level of wages, to which, despite variations, they would always revert, coincided with Malthus's belief that higher wages would in the long term only exacerbate the plight of the poor. When the market price of labour rises above its 'natural' price, the labourers produce more children. And so because 'the number of labourers is increased, wages again fall to their natural price', or even below it (p. 116). And what is this natural price? 'The natural price of labour is that price which is necessary to enable the labourers, one with another, to subsist and to perpetuate their race, without either increase or diminution' (p. 115). Ricardo is thus arguing that wages tend ineluctably not to rise much above the subsistence level — again a sharp contrast with Smith's expectation that all classes would share in the growing wealth produced by an expanding economy.

But despite his general endorsement of Malthus, Ricardo also apparently believes that if 'the labouring classes' can develop 'a taste for comforts and enjoyments', this will produce a fall in the birthrate: 'There cannot be a better security against a superabundant population' (p. 121). Yet, in practice, Ricardo adopted Malthusian attitudes. He was an opponent of the Poor Laws, and wished to see them abolished (pp. 126—7), and he declined to send James Mill a subscription for Brougham's Westminster Infants School because the children were to be given some dinner. He thought that this would 'give encouragement to excess of population'. [35]

What chiefly gives a dark hue to Ricardo's economic theory is that it is a theory not of the harmony of interests, but of fundamental conflicts of interest between three different groups or classes in society. These three classes are the landowners, the capitalists, and the workers, and the fruits of production accrue to these three groups under the three forms of rent, profits, and wages (p. 49). The principal conflict is that between landowners and the rest of the population. 'The interest of the landlords is always opposed to the interest of every other class in the community', he wrote in 1815, because they alone have an interest in high corn and food prices. [36] High food prices lead the workers to demand higher wages, and this leads to a squeeze on profits, because 'there can be no rise in the value of labour without a fall of profits' (pp. 76, 151). Thus both the working class and the manufacturers have an interest in low food prices, and therefore in the repeal of the Corn Laws, which kept the price of bread high to protect British agriculture. Ricardo thus gave the attempt to create a class alliance to campaign against the Corn Laws a sound theoretical basis.

But there was also a conflict of interests between capitalists and workers, and the capitalist always has an incentive to reduce labour costs. One way of doing this is to introduce labour-saving machinery. Ricardo's original belief was that the introduction of machinery was 'a general good' (p. 378). But in the third edition of the *Principles* (1821), he added a new chapter on machinery, in which he suggested that the advantages of machinery might be all on the employers' side: 'the opinion entertained by the labouring class, that the employment of machinery is frequently detrimental to their interests, is not founded on prejudice and error, but is comformable to the correct principles of political economy' (p. 384) — a view which was endorsed by Bentham. [37]

Thus the general picture of society presented by Ricardo was of classes — his use of this term is significant, and may partly account for his influence on early socialist economics — in conflict with each other over the distribution of the product of industry, trade and agriculture. Competition between conflicting classes over a limited amount of wealth, rather than a market-induced harmony between self-interested individuals and a prospect of unlimited growth, is Ricardo's theme, and it introduces a further note of harshness and pessimism into liberal political economy.

LAISSEZ-FAIRE AND THE LIMITS OF INTERVENTION

As we noted at the beginning of this chapter, recent discussion of classical political economy has been dominated by a sustained campaign of revision and rehabilitation. Like many campaigns, this one has not been free from special pleading and even a degree of absurdity. Thus, much has been made of the fact that the term *laissez-faire* is not much used by the classical writers, and that only Mill offers an explicit defence of it: '*laisser-faire*, in short, should be the general practice: every departure from it, unless required by some great good, is a certain evil.'[38] One commentator has pointed out triumphantly that the term does not appear once in the Corn Law Repeal debates of 1846.[39] But in themselves such semantic absences prove nothing. You do not show that Locke is not a liberal thinker by pointing out that 'liberal' did not exist as a political term in the seventeenth century. And it is clearly possible to discuss, or to hold views, on the proper limits of government action without using the term *laissez-faire*.

Similarly, nothing is gained by showing that none of these thinkers argued for total inactivity on the part of government.[40] They were not anarchists. Nor is it particularly significant that McCulloch and some other economists supported Shaftesbury's legislation to prevent the exploitation of children in factories, and to limit the hours they might work. Children could obviously be excepted from the general rules of economic life without undermining the rules, as McCulloch himself recognized: 'I would not interfere between adults and masters; but it is absurd to contend that children have the power to judge for themselves, as to such a matter.'[41] It need not be doubted that the classical economists allowed a significant role for government activity in both social and economic matters. The New Poor Law, of which Chadwick and Naussau Senior were two of the chief architects, is proof enough of that. Nor need we deny that particular economists were ready to support particular acts of intervention which contravened the general principle of *laissez-faire*. The question is whether, and in what respects, they espoused a *general principle* of non-intervention, with whatever limitations or qualifications.

Not many of them shared the extreme hostility to government action and legal regulation displayed by, for example, the popularizer Harriet Martineau, or later on by Herbert Spencer. I think, though, that it is broadly true to say that they wished to see government intervention confined to the social sphere, while the economy was left to function as a free market. It was always unclear where this distinction was to be drawn, and as intervention increased the line became ever more blurred. But even when the sanctity of market principles were proclaimed, there was still considerable scope for government action. Smith, as we have seen, was anxious to see the public provision of education extended, as was McCulloch, and Senior was clear that government has a right and a duty to protect the health of the people. Senior is also believed to be the chief author of the official Report on the conditions of hand-loom weavers, issued in 1841, which made recommendations about housing on very similar lines: 'With all our reverence for the principle of non-interference, we cannot doubt that in this matter it has been pushed too far.'[42] Such proposals undoubtedly implied an interference with property rights which many contemporaries found objectionable. Senior did not. However, the qualification must be noted. There *was* a 'principle of non-intervention', and it was one which the Commissioners revered. Coupled with this went a fundamental suspicion of the state and its activities. Or, as Bentham put it, 'The request which agriculture, manufactures and commerce present to governments is . . . "Stand out of my sunshine." We have no need of favour — we require only a secure and open path.'[43]

It is thus quite irrelevant for apologists for the liberal economists to point out that they — or some of them — favoured high wages.[44] They hoped that free market processes would produce high wages, but if they did not, the economists were opposed to any attempt to boost wages 'artificially', that is, by state action.[45] What is more, when we turn to consider the kinds of legislation and intervention which the liberal economists favoured, we discover that usually such action is to be guided by a strict regard for the laws of the market, and indeed, as in the case of the New Poor Law, had as its purpose the *reinforcement* of market principles. Old forms of local or national provision for the relief of distress were believed to undermine the incentive to work. They were therefore to be swept away, and a system imposed which would conform to the recently discovered 'laws' of economics.

It therefore seems mere mystification to portray the tradition of classical liberal economics in such a way as to suggest that it was completely 'pragmatic' or 'non-doctrinaire' in its attitudes towards the general issues of intervention and the market. Indeed, as we shall see, the New Poor Law and the British Government's response to the Irish famine of the 1840s suggest that words such as 'dogmatic' are only too apt when considering how the doctrines of liberal economics were often applied to practice. Nor can practice be cleanly separated from theory. We have already noted Malthus's willingness to make practical policy proposals, and the involvement of Senior and Chadwick in the devising and implementation of the New Poor Law further illustrates the close involvement of many of the liberal economists with government policy in the early nineteenth century. In any case we are concerned with liberal practice as well as liberal theory, and as to this, there can hardly be any doubt that the theory was interpreted as a doctrine of non-intervention. Lord Liverpool, the Prime Minister, summarized the position in 1812: 'it was undoubtedly true that the less commerce and manufactures were meddled with the more they were likely to prosper' — a view which was echoed in similar terms by the Russian reformer, Speransky.[46] And it was a corollary of letting industry and commerce alone that the state itself should confine its own activities and spending to a minimum, lest it should become a burden on the economy itself:

> Our rulers will best promote the improvement of the nation by strictly confining themselves to their own legitimate duties, by leaving capital to find its own most lucrative course, commodities their fair price, industry and intelligence their natural reward, idleness and folly their natural punishment, by maintaining peace, by defending property, by diminishing the price of law, and by observing strict economy in every department of the state. Let the government do this: the people will assuredly do the rest.[47]

We are then faced with the paradox that, as the nineteenth century went on, the interventionist role of the state increased, steadily if unevenly; more and more exceptions were made to the general rule of allowing economic life to follow its 'natural' course. But what is significant is that these continued to be seen as exceptions. No coherent philosophy of intervention was developed until the second half of the century. At the same time, the principles of liberal economics hardened, in the minds of many, into dogmas, rigidly adhered to however distressing the results of such adherence might be. The economic 'laws' whose discovery should, as in other sciences, have led to an increase of human control over the environment, turned into a straitjacket of prohibitions. Particularly under the influence of Malthus, a hard, brutal fatalism developed. If the laws of economics dictated that the mass of the poor must continue poor, so be it. There was nothing to be done. This was the frame of mind of the liberal Thackeray in 1848, when he wrote: 'the question of poverty is that of death disease winter or that of any other natural phenomenon. I don't know how either is to stop.'[48]

When Dickens launched his fierce and brilliant attack on utilitarianism and liberal economics in *Hard Times* in 1854, he ran into a hail of criticism. Macaulay denounced the book for its 'sullen socialism', while an American critic found Dickens' attitude 'childish', because he failed to see that 'the established laws of political economy' were of the same status as 'the established laws of the physical universe'.[49] This was the attitude still being maintained by *The Times* in the 1860s, when it said of the poverty of the East End of London: 'There is no one to blame for this; it is the result of Nature's simplest laws!' — an observation which Matthew Arnold (a significant figure in the shift of thought towards interventionism) particularly derides in *Culture and Anarchy*. This was the frame of mind, of 'self-cancelling Donothingism and *laissez-faire*' against which Carlyle had railed a quarter of a century earlier in his essay on *Chartism* (1839), and which even Samuel Smiles, the apostle of *Self-Help*, bitterly attacked.[50] Critics of such policies stand outside the mainstream of liberalism, and it was against the increasing harshness and complacency of that mainstream that they directed their angry and eloquent onslaughts.

14

Liberal Political Economy: Practice

THE TREATMENT OF POVERTY AND THE NEW POOR LAW

The emergence, in the seventeenth and eighteenth centuries, of harsh and hostile attitudes towards poverty and the poor, and their connections with liberal economic doctrine and the liberal concern for property, has already been noted (in chapters 8 and 9 above). These attitudes attained their fullest development, and their most complete dominance over policy, in the early nineteenth century. Reinforced intellectually by the new 'science' of political economy and the gloomy calculations of Malthus, and socially by bourgeois fears of revolutionary ferment among the new industrial working class, these attitudes achieved their greatest single triumph in Britain in the New Poor Law of 1834 and the system of workhouses which it set up.

It was one of the costs of freedom, and of the free market, that some must suffer. In a race not everyone can win, or gain a prize: 'It is one of the natural consequences of freedom that those who are left to shift for themselves must sometimes be reduced to want . . . Manufactures and commerce are the true parents of our national poor.' Edwin Chadwick said much the same 40 years later: 'as labour is the source of wealth, so is poverty of labour. Banish poverty, you banish wealth.'[1] This was no doubt regrettable. But what was the alternative? The alternative was governmental interference. There were three main lines of objection to such interference. The first was that it represented a restriction of the freedom of choice of individuals. The second was that it removed not only the responsibility, but also the incentive from the individual to find work. The third was that all interference represented a misguided attempt to tamper with the laws of the market, which like other natural laws were the discoveries of objective science. Freedom, individual responsibility, and science were the three grounds on which the poor were to be left to fend for themselves.

Burke, the conservative champion of the organic community, invoked those laws when arguing against the governmental alleviation of poverty. He urged his readers 'manfully to resist the very first idea, speculative or practical, that it is within the competence of government, taken as government, or even of the rich, as rich, to supply to the poor, those necessaries which it has pleased the Divine Providence for a while to with-hold from them.'[2] This sanctification of the market naturally proved to be extremely popular: the combined authorities of God and science dictated the futility of helping the poor. On this matter a political radical like Joseph Priestley was in agreement with Burke: 'the greater is the provision that is made for the poor, the more poor there will be to avail themselves of it.'[3]

Many people shared this view, and were campaigning in the early years of the nineteenth century, not only for the abolition of outdoor relief, but for an end to any kind of support for the poor, including the workhouses or poor-houses. Workhouses antedated the New Poor Law, and were always viewed with horror by the poor themselves, as George Crabbe recorded:

> Those gates and locks, and all those signs of power:
> It is a prison, with a milder name,
> Which few inhabit without dread or shame.
> (*The Borough*, 1810)

So the New Poor Law was, for those who like Malthus wanted an end to all poor relief, a compromise measure. Nevertheless, both it and the Report on which it was based were monuments to the new 'scientific' approach to social policy based on liberal economic theory and utilitarian moral principles. It was, said Chadwick, 'the first great piece of legislation based upon scientific or economical principles'.[4] It was not the fault of the Elizabethan originators of the Old Poor Law that they knew nothing of 'political science', said Lord Brougham, when defending the Bill in 1834: 'They could not foresee that a Malthus would arise to enlighten mankind upon the important branch of science — they knew not the true principle upon which to frame a preventive check to the unlimited increase of the people.'[5] The guiding principle of the new legislation was a simple deduction from liberal political economy. It was that whatever relief was offered for poverty, it should in no way undermine the monetary incentive to seek work. And indeed the plan was that the workhouses — henceforth to be the only source of relief — should be so forbidding as to act in themselves as a deterrent. Workhouses should be 'objects of terror',[6] and there should be attached to pauperdom a sense of disgrace which would operate as a 'check of shame' (p. 377) on those who might otherwise be tempted to opt out of the labour market.

Liberal political economy did not allow the recognition that poverty and unemployment had structural causes; they were seen as misfortunes whose remedy lay within the power of the individual. The Commissioners' investigations predictably confirmed this assumption: 'One of the most encouraging of the results of our inquiry is the degree in which the existing pauperism arises from fraud, indolence, or improvidence. If it had been principally the result of unavoidable distress, we must have inferred the existence of an organic disease' (p. 393). So the Commissioners based their recommendations on the premise that the workhouse should function as a deterrent and a punishment to the idle: 'Every penny bestowed that tends to render the condition of the pauper more eligible than that of the independent labourer, is a bounty on indolence and vice' (p. 335). They commended the policy adopted at Cookham in Berkshire, where the labourer found 'that the parish is the hardest taskmaster and the worst paymaster he can find' (p. 337), and recommended that a maximum level of consumption per head in workhouses be fixed nationally, 'leaving to the local officers the liberty of reducing it below the maximum if they can safely do so' (p. 419).

The dreadful consequences of the enactment of the New Poor Law are well known. It rapidly became one of the most hated pieces of legislation ever enacted in Britain. Within less than three years of its passing into law, Dickens, in his second novel *Oliver Twist*, was directing his genius for savage satire at the new workhouses and at the 'philosophers' who had inspired them and presided over them. The miserable diet against which Oliver naively protests was scarcely an exaggeration,[7] and the separation of wives and husbands was a Malthusian measure designed to keep down the population. It was by an appropriate irony that these institutions of liberal political economy came to be known as 'Bastilles'. The notorious scandal of the Andover workhouse, where paupers in the 1840s were so starved that they were reduced to gnawing the bones which they were supposed to be crushing for use as land fertilizer, was neither unique, nor did its uncovering put an end to the miseries and tyrannies of workhouse life. When, in *A Christmas Carol*, Scrooge refuses to give charity on the grounds that as a taxpayer he already supports the workhouse, the collector replies: 'Many can't go there; and many would rather die.' To this Scrooge replies in Malthusian vein: 'If they would rather die . . . they had better do it, and decrease the surplus population.'[8] There were those who took his advice. Mrs Dorothy Tompkins recalled, a few years ago, how her great-grandfather Jesse Craft, who had lost most of his sight in an accident at work, was refused outdoor relief in 1891 and offered the alternative of the workhouse. Jesse Craft 'replied that he would rather die. He went home and hanged himself.'[9]

To enquire into the kind-heartedness or otherwise of the Poor Law Commissioners would be as futile as discussing Malthus's good nature. These men were not inspired by personal viciousness but by principles. As Carlyle pointed out in 1839: 'They are not tigers; they are men filled with an idea of a theory.'[10]

Can liberalism really be identified with such harsh and repressive legislation? Is not the core of liberalism the belief in personal freedom? How is that to be reconciled with the draconian regime of the workhouse? Yet, as we have seen, many writers saw no conflict between freedom and poverty, and in the view of Malthus and of the Commissioners, those who entered the workhouse were those who *chose* not to work. Besides, liberalism had other concerns: property, which had to bear the cost of poor relief; and the market, whose laws could not be defied. Opposition to the New Poor Law came from radical Tories, like Michael Sadler, whose views were ridiculed by the Whig Macaulay,[11] and populist radicals like William Cobbett and Dickens. 'Enlightened' liberal opinion generally supported it, and had, indeed, fought long and hard to destroy the comparatively benevolent provisions of the old Poor Law.[12] Harshness towards poverty and the poor has been part of the hidden, unadvertised history of liberalism — but we do not have to explore very far to uncover it.

THE BRITISH GOVERNMENT AND THE IRISH FAMINE

In the autumn of 1845 the potato crop in Ireland, the basic food of the people, was struck by blight and largely destroyed. The crop failed even more completely in 1846, and there was another total failure in 1848. These were the years of the great famine, perhaps the most terrible of all disasters in the unhappy history of Ireland under British rule. Britain could not be held responsible for the failure of the potato crop, but it fell to the British authorities to devise policies to cope with the consequences of this failure. The policies they followed were, by and large, dominated not by the elementary human concern to save people from starvation, destitution and disease, but by adherence to the principles of free trade and *laissez-faire* economics.

This was particularly true of the Whig ministry, headed by Lord John Russell, which replaced Sir Robert Peel's administration in June 1846. Peel, although he shared the general faith in market principles, was sufficiently flexible to accept the need for a positive government strategy. His plan was to keep down the price of food by selling a limited quantity of Indian corn (maize) at a low price, and to provide employment, and hence the wages with which food could be bought, through a programme of public works. Neither of these policies was intended as a comprehensive solution to the relief problem. Peel shared the general view that such a response was neither possible nor desirable. The Irish must shift for themselves, and the landlords must bear their share of the burden.[13]

Once the Whigs were in office, however, even these fairly modest palliatives were rapidly discarded. Charles Trevelyan, Assistant Secretary of the Treasury, 'now became virtually dictator of relief for Ireland', and within days of Peel's fall he was writing to Sir Randolph Routh, chairman of the Relief Commission in Dublin, urging an end to the sales of maize: 'The only way to prevent the people from becoming naturally dependent on Government, is to bring the operations to a close.' Meanwhile the hungry Irish were enraged by the spectacle of wheat, oats and barley being exported from Ireland, often under the protection of the British army. But this, too, did not perturb Trevelyan: 'Do not encourage the idea of prohibiting exports', he wrote to Routh, 'perfect Free Trade is the right course.'[14] As for the Government importing food into Ireland, Russell told the Commons during the dreadful winter of 1846—47, 'we think it far better to leave the supplying of the people to private enterprise and the ordinary trade.' Nor should the price of food be regulated: 'We must abstain from any attempt to tamper with prices', Routh wrote to Lord Monteagle, one of the most actively humane landlords in Ireland, in October 1846, 'We must pay the true values for each article of food and encourage its importation upon that principle. Any other line of conduct would expose us to the most fatal consequences.'[15] Routh's words were unfortunate. Literally fatal consequences followed from the policies he recommended, and even as he wrote, people were being reduced to living on nettles and weeds, or, in the case of 7,500 people in Roscommon, on cabbage leaves boiled once every 48 hours. Reports of terrible distress flooded in from all over Ireland, with local relief officers repeatedly begging their superiors to send supplies of food. The Government remained unmoved. In 1849 Clarendon, Lord Lieutenant of Ireland, wrote to Russell: 'I don't think there is another legislature in Europe that would disregard such suffering as now exists in the west of Ireland, or coldly persist in a policy of extermination.'[16]

It is striking to find Britain's chief representative in Ireland speaking of 'a policy of extermination', if only because it is so easy to dismiss the accusation of genocide as the understandable, but ultimately unfair, product of Irish nationalist bias. I do not think the British Government had the intention of letting the Irish starve to death. But they were influenced decisively in their policies and their inaction, by the dominant tradition of liberal economics. On the one hand this tradition told them that intervention was futile if not positively harmful, and this belief had acquired a moral as well as a scientific sanction. People *ought* to fend for themselves. Habits of dependence were not to be encouraged. 'The more I see of government interference', wrote the Chancellor of the Exchequer, Sir Charles Wood, to Monteagle in November 1848, 'the less I am disposed to trust to it, and I have no faith in anything but private capital employed under individual charge.'[17]

In addition the Malthusian contribution to the tradition told them that Ireland was grossly over-populated in relation to the available capital. The Malthusian approach had made it quite normal for economist-politicians like Torrens to talk about Ireland's 'redundant population',[18] as well as domesticating famine as the final means through which nature restores the proper balance between population and food supplies. All this could only encourage at best fatalism. At worst it produced the response which Benjamin Jowett attributed to Naussau Senior: 'I have always felt a certain horror of political economists, since I heard one of them say that he feared the famine of 1848 in Ireland would not kill more than a million people, and that would be scarcely enough to do much good.'[19] In fact it is estimated that it killed about a million and a half people, quite apart from the one million who emigrated between 1846 and 1851.[20]

In February 1849 the diarist Greville reported, in some bewilderment it seems, that 'Nobody knows what to do . . . Charles Wood has all along set his face against giving or lending money . . . and he contemplates (with what seems very like cruelty, though he is not really cruel) that misery and distress should run their course.' Once again, it was not a question of personal hard-heartedness. It was that the ministers and officials most responsible for policy in Ireland — above all Trevelyan, Wood and Russell — were committed to an ideology which frowned on intervention and even resigned itself to famine as, in some circumstances, an unavoidable evil. Routh wrote to Trevelyan in 1846: 'You cannot answer the cry of want by a quotation from political economy.' But this is precisely what the Government did do. As Cecil Woodham-Smith wrote in her magnificent, moving study: 'The influence of *laissez-faire* on the treatment of Ireland during the famine is impossible to exaggerate.'[21] It is the only thing that renders the apparently cruel behaviour of the British ministers at all intelligible.[22]

Liberals in the twentieth century have made great play of the view that liberalism is essentially an empirical, undogmatic and unfanatical approach to politics; and that it is therefore more likely to respect human rights and happiness in the present than the 'utopian' creeds of socialists, communists and fascists. Thus Bertrand Russell once asserted that 'empiricist liberalism' was the only philosophy possible for someone who 'desires human happiness more than the prevalence of this or that party or creed'. It was a general rule of this approach that 'it is seldom justifiable to embark on any policy on the ground that, though harmful in the present, it will be beneficial in the long run.'[23] Russell might well have considered the conduct of his own grandfather in the years 1846—49. The policy he followed in Ireland transgressed both these principles. It elevated a creed above human happiness and it asserted that present sufferings were justified for the sake of long-term benefits. And much the same might be said of the New Poor Law, with which Russell as a minister was also associated.[24] Liberalism has shown itself at times to be quite as dogmatic and inhumane as its ideological rivals. It also has its massacres and cruelties to answer for.

MANCHESTER AND ITS SCHOOL

One city above all others came to symbolize the achievement of capitalist industrialization in all its grandeur and grimness: Manchester. Manchester between about 1815 and 1850 was the essence of modernity, 'the most wonderful city in modern times', according to a character in Disraeli's *Coningsby*, the place to which people came to see the shape of the future.

But visitors marvelled at its squalor as much as at its productivity, and at the interrelation between them: 'From this foul drain', wrote de Tocqueville, 'the greatest stream of human industry flows out to fertilise the whole world. From this filthy sewer pure gold flows.' And Engels has a famous anecdote about a bourgeois to whom he spoke at length about the appalling living conditions of the working class in the city: 'The man listened quietly to the end, and said at the corner where we parted: "And yet there is a great deal of money made here; good morning, sir."' Tocqueville believed that what the city demonstrated was 'the individual powers of man' and the 'capricious creative force' of 'human liberty'; but there was no sign of 'the directing power of society' or 'the slow continuous action of government'.[25] The condition of Manchester, in other words, was a monument to economic freedom.

The association of Manchester with economic liberalism is not misplaced. It was to Manchester and the cotton industry that Richard Cobden came in 1828, because, as he said, this is 'the place for money making business'.[26] And when in the mid-1830s he turned to writing pamphlets, he signed them simply 'A Manchester Manufacturer'. It was from Manchester that the campaign to repeal the Corn Laws was launched, and largely directed. 'The League is Manchester', Cobden once remarked. They built the Free Trade Hall, which still stands on the site of Peterloo, and it was there that John Bright in 1852 declared 'We are called the Manchester party . . . and this building, I suppose, is the schoolroom of the Manchester School. . . . I do not repudiate that name at all.'[27]

Neither Cobden nor Bright were in any doubt about the historical significance of the battles they fought. Bright waged what he saw as a class struggle: 'I believe this to be a movement of the commercial and industrious classes against the lords and great proprietors of the soil', he said at an Anti-Corn League meeting in 1845.[28] Bright saw the free traders as crusaders, challenging the *ancien regime* of the great landowners in England, and he believed that the two Reform Acts of 1832 and 1867 achieved a transfer of power from the nobility to 'the people'. His rhetoric is anti-feudal rhetoric, full of denunciations of 'palaces, baronial castles, great halls, stately mansions', as well as 'crowns, coronets, mitres, military display, the pomp of war, wide colonies, and a huge empire.'[29]

Cobden too was conscious of the class dimension of the struggle for free trade, although he may have found it expedient to play it down in public. 'Most of us entered upon the struggle with the belief that we had a distinct class interest in the question . . . it has eminently been a middle class agitation.'[30] After Repeal he urged Peel to accept his historical role as representative of 'the *idea* of the age' and govern 'through the bona fide representatives of the middle class'. That was the only way in which the country could be governed in the wake of the Reform Act and Repeal. At the same time he sought to reassure Peel, the Tory, about the respectability of the middle class: 'Are you afraid of the middle class? You must know them better than to suppose that they are given to extreme or violent measures. They are not democratic.' He was not uncritical of the middle class, and deplored its lack of cultivation. But what he chiefly regretted was its lack of self-confidence, its habit of 'toadying' to 'a clodpole aristocracy, only less enlightened than themselves'.[31] Cobden knew, too, that many of the manufacturers who had supported the League did so on grounds of plain self-interest. For them it was, as he put it, a 'gross pocket question', and he disliked that. For Cobden saw the battle for free trade in a grand historical perspective, as the latest in a long historical sequence of struggles for freedom: 'In one century we had the contest for religious freedom — another century marks the era of political freedom — another century comes, and the great battle of commercial freedom has to be fought; and Manchester, and those free cotton districts around it . . . were pledged to take the lead in this great contest.' He was clear, then, about the liberal tradition to which Manchester and its school were the inheritors.

Cobden believed that the principle of free trade was 'eternal in its truth and universal in its application'. It was the key to global harmony and peace: 'the triumph of free trade was the triumph of pacific principles between all the nations of the earth.'[32] Like Paine, who argued that unrestricted commerce would 'extirpate the system of war',[33] he believed that war and conflict were the work of governments, whereas the interaction of societies and economies could only be mutually beneficial. So his watchword was: 'As little intercourse as possible betwixt *Governments*, as much connexion as possible between the *nations* of the world!'[34] He deplored the 'spirit of interference with other countries' and 'the wars to which it has led',[35] just as Bright disliked the idea that we should 'become knight-errants in the cause of freedom to other nations'.[36] It was quite logical, therefore, that both Cobden and Bright should have opposed the Crimean war, although neither of them, not even Bright, who was a Quaker, was a total pacifist. They paid a political price for this, both losing their seats in Parliament in the 1857 election. Cobden recorded his admiration for Fox's stand against the war with France in the 1790s.[37]

The futile sufferings of the Crimea did much to vindicate their stand, and the chauvinistic jeers of Tennyson (in *Maud*) among others look shabby in retrospect. Yet Palmerston, the war leader, also represented a strand in the liberal tradition. His jingoistic assertion of British rights was still intermingled with a spirited concern for the rights and independence of nations still struggling against the old European empires. It was Palmerston's view that 'constitutional states' were 'the natural allies of this country', and therefore that 'the independence of constitutional states . . . never can be a matter of indifference to the British Parliament'. What is more, Palmerston saw a clear link between constitutionalism, prosperity and property: 'It is impossible without a constitution fully to develop the national resources of a country and ensure for the nation security for life, liberty and property.'[38]

As it had emerged in the period of the French Revolution, nationalism and internationalism had been two sides of one coin. A stable international order required the dissolution of the old dynastic empires and a respect for the universal right of national self-determination. Hence the energetic support which British liberals, among others, gave to national independence struggles in Greece, Italy and South America. Liberal nationalism was not aggressive or expansionist. It sought only autonomy for itself, not domination over others. Therefore, a world composed of independent self-governing, and, it was hoped, liberal and constitutional states, would be a world at peace.

But now liberal internationalism was dividing into two separate streams. Idealism was giving way to two different versions of self-interest. Cobden and Bright kept alive the principle of opposition to imperialism and aggression, but combined it with a degree of insularity. Palmerston upheld the commitment to national independence, but increasingly manipulated it as simply a sentiment to support a chauvinist foreign policy. It would be wrong to doubt Cobden's sincerity, yet however idealistic *he* might be about free trade, others noted even at the time that the policy did appear to coincide remarkably with the interests of British trade and industry. An American commentator declared in 1866 that 'free trade was a system devised by England to 'enable her to plunder the world.'[39]

As for economic policy at home, the Manchester school, and Bright in particular, generally shared the anti-interventionist outlook of the class they spoke for. Bright was a lifelong opponent of all legislation that regulated hours of work, or terms and conditions of employment, and as late as 1875 opposed Forster as a possible Liberal Party leader because Forster was 'very fond of Factory Bills and the rotton legislation which has come so much into favour of late years'.[40] Both Cobden and Bright generally viewed trade unions with hostility, although in the Reform campaign of the 1860s both turned more towards the unions in the belief that working-class support was necessary to achieve political change. For the unions to attempt to obtain higher wages by organized pressure, however, was utterly futile. It was to defy nature itself: 'They might as well attempt to regulate the tides by force, or change the course of the seasons, or subvert any of the other laws of nature, for the wages of labour depend upon laws as unerring.'[41] In saying this Cobden was merely echoing what had by then become the conventional wisdom: 'To buy in the cheapest and sell in the dearest market, the supposed concentration of economic selfishness, is simply to fulfil the command of the Creator, who provides for all the wants of His creatures through each other's help.'[42] When Bright contemplated closing down his cotton mills in the bad times of the early 1840s, he commented 'Self-preservation is the first law of nature.'[43]

Bright enjoyed a nearly lifelong reputation as a radical, and both he and Cobden were regarded by the established upper class as 'outsiders'. Theirs was a radicalism within strictly liberal limits. It remained anti-interventionist and anti-statist long after the climate of opinion was moving away from these inflexible principles. By the 1870s Bright was looking sufficiently old-fashioned for Walter Bagehot to publish an essay teasingly entitled 'The Conservative Vein in Mr Bright'. Even in relation to the 1860s campaign for parliamentary reform it would be wrong to overestimate their radicalism. Bright echoed Cobden's remark about the middle class when he protested 'I do not pretend myself to be a democrat. I never accepted that title.' And on another occasion: 'I have never said anything in favour of universal suffrage.'[44] Despite voting for Mill's amendment in favour of votes for women in 1867, he was fundamentally opposed to women's emancipation, and disliked any sign of independence on the part of women.[45] Like Burke and other conservative strategists, he saw reform as a way of avoiding more radical or revolutionary changes. He told Disraeli that a Reform Bill was needed to 'so far content the people as to extinguish the associations now agitating the question'.[46] Not even radicals like Bright were free from that fear of democracy and of the working class which was so conspicuous a feature of mid-nineteenth century liberalism, and to which we must now turn.

15

The Fear of Democracy

Fear of the 'Mob', of the propertyless, is, as we have seen, a constant theme within liberalism. After 1789 this issue assumed a significantly different shape. It was no longer a question of popular discontents surfacing in occasional eruptions of anger and desperation, but of 'the people' as a constant force to be reckoned with, one conscious of its own distinctive existence and confident of the legitimacy of its rights and demands. Among the industrial proletariat, class consciousness had developed, and with it the first forms of trade unionism and socialism.

Liberalism was thus faced with a double challenge. There was the popular demand for participation in the political process on equal terms — for democracy. There was also the developing socialist critique of capitalism, coupled with the demand for social and economic changes which challenged some of the most basic principles of the liberal capitalist economy. The two pressures were not distinct from one another. It was widely believed by the fearful bourgeoisie that democracy would lead inexorably to the supremacy of the working class, and from that to socialism and the destruction of all private property. Nor was this belief without foundation. Popular demands for the vote were often based on the assumption that political reform was the prelude and precondition of social and economic change. This was the premise of Chartism, and the reason for the great *popular* support for parliamentary reform in Britain in the period 1815—32, and again in the 1860s. As Cobbett said of the 1832 Reform Act, the people wanted the Bill 'that it might do us some good; that it might better our situation . . . and not for the gratification of any abstract or metaphysical whim.'[1]

Middle-class liberals were fearful, not only for wealth and property, but also for the position and values of their class. In the minds of many of them, culture and enlightenment were threatened by popular rule, and some, such as James Mill and Richard Cobden, even gave explicit expression to the widely shared belief that the middle class was peculiarly fitted to provide leadership and government for the whole of society. No issue has so clearly revealed the class character of liberalism as an ideology.[2]

JAMES MILL AND THOMAS MACAULAY

James Mill's *Essay on Government*, which appeared in 1828, had not long been published when it had the misfortune to be subjected to a particularly thorough and savage attack by the young Thomas Babington Macaulay, and this attack rather than the *Essay* itself has tended to attract the attention of posterity. Mill presented a utilitarian case in favour of democracy, or at least manhood suffrage; and it was against this as well as against Mill's *a priori* method that Macaulay directed his fire. Throughout his life Macaulay held the view that universal suffrage was incompatible with the very existence of government and even of civilization, as he stated in his speech of opposition to Chartism on 3 May 1842. He argued that Mill's democracy would lead to the rich being 'pillaged', and that such an attack on property would lead in turn to the destruction of civilization and a reversion to barbarism.[3]

Macaulay's opposition to Mill on the question of democracy, and his empiricist criticisms of Mill's utilitarian logic have tended to obscure what the two writers have in common. For example, Macaulay ridicules Mill for excluding women from the franchise: 'he placidly dogmatises away the interest of one half of the human race' (p. 385), but then proceeds to do almost exactly the same himself: 'The interest of a respectable Englishman may be said, without any impropriety, to be identical with that of his wife' (p. 386).

More important is their consensus on the key role they allot to the middle class in society. Mill was clearly anxious to assure his readers that democracy would not mean the end of the hegemony of the middle class, 'the class which is universally described as both the most wise and the most virtuous part of the community', since the lower orders accepted that hegemony: 'Of the people beneath them, a vast majority would be sure to be guided by their advice and example.'[4] Macaulay disagreed with this expectation, but he broadly shared Mill's opinion of the middle class, though not all of Mill's anti-aristocratic bias: 'the higher and middling orders are the natural representatives of the human race. Their interest may be opposed in some things to that of their poorer contemporaries; but it is identical with that of the innumerable generations which are to follow' (p. 393). In the light of subsequent experience it is clear that Mill's prediction was more acute than Macaulay's apocalyptic expectations.

However, Macaulay's fear was to become the more common liberal response as the confidence of the early nineteenth century drained away. He believed that to enfranchise the poor and propertyless would threaten property and hence civilization, for 'where property is insecure, no climate however delicious, no soil however fertile, no conveniences for trade and navigation, no natural endowments of body or of mind, can prevent a nation from sinking into barbarism.' It was likewise important to preserve not only property, but also its radically unequal distribution: 'The inequality with which wealth is distributed forces itself on everybody's notice. It is at once perceived by the eye. The reasons which irrefragably prove this inequality to be necessary to the wellbeing of all classes are not equally obvious.'[5] Here Macaulay was following Burke, whom he once described as 'the greatest man since Milton'. Typically, while he admired Burke, he was decidedly ambivalent about Fox, and had no time at all for Paine, whom this 'moderate' once described as 'that stupid worthless drunken dirty beast'.[6] There is an echo of Burke's attacks on 'political arithmetic' in Macaulay's contention that 'it is not by mere numbers, but by property and intelligence, that the nation ought to be governed', and it is revealing that this assertion came in the context of a speech in support of the first Reform Bill. Macaulay's slogan was 'Reform, that you may preserve.'[7] Reform was the means of saving property, and indeed society itself; it was the one sure way to avert revolution.

This liberal flexibility was indistinguishable from Burkean conservatism. Macaulay is one of those figures through whom Whig conservatism is carried through into the mainstream of parliamentary liberalism. He was securely Whig in his enthusiasm for 1688, but the terms in which he defended it revealed the conservatism of the Whigs: 'The highest eulogy which can be pronounced on the revolution of 1688 is this, that it was our last revolution.'[8] And, paradoxically, even that revolution was a conservative one: 'It is because we had a preserving revolution in the seventeenth century that we have not had a destroying revolution in the nineteenth.' Revolution in his own day would inevitably lead to socialism, and socialism was a high-flown name for robbery. Thus Macaulay's reaction to 1848, the year of revolutions, was one of fear and horror: 'I stood aghast', and he trembled for the survival of 'civilization'. Civilization was saved, 'but at what a price!' — the price, in fact, of the despotism of Napoleon III. Macaulay disliked despotism, but less than he feared the 'red republic'.[9] Hence the price had to be paid, even by liberals.

Macaulay was not universally admired, even by liberals. Lord Acton placed him beside Burke as one of 'our two greatest writers', but Matthew Arnold dubbed him 'the great apostle of the Philistines', and John Morley agreed: Macaulay was 'one of the middle-class crowd in his heart'.[10] It was typical of his conventional cast of mind that he should have jeered at Southey's *Colloquies* with their criticisms of industrial capitalism, and defended Malthus against his critics.[11] Part of his philistinism may be seen in his view of poetry, which, in his essay on Milton, he argued, in the manner of Locke, was essentially the product of primitive rather than advanced societies: 'the vocabulary of an enlightened society is philosophical, that of a half-civilized people is poetical.'[12] Progress leaves poetry behind. Once again orthodox liberalism fails to find a role in its scheme of things for imagination and art.

1848 AND THE LIBERALS

The year 1848 was a watershed in the development of liberalism. What made it so was the independent role played by the workers in Paris and other European cities in the revolutions of that year. Their demands challenged both property and the 'laws' of the market. Many liberals had been happy to consider themselves 'friends of the people' so long as the people confined themselves to making essentially liberal demands. In 1848, however, the demand was for social revolution, for the 'red republic'. Confronted with this, Macaulay was by no means the only liberal to identify himself with the forces of order and authority. Indeed, 'The liberals, prizing the rights of 1789, saw these endangered by the intrusion of the masses and were thus driven on to the side of the counter-revolution; indeed, in most of Europe, the defeat of the revolution was achieved by liberals, to their own subsequent ruin.'[13]

There were some more sympathetic responses. George Eliot, who was to respond very differently to the prospect of parliamentary reform in the 1860s, greeted the French Revolution with enthusiasm. 'I feared that you lacked revolutionary ardour', she wrote to a friend, 'But no — you are just as *sans-culottish* and rash as I would have you . . . I thought we had fallen on such evil days that we were to see no really great movement . . . but I begin to be glad of my date.'[14] Matthew Arnold, in his two sonnets *To a Republican Friend, 1848*, begins by expressing a kind of solidarity — 'God knows it, I am with you' — but immediately follows this with an 'if', and devotes the remaining 27 lines to a whole series of doubts and qualifications. Arnold's friend, Arthur Hugh Clough, was in Rome in 1849, and brilliantly reported his responses to the brief life of the Roman Republic of that year in his *Amours de Voyage*.

Clough's sympathies are with the republicans, but as for becoming actively involved — that brings out hesitations very like Arnold's. Would he be prepared to die defending the English girls he has been dallying with, he asks himself:

> No, if it should be at all, it should be on the barricades there;
> Should I incarnadine ever this inky pacifical finger,
> Sooner far should it be for this vapour of Italy's freedom,
> Sooner far by the side of the d--d and dirty plebeians.
> (Canto II, iv)

Yet freedom is a vapour, and the people are dirty plebeians. Byron may have found the people dirty, but he did not treat freedom as a vapour. Clough, by contrast, shrinks from the very notions of action and commitment:

I do not like being moved: for the will is excited; and action
Is a most dangerous thing; I tremble for something factitious,
Some malpractice of heart and illegitimate process;
We are so prone to these things with our terrible notions of duty.
                                                          (II, xi)

Clough's self-awareness, through which he observes and analyses his own
behaviour, impulses and motives, seems to us very modern. It is usually interpreted in terms of his own biography, and his personal alienation from the
bourgeois liberal ethic of 'getting on':

Each for himself is still the rule,
We learn it when we go to school —
   The devil take the hindmost, o!

But this is also an episode in the development of liberalism, in its growing loss
of assurance, and its consequent fastidious withdrawal from a public world
dominated by class conflicts it neither likes nor understands, into a private world
of individual self-cultivation and personal relationships.

                          ALEXANDER HERZEN

Although many of his writings, including his memoirs, are now translated into
English, Herzen has never received the attention or achieved the reputation
he deserves. Perhaps it is his fate, like that of many other brilliant figures in
Russia's pre-revolutionary culture, to be forever overshadowed by the great
geniuses of the Russian novel. As it is, most readers of English are as likely
to have encountered him mediated through the essays of Isaiah Berlin as to
have met him face to face, as it were. This is a mixed blessing. Berlin is generally
over-anxious to claim Herzen for his own tradition of empiricist liberalism,
as someone committed primarily to 'the preservation of individual liberty',
and impacably opposed to the sacrifice of individuals and their happiness 'upon
the altar of idealised abstractions'. Berlin links Herzen's name with those of
Erasmus, Montaigne and Montesquieu, and sees him as hostile to utopianism
and to socialism: 'The dogmas of socialism seem to him no less stifling than
those of capitalism.'[15]

   This is somewhat misleading, since Herzen certainly regarded himself as
a socialist, and also a little odd, since in another essay, 'Herzen and his
Memoirs', Berlin refers to Herzen's 'socialist beliefs' and his 'revolutionary
temperament and instincts'. He also says, quite rightly, that 'he did not, despite
all his distrust of political fanaticism . . . turn into a cautious, reformist liberal

constitutionalist. Even in his gradualist phase he remained an agitator, an egalitarian and a socialist to the end.'[16] Herzen, like Heine, is in fact a transitional, ambivalent figure: 'I hate, especially since the calamities of the year 1848, democrats who flatter the mob, but I hate still more aristocrats who slander the people.'[17] In his memoirs, Herzen records how he grew up to identify himself with the liberal tradition and with the cause of the Decembrists of 1825. He read Pushkin, whose works circulated in manuscript form (samizdat), and Schiller. His favourite Schiller character was the Marquis of Posa, the man of liberal principle who in *Don Carlos* defends the cause of the Flemish rebels against Spanish and Catholic domination. Like so many others he read, and was impressed by, de Tocqueville's *Democracy in America*. He also responded to the ideas of the Saint-Simonian socialists.

The remarkable series of essays on the events of 1848 which Herzen published under the title *From the Other Shore* is as much a critique of liberalism as anything else. It is also a mirror of Herzen's varying moods and reactions. There are moments when he advises withdrawal, and when he suggests that the only possible ideal is that of isolated individual integrity, to be a 'free man' and defy the pressure to align oneself with any particular political movement. This is Herzen in his liberal aspect, alarmed because the masses are concerned with bread rather than freedom: 'They are indifferent to individual freedom, to freedom of speech; the masses love authority' — and appalled at the thought of generations of human beings being sacrificed for the sake of a future utopia which recedes even as it is approached: 'Do you truly wish to condemn all human beings alive to-day to the sad role of caryatids supporting a floor for others some day to dance on? . . . an end that is infinitely remote is not an end, but, if you like, a trap; an end must be nearer.'[18]

Yet these misgivings and resistances do not, finally, force Herzen into an anti-revolutionary or anti-socialist position. He is convinced that a social revolution, a revolution against capitalism, is both necessary and inevitable: 'It is plain to us that things cannot continue as they have been in the past, that the exclusive rule of capital and the absolute right of property has come to its end just as had the reign of feudalism and the aristocracy in its time.' Liberalism has achieved what it can, and its liberating potential is now exhausted: 'The political revolution which modifies the forms of the state without affecting the forms of life has gone as far as it possibly can.'[19] He sees the achievements of liberalism, 'the development of the middle class, a constitutional order' as 'transitory forms linking the feudal—monarchic world with the social-republican one'; and he puts his finger on many of the basic weaknesses of liberalism: 'They want freedom and even a republic provided it is confined to their own cultivated circle. Beyond the limits of their moderate circle they become conservatives.' They 'played happily with the idea of revolution', but in 1848 retreated in terror before the 'hurricane' of the popular upheaval, 'and then they hid from their *brother* behind the bayonets of martial law in their effort to save *civilization and order!*' [20]

Liberal capitalist civilization is full of contradictions: it is 'a civilization of the minority . . . made possible only by the existence of a majority of pro-letarians.' It proclaims both 'the absolute right to property, on the one hand, and the inalienable right to life, on the other'. [21] And to the great material question of the day, 'the question of daily bread liberalism did not give much serious thought'. It is doomed, and Herzen urges his son not to identify himself with the old order: 'do not, I beg, remain on *this shore*. . . . Better to perish with the revolution than to seek refuge in the almshouse of reaction.' [22]

Herzen himself remained stranded between the old and the new worlds, 'belonging neither to the one nor to the other', [23] like Matthew Arnold contem-plating the monastery of the Grande Chartreuse: 'Wandering between two worlds, one dead / The other to be born' — although Herzen's mood is far more positive and energetic than Arnold's. Herzen is remarkable precisely because he does not follow the liberal path of retreat into privacy and political reaction, because he is so powerfully aware of the limits of liberalism and the justice of the people's cause. Yet he is sufficiently a part of bourgeois liberal culture to regret its anticipated demise, and to fear the authoritarian tendencies he detects within socialism and the workers' movement. No one understood better than Herzen himself his own ambivalent and transitional, yet finally committed position. If Herzen is a liberal, he is also one of liberalism's most acute critics.

DE TOCQUEVILLE

The liberal position which Herzen attacked, that of retreat into repression in the face of the popular challenge, has its most distinguished representative in Alexis de Tocqueville. Tocqueville was depressed and horrified by the outbreak of the revolution in France on 24 February 1848, even though it was something he had himself predicted. What dismayed him was not the collapse of the bourgeois monarchy of Louis Philippe — a regime he despised — but the emergence of socialist leaders and the demand for social and economic revolu-tion. He strongly supported the suppression of the workers' movement in the June Days. He was disappointed by the failure of General Cavaignac, the 'hero' of that suppression, to beat Louis Napoleon in the presidential election of December 1848; but he was nevertheless willing to serve as foreign minister under Louis Napoleon for some months in 1849. Like Macaulay, he supported a reactionary dictatorship when the alternative appeared to be a 'red republic'. 'He had fallen victim to the doctrine of "the lesser evil". . . . The social peril threw him off his balance.' [24] It was liberalism itself which was thrown off balance.

The irony was that so much of Tocqueville's writings, above all *Democracy in America*, was devoted to persuading himself as well as his readers that there could be no turning back the clock, no halting the advance of democracy and equality. This represented a triumph of historical objectivity over personal sentiments and values. Tocqueville was an aristocrat. Born in 1805, his childhood was lived in the shadow of the Revolution and of the terror, in which several of his relatives had been executed. His political realism early brought him into conflict with his own family and friends, yet he wept when the last of the Bourbons was driven into exile in 1830, and he despised the timid and mediocre character of the middle class which was brought to power in that year.

Moreover, his natural attachment to his own class was reinforced by his rational conviction that a strong, self-confident aristocracy supplied the most powerful bulwark against the despotism of a king or state, and so acted as a guarantee of freedom for the whole community. For it is the state or government which has absorbed the powers which formerly belonged to the nobility, leaving society as a whole more powerless than ever. He believed that there was 'far more freedom' before 1789 'than there is today', even if it was, as he admitted, 'a curiously ill-adjusted, intermittent freedom, always restricted by class distinctions and tied up with immunities and privileges'.[25] In his belief in the functional virtues of the aristocracy, as in many other respects, Tocqueville was consciously following in the steps of his equally aristocratic predecessor, Montesquieu.

Nevertheless Tocqueville was convinced that the whole of modern history showed equality gaining ground. He treats the terms 'democracy' and 'equality' as virtually synonymous, and, as Hugh Brogan has suggested, his book might more aptly have been called *Equality in America*.[26] By equality he meant social equality, or equality of status, but not economic equality which, as an orthodox liberal in economics, he regarded as an utter impossibility. But while outright opposition to the direction of history was useless, there was no cause for despair: 'The first duty which is at this time imposed upon those who direct our affairs is to educate the democracy', says Tocqueville in a phrase which found many echoes in this period.[27]

He believed that there was a radical tension between democracy and liberty, and this was a point which other worried liberals took up. It should be noticed though that Tocqueville's conception of liberty was by no means the merely negative one of an absence of constraint or restrictions. Freedom means, or at least involves, active participation in public political life:

only freedom can deliver the members of a community from that isolation which is the lot of the individual left to his own devices and, compelling them to get in touch with each other, promote an active sense of fellowship. In a community of free citizens every man is daily reminded of the need of meeting his fellow men, of hearing what they have to say, or exchanging ideas, and coming to an agreement as to the conduct of their common interests.[28]

Thus Tocqueville does not make the definitional separation of democracy from freedom that many twentieth-century liberals have made. On the contrary he explicitly associates freedom with participatory democracy, and in so doing shows his links with the old republican tradition, in which freedom is bound up with participation and civic spirit.

Tocqueville was by no means despondent about the possibilities of a democratic or egalitarian society preserving freedom. Nevertheless, democratic society contained serious dangers, among which he numbered its characteristic climate of opinion, which he believed to be overpoweringly conformist, to the extent that he coined his best-known phrase, 'the tyranny of the majority', to describe it. This was a melodramatic term, and Tocqueville does not provide the evidence to justify it, but he does give a very subtle and perceptive account of the ways in which public opinion as a force can restrict the range of options really open to individuals: 'The will of man is not shattered, but softened, bent, and guided . . . such a power . . . does not tyrannize, but it compresses, enervates, extinguishes, and stupifies a people, till each nation is reduced to be nothing better than a flock of timid and industrious animals, of which the government is the shepherd.'[29] Tocqueville believed that what he saw as the lack of outstanding individuals in America was the product of this passion for conformity, and that the life of society as a whole suffered as a result. This was a theme which was to be taken up by one of the many worried liberals who read *Democracy in America* when it appeared in the 1830s, John Stuart Mill.

What is strange, at first sight, is that Tocqueville, who understood so well the democratic passion for equality, should have failed to see that it would inevitably involve a measure of economic equality as well. For Tocqueville, unlike Herzen, could see neither justice nor rationality in the philosophy of socialism or the grievances of the masses. He was an uncritical believer in *laissez-faire* economics, and he believed that the demands for work, and for unemployment relief, raised in Paris in 1848, rested upon a simple failure to understand that economic laws doomed such enterprises to failure.[30] But he also feared the masses, and saw their rebellion in June as a threat to the whole order of civilized society.

It is, I think, misleading to call him 'a sincere democrat'.[31] He accepted democracy because he thought there was no choice; and the account of his mock-modest participation in the election under universal male suffrage of 1848 is strikingly similar to an episode in Giuseppe di Lampedusa's great novel *The Leopard*, in which another mid-nineteenth century aristocrat, the Prince of

Salina, makes the same necessary adjustment to the arrival of democracy in Sicily in 1860. In truly Tocquevillian style, Tancredi, the Prince's nephew, tells his uncle 'If we want things to stay as they are, things will have to change. D'you understand?'[32] But when democracy threatened to open the way to socialism, Tocqueville drew back and joined the side of 'order', which, in 1848, was a euphemism for direct, brutal repression of the urban poor. It was not a mere personal aberration or failure. It represents the liberal crisis of 1848, and one kind of liberal response to that crisis.

BRITAIN'S 'LEAP IN THE DARK': 1867

Apart from an inflated panic among the propertied classes over the Chartist demonstration on Kennington Common, nothing happened in Britain in 1848. The liberal crisis over democracy did not fully emerge until the 1860s, when the prospect of a second enlargement of the male electorate brought many fears and misgivings into the open. As we have seen, even Bright, a leader of the agitation for a second Reform Bill, was anxious to disclaim the label of 'democrat', while Gladstone, who reaped the political harvest of the Reform Act, was even more circumspect. In a debate on the franchise in 1864 he spelt out what he regarded as essential qualifications for having the vote: 'self-command, self-control, respect for order, patience under suffering, confidence in the law and regard for superiors'. It was because he believed that the working class had by the 1860s come to display these appropriately conformist characteristics that he came round to the idea of the further extension of the franchise. It was, in fact, the decline of Chartism and the turning away of the working class from 'political agitation' which reconciled many Liberals to further reform. Edward Baines, who introduced a Reform Bill into Parliament in 1864, had been an opponent of household suffrage in the 1840s. Twenty years later he was less worried about its consequences: 'we need not fear that the Parliament will ever be composed of low class men', he wrote privately.[33] Middle-class hegemony was safe.

GEORGE ELIOT AND 'FELIX HOLT'

There were still those who drew back from the prospect of democracy. One of these was George Eliot. By the time she wrote *Felix Holt*, in the mid-1860s, her '*sans culottish*' mood of 1848 was a long way behind her. The political dimension of this novel, set in and around the year 1832, constituted a warning against popular radicalism and 'mob' excitements. Felix Holt 'The Radical', is in reality Felix Holt the cautious, conservative working man, urging restraint and good behaviour on his supposedly less rational and far-sighted comrades. Holt's view is that the question of the vote is unimportant: a wider franchise will not improve matters so long as working men are 'drunken and stupid',[34] for 'Ignorant power comes in the end to the same thing as wicked power; it makes misery' (p. 399).

This message was spelt out even more clearly in Holt's 'Address to Working Men', which Eliot wrote as a pendant to the novel in 1867. The Address warns against 'a too hasty wresting of measures which seem to promise an immediate partial relief' (p. 613), but actually do fatal damage to the delicate, elaborate network of social life. It warns against class antagonisms, for 'any attempt to do away directly with the actually existing class distinctions and advantages' (p. 616) is futile; and, indeed, to attack the rich and the 'leisure and ease' of the rich is, in effect, to threaten the inheritance of culture and knowledge itself (pp. 621—2).

The Address warns against disorder, often fomented by 'dishonest men', and engaged in by 'Roughs' at 'the hideous margin of society' (p. 618). Such disorder could even lead to 'civil war'. Working men must understand that 'the fundamental duty of a government is to preserve order, to enforce obedience of the laws' (p. 619). All this is so deeply conservative that the most striking thing is that Eliot still apparently thinks of Holt as a radical. Liberalism, still seeing itself as liberalism, is steadily adopting a conservative stance.

George Eliot had the ability to watch this process at work; in the character of Daniel Deronda, she portrays, analyses and explains just how the liberal temperament and mind can become withdrawn from political action and fall into a state of honest, sensitive indecision and ineffectiveness:

> His early-wakened sensibility and reflectiveness had developed into a many-sided sympathy, which threatened to hinder any persistent course of action . . . his fear of falling into an unreasoning narrow hatred made a check for him: he apologised for the heirs of privilege; he shrank with dislike from the loser's bitterness and the denunciatory tone of the unaccepted innovator. A too reflective and diffusive sympathy was in danger of paralysing in him that indignation against wrong and that select-ness of fellowship which are the conditions of moral force.[35]

The whole passage, too long for quotation here, may be taken as a classic statement of the ever-sharpening liberal dilemma in the twentieth century.

MATTHEW ARNOLD

Arnold's complex political responses reveal him as in some ways a transitional figure between traditional liberalism and the 'New Liberalism' of Britain in the period between 1880 and 1920. Arnold called himself a liberal — with qualifications: 'I am a Liberal, yet I am a Liberal tempered by experience, reflection, and renouncement, and I am, above all, a believer in culture',[36] he declares in the Introduction to *Culture and Anarchy* (1869). This was very much to the point, since much of that book is an attack on the conventional liberalism which he associated especially with politicians like Bright, Roebuck and Robert Lowe: 'the great middle-class liberalism, which had for the cardinal points of its belief the Reform Bill of 1832, and local self-government, in politics; in the social sphere, free-trade, unrestricted competition, and the making of large industrial fortunes' (p. 62). In particular he attacks the inadequacy of the orthodox liberal idea of freedom, which he calls 'Doing as one likes'. Free speech, for instance, is not a sufficient principle 'unless what men say, when they may say what they like, is worth saying' (p. 50). Similarly he mocks the idea of 'the blessedness of the franchise' (p. 65), and suggests that Bright believes 'that the having a vote, like the having a large family, or a large business, or large muscles, has in itself some edifying and perfecting effect upon human nature' (p. 64). Free trade, which Arnold, (our latter-day scholars should note) uses as virtually a synonym for *laissez-faire*, is also attacked: 'the mere unfettered pursuit of the production of wealth, and the mere mechanical multiplying, for this end, of manufactures and population, threatens to create for us, if it has not created already, those vast, miserable, unmanageable masses of sunken people' (p. 193).

It is clear, however, that one thing that troubles Arnold is that orthodox liberalism has nothing to offer which might 'civilize' and restrain the rising tide of popular democracy. Liberalism has no conception of authority. Feudalism, 'with its ideas and habits of subordination' (p. 74) did. But now it is dying out, and 'we are in danger of drifting towards anarchy' (p. 75). The working class has taken over the liberal idea of doing as one likes, and the consequences fill Arnold with fear and even hatred: 'this and that body of men, all over the country, are beginning to assert and put in practice an Englishman's right to do what he likes; his right to march where he likes, meet where he likes, enter where he likes, hoot as he likes, threaten as he likes, smash as he likes. All this, I say, tends to anarchy' (p. 76). A demonstration in favour of parliamentary reform in July 1866 had led to scuffles with the police and the railings around Hyde Park had been trampled down. This was the occasion which stirred Arnold's fear of 'the mob', and prompted his tirades against 'rioters' and 'roughs', 'smashing' and 'threatening'.

What does Arnold suggest as a response to the threat of anarchy which he like so many others, saw in the popular pressure for democracy? At one level his answer is 'culture'. The diffusion of civilized values throughout society will temper the coarseness and militancy of the masses. This is comparable to Mill's concern to see people educated before they acquired the vote, and with the

sentiment summed up in the familiar phrase 'we must educate our masters'.
But to restore, or sustain 'that profound sense of settled order and security,
without which a society like ours cannot live and grow at all' (p. 82), new forms
of *authority* are also required. Arnold suggests two. Within the field of culture,
narrowly conceived, he promotes the conception of an academy, along the lines
of the French model, to uphold standards, and constitute 'a paramount right
reason' (p. 118). Arnold was no more troubled than Mill by relativist doubts
about how such intellectual distinction might be identified.

On the more general level, it is the state to which Arnold looks to provide
the authority and firm control necessary to prevent democracy from sliding
down into anarchy: 'We want an authority, and we find nothing but jealous
classes, checks, and a deadlock; culture suggests the idea of *the State*' (p. 96).
Arnold had already put forward this kind of idea in 1861 in his essay on
Democracy, in which he had made a strong case for a change of attitude towards
the state, as the only force which can, in a more democratic society, 'give a
high tone to the nation'. He used this general argument to urge an expansion
of the system of state schooling. Thus, both at the general and the particular
levels, he moves away from the traditional liberal suspicion of the state, and
puts forward instead a rather idealist conception of the state as 'the representative acting-power of the nation',[37] which anticipates the thinking of T. H.
Green and the 'New Liberalism'.

Arnold's view of the state leads to another and less benign conclusion. Our
'best self, or right reason' also urges us 'to set our face against' demonstrations, processions, meetings — 'whatever brings risk of tumult and disorder'
— and to support 'the occupants of the executive power, whoever they may
be, in firmly prohibiting them' (p. 97). Not only is culture 'the external
opponent' of Jacobinism (p. 66); it also requires a 'profound sense of settled
order and security'. All this is more conservative than liberal, and it is not
surprising to find that Arnold, like Macaulay, was one of those nineteenth
century liberals who cherished a special veneration for Burke: 'Burke is so great
because, almost alone in England, he brings thought to bear upon politics,
he saturates politics with thought.'[38]

Arnold was of course right to sense that the old *laissez-faire* liberalism was
running out of political ideas, and had no answer to the social problems of
the day. His own response, couched in terms of culture and the state, had the
two aspects of enlightened paternalism and resolute authoritarianism. In another
essay, on 'Equality', he argued that social inequality and class structures were
obstacles to a truly civilized society, and 'to live in a society of equals' was
bound to nourish the confidence and self-respect of the majority of individuals.[39]
Yet when the people demanded their rights, he called for repression and talked
of the need for authority.

All this makes an ironic contrast with the confessions of uncertainty, doubt and hesitation which abound in his poetry. Arnold's mood there contrasts sharply with the commitment of the poets of the revolutionary moment, such as Shelley:

> Thou waitest for the spark from heaven! and we,
> Light half-believers of our casual creeds,
> Who never deeply felt, nor clearly will'd,
> Whose insight never has borne fruit in deeds,
> Whose vague resolves never have been fulfill'd;
> (*The Scholar-Gipsy*)

This sense of loss and yearning, an awareness of a 'buried life' beneath ordinary existence, reflects, no doubt, Arnold's personal biography as well as the loss of faith in Christianity which plainly troubled him. But it also has a political dimension. Like Clough, he felt deeply alienated from the more philistine aspects of liberal capitalism — the celebration of wealth and the ethic of competition and 'getting on'. His sense of isolation was enhanced by his inability to share in the old liberal hope and confidence, as revealed in his 1848 sonnets, and his keen awareness that neither industrial capitalism nor secular liberalism had found a role for culture or imagination. Arnold uses the old liberal image of the prison, but, as Trilling points out, in a deeply fatalistic way: 'Most men in a brazen prison live' suggests that this is 'the ineluctable condition of life in society' rather than a condition from which liberation is a real possibility.[40] In these circumstances, the only refuge lies in personal relations: only there can the 'buried life' be occasionally recovered. *Dover Beach*, besides being a classic expression of the mid-nineteenth century crisis of religious doubt, is also a classic expression of the mood of liberalism in retreat, withdrawing from 'a darkling plain / Swept with confused alarms of struggle and flight' into the private life: 'Ah, love, let us be true / To one another!'

JOHN STUART MILL

To incorporate Mill under the heading of this chapter does justice neither to the detail of his thinking on the issue of democracy, nor to the scope and subtlety of his thought as a whole. Nevertheless, this issue may serve as a starting-point in considering this central figure in modern liberalism. He is central if only on account of his lasting popularity and influence. In the English-speaking world no name is more habitually linked to that of liberalism than Mill's, and no single liberal text is better known than *On Liberty*. Isaiah Berlin described Mill as 'the man who . . . founded modern liberalism', and *On Liberty* as 'the classic statement of the case for individual liberty'.[41] That is a fair indication of his continued standing.

Perhaps, too, no thinker illustrates more clearly and fully the characteristic ambiguities in the liberal response to democracy. Both his father, James Mill, and Bentham were thoroughgoing advocates of the principle of representative democracy, at least for men, and the younger Mill had this principle among others firmly instilled in him. But after the mental breakdown and personal crisis he went through at the age of twenty, Mill became receptive to the ideas of Coleridge and Carlyle, and those of Comte and the Saint-Simonian socialists. What these very different tendencies had in common was their lack of interest in democracy, and the importance they attached to the role of intellectuals in society. These ideas were reflected in Mill's essays of 1831 on 'The Spirit of the Age', in which he lamented that the normal state of affairs, in which 'the uninstructed have faith in the instructed' did not prevail, with the result that 'The multitude are without a guide, and society is exposed to all the errors and dangers' which follow from the ignorant dabbling in matters of which they are ignorant. [42] The right order of things is, as Mill put it in a letter of 1829, that 'the intellectual classes lead the government, and the government leads the stupid classes.' [43]

But it was the first volume of Tocqueville's *Democracy in America*, published in 1835, which, according to Mill himself, awoke him to the dangers as well as the virtues of democracy, and began the move away from 'pure democracy' to the 'modified form of it' which he expounded most fully in *Representative Government* in 1861. Mill became increasingly concerned about Tocqueville's 'tyranny of the majority'. He was not uncritical of the Frenchman's treatment of this idea. He noted the absence of examples and detail, and he noted, too, the eagerness with which the phrase had been taken up by Conservatives, including Peel. [44] What Mill understood by the phrase was, essentially, the dominance of a monolithic and intolerant public opinion. This, in his opinion, constituted a threat to both liberty and individuality, and therefore to progress and development in society. By the time he came to write *On Liberty* in the late 1850s, he was more anxious about the restrictive effects of 'society' than about the power of the state itself. This 'social tyranny' he saw as 'more formidable than many kinds of political oppression, since . . . it leaves fewer means of escape, penetrating much more deeply into the details of life, and enslaving the soul itself.'

There were two main grounds for this anxiety. First he was firmly convinced of the virtues of the individual thinking for herself. That is the ideal of the rational person. And it is only through making our own choices that we achieve intellectual and moral health. People are naturally diverse, and should not be rendered uniform by social pressures. However reluctant he may have been to admit it, for it was not consistent with utilitarianism, individual independence is something which Mill values in itself. But personal freedom is also important from the point of view of society and human progress, because it is through deviant and dissenting individuals that progress and change are achieved: 'The unlikeness of one man to another is not only a principle of improvement, but would seem almost to be the only principle.'[45] On another occasion he wrote that 'what the improvement of mankind and of all their works most imperatively demands is variety, not uniformity.' The inherent tendency of democracy, according to Mill, was not towards anarchy or social disintegration but, on the contrary, towards stagnation and 'a general torpidity and imbecility'.[46] These could only be counteracted by ensuring a general tolerance of dissent and eccentricity, and by providing mechanisms which would ensure that deviant minorities enjoyed not merely toleration, but influence within society.

But who are these few innovative individuals who are the 'salt of the earth', in Mill's phrase? Leaving aside the slide from 'the individual' to 'the exceptional individual', which is perhaps inherent in the concept, we find that Mill tends to associate the cause of individuality with the cause of the hegemony of intellectuals, as when he speaks of 'the decay of individual energy, the weakening of the influence of superior minds over the multitude',[47] or when he urges that the power of the majority should be 'tempered by respect for the personality of the individual, and deference to the superiority of cultivated intelligence'.[48] Similarly he tells us in *On Liberty* that 'No government by a democracy or a numerous aristocracy . . . ever did or could rise above mediocrity except in so far as the sovereign many have let themselves be guided (which in their best times they always have done) by the counsels and influence of a more highly gifted and instructed *one* or *few*.' This is immediately followed by 'The initiation of all wise or noble things comes and must come from individuals; generally at first from some one individual.' Mill's move away from 'pure' democracy was inspired by the familiar fear of the masses: 'We dreaded the ignorance and especially the selfishness and brutality of the mass' he recalled[49] — and by his concern that the sources of enlightenment and progress should be safeguarded.

How was this to be done? At different times Mill put forward a number of different ideas. In his first essay on Tocqueville he defended 'the existence of a leisured class': 'a numerous class possessed of hereditary leisure' could provide 'the great and salutary corrective of all the inconveniences to which democracy is liable'. A few years later he praised Coleridge's notion of a 'clerisy', of 'an endowed class, for the cultivation of learning, and for diffusing its results among the community'.[50] Subsequently, however, he seems to have become convinced that more than this was needed, and that political institutions themselves would have to be constructed in such a way as to restrict the power of the majority. One such device was to ensure that the function of the popularly-elected parliament or assembly was 'not to make the laws, but to see that they are made by the right persons, and to be the organ of the nation for giving

or withholding its ratification of them.'[51] This was in line with his conception
of a 'rational democracy', which was

> not that the people themselves govern, but that they have *security* for good
> government . . . Provided good intentions can be secured, the best
> government, (need it be said?) must be the government of the wisest,
> and these must always be a few. The people ought to be the masters,
> but they are masters who must employ servants more skilful than
> themselves . . .[52]

The device to which Mill probably attached most importance was that of
a weighted voting system, in which everyone, including women, would have
one vote, but some people would have more than one vote, this privilege being
'annexed to education, not to property'.[53] Mill was clear that universal suffrage
was the precondition of such a scheme: everyone has the right to participate
in politics, but not equally, for 'It is the fact, that one person is *not* as good
as another.'[54] And, 'It is not useful, but hurtful, that the constitution of the
country should declare ignorance to be entitled to as much political power as
knowledge.'[55] Mill's scheme would secure the 'superiority of weight justly due
to opinions grounded on superiority of knowledge.'[56]

Mill's attitude towards democracy is thus deeply ambivalent. On the one
hand he, like Tocqueville, is a firm believer in participatory citizenship, and
wishes to see as much popular involvement in decision-taking as possible. In
one very important respect he was a more consistent and thorough democrat
than many who claimed that title: he made no distinction betwen men and
women. By universal suffrage he meant universal suffrage, and not male
suffrage, and, true to this view, he moved an amendment to the 1867 Reform
Bill in favour of women's suffrage.

On the other hand, he shared middle-class fears of the working class and
the 'mass of brutish ignorance' which it supposedly embodied. He was always
very free with his references to 'the common herd', 'the uncultivated herd',
and so on, and he believed that democracy could become 'a mere mob-
government'[57] if it were not curbed and qualified. Mill was a Platonist, not
only in so far as he believed in government by the best, but also in his absolute
confidence that the 'best' and the 'wisest' could be readily identified. It is
therefore misleading to suggest, as Berlin does, that he was exempt 'from the
elitist tendency of his Fabian disciples'.[58] Even if Mill does not believe that
the intellectual, educated minority should govern (and this is not certain), he
certainly believed that they should enjoy a special influence within the political
system, and a special deference from the 'less-instructed' masses.

Yet Mill stood well within the tradition of liberal political economy in his
belief in competition and in the efficacy of individual exertion: 'It is the common

error of Socialists to overlook the natural indolence of mankind...Competition may not be the best conceivable stimulus, but it is at present a necessary one, and no one can foresee the time when it will not be indispensable to progress.'[59] In similar vein, he argued that the best 'mode of distributing the produce of industry' was that of 'letting the share of each individual (not in a state of bodily or mental incapacity) depend in the main on that individual's own energies and exertions'.[60] He opposed taxation of larger incomes at a higher percentage on the grounds that it was 'to lay a tax on industry and economy to impose a penalty on people for having worked harder and saved more than their neighbours.'[61] The famous passage, quoted above, in which he laid down his rule that *laissez-faire* should be the 'general practice', was left to stand in every edition of the *Principles of Political Economy*, despite many other revisions.

All this is impeccably orthodox. Yet Mill could not rest there. He was unhappy, as Clough and Arnold were unhappy, with the selfish, competitive ethos which these principles encouraged. He could not believe 'that the trampling, crushing, elbowing, and treading on each other's heels, which form the existing type of social life, are the most desirable lot of human kind, or anything but the disagreeable symptoms of one of the phases of industrial progress.'[62] Mill could not share the confidence of an earlier generation that the pursuit by each of his/her own advantage would automatically produce the general good. Mill shows the liberals beginning to falter in their faith in capitalism and economic individualism. But these misgivings were not enough to dislodge either competition or individualism from their central positions in his social and economic thought.

Mill did not stray all that far from the paths in which he was brought up. As we have seen, he was a youthful enthusiast for Malthusianism, and he remained a defender of Malthus's doctrines throughout his life.[63] He supported the separation of the sexes within workhouses on Malthusian grounds, and he defended the New Poor Law, not only when it was introduced, but also later on in the 1840s when it had fallen into considerable discredit, jeering at 'the new philanthropists' who 'cannot bear that even a workhouse should be a place of regulation and discipline', and referring in his *Autobiography* to 'the numerous sentimental enemies of political economy'[64] as if the Irish famine and the scandal of the Andover workhouse had never happened. In 1845 he was still urging the poor 'to help themselves' and suggesting that through education the working class might improve its condition 'by the exercise of the same degree of habitual prudence now commonly practised by the middle class'.[65] (Mill, like his father, had a considerable faith in the middle class and its virtues.) There is a streak of the characteristic harshness of the political economists in Mill, especially in these denunciations of 'sentimentality'.

Nevertheless, Mill sometimes considered himself a socialist, even if others did not, and certainly responded with interest and sympathy to some of the ideals of socialism, and some of its criticisms of capitalist society.[66] He was an eclectic, lacking the clarity and logic of Bentham or his father. But this eclecticism and confusion — with all the scope it offers for varied interpretations of his 'real' position — is a mirror of the uncertainties and doubts of mid-nineteenth century liberalism. Yet whatever may be said about his thought, his political record, particularly during his brief period as an MP, was one of courageous, consistent liberalism. He helped to defeat a Bill designed to prohibit political meetings in the London parks, and another to facilitate the extradition of political refugees. He supported Bradlaugh, the MP who was barred from his seat because he refused to take a religious oath. He spoke out against the atrocities for which the British Governor of Jamaica, General Eyre, was responsible. He defended the cause of the Irish. Above all, he spoke up for women. He argued the case for equality of the sexes, and by doing so showed up the inconsistency and conservatism of most of his fellow liberals, as well as most socialists of that time. For this alone, Mill would deserve a special and honourable place in the history of liberalism.

AFTER MILL

The issue of democracy remained even after 1867 to torment and divide the British Liberal Party. The 1884 Reform Act, and Gladstone's schemes for land reform and home rule in Ireland, revived all the earlier doubts and debates. James Fitzjames Stephen, the Liberal whose experience of imperial administration in India led him to turn against Mill and write his critique, *Liberty, Equality, Fraternity*, lamented that 'The old maxims of government, the old Liberalism . . . have been and are being utterly given up, and in their place is being erected a tyrannical democracy, which will change the whole face of society and destroy all that I love or respect in our institutions.'[67] The historian Lecky looked back from the 1890s to 'the days of middle-class ascendancy' when 'every politician found it necessary to place himself in general harmony with average educated opinion.' Popular democracy, he predicted, would lead to 'a weakening of private enterprise and philanthropy; a lowered sense of individual responsibility; diminished love of freedom' and a growth of state power.[68]

The late Victorian figure who expressed liberal doubts about democracy with the greatest sophistication was Gladstone's friend, the liberal historian Lord Acton. Acton, as we saw earlier, made a clear distinction between the liberal and the democrat. He was a liberal. And he noted that 'the ablest political writers' of the mid-century, among whom he counted Tocqueville and Mill, had made 'in the name of freedom, a formidable indictment' against democracy. He seems to have believed, too, that social and economic equality was not compatible with liberty, and that the French Revolution's 'Reign of Terror' was the logical outcome of trying to combine the two.[69]

And yet he recognized that the unrestricted reign of property had come to an end, and that it was right and inevitable that it should be so: 'Justice required that property should — not abdicate, but — share its political supremacy.' He accepted that the principles of liberalism had not changed the conditions of the masses:

> For the óld notions of civil liberty and of social order did not benefit the masses of the people. Wealth increased, without relieving their wants. The progress of knowledge left them in abject ingorance. . . . Society, whose laws were made by the upper class alone, announced that the best thing for the poor is not to be born, and the next best, to die in childhood, and suffered them to live in misery and crime and pain. . . . Liberty, for the mass, is not happiness.[70]

Acton, like Tocqueville, whom he so much admired, was a liberal aristocrat who did not find it easy to adjust to democracy and equality; yet even more clearly than Tocqueville he was able to recognize both the inevitability and the rightness of the changes that were taking place. Acton, like Herzen, represents liberalism beginning to acknowledge openly its own limitations. It was left to a later generation of liberals — the modern liberals so disliked by Lecky and others — to try to remedy those limitations, while preserving the essential essence or framework of liberal values. It is to that episode that we must now turn.

16

A 'New Liberalism'?

In the later nineteenth century, liberalism was running out of ideas and steam. The great onslaught on feudal and aristocratic privileges, launched in 1789, had been widely successful. Many of the classic liberal demands, for political and legal equality (for men), for freedom of opinion and its expression, had been quite substantially achieved. It hardly seemed appropriate for what had been a movement and a party of reform, if not of revolution, to become a prop of the status quo. Yet the preoccupation of a major liberal politician like Gladstone with the problem of drink, and the disestablishment of the Church in Wales, suggested that liberalism was coming to the end of its original programme. Gladstone himself sensed this. Towards the end of his long life, in 1896, he described himself as 'a dead man, one fundamentally a Peel—Cobden man'. And a few years earlier another leading Liberal, R. B. Haldane, had declared 'the Liberal party has accomplished the main part of what it has to do in the way of establishing more freedom from intereference for the individual.'[1]

What then was to be done next? Increasingly it was the question of 'the condition of the people', rather than the 'freedom of the individual', which was coming to dominate politics. 'The politics of the future are social politics' said Joseph Chamberlain in 1883.[2] This was in part the result of the widening of the franchise, to which Liberals had been committed, and the consequent need of the political parties to develop policies which would attract popular support. The British Liberal Party in the 1880s and 1890s was a party which was searching for a new role and new objectives, or at the least a broadening and updating of its traditional role and objectives. 'Politicians in search of a cry' was how Chamberlain characterized the Liberals of the 1890s. They were conscious that great issues of principle and philosophy were at stake. 'The nineteenth century might be called the age of Liberalism, yet its close saw the fortunes of that great movement brought to their lowest ebb', wrote L. T. Hobouse in 1911, 'Its faith in itself was waxing cold. It seemed to have done its work. It had the air of a creed that is becoming fossilized as an extinct form.'[3]

Hobhouse was prominent among those Liberals who devoted much intellectual and political energy to reviving 'that great movement'.

At the heart of the problem lay two connected issues: the nature of freedom, and the role and functions of the state. The nineteenth century had witnessed an uneven, but steady and cumulatively vast expansion of the activities and responsibilities of both the state and local authorities. More and more aspects of economic and social life came under legal regulation and restriction. Much of this legislation had been the work of liberal governments; yet liberals could not avoid feeling uneasy about these developments. They ran counter both to their belief in the minimal state, and to their belief that freedom consisted essentially in the absence of all but a minimum of law, regulation and compulsion. Was not the historic task of liberalism to abolish restrictions, limitations and obstructions? No wonder that the veteran Whig, Palmerston, when asked in 1864 what the government's plans were for domestic politics, replied irritably: 'there is really nothing to be done. We cannot go on adding to the Statute Book *ad infinitum*. Perhaps we may have a little law reform, or bankruptcy reform; but we cannot go on legislating for ever.'[4] The legislating went on nevertheless.

But the advance of intervention was not accompanied by a corresponding adjustment of liberal theory. Liberals continued to pay lip-service to the principles of non-intervention, free trade and *laissez-faire*, and acts of intervention were sanctioned only as exceptions to the general rule — as Mill had said. Nineteenth-century liberals attached great importance to the principle of 'voluntaryism', as Ian Bradley has stressed. Moral virtue attached only to acts performed voluntarily; there was no virtue in doing what you were compelled, or ordered, to do. Therefore compulsion was inherently undesirable. And such arguments were reinforced by the established liberal individualist belief that the individual is generally the best judge of her or his interests. Thus the whole climate of liberalism was unsympathetic to the growth of legislation and intervention which was actually taking place, and which many people, including some socialists, identified with socialism. Gladstone might, as a Liberal of the old school, grumble about 'the leaning of both parties to socialism, which I radically disapprove', but that certainly appeared to be the direction in which history was moving, and it threatened to leave the liberals behind, clinging anachronistically to principles which they didn't even practise any longer. Elsewhere in Europe, liberal parties were already in decline.

This was the situation in Britain in which a sustained and concerted effort was made to rethink the liberal concept of freedom and the liberal philosophy of the state. Matthew Arnold had pointed in this direction; but it was left to the idealist philosopher T. H. Green to develop these ideas in a systematic and influential manner. Green took from Hegel and the German idealist tradition more positive conceptions of both the state and society than liberalism could provide. He rejected the old liberal ontology according to which individuals were the primary units, and society was either their secondary creation, or else no more than a collection of individuals: 'Without society, no persons; this is as true as that without persons . . . there could be no such society as we know.'[5] He rejected the idea that 'the individual brings with him into society certain rights which he does not derive from society'. Rights could not exist apart from society: 'There can be no right without a consciousness of common interest on the part of members of a society.'[6] Similarly he suggested that the traditional liberal antithesis between freedom and law was misconceived. 'In one sense no man is so well able to do as he likes as the wandering savage', yet 'he is the slave of nature' and his 'actual powers . . . do not admit of comparison with those of the humblest citizen of a law-abiding state.' Laws and the state can confer and enlarge freedom as well as restrict it. This was more than ever possible since the state had by then been effectively democratized, in Green's view, and therefore 'The danger of legislation, either in the interests of a privileged class or for the promotion of particular religious opinions, we may fairly assume to be over. The popular jealousy of law, once justifiable enough, is therefore out of date.'[7]

This was the theme which he developed in his famous lecture on *Liberal Legislation and Freedom of Contract*. Written in 1880, this was a response to old-style liberal arguments that such acts as the recent Employers' Liability Act (which gave workers a legal right to compensation if they suffered injury at work) constituted an interference with free contracts and tended to weaken the 'self-reliance' of the workers. Green in fact admitted that this and other pieces of 'reforming legislation' had in fact 'put restraints on the individual in doing what he will with his own', but went on to argue that these restraints were nevertheless justified in terms of freedom itself, understood in broader and more ethical terms.

Green was in no doubt that 'freedom, rightly understood, is the greatest of blessings'; but he was concerned that freedom should not be defined as 'merely freedom from restraint or compulsion', or 'merely freedom to do as we like irrespective of what it is that we like': 'When we speak of freedom as something to be so highly prized, we mean a positive power or capacity of doing or enjoying something worth doing or enjoying, and that, too, something that we do or enjoy in common with others', and he added to this the further statement that 'the ideal of true freedom is the maximum of power for all members of human society alike to make the best of themselves.'[8]

There are three ways in which this conception makes a radical departure from, or at least enlargement of, the traditional liberal idea of freedom. Green turns freedom from a negative conception — the *absence* of restraint — to a positive one, the actual power or ability to do things: freedom is bound up conceptually with power. Second, there is a moral element in Green's thinking.

The things which people ought to have the power as well as the opportunity to do should be things *worth* doing. Third, there is an explicitly egalitarian element: all alike should have this power 'to make the best of themselves'. It was argued by Green and the New Liberals that it was through state action that the power or capacity of people could be increased, and that although such action might restrict the freedom of some individuals — property owners, for example — this was justified by the egalitarian principle that all alike were entitled to have their real freedom increased.

This was the way, then, in which Green and those who followed after him tried to justify interventionism in liberal terms, and break down the old liberal hostility to state activity. Green contended that such a position was not incompatible with a commitment to individualism. The fact that people were relieved of responsibility in respect of, for example, obtaining decent housing conditions, meant that they had more opportunity to develop self-reliance in other areas. Green was as concerned as any nineteenth-century liberal with the moral life of the individual, and in some important respects he did not differ from his predecessors in his view of what self-reliance involved. Thus he seems to have shared the view of his pupil Arnold Toynbee that outdoor relief under the Poor Law should be abolished, because it undermined self-reliance. Green was anxious to stress the continuity of the 'New' liberalism with the old. Behind differences over specific policies lay 'the same old cause of social good against class interests for which, under altered names, liberals are fighting now as they were fifty years ago.'[9] This stress on the general good as opposed to sectional and class interests was one way in which the New Liberals sought to distinguish themselves from both Conservatives and Labour, both parties representative primarily of particular class interests, in the liberal view.

Others were even more emphatic in stressing continuity with the liberal tradition and in differentiating their position from that of the 'collectivist' socialists. Thus Toynbee, writing in 1882, was adamant that 'nothing must be done to weaken those habits of individual self-reliance and voluntary association which have built up the greatness of the English people.' What Toynbee called his 'radical socialism' differed from 'Continental Socialism' because 'we accept the principle of private property and repudiate confiscation and violence', and because it conceded only 'a reluctant admission of the necessity for state action'.[10]

Green was not alone in developing these new attitudes. Thus Cliffe Leslie wrote in 1879 that 'Practical freedom involves much more than the absence of legal and social restraint; every limitation of power is an abridgement of positive liberty.' And D. G. Ritchie developed the implications of these ideas with considerable thoroughness in his *The Principles of State Interference* (1891). These ideas were taken up by Liberal politicians, such as Asquith, who

declared in his 1892 Election Address: 'I am one of those who believe that
the collective action of the community may and ought to be employed positively
as well negatively . . . to make the freedom of the individual a reality and
not a pretence.'[11] becuase, as he explained ten years later in his Introduction
to Herbert Samuel's *Liberalism*, for people 'to be really free, they must
be able to make the best use of faculty, opportunity, energy, life.' Samuel
himself endorsed the fundamental liberal view that 'Liberty is of supreme
importance', but added that 'State assistance, rightly directed, may extend
the bounds of liberty'. Hobhouse said much the same: 'There are many enemies
of liberty besides the state and it is in fact by the state that we have
fought them.'[12]

Here then was a philosophy which justified state intervention and social
reform in essentially liberal terms; that is, in terms of freedom, albeit freedom
defined more broadly — some would say more loosely — than it had been
by classical liberalism. It looked as if the way was now clear for the adaptation
of the British Liberal Party to the changed political needs of the twentieth
century, and so for its political survival. This seemed to be confirmed by the
triumphant return to power of the Liberal Party in 1906, and its commitment
to reforms which can be seen in retrospect as marking the first stage in the
creation of the welfare state. The New Liberalism, as one of its leading politicians, Charles Masterman, pointed out, was not socialism; but neither was
it the old commitment to *laissez-faire* capitalism either: 'It believes in property,
possession, competition for attainment above a standard of life. It believes in
a capitalism widely diffused amongst a whole community . . . it believes in
the reform and not the destruction of the existing order.'[13]

It has been argued by Michael Freeden that this balance, or synthesis, made
liberalism at this time 'intellectually better equipped than any other ideological
force' to cope with the social problems of the day, and therefore that whatever
explanation is found for the collapse of the Liberal Party in Britain, it cannot
be one in terms of 'the intellectual failure of its theorists'. Another historian
of the early twentieth century, Peter Clarke, has argued similarly that the
Liberal Party had made the necessary adjustments by around 1910. Those who
remained committed above all to *laissez-faire* had by then moved over to the
Conservative Party; those who stayed with the Liberal Party, even if they were
businessmen or manufacturers, had accepted the principles of the New
Liberalism.[14]

Such arguments, if correct, would only deepen the mystery of the sudden,
rapid decline of the Liberal Party in the decade or so after 1914. How could
a party, which adjusted both intellectually and politically to the realities and
issues of the day, collapse and be replaced in so short a time by a party which
in 1914 was at best a very junior partner in the 'progressive' alliance? One
response, the most untheoretical and 'empirical', is to concentrate on the impact

of the First World War, and, even more narrowly, on the havoc wreaked by Lloyd George's manoeuvrings and ambition. Had it not been for these essentially fortuitous events, the Liberal Party might have stood a chance of surviving as *the* radical party in British politics.

This seems implausible. There is, after all, a general pattern of the replacement, or displacement in radical politics of liberal parties by socialist, social democratic or communist parties in the late nineteenth and early twentieth centuries. Could the British Liberal Party have escaped this fate? It seems doubtful, for two reasons. First, I think we should be sceptical of the suggestion that the Liberal Party made a complete and thorough adaptation to the philosophy of the New Liberalism. What that required was not much less than a *reversal* of the traditional liberal view of the state and of its relation to society. What is more, when we look at the history of the Liberal Party, we find that the old beliefs lingered on for many years, and not merely in the obscure backwoods of the party. Thus, as late as 1950, Sir Andrew McFadyean wrote in *The Liberal Case* that 'Liberals stand alone in demanding free trade . . . Liberals object to protection not merely as wrong in the circumstances of today. They believe that it destroys enterprise, restricts the consumer's freedom of choise, is a reprehensible method of invisible taxation, and is a fertile source of international friction.'[15] Similarly, there was resistance within the party to the efforts of Lloyd George, Keynes and others to commit the party to interventionist measures to counteract the slump of the inter-war years. Finally, as we shall see, when a revival of liberalism as an ideology did take place, in the Cold War period after 1945, it reappeared in forms closer to the classic nineteenth-century model than to the New Liberalism of Green, Hobhouse, Samuel and the rest. I believe that the adjustment to the New Liberalism was less complete, and more superficial than has been suggested, and that the New Liberals ultimately failed to redirect the whole tendency of liberalism away from its traditional channels.

It is clear, too, that the party's commitment to intervention and social reform did alienate many traditional supporters of liberalism and drive them into the Unionist, or Conservative camp. They clung to the tradition of self-help and non-intervention, and when it seemed to them that the Liberal Party had abandoned these old principles, they took them with them into the Conservative Party. The apostle of undeviating non-interventionism in England in the later nineteenth century, Herbert Spencer, writing in 1884, had in fact attacked Liberal interventionism as 'The New Toryism'. However, by 1891 he was noting with approval the degree of Conservative support for the Liberty and Property Defence League (for which another suggested name had been the 'State Resistance Society'), with its motto of 'Individualism versus Socialism', and suggesting that 'it may by and by really happen that the Tories will be defenders of liberties which the Liberals . . . trample under foot.' The converse of this was that 'Most of those who now pass as Liberals, are Tories of a new type.'[16]

Spencer held fast to the old belief that liberty consisted in the absence of restraints, and that the rights of the individual, including the institution of private property, are morally and actually prior to the existence of government. In addition he was the leading translator of Darwin's principle of the survival of the fittest into social terms which meant that the sufferings of 'the incapable', 'the imprudent', 'the idle' and 'the weak' were not only deserved, but part of the inevitable price to be paid for the progress of the species as a whole. It was misguided benevolence to interfere with these processes: 'Instead of diminishing suffering, it eventually increases it. It favours the multiplication of those worst fitted for existence, and, by consequence, hinders the multiplication of those best fitted for existence — leaving, as it does, less room for them.' Not all suffering 'ought to be prevented'. Much of it is 'curative', and much is simply unavoidable. Hence 'the tacit assumption that Government should step in whenever anything is not going right' is based on false assumptions about what is possible and what is beneficial.[17]

Such doctrines, with their echoes of Malthus, were music to the ears of those sections of the bourgeoisie who wished to believe that the contemporary concern to improve the condition of the poor was not only expensive but mistaken. Social Darwinism, even more emphatically in the USA than in Europe, provided a timely set of arguments to justify policies of harshness and inactivity in the face of poverty and misery, as well as giving the old principles of competition and *laissez-faire* a new seemingly scientific foundation.

It is customary to represent this version of traditional liberalism as the polar opposite of the New Liberalism, with its concern for welfare and its commitment to intervention. This is somewhat misleading. Leading exponents of the New Liberalism, from Toynbee to Churchill and Masterman, were explicit about their commitment to competition, self-reliance and private property, even if these commitments were somewhat qualified. It is true that Hobouse attacked Social Darwinism: 'Just as the doctrine of Malthus was the main theoretical obstacle to all schemes of social progress through the first two-thirds of the century, so the doctrine derived in part from Malthus by Darwin has provided a philosophy for the reaction of the last third.'[18] as well as the fallacious equation of evolution with progress. Not all his allies were so unequivocal. J. A. Hobson endorsed the principle of the 'selection of the fittest' and believed that government would therefore be wrong to 'abandon the production of children to unrestricted private enterprise', while William Beveridge, so much honoured as one of the pioneers of the welfare state, and a lifelong member of the British Liberal Party, expressed in 1906 some strikingly callous views on what should happen to 'surplus' population: 'To those . . . who may be born personally efficient, but in excess of the number for whom the country can provide, a clear choice will be offered: loss of independence by entering a public institution, emigration, or immediate starvation.' Freeden finds this 'inexplicable' coming from 'a liberal social reformer', but that is precisely because he consistently underestimates the continuing hold of the classic liberal ideas of competition and self-help. [19]

The New Liberalism, in other words, was not as totally new as many supposed. And indeed many of its leading figures cherished the links with their liberal forbears. Hobhouse grew up believing that J. S. Mill was 'the greatest and best man of this century' and always acknowledged how much he owed to Mill and Green, even suggesting that Mill gives in his *Autobiography* 'perhaps the best summary statement of Liberal Socialism that we possess'. [20] J. L. Hammond's first book was a study of Charles James Fox, and Hobson edited Cobden's papers on international affairs. There was, nevertheless, a natural tendency to identify the New Liberalism with socialism, and if there was one thing which the middle class knew that it detested, that was socialism. Not surprisingly, therefore, the Liberal Party lost much of its middle-class support once it turned in the direction of social reform. It had ceased to be the undisputed party of *laissez-faire* capitalism.

If the Liberal Party was no longer capitalist enough for the capitalists, it remained far too middle-class in character to win unqualified working-class support. Its ditherings over the issue of the eight-hour day in the 1890s illustrate this very well. On the one hand its commitment in 1891 to an eight-hour day for miners antagonized the Liberal mine-owners; on the other its refusal to extend the principle to other groups of workers left labour dissatisfied. It was a matter of ethos as well as policies. The Party was obviously anxious not to be outflanked by the newly-formed Labour Party, yet it remained difficult for working-class men to get adopted as Liberal candidates, even in obviously working-class constituencies. But the party may in any case have been too compromised by its past as a party of manufacturers and Manchester economics to satisfy the desire of the working class for a party of their own. Some historians have argued that this period was one of growing class-consciousness, and that 'As political allegiance became more and more determined by class self-awareness, the Liberal Party found it could make no claim on the loyalties of any class.' [21]

The New Liberalism was a remarkable, perhaps unique attempt by committed liberals to adapt the old creed to new realities. If it failed, it was not without influence, but its heirs were the social democrats of the Labour Party, and, as Peter Clarke's study made plain, many of the New Liberals experienced little difficulty in making the move from Liberal to Labour. Indeed, while some liberals had been anxious to stress what distinguished the New Liberalism from socialism, others, and notably Hobhouse, dwelt on what they had in common, partly in an attempt to undercut the appeal of Labour.

Hobhouse argued that 'true Socialism' was in fact the heir of liberalism. It 'is avowedly based on the political victories which Liberalism won, and as I have tried to show, serves to complete rather than to destroy the leading Liberal ideals.' And he suggested that the actual policies of the German Social Democrats, as opposed to their Marxist professions of faith, contained nothing which a Liberal could not support, since there was nothing which implied a 'revolutionary attack on property'. So it comes as no surprise to find him expressing the view that the first minority Labour Government of 1924, 'moderate Labour in office — has on the whole represented essential Liberalism, not without mistakes and defects, but *better* than the organised party since C. B.'s [Campbell-Bannerman's] death.'[22]

Hobhouse, and others, had a particular kind of socialism in mind, of course. It was not rampantly anti-capitalist or anti-property, nor was it class-based. Hobhouse noted with relief in *Democracy and Reaction* that 'There is in this country at present no sign of the kind of class war to which German Socialists appealed.' He hoped for 'a distinctive kind of Socialism . . . based not on the Trade Unions but on the community and social service'. It was 'a most serious defect' that the Labour Party was tied to the trade unions '& their sectional selfishness'.[23] Liberals had contended, in Green's words, for the 'social good against class interests'. If Labour could do the same, it would make a worthy heir to liberalism.

THE CASE OF KEYNES

One final effort was yet to be made to restore Liberalism's position in Britain as the principal stream of progressive thought and action. It was that of Keynes, but here too it was, in the end, social democracy which inherited the legacy of his thought. There was a considerable irony in this; for Keynes was not only a convinced Liberal — to the question he asked himself, 'Am I a Liberal?', he answered in his own terms, 'yes'. He was also an economist working within, or in relation to, the tradition of classical and neo-classical economics; and his theoretical and practical innovations were explicitly intended to rescue and restore capitalism at a moment when it was threatened with disaster, both by the incompetence of capitalist governments and the contrasting success of state socialist planning.

The General Theory of Employment, Interest and Money was intended as a challenge to the theoretical orthodoxy of economics at that time. Keynes called this orthodoxy 'the classical theory', but what he was really attacking was neo-classical economics, and in more than one respect he was returning to the classical liberal economists and making a heroic attempt to revive their outlook and philosophy. Neo-classical economics had concerned itself largely with the proper distribution of a quantity of resources which it took as given; but Smith's primary concern had been with the expansion of production itself, and this was Keynes's concern as well. For some years before writing the *General Theory* Keynes had been convinced that it was wrong to suppose that demand could not be stimulated or generated by skilful management of the economy, or to suppose that such stimulation would disturb or destroy the basic equilibrium between supply and demand in the economy. Hence he rejected the fatalistic response to the slump of the inter-war years. He believed in the possibility of human control over economic life, and in that respect he represents a return to a more positive and, indeed, rational version of political economy than the nineteenth-century belief that the 'laws' of economics were as unchallengeable as any other natural laws. Keynes never ceased to be optimistic, in so far as he believed in the possibility of economic recovery and continued growth and progress. He wrote in 1931 of his 'profound conviction that the Economic Problem . . . the problem of want and poverty and the economic struggle between classes and nations, is nothing but a frightful muddle, a transitory and *unnecessary* muddle.' That term 'muddle', where others were talking of crisis and doom, perfectly expressed his rational confidence in the possibility of 'sorting things out'. And only a year earlier, in the depths of the slump, he outlined his vision of *Economic Possibilities for our Grandchildren*, asserting that 'in the long run . . . *mankind is solving its economic problem*', and that 'the standard of life in progressive countries' would be four to eight times higher in a hundred years time. He believes in the middle way of enlightened gradualism, and rejects equally 'the pessimism of reactionaries' who see terrible dangers in any kind of novelty or experiment, and 'the pessimism of revolutionaries who think that things are so bad that nothing can save us but violent change.'[24]

Like Smith, he believed that capitalism was in principle a beneficent economic system, provided that its grosser inequalities and instabilities could be removed, as he was sure they could. Yet again like Smith, he viewed capitalism, and even more, capitalists, with a marked degree of critical detachment. If on the one hand he suggested that 'dangerous human proclivities' could be usefully diverted into the 'comparatively harmless' business of making money (and went out of his way to praise 'the traditional advantages of individualism' in the final pages of the *General Theory*),[25] on the other he looked forward to a future time when 'the accumulation of wealth is no longer of high social importance'; and when, therefore, 'the love of money as a possession . . . will be recognised for what it is, a somewhat disgusting morbidity.' It was for this reason that, although he always regarded Marxism as a nineteenth-century irrelevance, he was interested in the great experiment of the Soviet Union. He did not believe that 'Russian communism' had any useful economic lessons to teach, but he was intrigued and a little attracted by what he interpreted as an attempt to create a society which did not revolve around the profit motive. That might give communism the public spirit, or 'religion', which modern capitalism so conspicuously lacked — 'often, though not always, a mere congerie of possessors and pursuers'.[26]

Finally, though, he rejects communism for two essentially liberal reasons. The first is that it is oppressive and repressive: 'I am not ready for a creed which does not care how much it destroys the liberty and security of daily life.' The second is that it is 'a creed which, preferring the mud to the fish, exalts the boorish proletariat above the bourgeoisie and the intelligentsia who, with whatever faults, are the quality in life and surely carry the seeds of all human advancement.' Here Keynes, with remarkable candour, restates that faith in the middle class enunciated a century earlier by James Mill and Macaulay. His grounds for not joining the Labour Party were similar. Labour is a class party 'and the class is not my class' . . . 'the *class* war will find me on the side of the educated bourgeoisie', although, somewhat contradictorily, he claims that the 'progressive Liberal' does not believe in the class war, and believed, at least in 1925, that 'there is room for a party which shall be disinterested as between classes', the Liberal Party being such a party.[27]

Keynes thus recognized the Liberal Party as his natural habitat, even though he was not optimistic about its future prospects; and at the same time as he was announcing 'The End of *Laissez-Faire*', he also reaffirmed his belief in free trade. Yet he was convinced that liberalism had to adopt a more positive and interventionist approach to the economy, and that 'the true destiny of New Liberalism' was to seek to solve the problems involved in 'the transition from economic anarchy to a régime which deliberately aims at controlling and directing economic forces in the interests of social justice and social stability.'[28] He was therefore closely identified with the programme of positive action to counteract the slump and unemployment presented by Lloyd George and the Liberal Party in the 1929 election; and for the same reason he had some sympathy with Oswald Mosley and his New Party at the moment when they represented an interventionist protest against the fatalistic orthodoxy which dominated the Labour Government of 1929—31.[29]

After the Second World War, Keynesianism provided the rationale for the widespread acceptance by Western governments of a responsibility for maintaining full employment and achieving economic growth. In most Western countries, however, liberal parties were no longer of any great significance, and it was social democratic and labour parties which embraced Keynes's ideas most wholeheartedly. This process had begun in the 1930s. Even before the *General Theory* was published, the then-socialist A. L. Rowse was urging Keynes to ally himself with the Labour Party, and after 1936 Labour Party economists like Douglas Jay and Evan Durbin found in Keynes additional support for the socialist case for a planned economy. John Strachey, a leading British Marxist of the 1930s, embarked on what was intended as a critique of the *General Theory*, but ended up accepting the basic Keynesian case, and producing *A Programme for Progress*, which he later described as 'a programme for the application of his [i.e. Keynes's] ideas by a British Labour Government'.[30] Both Richard Crossman and Strachey, writing in the 1950s, interpreted Keynes as having provided a theoretical foundation for socialist gradualism, although Strachey recognized that this was not what Keynes himself had intended.[31]

There is both logic and irony in this development. The logic is that social democracy has never suffered from liberalism's misgivings about the use of state power to rectify the injustices of capitalism. It could therefore be expected that they, rather than the Liberal Party, would accept Keynes's ideas. The irony is that Keynes was never a socialist, and did not see his policies as a strategy for socialism, but as the adaptation of capitalism that would enable it to survive crisis and retain the precious legacy of individualism. Hobhouse and Keynes were among many early twentieth-century radicals and liberals who did not consider themselves socialists because they were not, in the final analysis, anti-capitalist even if they were anti-*laissez-faire*. By the middle years of the century, however, the dominant strand of social democracy had also ceased to be socialist in that sense. It did not want to abolish capitalism outright but to modify and reform it. It was then not difficult to reinterpret Keynes as someone who was a socialist, or at least a social democrat, without knowing it. Keynes once complained that the Labour leaders failed to see that they were, or ought to be, 'the heirs of eternal liberalism'. Some leading figures of the Left were happy to accept this version of what they represented. 'Many of my friends call me a "liberal"', wrote Kingsley Martin, soon to be editor of the *New Statesman*, in 1927. 'I doubt if there is any difference of substance between my views and those of Keynes, for instance.'[32] That version of social democracy which accepts as its ideal a restrained capitalism combining the mixed economy with the welfare state is clearly one legitimate heir of the New, if not eternal, Liberalism.

PART III

Liberalism in Decline

17

Twentieth-Century Liberalism: The Mood of Withdrawal

The dominant character of twentieth-century liberalism has been very different from what Hobhouse, or even Keynes, might have hoped for. It has taken two related forms. First, a pattern of doubt and even disgust leading to withdrawal and a deep loss of hope. Second, doubt and disgust generated a militant moderation and an aggressive defence of a strongly conservative version of the liberal tradition. Both are responses to what became known as 'totalitarianism', a term the liberals helped to popularize, and in particular to the challenge of communism and social revolution. Both, but especially the second, hinge on the development of the Cold War, particularly in the period between 1945 and the early 1960s.

THE MOOD OF WITHDRAWAL

The impulse of the sensitive liberal to withdraw from a world dominated by values and social forces with which she finds herself out of sympathy dates back, as we have seen, at least to 1848. The 'year of revolutions' showed that when challenged from 'below', liberals might end up, as de Tocqueville did, on the side of order and repression. From this moment on, many liberals felt increasingly the impossibility of taking sides in a conflict in which, as it seemed to them, 'ignorant armies clash by night.'

When, in our own century, aggressive, expansionist nationalism or imperialism, and militant socialism came to dominate politics, especially after the First World War, this liberal sense of alienation and isolation was greatly enhanced. It was not only the content, but also the ethos and temper of these movements that repelled the liberal. She found herself out of sympathy with their militancy and conviction, their apparent readiness to impose their beliefs and visions upon humanity, even, if necessary, against its will. The religious

fanaticism and dogmatism against which the liberal Enlightenment had fought
— not without success — seemed to be reappearing in sinister secular shapes
— the more dangerous because the technology and organization for imposing
conformity and persecuting dissent were now so much more effective and
extensive. The twentieth century looked like another Age of Faith, or what
Bertrand Russell called 'an epoch of wars of religion, but a religion is now
called an "ideology".'[1] Most liberals agreed with E. M. Forster in finding
it uncongenial — 'extremely unpleasant really' — because, like him, they did
not 'believe in Belief'.[2]

The liberal, according to Russell, has opinions, but holds them 'tentatively',
in 'the way in which opinions are held in science'. Russell virtually parodies
his own recommendation when he suggests that 'the genuine liberal does not
say "this is true", he says "I am inclined to think that under present circumstances this opinion is probably the best." Nevertheless, he was undoubtedly
serious when he wrote at that time that 'only through a revival of Liberal tentativeness and tolerance can our world survive.'[3] Isaiah Berlin wrote in similar
vein that 'What the age calls for is not (as we are so often told) more
faith. . . . Rather is it the opposite — less Messianic ardour, more enlightened
scepticism, more toleration of idiosyncrasies' — and so forth.[4]

The liberal outlook, as Russell conceived it, did indeed generate scepticism
about all but the most negative and limited kinds of politics. As Forster put
it in 1941: 'Each time Mr Wells and my other architectural friends anticipate
a great outburst of post-war activity and world-planning my heart contracts.
To me the best chance for future society lies through apathy, uninventiveness
and inertia.'[5] This was not altogether representative of Forster's political
outlook, and was no doubt intended to deflate those who shared Wells's brisk
rationalist confidence in planning. But it strikes one authentic note of mid-
twentieth century liberalism, as does Forster's comment on George Orwell:
'A true liberal, he hoped to help through small things. Programmes mean
pogroms.'[6]

Where Russell was mistaken was in suggesting that this tentative, sceptical
attitude was always typical of liberalism. On the contrary, the image of the
liberal as at best open-minded and coolly reasonable, and at worst hesitant,
vacillating, non-commital and ineffectual, is essentially a twentieth-century
phenomenon. Gladstone did not conform to it, neither did Mill. It is even less
well-matched to the militant liberalism of Voltaire or Condorcet, Hazlitt or
Shelley. And Russell, in his actual politics, was usually closer to them than
to the pattern of tentativeness he outlined in that particular essay. In fact until
recently this general scepticism about positive beliefs and political action has
been characteristic of secular conservatism. Liberalism, by contrast, was seen
as positive in its belief in the possibility and desirability of reform and progress,
even at times of revolution.

There can be no doubt that, for those who grew up before 1914 — and Russell and Forster both belong in this category — the First World War marked the end of an era, and the collapse of many of the old liberal hopes and certainties: 'the war of 1914 had destroyed the hope that human beings were becoming civilized — a hope not unreasonable at the beginning of the twentieth century', wrote Leonard Woolf, looking back more than 50 years later.[7] The war, and what followed — the triumph of Bolshevism in Russia and the rise of fascism in many other parts of Europe — shattered the dream of progress, and the perspective of the steady humanizing and liberalizing of social life and its institutions. The forces that had taken over the public world of politics not only had the effect of dwarfing 'the individual' and inducing a sense of helplessness amounting at times to despair; they also appeared as inhuman and anti-human, encased in uniforms and cruel metal, talking a mechanized language in which neither individuality nor ordinary human feeling had any part. Small wonder that in these circumstances so many liberals should have felt that it was only within the surviving enclosures of private life and personal relations that the humanist tradition could be kept alive. Privacy and private life acquired a higher value than had ever before been attached to them.

E. M. FORSTER AND 'BLOOMSBURY'

E. M. Forster was perhaps the most articulate and persuasive representative of this position of modest yet defiant withdrawal, in his novels, especially *Howards End*, as well as in his broadcast talks and essays. 'I have lost all faith in positive militant ideals; they can so seldom be carried out without thousands of human beings getting maimed or imprisoned', wrote Forster in 1941.[8] What did he put in their place? Above all, personal relations. 'I know that personal relations are the real life, for ever and ever', says Helen Schlegel, to which her sister responds 'Amen!' And so, when every qualification has been made by the events and dialectic of *Howards End*, does Forster. Only within that area, of particular and individual relationships, can one hope to do good:

> Others had attacked the fabric of Society — Property, Interest, etc.; she only fixed her eyes on a few human beings to see how, under present conditions, they could be made happier. Doing good to humanity was useless: the many-coloured efforts thereto spreading over the vast area like films and resulting in a universal grey. To do good to one, or, as in this case, to a few, was the utmost she dare hope for.[9]

Forster said that his books 'emphasize the importance of personal relationships and the private life, for I believe in them'.[10] This may be contrasted with

George Eliot's famous observation in *Felix Holt* that 'there is no private life which has not been determined by a wider public life.'[11] In *Howards End* in particular Forster shows himself to be well aware of this, yet, like the Schlegel sisters, we feel it is something that he faces only with reluctance. His friend and contemporary Virginia Woolf noted justly that 'He has no great interest in institutions' and no 'wide social curiosity'.[12]

Forster was never entirely at one with the mainstream of Cambridge—Bloomsbury liberal thinking, yet it is striking how closely the outlook of the Schlegel sisters corresponds to the ethic of Cambridge—Bloomsbury as it was recalled by Keynes in his memoir 'My Early Beliefs'. G. E. Moore, the philosopher, was one major source of these beliefs, and his conclusion in *Principia Ethica* that among those things that can be considered as good in themselves, 'By far the most valuable . . . are certain states of consciousness, which may be roughly described as the pleasures of human intercourse and the enjoyment of beautiful objects,'[13] or, in other words, 'personal affections and aesthetic enjoyments', is clearly reflected in Keynes's summary: 'Nothing mattered except states of mind, our own and other people's of course, but chiefly our own.' Meanwhile 'social action as an end in itself . . . had dropped out of our Ideal.'[14] As Leonard Woolf, another member of this group, later wrote, 'we were not proselytizers, missionaries, crusaders, or even propagandists.' Woolf also expressed an even more fundamental version of the scepticism recommended by Russell: 'The belief in the importance of truth and the impossibility of absolute truth, the conviction that, though things rightly matter profoundly to you and me, nothing matters, this mental and emotional metaphysic or attitude towards the universe produces the sceptical tolerance which is an essential part of civilization.'[15]

Yet here is the paradox: each of these proponents of scepticism, of helping through small things, of self-cultivation and personal relations, in practice engaged actively in the life of politics, in the 'outer life' of 'telegrams and anger', as Forster called it. Woolf was a lifelong propagandist against imperialism and for Fabian socialism; the crusading activities of Russell, and, in a more establishment style, Keynes, are well known, while even the more elusive Forster was for many years actively involved with the National Council for Civil Liberties, and became a public spokesperson for the liberalism which he 'found . . . crumbling beneath him' but nevertheless refused to abandon.

The paradox is not quite as sharp as it appears at first sight. Forster remains true to himself, an individual voice and a private face in public places. He takes up no large cause or ideal, but speaks up for liberal values — tolerance, freedom from censorship — when they are threatened. Keynes, Woolf and Russell were all, in different ways, compelled to go beyond this modest pattern in their politics, towards socialism or social democracy. That is what any involvement which was more than defensive in Forster's manner required.

Organized liberalism no longer offered a basis for active, reforming politics. Woolf and Russell had little choice but to orientate themselves towards the Labour Party, and even Keynes would have had to do the same had he survived long into the post-1945 era.

At the same time the *principle* of scepticism was maintained, and we find both Forster and Woolf invoking and thus constructing a tradition of liberal scepticism as a prop to what they see as their own beleaguered situation. 'My law-givers are Erasmus and Montaigne, not Moses and St Paul' declared Forster. Woolf too pays homage to Montaigne, and goes on to associate him with Erasmus, Voltaire and Paine. [16] He was also the author of an essay on Erasmus entitled *A Civilised Man*. It is significant, however, that a liberal socialist like Woolf can share his admiration for Erasmus with a Tory like H. R. Trevor-Roper. [17] The modern liberal's dislike of what he sees as fanaticism brings him closer to the moderate sceptical Tory.

Liberal scepticism was reinforced, not only by illiberal politics but also by intellectual developments. The tendency of much modern moral philosophy, including Moore's, was to stress the subjective and individual nature of judgements about goodness. How was one such judgement to be preferred to another? All Keynes could suggest was that some people have 'an acuter sense of judgment, just as some can judge a vintage port and others cannot.' Matters of moral judgement are thus reduced to questions of taste, subjective and ultimately beyond resolution. Keynes claimed that 'We entirely repudiated a personal liability on us to obey general rules', and that 'we repudiated entirely customary morals, conventions and traditional wisdom.' [18] This undoubtedly exaggerates the personal and intellectual radicalism of his Cambridge generation. But it has an interesting affinity with the later existentialist approach to morality, which in Sartre's version stressed the impossibility of formulating general rules and the inescapable obligation of each individual to *choose* his or her own values. Such an approach not only pushes individualism in morality to its farthest possible extreme. It must also make the individual hesitant in applying her moral judgements to others beside herself. In these philosophies we find one root of the modern liberal's indecisiveness and lack of conviction in relation to so many public issues.

Another lies in the greater historical and social self-awareness of contemporary liberalism — a development which reflects the impact of Marxism and other theories of history and ideology. If they were not *more* aware than their forbears of the class basis and class character of liberalism, they were certainly more *uneasily* aware of them. Forster, once again, embodies this complex awareness. He knows that the limits of the world encompassed in his novels are the limits of his class; and he treats this with characteristic self-mockery, as when he says in *Howards End*, 'We are not concerned with the very poor. They are unthinkable, and only to be approached by the statistician or the poet. The story deals with gentlefolk.'[19] But limitations do not cease to be limitations simply because we are aware of them; and such ironies are only possible for a writer who is consciously addressing his own class, rather than the 'unthinkable' very poor, who might not be amused by such a dismissal.

Forster is well aware of the material basis of the civilized life he prizes: 'In came the nice fat dividends, up rose the lofty thoughts, and we did not realize that all the time we were exploiting the poor of our own country and the backward races abroad, and getting bigger profits from our investments than we should.' The importance of money is a central theme in *Howards End*. Margaret Schlegel tells her aunt, in terms close to the arguments of the New Liberals of that period:

> You and I and the Wilcoxes stand upon money as upon islands. It is so firm beneath our feet that we forget its very existence. It's only when we see someone near us tottering that we realize all that an independent income means. Last night, when we were talking up here round the fire, I began to think that the very soul of the world is economic, and that the lowest abyss is not the absence of love, but the absence of coin.

Her aunt finds that all this talk about money smacks of socialism, and she is, of course, quite right. Forster's own answer was to plead for a combination of political liberalism with economic socialism: 'we must manage to combine the new economy and the old morality.'[20] But awareness of 'the basis of golden sovereigns' on which the liberal outlook was once founded induced doubt, at least about its capacity to survive the collapse of empire and the demand for greater equality. As Patricia Stubbs has written: 'He gives up, if you like, the public and economic aspects of liberalism, but clings to its private morality. . . . Forster appears to us now as the artist of liberalism in retreat.'[21]

REX WARNER'S FABLE OF THE 1930s

In *The Professor*, one of three political fables which Rex Warner wrote in the late 1930s, we have the portrait of a scholarly liberal who finds himself for a moment hoisted into political prominence as Chancellor of a central European state threatened by fascism both internally and externally. The portrait is admittedly drawn from a relatively unsympathetic point of view, and the moral of the story is that in an extreme political situation conventional liberalism is 'not enough': 'you would not arm your own ideas', one of his critics tells him when the chief of police launches his coup, 'Now we shall have to run for it.'[22] Before his death at the hands of the fascists, 'shot, as on the following day the newspaper reports declared, "while attempting to escape"' (p. 171), the

Professor (he is never given any other name) comes to see the necessity of revolution, 'a word which throughout his life he had regarded as most distasteful' (pp. 156—7), if even his own cherished liberal values are to be preserved. The overt message of the book, then, is that of Stephen Spender's title, *Forward from Liberalism*. This implies that liberalism is the starting point from which we move on. And so it proves in Warner's case.

The Professor does indeed embody what we can now recognize as the stock characteristics of the modern liberal. These traits are in some respects admirable, and certainly likeable because they are essentially humane and decent. Yet the structure of the story is designed to show that they are inadequate to the conditions of political crisis; and when every objection has been made to the inevitably schematic nature of Warner's fable — it is closer in style and construction to an outright allegory like *Animal Farm* than it is to the traditional realist novel — Warner's delineation of the liberal academic, the man of reason trapped in a situation where the rules of reason do not operate, is extremely convincing. His mildness — 'He was accustomed, however, rather to smile at folly than to condemn it' (p. 25) — and reasonableness are more than plausible. When he is warned by the Leftists of the danger of a fascist coup, he is naturally sceptical: 'Extremists, thought the Professor . . . are always apprehensive of some great disaster' (p. 57); and he continues to believe up to the last moment 'that even at this hour persuasion may be proved more powerful than violence' (p. 94). Only in the hour of defeat and failure does he come to see the necessity of resisting violence with violence: 'if love, he saw clearly now, were to exercise itself in action, love itself would have to be armed' (p. 146).

THE POST-WAR LIBERAL NOVEL:
ANGUS WILSON AND LIONEL TRILLING

It is not until the dark days of the post-1945 Cold War that we reach the nadir of this liberal scepticism about not only the possibility of progress but about the usefulness of any kind of radical political activity. Two further novels may be taken as expressive of this deeply pessimistic style of liberalism, Angus Wilson's *Hemlock and After* (1952), and the critic Lionel Trilling's only novel, *The Middle of the Journey* (1947). Wilson's novel in particular should be taken as representative of its time rather than its author, since the mood of some of his subsequent work was markedly less despondent than this full-length study of a liberal humanist in crisis and despair.

Bernard Sands is an elderly writer who has in the past been identified with liberal and progressive causes, but has gradually withdrawn from politics into self-examination and self-criticism. This move to inwardness is inspired by the desire for self-knowledge, but, as Wilson himself said of Sands, in this case

'Self-knowledge brings paralysis of the will.'[23] Bernard comes to doubt the probity of his own motives, and this becomes so much of an obsession that he even allows it to dominate a public speech at one of those disastrous public occasions which provide several set-pieces in Wilson's novels: 'Motives were so difficult, so double, so much hypocrisy might spring from guilt, so much benevolence from fear to use power, so much kindness overlay cruelty, so much that was done didn't matter.'[24] Sands is also obsessed with the consequences of action, with the unintended, unpredictable consequences which can negate or at least qualify the actor's intention.' "I wish" ' says his wife Ella after his death, ' "that one could act in single things without involving so many others. Such a lot of wicked things get mixed up with any good one does" ' (p. 235). These two doubts, about the purity of motives and the unpredictability of consequences, inhibit Bernard Sands from taking all but the most limited moral actions. As he says, ' "Being good to people . . . is a dangerously complicated process" ' (p. 184). That *inaction, not* being good to people, also has its consequences, is something which he also understands, but it is a truth which makes less impact on his actual behaviour. His impulse is to act as little as possible. When his still politically active sister tries to draw him back into public campaigning, he replies ' "I don't think making stands is quite so easy as you think, Isobel" ', and to himself he reflects that she belongs to 'a world of never-grow-ups' (pp. 73—4), while the more militantly Left politics of Isobel's friend Louie Randall he regards as simply 'pathological'(p. 107).

Thus Bernard's doubts extend beyond himself to others. Not only can he no longer share their certainties, but he regards those certainties as evidence of immaturity and psychological imbalance. It would be untrue to say that the whole weight of the book is tilted towards Bernard's 'despair' (his word). The book ends with a few notes of muted hope. Nevertheless C. B. Cox, in his valuable study of liberal humanism in the English novel, is right to relate *Hemlock and After* to a general mood of scepticism about political idealism and political action which prevailed in the years after 1945.[25]

In his discussion of Angus Wilson, Cox quotes, aptly enough, an essay of 1947 in which Lionel Trilling made a plea for what he called 'moral realism', by which he meant 'the perception of the dangers of the moral life itself'. It is necessary to 'be aware of the dangers which lie in our most generous wishes. Some paradox of our natures leads us, when once we have made our fellow men the objects of our enlightened interest, to go on to make them the objects of our pity, then of our wisdom, ultimately of our coercion.'[26] Political idealism leads ultimately to dictatorship and repression. Thinking of this kind has become a part of Western conventional wisdom. What Trilling failed to see was that the paradox lay, not in 'our natures', but in his formulation of the supposed development. Certainly, if we make people the 'objects' of any condescending attitude, we shall probably end by treating them as objects; and if we begin by assuming our own enlightenment, and others' lack of it, we shall be well on the way to paternalism or worse. But why assume that moral and political action must necessarily take such a form? Why not think in terms of solidarity and collective action? Trilling's formulations, and the misgivings which flow from them, tell us more about the modern liberal view of politics than they do about politics as such.

And so, it can be said, does Trilling's own novel of politics and anti-politics, *The Middle of the Journey*. This appeared in the same year as the essay just referred to, and has the same message: radicals are seeking, consciously or otherwise, to impose their will on humankind: '*Democracy* and *freedom*. And in the most secret heart of every intellectual, where he scarcely knows of it himself, there lies hidden the *real* hope that these words hide. It is the hope of power, the desire to bring his ideas to reality by imposing them on his fellow men.'[27] These words are given to Gifford Maxim, the ex-Communist Party activist turned reactionary Christian, a figure modelled, as Trilling subsequently acknowledged, on Whittaker Chambers, the principal prosecution witness in the celebrated case of Alger Hiss. Trilling does achieve a genuine dialectical interplay of ideas, experience and character between his major characters, or at least between Maxim and the story's central character, the reflective liberal, John Laskell. Not everything that Maxim says is endorsed by his creator, that is clear. But on this issue Laskell, whose political enlightenment-cum-disillusionment is the central process of the novel, comes to the same conclusion. He comes to see in Nancy Croom, his still radical, even fellow-travelling friend, a sinister and potentially ruthless passion:

> a passion of the mind and will so pure that, as it swept through her, she could not believe that anything that opposed it required consideration. When one had a reference as large as Nancy's, when it was something as big as the future or reality to which one conceived oneself dedicated, nothing could possibly have the right to call it to account. (p. 238)

That this *is* the nature of Nancy's passion is less than self-evident to this reader, at least, but that certainly is the way that Trilling wishes us to think of her. She in particular, and her husband Arthur to a lesser extent, are presented in a deeply unsympathetic light.

Laskell has come at their invitation to recuperate in the country after an illness during which he nearly died. He has also experienced the death of his girl-friend, and has been confronted by Maxim going in fear of his life. But the Crooms are protrayed as unwilling to face, or even discuss, the fact of death. It is 'as if you thought that death was politically reactionary', charges Laskell, and to this Nancy has nothing to say (p. 116). We are left in no doubt that Trilling believes that the price of the Crooms' radicalism, or utopianism, of their being 'committed to life' and to a 'passionate expectation of the future' (p. 17), is that they live in a world of foolish delusions. They avert their eyes not only from death, but also from 'the evil and hardness of the world' (p. 108). They refuse to believe anything of what Maxim tells them about the Communist Party. They refuse to face unpleasant truths about individuals they admire. They, or she at least, refuse to accept 'human nature': 'a profound dissatisfaction with the way human beings had ever been', lies 'at the root of her political feelings' (p. 179). Laskell, the moderate liberal, rejects Maxim Chambers' abrupt lurch from communism to religious conservatism. He also rejects the Crooms: 'Laskell saw that the intellectual power had gone from that system of idealism. . . . The time was getting ripe for a competing system' (pp. 306).

The Middle of the Journey, despite its wordiness ('to which one conceived oneself dedicated') and its over-explicit conceptualization, is not a dramatized debate, but a genuine novel of politics and political ideas. It reflects exactly the moment at which it was written. It demarcates the boundaries and norms of post-1945 respectable political debate. Radicals, socialists, communists lie outside those boundaries. They inhabit a world of falsely optimistic illusions which issue finally in dictatorship and murder. The real debate is between moderate, undoctrinaire liberalism and dedicated, quasi-religious anti-communism. In this novel, as in much of his critical writing, Trilling helps to create the ethos and principles of liberalism in one of its last and least creditable forms — Cold War liberalism.

18

Cold War Liberalism

While we re-live the horrors of the Dark Ages, of absolute states and ideological wars, the old platitudes of liberalism loom up in all their glory, familiar streets as we reel home furious in the dawn.[1]

LIBERAL ANTI-COMMUNISM

Cyril Connolly's wartime (c. 1942) dictum brilliantly encapsulates the essence of the revived liberalism of the years after 1945, illuminating both its appeal and one fundamental cause of that revival. The sentiment is essentially the same as Forster's, whose 'golden pamphlet' (*What I Believe*) Connolly wrote of enthusiastically when reviewing Trilling's study of Forster:[2] in a world dominated by rival authoritarianisms, liberalism may look weak and outdated but it actually becomes more urgently relevant than ever. Forster and Connolly were opposing the collectivist intolerance generated by total war, as well as the evil of fascism, with its open contempt for every aspect of liberal humanism.

But in 1945 fascism was finally defeated, and 'totalitarianism' was henceforth identified almost exclusively with communism. The term 'Cold War Liberalism' is appropriate because the dominant characteristic of the liberalism which achieved a kind of revival after 1945 was its anti-communism. It is the *dominance* which is distinctive. Given that communism was both socialist (by profession) and authoritarian (in practice) liberals were bound to be, and had always been, opposed to it — even if, like Keynes, a few of them had recognized its power and historical significance. But in the Cold War period this single attitude so shaped the overall character of liberalism that some of its more fundamental principles were sacrificed or lost sight of. Freedom of speech and opinion, tolerance and diversity, were suddenly discovered to be principles which need not be applied to communists, or even those who *might* be communists, or who had, to use one of the conveniently elastic phrases of the time, 'communist sympathies'. By the same token, a blind eye could be turned to illiberal and repressive regimes which happened also to be anti-communist; or, worse still, specious justifications could be produced for them. Cold War liberalism, it can be argued, was not 'true' liberalism at all, but a betrayal of it. But it was a betrayal perpetrated and endorsed by people who claimed to be liberals, inheriting and invoking the tradition of Locke and Montesquieu, de Tocqueville and Mill.

At more than one level the quintessence of this corrupted liberalism can be found in a single place — the files of the monthly magazine, *Encounter*. *Encounter* made its first appearance in October 1953, and was expected by some to fill the gap left by the demise of Cyril Connolly's literary and cultural monthly, *Horizon*. It was at once clear, however, that *Encounter* was to be as much political as literary — as was indicated by the dual editorship of the English poet Stephen Spender and the American political writer, Irving Kristol — and its politics were the politics of anti-communism. This was noticed by several reviewers of the first issue, including the *Times Literary Supplement*, which observed that many of the non-literary articles were 'characterized by negative liberalism, or by a liberalism whose main positive feature, at least, appears to be a hatred and fear of communism.'[3]

The first issue opened with an editorial, 'After the Apocalypse', in which it was claimed that the workers' protests of that year in Czechoslovakia and East Germany had achieved 'the destruction of the Marxist—Leninist creed', although it was also announced that the magazine 'seeks to promote no "line"'. The issue also contained an attack on Isaac Deutscher's most recent book on Russia, and Leslie Fiedler's long article on the trial and execution in the USA of Julius and Ethel Rosenberg, convicted of spying for the Soviet Union. Although Fiedler suggested in his final paragraph that they should have been 'granted mercy', the bulk of his article was given over to an attack on their integrity and the integrity of those who campaigned on their behalf. 'The suffering and death of the Rosenbergs were willed by the makers of Communist opinion and relished by them, as every instance of discrimination against a Negro in America is willed and relished' (p. 14) — a formulation that neatly implied that the communists themselves were partly responsible for both phenomena.

These attitudes and tones were consistently sustained in subsequent issues. The second included an enthusiastic article on Montaigne — 'this deeply liberal spirit' — and an equally uncritical review of Isaiah Berlin's *The Hedgehog and the Fox*, by Arthur Schlesinger Jr. In the fourth issue Irving Kristol replied defiantly to the *Times Literary Supplement*, suggesting that it had made an 'unwitting . . . concession(s) to Communist ideology', which 'had induced in the West, and particularly among Western intellectuals, a bad conscience about opposing Communism'. This was the authentic style of argument of the Cold War: not to be unhesitatingly anti-communist was to reveal yourself as infected, even if 'unwittingly', by communist 'propaganda'.

Cold War liberalism, ever vigilant for signs of incipient or covert 'totalitarianism', was apt to assert that to judge and interpret literature and the arts in political terms was at least potentially 'totalitarian', in that it denied to the arts the autonomy essential to their well-being. But in this respect Cold War liberalism failed to conform to its own precepts. *Encounter* persistently judged the arts in political terms, and rarely failed to attack any Marxist writer or artist whom they thought might be becoming dangerously influential. And so Brecht, Sartre, Lukács, John Berger and many others were fiercely, and in some cases repeatedly, attacked in its pages.

In international politics *Encounter* epitomized the selective vision of Cold War liberalism. Cuba provides a good example. Before .its overthrow by Fidel Castro's guerillas in 1959, Cuba was under the corrupt, reactionary dictatorship of Batista. This regime received no critical attention from *Encounter*. But once the Castro regime was established, Cuba became the subject of a whole series of articles, which, it need hardly be said, found little to praise and much to condemn. The magazine's casual, even flippant treatment of the issue of race, whether in South Africa or the USA was adequately commented on by Conor Cruise O'Brien in a properly sharp review of *Encounter*'s first ten years.[4]

The final ironies, if that is not too mild a word, of *Encounter*'s record relate, not to its contents but to its funding and sponsorship. The magazine first appeared under the auspices of that liberal-sounding body, the Congress for Cultural Freedom. Like many another fine-sounding organization, the Congress had a rather less elevated specific purpose: the mobilization of Western intellectuals against communism and the Soviet Union.[5] Its first conference in 1950 took place, typically enough, in West Berlin, and thereafter it staged regular conferences around such high themes as 'The Future of Freedom', at which a spectrum of intellectuals ranging from the Right to the social democratic centre would deliver hortatory addresses about the dangers of socialism and all forms of radicalism.

Zealous anti-communists of those days were always on the look-out for what were called 'front organizations', bodies with noble names, fronted by a bevy of progressive or leftish 'names', behind which lurked the local Communist Party or even perhaps the Comintern. Daniel Bell described these 'papier-mâché front organizations' as 'the greatest triumph of Communist propaganda'.[6] Behind the Congress for Cultural Freedom there lurked the American Central Intelligence Agency (CIA), as was finally revealed in 1967. Funds from the CIA had been channelled to the Congress via various respectable institutions such as the Ford Foundation, and then passed on the various journals which the Congress subsidized — *Encounter, Preuves, Tempo Presente*, and so on. When rumours about the CIA connection circulated in 1966, *Encounter*'s editors published a denial: 'we are our own masters and are part of nobody's propaganda', and leading liberal intellectuals, including J. K. Galbraith and

Arthur Schlesinger Jr, defended the record and supposed independence of the Congress.[7] The full story of the CIA's relations with the Congress and the magazine was then revealed by former CIA administrator, Thomas Braden. This led to the resignations of the two British editors, Spender and Frank Kermode, both of whom had made public denials of the CIA connection, and now claimed that they had been 'misled'. The American editor, Melvin Lasky, who did know about the link, did not resign, however, and is still an editor of *Encounter* at the time of writing.

In the wake of these disclosures, the American monthly *Commentary* conducted a symposium on 'Liberal Anti-Communism Revisited' (September 1967), in which contributors were asked to comment on the CIA connection, and on the suggestion that the 'anti-communism of the Left' helped to make the Vietnam War possible. Spender condemned covert funding as involving 'methods all too similar to those of the totalitarianism we were opposing', and as bringing freedom into discredit. Richard Rovere was another from whose eyes the scales had fallen. In the 1950s he had defended the Congress as 'generally libertarian in outlook and associated with no government',[8] and had been a member of the American Committee for Cultural Freedom, 'but quit when it became clear that the organization was anti-Communist and little else.' Murray Kempton declared bluntly that 'Vietnam is a liberal's war.' It was the outcome of America's global liberalism, of the assumption that the USA had the responsibility to defend freedom everywhere, as President Truman had announced in March 1947: 'The free peoples of the world look to us for support in maintaining their freedoms'[9] — which in practice had meant the propping up of each and every anti-communist regime, however unfree it might be.

It was equally significant, however, that other leading liberals were neither penitent nor embarrassed about the CIA revelations. Diana Trilling launched a fresh attack on 'anti-anti-Communism'. Daniel Bell defended the Congress, formed 'to stand as a symbol of free inquiry and common discourse for intellectuals in all countries', and its conferences, which 'were never propaganda jamborees, but discussions enlisting some of the best minds of our time'. Sidney Hook contended that 'no one can honestly impugn the intellectual independence of the Congress and its magazines.'

We do not have to ask how these protagonists of intellectual freedom would have reacted if they had discovered other intellectuals to be taking part in conferences covertly funded by Soviet government agencies, thus becoming, in Bell's words 'pliable tools of the Communist manipulators behind the scenes.'[10] We need only consider the reaction to the Cultural and Scientific Conference for World Peace held at the Waldorf-Astoria Hotel in New York in 1949. As its name suggests, this event was connected with the international peace campaign then being promoted by Communist parties. It provoked outrage among the Cold War liberals. Sidney Hook set up an alternative conference which was supported by Schlesinger among others. Dwight Macdonald, Mary McCarthy and Norman Cousins were among those who picketed the conference and tried to disrupt it.[11] It was exactly the same *type* of event as the CIA-financed conferences which Hook and Bell were still defending 20 years later.

Encounter and the Congress for Cultural Freedom were junctions at which the intellectual concerns of the Cold War liberals intersected with the real politics of anti-communism, and, in particular, the foreign policy interests of the USA. At that point even Montaigne could be used, or Brecht abused, to reinforce hostility to communism and the Soviet Union. Few of those involved can have realized how they were being 'used', but even those who were ignorant or disbelieving of any 'propagandist' connections were ready and willing to identify liberalism with anti-communism.

THE LIBERALS AND 'McCARTHYISM'

It has often, and I think necessarily, been stressed in this study that liberalism is not and never has been as totally benign a creed as its protagonists would like us to believe. Both the theory and practice of liberalism have their darker aspects. But it is hard to think of another occasion on which professed liberals have so abjectly betrayed their own principles as that moment of obsession with communism, between 1945 and around 1960, which turned at least some of them into advocates and apologists for political inquisition and persecution.

This is the phenomenon usually called McCarthyism, after its most frighteningly influential incarnation, Senator Joe McCarthy of Wisconsin. Like other personalized 'isms', this is a misnomer which distracts attention from the real nature and extent of the thing itself. The hunting out of communists and suspected communists was not initiated by McCarthy: it was set in motion by the Democrat administration of President Harry Truman. The bandwagon had been rolling for at least three years before McCarthy climbed aboard — as the Democrat presidential candidate in 1952, Adlai Stevenson, boasted in the course of his campaign.[12]

Once this climate of hysteria and insecurity had been established, only a handful of liberals and radicals, including the incorruptible journalist I. F. Stone, could be found ready to withstand the stampede to abandon liberal principles in the name of national security, or even — freedom! It became commonplace among American liberals to accept that committed communists had, by virtue of their commitment, forfeited certain normal rights and freedoms. Communists were not entitled to the same rights as other dissenting groups, since the communist movement was, in Bell's words 'a conspiracy, rather than a legitimate dissenting group'. This was also the view of Irving

Kristol, who said that communism was not an 'opinion' but 'a fanatical conspiracy', and of Sidney Hook, whose pamphlet, *Heresy, Yes — Conspiracy, No!*, was published by the American Committee for Cultural Freedom. [13]

It was generally accepted, and publicly argued by the ACCF, that communists had no right to be employed, or to remain employed as teachers in schools or colleges. The ACCF report on academic freedom, produced by a group which included Hook and the noted historian of ideas Arthur O. Lovejoy, argued that 'A member of the Communist Party has transgressed the canons of academic responsibility, has engaged his intellect to servility, and is therefore professionally disqualified from performing his functions as scholar and teacher.' [14] James B. Conant, President of Harvard, who, according to O'Brien, 'was regarded by many as the epitome of the liberal, humanist intellectual', agreed that members of the Communist Party were 'out of bounds as members of the teaching profession', and both he and the President of Yale gave undertakings not to appoint communists. Conant's successor, Nathan Pusey, took the same line. [15]

Some went even further than this. Leslie Fiedler, whose highly equivocal *Encounter* article on 'McCarthy and the Intellectuals' was written explicitly from the standpoint of a 'liberal intellectual', spoke approvingly of 'the firing of proven Communists, in which many anti-McCarthyites would concur'; [16] while Sidney Hook held that anyone who, under interrogation, cited the Fifth Amendment, and thereby refused to answer questions about him/herself, was virtually sure to have been a communist: 'almost all who invoked the privilege, independent evidence shows, were present or former members of the Communist Party.' [17]

Once the principle was conceded, that communists automatically forfeited certain civil rights, where was the line to be drawn? Why should former communists be trusted? Why should fellow-travelling non-party members escape the net? Why not presume, with Hook, that those who refused to answer questions must have something to hide? And so we find Fiedler referring to 'the evasion of the non-cooperators', as if there were something cowardly or dishonourable in refusing to submit to the McCarthyite inquisition, and suggesting that the 'truly liberal' course *would* involve the naming of names. We are here at the furthest possible remove, in practice, from Forster's principle of loyalty to one's friends. Friends denounced friends, sister (Ruth Fischer) denounced brother (Gerhard Eisler), and this behaviour commanded approval in some liberal circles. And we find Kristol arguing that because 'the existence of an organized subversive movement such as communism is a threat to the consensus on which civil society and its liberties are based', communists *and* fellow-travellers have forfeited their civil liberties. Someone who argues that 'we can defend our liberties only by uncritically defending theirs . . . will be taken as speaking as one of them.' [18] Once again — guilt by association. To claim that communists had the same civil rights as other members of society, was to be in effect, a communist.

Thus was the civil liberties posture discredited. Even to protest at the extent of the inquisition and the fear it generated was to reveal yourself as tainted with communism, for, as Diana Trilling put it, 'an intense fear of McCarthyism has been nurtured by the Communists and directly serves the Communist purpose', and 'the idea that America is a terror-stricken country in the grip of hysteria is a Communist-inspired idea.'[19]

Given the readiness of these liberal intellectuals both to endorse the witch-hunt *and* to play down its extent, it is appropriate to recall a few facts and figures. David Caute estimates that between 1947 and 1956 there were around 2,700 dismissals and around 12,000 resignations from the federal civil service as a result of the 'loyalty' investigations. About 600 school and university teachers lost their jobs for political reasons, and Caute calculates that there were around 5,000 dismissals in private industry for the same reasons. The Hollywood blacklist included 250 names of directors, writers, actors and others. Forty trade unions banned communists from membership, and several trade unions with a Leftist record were harassed and destroyed — a process in which the future President John F. Kennedy played a prominent part.[20] If political purges on that scale had occurred under any socialist regime, it is unlikely that Sidney Hook and Diana Trilling would have found it inappropriate to use words like hysteria to describe what inspired them.

Furthermore, the logic of the situation meant that the liberals themselves would in the end come under suspicion and attack. A process which found it hard to distinguish between communists and those with communist 'sympathies', was hardly likely to be more sensitive to the fine distinctions between social reformers and social revolutionaries, or between democratic socialism and revolutionary Marxism. Given the American use of the term 'liberal' to signify Left and progressive opinion of all persuasions, it is hardly surprising that many people believed that 'A liberal is only a hop, skip, and a jump from a Communist. A Communist starts as a liberal.'[21] Whittaker Chambers, the ex-Communist turned informer who sent Alger Hiss to jail (later canonized by Lionel Trilling as 'a man of honour' and of 'magnanimous intention'), gave it as his opinion that the New Deal was a socialist revolution disguised as liberalism.[22] Irving Kristol went some way to endorsing this line of argument when he wrote that 'the American people' at least know that McCarthy 'like them, is unequivocally anti-Communist. About the spokesmen for American liberalism, they feel they know no such thing.'[23] Given this climate of opinion, it was only to be expected that the more timid liberals, above all those with a communist or radical past, should fall over themselves to prove that they were as loyal and as dedicatedly anti-communist as the heresy-hunters themselves. So they abandoned liberal principles in their eagerness to prove their anti-communist credentials.

There *were* liberals who stood and spoke out against McCarthyism and the erosion of civil liberties, among them Richard Rovere and Arthur Schlesinger Jr, the latter stating pointedly that 'I cannot go along with those who profess a belief in cultural freedom, on the one hand, and refuse to condemn McCarthyism, on the other.'[24] In general, though, it has to be said that the American liberals fared badly in this sharp test of their true convictions.

It is often suggested that McCarthyism, like Watergate — and like, it sometimes seems, any other discreditable episode in American history — was an aberration, a temporary lapse which failed to divert the mainstream of American progress from its true liberal course. Such an account is really the reverse of an explanation; but in any case, as far as McCarthyism is concerned, it certainly underestimates the lasting impact of this episode. Not only does it fit into a pattern of recurring 'red scares' in twentieth-century American history: McCarthyism, by destroying left-dominated trade unions, by bringing the socialism and radicalism of the 1930s and 1940s into discredit, by creating a climate of intolerance, fear and conformity, constituted the grim but necessary prelude to the very different climate of opinion which was being celebrated in the USA at the end of the 1950s: the end of ideology. Ideology had not simply died a natural death; it had been driven out, or driven underground, by the inquisition and purges of the years of the Great Fear.

LIBERALISM AGAINST 'IDEOLOGY'

Cold War liberalism was, then, polemical, topical and involved, and its involvement was with the politics of anti-communism. Beyond the responses to particular issues and crises, the Cold War liberals built up a formidable and comprehensive defence of their position. Much of this was developed negatively, in the form of an immense and elaborate theory of 'totalitarianism' and of its supposed historical and intellectual roots. In particular, of course, they wanted to uncover the pedigree of *Left* totalitarianism; to expose the fundamental philosophical errors which, they believed, had set the Left on the path which led in the end to Lenin and Bolshevism; Stalin, the labour camps and mass purges; the world of Koestler's *Darkness at Noon* and Orwell's *Nineteen Eighty-Four*. On the positive side, there was the re-presentation of liberalism as above all an empiricist and pluralistic doctrine, and a very drastic revision of classical democratic theory. In what follows we must consider briefly the various elements in this revised and revived liberalism of the post-1945 West.

'TOTALITARIANISM'

The concept of 'totalitarianism' is not easy to define, the word having become an all-purpose term of abuse. The term was coined, it seems, in the 1920s, and was quickly taken up by Mussolini to describe the aims and even the actual nature of the Italian fascist state. Somewhat surprisingly, many later theorists have been prepared to take Mussolini at his own word. Essentially the term has been used to describe, or to categorize, what was taken to be a new type of authoritarian regime, one with unprecedently comprehensive ambitions.

What became the dominant 'typology' of totalitarianism was outlined by Carl Friedrich and others at the height of the Cold War in the early 1950s. A conference held in 1952 produced a symposium which revealed general acceptance of the concept among political theorists and scientists, despite differences over its proper definition and application. Friedrich himself listed five central 'factors or aspects which basically are shared by all totalitarian societies of our time'. They were: 'an official ideology . . . covering all vital aspects of man's existence' — this ideology, he added, 'is characteristically focused in terms of chiliastic claims as to the "perfect" final society of mankind'; 'a single mass party'; a 'near-complete monopoly' of force; and the same of the means of mass communication; and, finally 'a system of terroristic police control'.[25] The influence of this characterization is illustrated by the fact that nearly 20 years later Leonard Schapiro's brief textbook on *Totalitarianism* took it as its starting point.[26] To these five features a sixth was sometimes added: 'central control of the entire economy'. Other writers have made much of what is referred to as 'mass mobilization' or 'mass enthusiasm', and have suggested that totalitarianism has its roots in, or even is, as Schapiro puts it, 'an aspect of mass democracy',[27] Finally, there is the question of definition — a concise summary has been supplied by Barrington Moore: 'As the root "total" suggests, writers who use this term usually have in mind a society all of whose activities, from the rearing of children to the production and distribution of economic goods, are controlled and directed from a single centre.'[28]

It was open to the proponents of the concept to put it forward as no more than an 'ideal type' or model, to which actual regimes only ever approximated, or *aimed* to achieve. Most of them went further, however, arguing that three political systems at least had conformed to the model: Nazi Germany, fascist Italy, and Stalin's Russia, or, more sweepingly, the Soviet Union at every stage in its history. No doubt there are some writers who would still maintain that position; and certainly outside academic circles it is still common to find these regimes and many others, especially communist or Marxist ones, described unhesitatingly as 'totalitarian'. However, the *description* of fascist Italy, or even Nazi Germany or Stalin's Soviet Union as totalitarian has come to seem less

and less plausible as more and more is known about them in detail. Even if
the ramshackle apparatus of Italian fascism is set aside, the monolithic facades
of the other two regimes are now seen to have concealed considerable contradictions, and their great power had narrower limits than the notion of 'total control'
implies. The 'planned economy' of the Nazis, for example, did not involve
much interference with the operations of private enterprise, beyond the racially
motivated expropriation of the Jews; and, as T. W. Mason has shown, even
the abolition of the trade unions did not suceed in preventing all strikes and
other forms of industrial unrest, including wage drift. [29]

The belief that totalitarian regimes, by virtue of their supposed total control,
possessed unique efficiency has also been attacked as a myth. Trevor-Roper
was the first of several historians who noticed that the Nazi regime was not
so much a streamlined monolith as a conglomeration of quasi-feudal baronies,
loosely held together by Hitler's leadership. [30] The divisions and tensions inside
Stalinist Russia are more thoroughly concealed by Soviet secrecy and censorship; but the dramatic changes that followed hard upon Stalin's death,
Khrushchev's astonishing speech to the twentieth Party Congress in 1956, and
the accumulated evidence of industrial unrest and intellectual dissent, indicate
that the Soviet Union is still a long way from conforming to the pattern of
Nineteen Eighty-Four.

In fact there has always been an unresolved contradiction in Western
coverage of communist affairs. On the one hand, the 'totalitarian' character
of communist regimes must be insistently stressed. On the other hand, there
is the natural ideological desire to show how unpopular such regimes are with
their own peoples, and therefore to report and magnify every indication of
opposition and dissent within communist societies. Yet how could such
opposition and dissent exist at all if the regimes were in fact totalitarian, and
had achieved 'total control' over society? It is even more difficult to explain,
from the 'totalitarian' angle, such events as the Prague Spring of 1968, when
communist leaders themselves made dramatic moves towards an open and
democratic style of government, or the repeated popular convulsions in Poland.

The actual troubled histories of communist regimes suggest, in other words,
that at most the notion of totalitarianism can only be used as a model, to which
such regimes may aspire, or even at times perhaps approximate. It cannot be
used as a simple description. Some of the more subtle exponents of the theory
of totalitarianism grasped this from the start. Hannah Arendt, for example,
wrote that 'What strikes the observer of the totalitarian state is certainly not
its monolithic structure', and she emphasized the confusion and inefficiency
of their actual structures and policy-making. [31]

Nevertheless, the image of communist societies as actual embodiments of
totalitarianism gained a widespread acceptance in the West, and still obtains
today. Yet the conception has undoubtedly lost a great deal of the academic

prestige it once enjoyed — so much so, indeed, that Herbert J. Spiro, who contributed the article on 'Totalitarianism' to the 1968 edition of the *Encyclopaedia of Social Sciences*, went so far as to suggest that 'the greatest problem for future research on the topic of totalitarianism is the utility of the concept itself', and to express the hope that it would not appear at all in the next edition of the *Encyclopaedia*.

I share that view, and believe that in the perspective of history, the term will be seen as belonging more to political propaganda than to political analysis. It is, though, impossible to deny its centrality to the revived liberalism of the Cold War period. The concept itself was liberal, since it implicitly disregarded the differences of aim, ideology and character between authoritarian regimes of the Left and Right, and implied that the crucial factor was that both denied the principles of liberal democracy. As Hayek put it, 'the opposite of liberalism is totalitarianism'. The concept itself did much to ease the transition from the actual war against fascism to the Cold War against communism. Were not the two enemies essentially one and the same? Such an indifference to the manifest differences between fascism and communism is possible only from a liberal point of view.

After 1945, fascism was generally assumed to be a thing of the past; it was communism which was the real enemy. Hence the weight of the liberal critique and analysis of 'totalitarianism', as it was developed in the 1950s, was directed essentially against communism, but also against the whole intellectual and political history of revolutionary socialism since the French Revolution. For was not totalitarian communism the final, and, it was suggested, logical outcome of that history? And, if that was so, was it not necessary to uncover the roots of totalitarianism, buried beneath the superficial attractions of left-wing utopianism? Other forms of repression and authoritarianism were not interpreted in the same way. But totalitarianism, according to the theory, was different. It allotted a special place to ideology, conceived of as an explicit doctrine with what were usually tendentiously called 'chiliastic' or 'millenarian' or 'utopian' aims. It was suggested that these aims extended, not just to the transformation of human society, but to the reconstruction of human nature itself. Hannah Arendt spelt out what she took to be the terrible consequences of that grandiose project: 'The concentration camps are the laboratories where changes in human nature are tested.'[32] These aims were the products of ideology, and since the official ideology of communist regimes is Marxism, or Marxism-Lenism, it followed that the critique of totalitarianism must involve an intellectual assault on Marxism and even its socialist predecessors. The other feature of the liberal intellectual attack on totalitarian politics followed equally logically from this analysis: it was a critique of all forms of 'ideological' politics, and even of the very concept of ideology itself.

THE ATTACK ON 'UTOPIANISM'

The intellectual source of communist totalitarianism was held to be the 'utopianism' of the Left. Conservatives from the time of Burke had always regarded the vision of a happy and harmonious future for humanity as a delusion, and perhaps a dangerous one. But in Burke's day it was radical liberals like Condorcet, Paine and Shelley who projected such visions. It is only in the twentieth century that liberals have joined with conservatives in seeing all forms of utopianism as sinister and potentially tyrannical. The tragedy of utopianism was that it was inspired by idealism, by well-intentioned dreams and plans for human welfare. But 'while it has its birth in the noblest impulses of man, it is doomed to be perverted into an instrument of tyranny and hypocrisy.'[33] J. L. Talmon was in fact a conservative theorist, and this quotation is from a pamphlet published in 1957 by the Conservative Political Centre. However, Talmon's book, *The Origins of Totalitarian Democracy*, published in 1952, was at once incorporated into the liberal critique of utopianism, and his approach is not substantially different from that of avowed liberals like Sir Isaiah Berlin and Sir Karl Popper: 'the Utopian attempt to realize an ideal state, using a blueprint of society as a whole, is one which demands a strong centralized rule of a few, and which therefore is likely to lead to a dictatorship.' One of Popper's most enthusiastic and uncritical disciples, the former Labour MP, Bryan Magee, has spelt out the message even more strongly in his short study of Popper himself. Both the reactionary and Utopian ideals 'are led into totalitarianism. This development is inherent from the beginning, though when it comes about people will say that the theory has been perverted.'[34] Thus Magee will not even allow that a perversion of the original ideal is involved. In similar vein, Berlin has written of 'the tyranny of the great altruistic systems' and of 'liberators who crush'.[35] The utopians are so obsessed with, so possessed by, their visions of future perfection that they become indifferent to the rights of individuals and the actual sufferings of actual persons in the present. 'What in fact does the sacrifice of individual men matter as long as it contributes to the salvation of all mankind!' is Albert Camus' sarcastic paraphrase of Marx's supposed attitude in another influential book of the 1950s, *The Rebel.*[36]

Thus by a terrible irony, vision and idealism turn out to be the parents of cruelty and tyranny. Contemporary liberals and conservatives are agreed on this. But this apparent paradox can be explained. For, as many of the anti-utopian writers have suggested, secular utopianism is a modernized version of an older religious vision, usually called 'chiliastic', 'millenarian' or 'messianic'. The heart of the 'Utopian dream' says Berlin, 'is the pattern of sin and death and resurrection . . . Its roots lie deep in the religious imagination of mankind.'[37] This theme was developed at length in yet another key text of the 1950s, Norman Cohn's *The Pursuit of the Millenium*, which, Cohn claimed, described 'the medieval beginnings of revolutionary messianism in Europe'. He contended that there was 'a hidden continuity' between medieval Christian and modern secular versions of 'the revolutionary apocalypse'.[38] Therefore a study of Christian millenarianism cast direct light on modern totalitarian movements. It became conventional to discredit any vision of a radically different society, and any conception of wholesale social change, by the use of quasi-religious terminology. We need 'less Messianic ardour' said Berlin. What rational person would dare to admit to anything so mad as Messianic ardour, with its overtones of fanaticism and intolerance?

If the irrational character of utopianism was partly indicated by its quasi-religious character, a related accusation was that it was essentially unscientific. This was the line of criticism developed, at length, by Popper. He argued that any attempt to change or reconstruct society as a whole — what he called 'Utopian social engineering' — rested on the assumption that we possess sufficient 'factual knowledge' to undertake such an enterprise, and this is invalid. Furthermore, it violates the principle of trial and error, which can only be applied in social experiments on a more modest, 'piecemeal' scale; and so contradicts the most elementary rule of science, 'since the whole secret of scientific method is a readiness to learn from mistakes'. As a result, the utopian, or 'holistic' method turns out also to be 'impossible'; it is, in the last resort, unworkable.[39]

What Popper calls 'holism' is similar to, or belongs to the same family as what Berlin calls 'monism'. This is the desire and determination to find a single pattern in or behind the multiplicity and variousness of events, and the belief that there is a single pattern of values, a single social order towards which humanity, half without knowing it, yearns and strives. Such a perspective inevitably denies the complexity and variety of human experience and human aims. Hence 'attempts to adapt individuals and fit them into a rational schema, conceived in terms of a theoretical ideal, be the motives for doing it never so lofty, always lead in the end to a terrible maiming of human beings, to political vivisection on an ever increasing scale.' This contrast between monism and pluralism is one of Berlin's central themes, and is elaborated in his well-known essay on Tolstoy in terms of the difference between the hedgehog who 'knows one big thing', and the fox who 'knows many things'. Berlin is on the side of the foxes. Reality itself is plural, complex, ultimately unintelligible, and not reducible or assimilable to a single comprehensive vision or pattern: 'Single-minded monists, ruthless fanatics, men possessed by an all-embracing coherent vision, do not know the doubts and agonies of those who cannot wholly blind themselves to reality.'[40] Monism leads to fanaticism. It provides the philosophical basis for utopianism and totalitarianism, while conversely, political pluralism is based on philosophical pluralism which asserts the diversity and complexity of reality itself.

Marxism was seen as a form of monism, and was inevitably the one which attracted most critical attention from the liberal theorists. Ironically, however, the tendency of these commentators was to underplay the complexities and contradictions within Marx's own work, to say nothing of the variety of trends within Marxism. Instead, Marxism was usually presented as a single monolithic creed of a determinist character. It was assumed that Marx claimed to have produced a science of society. It was also assumed that the test of science is its capacity to make accurate predictions about future events. Popper himself believed that he had not merely discredited 'historicism', of which Marxism is the leading example, but had in the end actually refuted it: 'I have shown that, for strictly logical reasons, it is impossible for us to predict the future course of history.' What is more, he held that 'with the elimination of the historicist doctrine, the theory of revolution becomes completely untenable.'[41]

Popper's supposed 'refutation' of Marx hinged upon his contention that Marx was a rigid determinist, who viewed human beings as 'mere puppets, irresistibly pulled by economic wires — by historical forces over which they have no control.'[42] It is fair to say, that although there may have been some Marxists who conformed to this picture, it is not a description of Marx's own theory which most Marx scholars would now accept. It was this same Marx, after all, who wrote in *The Eighteenth Brumaire* that 'Men make their own history, but not of their own free will; not under circumstances they themselves have chosen but under the given and inherited circumstances with which they are directly confronted.' And Marx himself was at pains in later years to disown such an interpretation of his theory.[43] The widespread acceptance of this interpretation and critique of Marx in the 1950s and 1960s was testimony less to its intellectual cogency than to the degree to which it endorsed the anti-Marxist ethos of the Cold War.

THE CRITIQUE, AND THE 'END', OF IDEOLOGY

'To denounce ideologies in general is to set up an ideology of one's own.'
(E. H. Carr)[44]

Cold War liberalism claimed to be both non-ideological and anti-ideological, and in the late 1950s and early 1960s it even claimed that ideological politics were dying out, and that we were entering a new era of rational, realistic, empirical politics. We had reached 'the end of ideology'.

The concept of ideology is now much more familiar and more widely used than it was in the 1950s, and it does not necessarily have an intrinsically derogatory meaning. As we have seen, it can be taken to mean no more than a comprehensive world-view with a social basis and important political implications. But the Cold War liberals always used 'ideology' as a term of disparagement with a much more restricted meaning. The term was not usually defined with any precision; it was simply used in a highly tendentious way which presumed that readers would share the hostility of the writer. Thus the chapter of Bernard Crick's widely read *In Defence of Politics* which is called 'A Defence of Politics against Ideology' is in fact entirely devoted to a consideration of totalitarianism, and the phrase 'totalitarian ideology' is used as if it were in fact a tautology: ideology is inherently and essentially totalitarian. From this kind of usage it is possible to distil a fairly clear picture of what these liberals meant by ideology, and why they opposed it so vehemently.

Whereas it is now generally accepted that an ideology can be a set of values or a world-view which is *implicit* in people's attitudes or behaviour rather than being consciously spelt out, in the 1950s liberal writers saw ideology as essentially explicit, consciously coherent, and systematic. As Edward Shils wrote (somewhat later): '*Ideologies* are characterized by a high degree of explicitness of formulation . . . As compared with other patterns of beliefs, ideologies are relatively highly systematized or integrated.' This explicitness and systematic character meant that they were also rigid. Because ideologies were so systematic and coherent, those who subscribed to them would be unreceptive to any new evidence or experience which did not fit into these preconceived patterns, and Shils referred in his article to 'the closure of the ideological disposition to new evidence'.[45] Or, as Hannah Arendt put it: 'Ideological thinking . . . proceeds with a consistency that exists nowhere in the realm of reality. . . . Once it has established its premise, its point of departure, experiences no longer interfere with ideological thinking, nor can it be taught by reality.'[46] Thus the very characteristics which in many situations are considered to be intellectual virtues — coherence, consistency and systematicness — are defects in a political creed, because they contradict 'reality' and promote an anti-empirical frame of mind. Ideologists, said Daniel Bell, were ' "terrible simplifiers" '. Ideology makes it unnecessary for people to confront individual issues on their individual merits. One simply turns to the ideological vending machine, and out comes the prepared formulae.' Implicit in these criticisms was the assumption of the 'foxes', that reality itself is pluralistic, even chaotic, and not to be understood in terms of a single coherent system of ideas or values. Politics too, therefore, were pluralistic, and no single doctrine could provide. a guide through the confusion. Individual issues had to be treated individually, on their individual 'merits'. Attempts to connect these separate events or problems, to fit them into a pattern, were mistaken and dangerous.

Ideology was seen as a form of 'secular religion',[47] and associated with fanaticism. It was seen as providing the intellectual basis for dogmatic, doctrinaire and extremist political attitudes, and above all for totalitarianism. To be ideological was *ipso facto* to be unreasonable, as Irving Kristol implied when he reported on the Vietnam War teach-in movement in *Encounter*: 'Within the "teach-in" movement there are many unreasonable, ideological types — pro-Castro, pro-Viet Cong, pro-Mao, anti-American.'[48] The reverse position, pro-American, anti-Mao, etc. was presumably not unreasonable or ideological.

If these writers felt no need to define ideology, that was perhaps because they believed that as far as the developed, industrialized Western World was concerned, ideological politics were on the way out. Apparently it was Edward Shils who coined the phrase 'the end of ideology', which he used in 1955 as the title for a conference report in *Encounter*. The conference, he said, 'had in part the atmosphere of a post-victory ball'. This was primarily due to the feeling that 'there was no longer any need to justify ourselves *vis-à-vis* the Communist critique of our society'; but also to the feeling that we had reached 'the end of ideological enthusiasm', and had learnt from 'the disasters of governing societies by passionate adherence to formulae'.[49] In similar vein, Bell announced in 1959 that 'In the last decade, we have witnessed an exhaustion of the nineteenth-century ideologies, particularly Marxism.'[50]

The 'end of ideology' had both a negative and a positive aspect. Negatively, it was suggested that the experience of authoritarian communism, as well as of fascism and the Nazis' Thousand Year Reich, had finally discredited utopianism and every grandiose vision of changing human nature and remaking human society. The horrors these had produced meant 'an end to chiliastic hopes, to millenarianism, to apocalyptic thinking — and to ideology'. What had also been demonstrated, at least in the democratic West, was the existence of consensus on a number of fundamental political principles, and the acceptance of compromise as a means of settling remaining disagreements: 'In the Western World, therefore, there is today a rough consensus among intellectuals on political issues: the acceptance of a Welfare State; the desirability of decentralized power; a system of mixed economy and of political pluralism. In that sense, too, the ideological age has ended.'[51] This political consensus reflected something even more profound and more remarkable, in the view of S. M. Lipset; namely, 'the fact that the fundamental problems of the industrial revolution have been solved. . . . This very triumph of the democratic social revolution in the West ends domestic politics for those intellectuals who must have ideologies or utopias to motivate them to political action.'[52]

Since the end of ideology itself came to an end quite soon after it had been announced by Bell, Shils, Lipset, Raymond Aron[53] and others, it is tempting to dismiss the whole episode as one of the absurdly misplaced moments of Western intellectual smugness. But its mood and outlook were not confined to a marginal intelligentsia. The abandonment of the socialist commitment to public ownership by the West German Social Democratic Party, and the comparable 'revisionist' tendency in the British Labour Party reflected this climate of opinion. Yet another influential book of the 1950s, Anthony Crosland's

The Future of Socialism (1956) was based on the same interpretation of Western politics: many of the traditional aims of socialism had been realized, and these achievements had been endorsed by a consensus of political opinion. Class struggle was at an end, and doubt was even cast on the very existence of class as a significant factor in politics. This perspective was adopted by the then leader of the Labour Party, Hugh Gaitskell, and, in a less overt and abrasive form, by his successor, Harold Wilson.

The belief that 'the fundamental political problems of the industrial revolution have been solved' was very soon made to look ridiculous. What was sometimes called 'the rediscovery of poverty' — the uncovering of persisting forms of deprivation behind the appearance of universal affluence — the coexistence of public squalor with private wealth to which J. K. Galbraith had drawn attention in *The Affluent Society* (1958) even before Bell and Lipset had published their celebratory texts, the emergence of the black civil rights movement in the USA, the deep political divisions created by the American war in Vietnam — all these destroyed the illusion of conflict-free, unideological politics almost as soon as it had been proclaimed a reality. The world depression of the 1970s and 1980s, the return of inflation and mass unemployment to the developed capitalist world, and the undermining of the welfare state, confirmed that the 'moment' of 'the end of ideology' was indeed no more than that — a political and intellectual reflection of the post-1945 capitalist boom which has now come to an end. It was itself an ideological episode.

Yet its importance to the evolution of contemporary liberalism was great. For the critique of utopianism and ideology developed by the Cold War liberals, and the concomitant advocacy of empiricism and piecemeal reform, are not in essence liberal at all: they are the stock-in-trade of established conservative argument and polemic:

> The less, therefore, man clogs the free play of his mind with political doctrine and dogma, the better for his thinking . . . what shams and disasters political ideologies are apt to be, we surely have had opportunity to learn . . . almost all ideologies vastly overrate man's capacity to foresee the consequences and repercussions of ideals forced on reality.[54]

These were the quintessentially conservative sentiments of the conservative historian, Sir Lewis Namier — sentiments which were no different from those being expressed at that same period by liberals like Berlin, Popper, Bell, Lipset, Aron and Camus. Nor would any of these liberals have wished to dissent from the conservative Talmon's contention that 'empiricism is the ally of freedom, and the doctrinaire spirit is the friend of totalitarianism.'[55]

Thus the liberal adoption of political empiricism and renunciation of utopianism and ideology brought liberalism into a much closer alliance with conservatism, and shifted the whole spectrum of Western politics to the Right. If it is not clear how liberal scepticism differs from the Tory version, it *is* clear that both are outlooks fundamentally unsympathetic to political radicalism.

DEMOCRACY REDEFINED

A further stage in this de-radicalization of liberalism was the wholesale rewriting of the conception and theory of democracy. This was not an altogether surprising development. Liberalism, as we have seen, has always been deeply ambiguous and hesitant about democracy; and the theoretical revisions of democratic theory promoted by such writers as Joseph Schumpeter, Robert Dahl and Seymour Martin Lipset represent a refined sociological version of the traditional liberal doubts and misgivings. Yet classic liberal writers like de Tocqueville and J. S. Mill never went so far as to try to redefine the very concept of democracy to accommodate their own anxieties. This bold enterprise was left to the sociological theorists of the twentieth century.

The motives which prompted this 'revisionism' were political as well as intellectual. On the one hand the revisionists were troubled by the extent to which democracy as it actually existed failed to conform to the aspirations and prescriptions of classical democratic theory, and felt compelled to find explanations for this disparity. This in itself might have led to a far-ranging critique of existing democratic practices in the light of the original ideal. But it did not. It led instead to the redefining of democracy itself in terms which accommodated the definition to existing practices. This was as much a political as an intellectual move, since it demonstrated that the liberal theorists were unwilling to allow that those Western societies which called themselves democracies might be faulted for their failure to live up to the original ideal. Better to change the definition than to criticize the reality.

The development of a sociological understanding of politics seriously undermined the classical liberal individualist picture of the electorate as a collection of discrete rational individuals. It was clear, for one thing, that there was a significant degree of correlation between social class and political allegiance, including what is usually called 'voting behaviour'. It was clear, too, that voters tended to give their allegiance, often a lifetime of allegiance, to a single political party, rather than making a conscious and specific decision about voting at each election. Sociological studies repeatedly revealed, indeed, that large numbers of voters were strikingly ill-informed about politics, and many of them were apparently indifferent or apathetic.

Nor were these the only ways in which the 'actually existing' democracies failed to conform to the classical model. It was far from clear in what way they embodied the old notion of 'government by the people'. Even if the factor of size ruled out actual participation in government by the mass of the citizens, and the idea of 'representative' democracy is developed as a (diluted) substitute, it was not apparent that this came very close to the original principle. How far were 'representatives' representative and accountable? Their accountability was almost entirely confined to the electoral process: the vote was the people's only sanction. In practice people voted, not for individuals but for parties. The range of parties was also very limited, often to two plausible candidates for government. The rejection of one government might, in practice, leave only one alternative: government by the other major party. How could such a narrow choice embody the popular will?

The major elite theorists of the early twentieth century went further. From their varying angles, Pareto, Mosca and Michels all argued that democracy was, judged by its own criteria, a fraud. It had failed to replace the age-old rule of the many by the few with the rule of the many by themselves. It had not succeeded in displacing oligarchy. Furthermore, they argued, it *could not* succeed in doing so. Oligarchy, rule by a few or by an elite, was an inevitable, unavoidable feature of politics. Democratic rule was simply an impossibility, almost a contradiction in terms.

Not all of the elite theorists went so far. Michels' argument in *Political Parties* was that there was a *tendency* towards oligarchy in democratic as in other kinds of politics, but that this tendency could and should be resisted. That was not, however, the kind of conclusion drawn by the mainstream liberal and conservative theorists of democracy. In general they accepted the line of argument which had been developed by the elite theorists: democracy on the classical model was an impossibility: 'The citizen in a democracy simply cannot play the role in which the classical philosophy has cast him.'[56] And it might be undesirable even if it were possible. Accordingly, if the credit of the term was to be rescued, 'democracy' would have to be redefined in a way which would accord with the supposedly unavoidable facts of life in advanced industrial societies. And since 'democracy' had become, since the beginning of the twentieth century, one of the most prestigious terms in the vocabulary of politics, it was clearly politically desirable that such a rescue should be undertaken.

The proposed redefinition was drastic — perhaps more so than some of its proponents realized. The root of it was the confining of the conception of democracy to a system of government, or, still more narrowly, to a system of choosing a government. Lipset, in *Political Man*, provides a representative definition in the new style: 'Democracy in a complex society may be defined as a political system which supplies regular constitutional opportunities for changing the governing officials, and a social mechanism which permits the largest possible part of the population to influence major decisions by choosing among contenders for political office.'[57] Schlesinger also offered an essentially electoral definition of democracy as 'a system in which the majority under constitutional procedures freely chooses among competing persons for limited-term control of the state'; while Robert Dahl's conception even omitted any reference to elections — '. . . what we call democracy — that is, a system of decision-making in which the leaders are more or less responsive to the preferences of non-leaders'[58] — and is so vague that it could be applied to virtually any regime that does not rule by brute force. All these definitions follow Schumpeter in treating democracy as a 'political method', or an 'institutional arrangement'[59] for deciding who shall govern, or for choosing leaders. As one critic, Jack Walker observed, 'Democracy is thus conceived primarily in procedural terms.'[60]

These writers also followed Schumpeter and the elite theorists in accepting a clear separation between the governors and the governed, the leaders and the led. Some of them did not flinch from the term elite. Thus Maurice Duverger laid down that 'The formula "Government of the people by the people" must be replaced by this formula: "Government of the people by an elite sprung from the people".'[61] Lipset declared that 'The distinctive and most valuable element of democracy is the formation of a political elite in the competitive struggle for the votes of a mainly passive electorate.'[62] Others believed that the distinctive feature of democracies was that they offered the possibility of choice between *competing* elites, as opposed to those systems where power was in the hands of a single homogenous elite.

Lipset's assumption that 'a mainly passive electorate' was entirely compatible with a working democracy, indicates another significant feature of the revised conception. Democracy was a system of choosing a government which gave everyone the *opportunity* to take part. But it required little more than voting by way of participation, and at least one writer suggested that there were sinister totalitarian overtones to arguments 'connected with the general theme of a Duty to Vote'. Participation on a large scale was not only unnecessary; it could even be dangerous, as Lipset suggested: 'The belief that a very high level of participation is always good for democracy is not valid.'[63] Bernard Crick suggested something similar when he wrote that the idea of popular sovereignty, 'if taken too seriously, is an actual step towards totalitarianism', because 'it allows no refuge and no contradiction, no private apathy even'.[64] Thus mass participation, coupled to the idea of popular sovereignty, was seen as at least potentially illiberal, and linked to the bogey of totalitarianism.

Was there then nothing more for the citizen of a modern democracy to do than to cast the occasional vote (provided that he or she did not feel coerced by too strong a sense of duty)? As if by way of compensation for the minimal role allotted to the individual in the central process of politics, the revisionist theorists discovered an alternative channel through which the individual could exercise some influence on the ruling elite. This was the pressure or interest group.

Here too there was a more or less complete reversal of classical democratic theory. Classical theory had advocated popular participation in politics and had exalted the popular will. It had looked askance at what the eighteenth century called 'factions' — groups which sought to promote particular interests, regardless of the general good. Old-fashioned democrats and egalitarians might regard pressure groups with suspicion, as the organized lobbies of the richest and most powerful vested interests in society. The liberal revisionists had no such misgivings. They saw pressure groups as central to the workings of modern democracy, and campaigned vigorously to have this view more widely accepted. 'Apart from Parliament itself', wrote Robert McKenzie, 'the interest group system could be considered the most vital feature of British democracy.' He concluded this newspaper article by asking 'is it not time to recognise that the interest group system and its healthy functioning . . . is of central importance in a pluralist society?'[65] John Plamenatz was, if anything, even more enthusiastic: 'In a country which has been democratic for a considerable time and where there is general literacy, every section of the people is spoken for by some organization or other. The voice of the people is heard everlastingly . . . through these spokesmen.'[66] Robert Dahl, for one, was confident that this ideal was realized in the USA, which possessed, he said, 'a political system in which all the active and legitimate groups in the population can make themselves heard at some crucial stage in the process of decision.' Although it should be said that Dahl rather undermined his own statement by admitting that in the USA of the 1950s 'Communists are not now a legitimate group', and also that 'neither individuals nor groups are political equals.'[67]

The argument in favour of recognizing the centrality of pressure groups to democracy had three strengths. First, it accepted and endorsed the pluralist conception of society: it harmonized with the characteristic liberal stress on the variety of human aspirations, interests, values, and commitments. Secondly, it had a sociological sophistication which classical liberal individualism conspicuously lacked: it recognized that human beings in society tend to function not as isolated, discrete individuals, but as members of groups — and not necessarily of one group, but of a variety of overlapping groups embodying different dimensions of their social life. Thirdly, it accepted the existence of pressure groups, and found a place for them within the framework of a theory of democracy. It was in tune with the realities of Western capitalist politics.

This last 'strength' was also part of the weakness of the revisionist redefinition of democracy: it tried to convert 'democracy' from an ideal, or a critical concept, into a mere description of politics in the West. The idea ceased to be a norm or principle against which reality could be measured; reality itself in Western societies *was* democracy. There was nothing left to be aimed at. Utopia had been reached. Democracy, said Lipset, 'is not only or even primarily a means through which different groups can attain their ends of seeking the good society; it is the good society itself in operation.'[68]

Even in its less grotesque forms, the revisionist conception of democracy was an impoverishment of the classical ideal. Those who wrote about, and fought for, democracy in the nineteenth century did not conceive of it as no more than an electoral system, just one method of choosing a government. They saw democracy as a principle which should permeate the whole of society. It was a social ideal, not merely a political mechanism. J. S. Mill, who had so many misgivings about the extension of the franchise, nevertheless believed that 'nothing less can be ultimately desirable than the admission of all to share in the sovereign power of the state', and meanwhile 'any participation, even in the smallest public function, is useful.'[69] That 'democracy' might be taken to imply that participation was in itself dangerous, that apathy might be more desirable, that the burden of political action could somehow be transferred to 'heroic leaders' — to Paine, to Shelley or Mill these notions would have been quite simply incomprehensible. The emphasis on popular political activity was seen by them as for better or worse central to the very meaning of democracy. The revisionists have only arrived at a conception of democracy satisfactory to contemporary liberalism by stripping it of that distinctive emphasis, and in so doing they have transformed 'democracy' from a radical into a conservative political idea.

Detailed criticism of the pluralist apologia for pressure groups is hardly necessary here. Powerful critiques began to appear within a few years of the celebratory articles and essays quoted above.[70] One can only marvel at the bland assumption of so sophisticated a theorist as Plamenatz that *every section* of the people is spoken for through some interest group or other, and at the failure of this writer and so many others to consider the quite blatant inequalities of influence and access between individual pressure groups. How, for example, are millions of the unemployed in the Western democracies represented through this system? How are the millions of retired old people represented? And where organizations do exist to lobby on behalf of such vast 'groups', how effective are they compared to, let us say, the professional organizations which lobby on behalf of lawyers, or doctors, or lorry-owners, or landowners, or the police? Such discrepancies reflect not only an important difference between interests which are organized and interests which by their very nature are virtually unorganizable; they reflect also the structure of inequalities of wealth and power within society.

Beyond these and other radical defects in the pluralist version of democracy, there lies a further fundamental issue. Are the pluralists right in assuming that there are no *general* interests of society, but only particular interests within it? Are not such concerns as health, education and the welfare services general interests? And is it not in the nature of such general interests that they will not be adequately catered for by the operations and interplay of pressure and interest groups and lobbies? Doctors, nurses, health service workers, all have their organizations and means of pressing their claims upon the state. But what of patients? Patients do not constitute a permanent, organizable group. We are all patients at one time or another. How are our interests as potential patients to be represented? How are they not to be lost sight of as the many organized groups jostle for attention and success?

Such questions are not altogether rhetorical. It is extraordinary that they were so little considered by the pioneers of pluralism and pressure group theory. Or it would be extraordinary, if it were not so clear that these revisionists were in fact more concerned to celebrate existing politics than to criticize them, more ready to act as apologists than as analysts. It need not have been so. It can readily be granted that the actual evolution of politics in the West posed a serious challenge to traditional thinking about democracy. But it did not follow that democratic theory had to be reconstructed simply to bring it into harmony with existing political practice. The question could have been asked, How under twentieth-century conditions could the classical democratic ideal be turned into a reality? But in the context of the Cold War, when 'democracy' was supposedly threatened by 'totalitarian communism', such a question would have been a political embarrassment. There were political as well as intellectual pressures to rewrite democratic theory to fit current Western practice.

Cold war liberalism now seems more than a little old-fashioned. The 'end of ideology' came to an end almost as soon as it was proclaimed, and it is now possible to use the term 'ideology' without being suspected of crypto-totalitarian tendencies. The notion of totalitarianism itself also looks rather shabby. We have reached 1984, and, in spite of many sinister developments, by no means confined to the communist world, Orwell's nightmare of total control has not been realized. People are, rightly, more frightened by the real possibility of nuclear war than they are by the spectre of universal Soviet expansionism. Like the 'end of ideology', the 'new democracy' of the revisionists came under attack almost as soon as it had been elaborated.

This is not to say that any more radical ideology has replaced Cold War liberalism; only that its dominance has been challenged and, to a significant extent, undermined. The revitalization of Western Marxism on the one hand, and of some forms of conservatism on the other, has produced a situation in which conventional mainstream liberalism has to compete for support with other doctrines, and changing circumstances have cruelly exposed its weaknesses.

Cold War liberalism represents, I believe, an almost terminal stage in the decline of Western liberalism. In this shape, liberalism ceased to retain any vestige of radicalism, ceased to pose any shadow of a challenge to the existing order of capitalist society. It became wholly defensive and fundamentally conservative. It assumed that its ideals had been realized in the Western World, and now needed only to be defended, against 'totalitarianism' from without, and against radical 'extremism' within. Cold war liberalism was more conservative than the 'New Liberalism' of the early twentieth century. Thus Maurice Cranston wrote of freedom in the 1950s as if it were still threatened principally by 'the state', whereas Green, Hobhouse and others had argued that the state could be used to extend freedom. And Berlin's discussion of freedom was in some ways less sophisticated than Mill's a century earlier. For Mill had seen that freedom could be as much endangered by social forces as by laws and overt governmental actions. Berlin's discussions, by contrast, revert to the older focus on the conflict between laws (any laws) and individual freedom.

Cold War liberals argued vigorously that we should recognize the multiplicity of values, aims and aspirations which human beings are likely to cherish, and therefore not seek to impose a single pattern upon society. Yet when it came to making judgements on actual politics, they showed that they attached absolute priority to the existence of liberal freedoms over all other considerations. Social and economic achievements such as the alleviation of hunger, poverty, disease, illiteracy and exploitation were never allowed to weigh so heavily. Thus, in the final analysis, the Cold War liberals emerged as opponents of social and economic revolution, and even of greater equality if this was seen as threatening individual freedom. All this largely explains the discredit of liberalism in the Third World, to which attention was drawn at the beginning of this book. The creed which once helped to inspire some of the greatest upheavals in world history — the French Revolution, the struggles for national liberation in Latin America, in Poland, Greece and Italy, and struggles for democracy throughout Europe; which had fired some of the supreme imaginations of European culture — Beethoven, Verdi, Goya, Shelley, Pushkin, and Byron — had dwindled to a doctrine so tame and conservative that its propaganda could be promoted and financed by the USA's Central Intelligence Agency.

19

Liberalism Today

In the second and third part of this book I have traced what I see as a clear overall pattern of rise and decline in the evolution of liberalism as a political doctrine or ideology. From that point of view it would be tidy to end the entire work on the sour note sounded at the end of the last chapter; and 20 years ago, when that brand of liberalism enjoyed such a wide measure of uncritical acceptance in the Western World, that ungenerous conclusion might also have been appropriate — polemically at least. But the recent history both of liberalism itself, and of the significantly more illiberal context in which it exists, means that a more complex summing up is called for. We must therefore consider briefly the nature and significance of some recent developments within the liberal tradition; and finally we must try to assess what the present and future prospects are for the survival of liberalism and liberal values.

LIBERALISM IN THE 1970s AND 1980s

There was something of a revival of liberal theorizing in the 1970s — a revival which took two rather different if overlapping forms. On the one hand there was the remarkable contribution made to the old tradition of social contract theorizing made by John Rawls's massive study, *A Theory of Justice*, published in 1971. Not for a long while had a creative work of political thought provoked more discussion and response, not only from other political theorists, but also from economists, legal theorists and political commentators generally. Rawls's work provided a unique stimulus to political and economic thinking within the liberal tradition.

Among the books which took issue with Rawls was Robert Nozick's *Anarchy, State, and Utopia*, another substantial work of political theory. Both works can be considered as contributions to liberal theory. But whereas Rawls's work was sufficiently open and even ambiguous to be given a fairly wide range of interpretations, Nozick's book belonged squarely within the tradition of right-wing 'libertarianism' represented a century earlier by Herbert Spencer in Britain and William Graham Summer in the USA. As such it constitutes a link with the second form taken by the revived liberalism of the 1970s — namely the return to some degree of academic and political influence of the long marginalized tradition of orthodox liberal economics, together with both Malthusian and Social Darwinist ideas. The veteran representative of this economic tradition, and its most wide-ranging and sophisticated advocate, was F. A. Hayek. He had been a critic and opponent of Keynes even in the 1930s, and had the satisfaction of living long enough to see Keynesianism itself lose its predominance, and his own ideas regain a measure of serious attention. In the popular mind the revival of liberal economics was, however, associated more readily with the cruder writings and prescriptions of Milton Friedman, another Nobel economics prizewinner of the 1970s, and leader of the Chicago school of liberal political economy, often called 'monetarism'.

RAWLS ON PLURALISM AND LIBERTY

John Rawls's *A Theory of Justice*, despite its meticulousness and length, could not be said to be a monolithic study. The wealth of critical, if respectful, commentary which Rawls's book immediately inspired, indicated only too clearly that his argument, or at least the implications of his argument, was open to a considerable range of differing political interpretations. The comments offered here can only be marginal to, and parasitical upon, that very substantial debate.

In one very important respect Rawls's book marks a significant advance, or at least renewal, within the liberal tradition, and that is indicated by its title. Rawls places the idea of justice at the centre of liberal thought, and in so doing revives a way of thinking which looks to Kant rather than to Bentham or J. S. Mill for its foundations in moral philosophy. The ideas of justice and rights have always presented a problem to the ethics of utility; and it is the utilitarian approach which has predominated within liberalism, at any rate in the English-speaking world.

In starting from the concept of justice — 'Justice is the first virtue of social institutions, as truth is of systems of thought'[1] — Rawls tries to remedy one of the defects of utilitarianism, but without abandoning the liberal view of 'the individual'. (Indeed, Rawls's Kantian approach implies *more* respect for the rights of the individual than classical utilitarianism allows for.) Rawls accepts the standard liberal ontology in which individuals are primary and society is secondary — a device created, or agreed to, by individuals, each of them for his or her own purposes. That is implicit in any version of contract theory, and Rawls, in reviving this rather fustian device, cannot escape it. Society is 'a cooperative venture for mutual advantage', but just in case that word 'cooperative' raises any false hopes, Rawls immediately adds that 'it is typically marked by a conflict as well as by an identity of interests' (p. 520). He also, as that sentence implies, accepts the orthodox liberal view of human nature: the human being is basically self-interested, yet — and this too is entirely orthodox — sufficiently rational to agree to abandon the hazards and opportunities of the state of nature in favour of the more restricted but more secure arrangements of human society and government. The rationality of Rawls's individuals is that type of rationality we have already encountered in the thinking of Hobbes, Hume and Bentham: the working-out of the most efficient means to whatever ends the individual may desire; the calculations of enlightened self-interest.

As has been pointed out by Robert Paul Wolff, this is much the same picture of human beings as we find in utilitarianism and neo-classical economics. That is to say, human beings are seen as 'utility-maximizers, seekers after gratification whose reason is employed in finding the most efficient allocation of their scarce resources.'[2] In other words, the gratification of desires, and, in economic terms, consumption, are seen as the fundamental human drives and motives. Human beings as producers, creators, as social beings finding their lives' meaning in their participation in society and interaction with others — these dimensions of human nature, which are so central to classical Greek thought and to socialist theories, are underplayed by Rawls, as they are by most liberal thinkers — with a few exceptions such as T. H. Green and his followers.

Thus Rawls's individualism is familiar and unsurprising. Equally conventional, in liberal terms, are the priority he assigns to liberty above other social values, and the importance he attaches to the establishment of legal and political rights in this respect — by contrast with his approach to economic and social equality. As far as the priority of liberty is concerned, only two points need to be made here. The first is that there are evidently many millions of people who clearly do not, in practice, accept Rawls's, and the liberals', view as to the priority of liberty. I am not thinking of those countless millions for whom food, warmth, freedom from disease and sickness, and minimal literacy, are clearly more urgent priorities than the 'basic liberties' listed by Rawls (p. 61). These millions are not overlooked by Rawls, since he allows that below a certain level of material well-being people cannot enjoy their basic liberties, and that therefore other goals must take priority. It is typically liberal, however, that he does not relent very far in that direction: 'The denial of equal liberty can be defended only if it is necessary to raise the level of civilization so that in due course these freedoms can be enjoyed' (p. 152). In other words, only liberty itself can justify a (temporary and limited) deviation from the principle that liberty takes priority over all other social goods. It is doubtful, to put it mildly, whether most people see food, warmth and good health as mere means to the enjoyment of liberties, however broadly defined. Nevertheless, what is still more relevant is that it is equally doubtful whether even those who have attained the necessary level of 'civilization' to enjoy these freedoms, do in fact attach such overriding importance to liberty as Rawls seems to think. Perhaps Rawls means to suggest only that if people were to think rationally about the issues, they 'will not exchange a lesser liberty for an improvement in economic well-being' (p. 152). But even this is debatable. Why should we suppose that those who do attach priority to 'an improvement in economic well-being' are thereby mistaken or irrational? Rawls's commitment to the principle of freedom is characteristic of the liberal intellectual. To others it may not be so obvious that liberty should enjoy the absolute predominance it does in Rawls's scale of values.

The second point to be made about Rawls and liberty is that within the careful structure of his argument it is clear that this is the way in which he establishes the principle of pluralism, or of what has been termed 'the open society'. In other words he wants to construct a society in which the only principles to which everyone must be committed are the liberal principles of freedom and individual rights. A society committed to other and further principles beyond these — such as community or economic equality, for example — would be one in which liberty and diversity would come under threat. But liberty, on this interpretation, is a minimally restrictive principle which allows individuals operating within its rules to pursue a wide diversity of objectives. And this is as it should be: 'Human good is heterogeneous because the aims of the self are heterogeneous' (p. 554). It is clear that, approaching the matter in a more systematic and philosophical manner, Rawls reaches conclusions about social goals very similar to those of liberals of an earlier generation, such as Berlin, Popper, Camus and Aron. It is a position with strong negative implications. It prohibits the pursuit of positive goals by, or even on behalf of, society as a whole. It puts a stop on utopianism and dreams and sketches of 'the good society' in any sense more positive than that of a society committed to liberty, and based on justice in Rawls's sense of that term.

This negative aspect of Rawls's theory gives it a natural appeal to theorists of the market such as Samuel Brittan, who welcomes Rawls's conception of justice as one 'which attempts neither to assess merit nor to aim at complete equality but nevertheless seeks to provide criteria for state action in the field of income distribution and elsewhere.'[3] And even Hayek, who has repeatedly denounced the notion of *social* justice, holds a very similar view as to the importance of justice as the foundation of liberal society: 'the limitation of all coercion to the enforcement of general rules of just conduct was the fundamental principle of classical liberalism, or, I would almost say, its definition of liberty.' Rawls also makes a link between justice and liberty, and Hayek's phrase about 'the end-independent character of rules of just conduct'[4] exactly expresses a principle which is common to Rawls and Hayek and which both see as the fundamental principle of a liberal society. Hayek associates this with Hume and Kant, just as Rawls builds his case upon a Kantian foundation. Here then is one point at which there is common ground between Rawls and the market theorists.

What Brian Barry has called the 'archaic' character of Rawls's liberalism provides another meeting point. For Rawls, like Hayek, attached great importance to legal and political equality as distinct from economic and social equality. 'In a well-ordered society', according to Rawls, the self-respect of the individual is 'secured by the public affirmation of the status of equal citizenship for all' (p. 545). 'The distribution of material means' is quite a separate matter. One's self-esteem does not depend upon 'one's income share', but upon enjoying equal status with everyone else as a citizen enjoying 'fundamental rights and liberties' (p. 544).[5] Once again this raises many puzzling empirical and historical doubts. For 200 years, since the Declaration of Independence and the French Revolution, liberals have believed that the establishment of equal legal and political rights for all would give everyone that sense of self-respect, of being equal, with which Rawls is concerned. Why then is it that in the liberal democracies, where such rights have been more or less achieved, people are manifestly dissatisfied with the continuing inequalities of wealth and status, and manifestly do not feel themselves to be equal in the way in which Rawls considers to be essential? At this and other points Rawls unwittingly exposes the abstract and unhistorical character of his liberal theorizing

It is true, of course, that Rawls's approach can be regarded as fundamentally egalitarian, for he starts from the assumption that it is equality which should, *a priori*, be the rule, and it is inequalities which have to be justified. This approach underlies his concern for the least well-off, the most deprived members of society. It is an approach with which most of the market theorists would have no sympathy, and which brings Rawls closer to social democratic thinking. Rawls's rule is that inequalities can be permitted so long as they are of benefit to the least fortunate members of society. Such a rule is plainly potentially radical and redistributive in its practical implications. Yet Rawls manages to interpret rule and reality in such a way that a high degree of inequality turns out to be quite tolerable — especially, as we have seen, since it will not generally damage the individual's self-respect. Barry's comparison of Rawls with Locke, as a thinker who starts from radical premises, only to reach rather tame and conservative conclusions, is not altogether unfair.[6]

The stress on equality as a central principle of liberalism is a theme which has been developed by another contemporary theorist of liberalism, Ronald Dworkin. Some confusion may arise over the use of the term 'liberal'. Dworkin uses it in the American sense to refer to the loosely 'progressive' or 'Left' side of USA politics. This makes it possible for him to assert, for example, that liberals 'demand that inequalities of wealth be reduced through welfare and other forms of redistribution financed by progressive taxes'.[7] From a British or European point of view this is a social democratic rather than a liberal position. It has been more typical of liberals, including even Keynes, to stress the inevitability, and to some extent also the desirability, of social and economic inequality.

However, what Dworkin offers as 'the liberal conception of equality' (p. 143), turns out to be something rather different from what is usually understood by that term. What Dworkin, like Rawls, means is an equality of respect for individuals, and for their choices of 'the good life'. On this question of 'the good life' government itself must be neutral (p. 127). Dworkin goes on to argue that in many ways it is the market which satisfies the diversity of people's choices of the good life, and that in so far as it does not, and fails to provide equal opportunities for people to pursue their chosen paths, limited government intervention is the answer. It is the so-called 'mixed economy' which best fulfils the requirements of this liberal conception of equality (pp. 128—33).

We thus arrive, by a route not so different from Rawls's, at a very similar conclusion. What Dworkin sees as a principle of equality (of respect) provides the basis for a commitment to pluralism, limited government, the renunciation of utopias, and a commitment to the market and the mixed economy. Although this is a liberalism which does not lack a sense of social justice and a concern to eradicate basic poverty and deprivation, it is essentially a liberalism which endorses the Western status quo. At its most radical, it supports limited social democratic interventionism and redistribution. At its most consesrvative, it provides advocates of the market with additional theoretical ammunition. It is a liberalism which remains suspicious of 'too much' economic and social equality, suspicious of 'positive' government, and attached, with however many misgivings and qualifications, to capitalism and the market.

Rawls's and Dworkin's requirement, that governments and the state remain neutral in relation to differing conceptions of the good life or the good society, is open to at least one very substantial objection: namely, that it is impracticable. It is almost impossible that any society which seeks to continue as such from one generation to another, could practice this neutrality in the entire field of the upbringing of children and of education, for example.[8] However much freedom and diversity are available in that area, a minimum of socialization is clearly indispensable. The idea of a wholly value-free education makes no sense. The same consideration must surely apply, if less strongly, to many other social institutions. No society can be as uncommitted and aimless as the liberal philosophers demand.

Robert Nozick's *Anarchy, State, and Utopia*, the other major text of liberal theory in the 1970s, stands in a dialectical relationship to *A Theory of Justice*. That is to say, it both rejects and builds upon some of Rawls's ideas. As Nozick himself says, having paid sustained attention to some of Rawls's arguments, Rawls represents, from Nozick's point of view, an 'undeniably great advance over utilitarianism'. [9] That is to say, Rawls, in starting from ideas of rights, liberty and justice, starts in the right place — as opposed to the concern of classical utilitarianism with the *sum* of well-being or happiness and its concomitant indifference to individual rights. The notion of rights is central to Nozick's theory of the minimal state and the autonomy of the individual.

But, unlike Rawls, Nozick is determined to make a clean sweep of all considerations of social justice, according to which, as Rawls recognizes, redistribution from the rich to the poor and progressive taxation can be justified. Whereas the practical political implications of Rawls's thinking are moderately social democratic, Nozick provides a theoretical justification for what the Americans like to call 'libertarianism', but which can only properly be called such if we adopt Herbert Spencer's view of what liberty is and what threatens it. Rawls provides a justification for state action to protect and help the least fortunate, if it should be necessary. Nozick's theory reinforces the old atavistic belief of the backwoods capitalist that the state is the great enemy of liberty, and that every interference with the rights of private property is a fundamental assault upon human rights. As Peter Singer suggested, when reviewing Nozick's book, 'if having gone half-way with Rawls we are forced by the logic of our position to go all the way with Nozick, it could be that we went wrong when we started out.' [10] For most of us, Nozick's profoundly reactionary conclusions can only enhance, by contrast, what often seem to be the fading attractions of utilitarianism — if that is what the continued existence of public services and welfare provisions requires.

THE REVIVAL OF LIBERAL POLITICAL ECONOMY

At this theoretical and highly abstract level, it is not such a great distance from the ideas of Rawls and Dworkin to the arguments of the proponents of market philosophy, such as Hayek and Brittan. Nozick provides one link. Yet, as Brian Barry pointed out, Rawls himself argues for a view of inequality and the market which may have seemed plausible a century ago, but which much of twentieth-century politics, most notably the development of trade unions and labour movements, has been committed to challenging: namely, the belief that, as a general rule, improvements in the situation of those best off will benefit rather than damage the conditions of the worst off (see, for example Rawls's comments on inherited wealth, p. 278). Either this is untrue, or is believed to be untrue on a very wide scale; for it is, as Barry points out, a central feature of contemporary politics that this faith, that if the rich get richer we shall all benefit, has steadily waned, certainly among the vast majority of the poor and deprived. [11]

One of the things which the revival of liberal political economy has included is an attempt to refurbish this nineteenth-century belief, and to persuade the working class that they will benefit automatically from the unhindered pursuit of wealth on the part of property-owners and the rich; while they can only damage their own interests by seeking to gain for themselves a proportionately larger share of the available wealth. Why greed on the part of capitalists is so beneficial, while it is so harmful on the part of workers, is one of the unexplained mysteries of this type of economic thinking. And while it may be that this Victorian revivalism may have attracted some converts among the relatively less privileged, it seems more likely that what are now habitually termed 'excessive' wage demands have been curbed not so much by faith as by fear — fear of unemployment and poverty. Like its classical predecessor, the new liberal economics relies, if less harshly, upon the threat of emiseration quite as much as upon its much advertised incentives to individual enterprise, in order to operate successfully.

And this, in the context of this study, is the most striking aspect of the current renewal of market theory — nor its novelty, but its lack of it. I cannot speak of the technical economics to which, it is claimed by some, Hayek, Friedman and others have made noteworthy, indeed Nobel-worthy, contributions. But that, in any case, is not what has given them their latter-day fame and influence. It is their general prescriptions, for policy and for basic attitudes, which have carried weight with right-wing governments in the USA, Britain and elsewhere. Whatever the intellectual merits of the theory, its current vogue is to be explained in historical and circumstantial, rather than purely intellectual, terms. Ideas have a history, and are part of history. We can only explain the attention presently given to the ideas of Hayek, Friedman and the market theorists in terms of the particular circumstances of the 1970s and 1980s, since it was certainly not the novelty of what they had to say that attracted attention.

On the contrary. Hayek had been writing in the same vein for 30 to 40 years prior to the current revival, and in the heyday of post-war Keynesianism he had been treated as something of a freak, an anachronistic survivor from an earlier lost age. George Lichtheim, for example, reviewed Hayek's *The Constitution of Liberty* when it appeared in 1960 under the title 'The Faith of a Whig'; and, after referring to the 'somewhat archaic ring' of the book, concluded that 'It does not seem possible any longer to state the case for *laissez-faire* in a manner that is at once logically consistent and socially relevant' — a conclusion with which virtually all his readers at that time would doubtless have agreed. [12] Milton Friedman's *Capitalism and Freedom* appeared only two years later, but his name, too, only acquired its present familiarity in the mid-1970s.

It was only at the end of the long post-1945 capitalist boom, in the context of the unforeseen combination of rapid inflation with high and rising unemployment, and in the absence of an economist of Keynes's originality and persuasiveness, that the antiquated nostrums of pre-Keynesian economics, thinly refurbished in the guise of 'monetarism', were able to re-enter the mainstream of both academic economics and the actual policies of capitalist governments. The practical and theoretical impasse of Keynesian and expansionist economics produced the vacuum into which 'monetarism' moved.

'Monetarism' is, for the economists, a specialized term used to refer to a particular theory about the causes of inflation and about how to control it through strict control of the money supply. That, of course, is not the way in which the term is commonly used. It is used to refer to the whole theory and practice of those capitalist governments (and their supporters) who reject Keynesianism, who reject the strategy of generating growth and demand as a way of counteracting stagnation and depression, and who assign to the control of inflation a far higher priority than the reduction of unemployment or the generation of growth. Indeed, if they follow Hayek, they will regard it as a mistake to make full employment a target of policy at all. [13] Whether calling this 'monetarism' is appropriate or accurate is not the point here. What is important is that 'monetarism' in its precise sense is a relatively small ingredient in a compound of policies and beliefs which, as a whole, represent a resuscitation of traditional liberal economics, rather than a new theory, let alone a notably sophisticated or technical one.

With one or two notable exceptions, such as the economic journalists Samuel Brittan and Peter Jay, the revival of liberal economics is in political as well as economic terms a right-wing phenomenon, even by conservative standards. Both Brittan and Jay are converts to 'monetarism' who bring with them from their previous centre and centre-left positions certain recognizably liberal political values and commitments. Brittan is unusual among the market enthusiasts in his commitment to liberal values in politics and private life as well as economics [14] — though, like them, he is no great friend of democratic government. Otherwise the commitment to what is called economic liberty is markedly dissociated from any comparable commitment to political freedom or civil liberties — as we noted at the beginning of this book. Yet at the theoretical level, the market theorists assign a high value to political freedom, and like many liberals of earlier generations, they make the two important claims that (1) it is allied to the existence of capitalism and economic liberty; and (2) it is distinct from, and even threatened by, what they tendentiously term 'unlimited democracy'.

The first claim is put forward with particular enthusiasm by Friedman in *Capitalism and Freedom*, where he suggests that 'competitive capitalism . . . promotes political freedom because it separates economic power from political power and in this way enables the one to offset the other.' [15] Whether capitalism has any inherent tendency to promote political freedom might be doubted in view of the large number of capitalist economies flourishing (or not flourishing) under fiercely repressive regimes in many parts of the Third World, to say nothing of the earlier coexistence of capitalism with fascism in Europe and Japan. Still, Friedman is careful to make the point that 'history suggests only that capitalism is a necessary condition for political freedom' (p. 10), not a sufficient one, which may be thought to let him off the hook of that 'promotes'.

Chile, since the military coup of 1973 destroyed elected government there, has been an example of a country where political repression has gone hand in hand with the adoption of 'monetarist' policies, under the guidance of a team of economists trained in Chicago by Friedman and his associates. In Chile the re-establishment of 'competitive capitalism', so far from 'promoting' any kind of political freedom, has required the suspension of civil and political liberties, and the repression of all organizations based in the working class, both trade unions and political parties. Friedman has expressed his 'profound disagreement with the authoritarian system of Chile',[16] but he has not explained what, from the point of view expressed in both *Capitalism and Freedom* and the more recent *Free to Choose*, is at least a paradoxical situation.

Hayek's grasp on the realities of Chile under military rule appears to have been rather slighter than Friedman's. In a letter to *The Times* (3 August 1978) he reported that 'I have not been able to find a single person even in much-maligned Chile who did not agree that personal freedom was much greater under Pinochet than it had been under Allende.' Since not even Friedman denied the existence of political repression in Chile, the most charitable assumption we can make is that for Hayek 'personal freedom' has become virtually identical with 'economic liberty'.

Hayek's remarks about Chile were placed in the context of two distinctions of considerable importance within the revived economic liberalism. The first is that there is a distinction between authoritarianism and totalitarianism — an idea popularized by Jeanne Kirkpatrick, a leading member of the Reagan administration with responsibility for foreign relations. Authoritarianism, for Hayek, is the opposite of democracy: it refers to a type of government or regime, not to the extent of its powers or activities. Totalitarianism is the opposite of liberalism: it denies or abolishes every kind of freedom. There can therefore be such a thing as totalitarian democracy, while 'it is at least conceivable that an authoritarian government might act on liberal principles.'[17] This careful hypothetical statement was replaced in his Chile letter by the blunt claim that 'there have of course been many instances of authoritarian governments under which personal liberty was safer than under many democracies' — although none of these benign dictatorships were actually named.

In the crude and predictable terms of Cold War politics this distinction is translated into a highly convenient difference between communist (or Marxist) dictatorships, and non-communist dictatorships. Marxist regimes are, of course, totalitarian; anti-Marxist and pro-Western dictatorships are merely authoritarian. And this is not such a distortion of the original idea as might be supposed, since it is often suggested that what makes a regime totalitarian rather than authoritarian is its control over the economy. Since socialism involves or aims at state control over the economy, socialism is either inherently or potentially totalitarian. This was the contention of what probably remains Hayek's best-known book, *The Road to Serfdom*, first published in 1944. The argument has a clear tendency to equate personal liberty with economic liberty.

The second important and related distinction is that between democracy and liberty or liberalism. This familiar liberal theme has received a new lease of life from the market theorists, who have gone beyond making a theoretical distinction between democracy and liberty, to restating the view that democracy, or at least 'unlimited democracy', constitutes a threat to liberty, and must therefore be curbed. Hence their demands for the setting of permanent fixed limits to the powers of elected governments by means of such devices as a written constitution or a bill of rights. Hence Brittan's view that what we need is not new economic theory but 'a revolution in constitutional and political ideas which will save us from the snare of unlimited democracy.'[18] In insisting on the importance of limited government, the market theorists are, of course, writing in the tradition of classical liberalism. It is, however, far from clear that 'unlimited democracy' is a real danger in Britain, or any other Western society. What *is* clear is that the fear of democracy is still very much alive within the liberal tradition.

Equally traditional is the highly abstract individualism which is characteristic of all the market theorists. As restated by Friedman, the individualist position is neither original nor sophisticated, but simply reiterates points made originally by Bentham and Mill, as if nothing had happened, and nothing had been said in the interim to cast any doubt on these propositions. 'To the free man', writes Friedman in *Capitalism and Freedom*, 'the country is the collection of individuals who compose it' (p. 1). It follows from this simple atomism that 'the individual' is also the key to social progress, as he/she was for Mill: 'The great advances of civilization . . . were the product of individual genius, of strongly-held minority views, of a social climate permitting variety and diversity' (p. 4). To Friedman, and to Brittan, economic life is composed, in the same way, of individuals each pursuing his or her own interest, yet also co-operating to produce general benefits, just as Adam Smith suggested, 200 years ago. Friedman even refers to 'voluntary co-operation of individuals' as 'the technique of the market place' (p. 13).

A charitable view might be to say that this individualistic picture does bear some relation to the process of buying and consumption, at least at the retail level. But it is clear that the market theorists do not intend it to apply so narrowly. They do genuinely offer it to us as a picture of economic life as a whole, as when Friedman states that 'the employee is protected from coercion by the employer because of other employers for whom he can work' (pp. 14—15). Let us leave aside, for the sake of argument, the present fact that unemployment gives employers a substantial advantage over those who are seeking work. Let us leave aside also the fact that such a view leaves unexplained the whole history of trade unionism under capitalism: why should such organizations ever have arisen if the worker enjoys this extraordinary freedom of choice? Let us simply note that it was against exactly this sort of argument that T. H. Green more than a century ago felt obliged to defend the British Liberal Government's latest legislation to protect working people against excessive exploitation in the 'labour market'. It seems scarcely credible that such a piece of mythology should survive, to be repeated by a Nobel-prizewinning economist a hundred years later.

The whole trend, in modern economic life, towards organization, concentration, co-ordination and oligopoly, if not monopoly, however regrettable or otherwise it may be, is not merely left unexplained by this individualist mythology; it is totally ignored. And this is surely the most obvious weakness of the 'new' liberal economics: its blithe doctrinaire disregard for fact. Liberals constantly remind us of the virtues of empiricism and the dangers of the systematic and the abstract (see, for example, Rawls, p. 554). Yet there is surely no better contemporary example of unempirical abstraction than the picture of economic life as consisting of the actions and interactions of 'individuals', presented to us by today's liberal economists.

Nor is this theorizing devoid of the inhumanity which characterized its nineteenth-century prototype. In the Preface to *Free to Choose*, Milton and Rose Friedman 'reject utterly' this criticism. In response they choose the example of health care. They suggest that waiting lists for medical operations are an intrinsic defect of a public health service, that no such waiting periods occur in the USA, and that 'there would be none in a United Kingdom voluntary system'. Therefore to reduce 'the tax burden now imposed to support the health service in order to enable individuals to buy their own health care' is not an inhumane recommendation.[19] Perhaps if a 'voluntary' system had the results they so confidently predict, this might be plausible. But we do not have to speculate about the future. We need only stop to enquire what happened in Britain before the National Health Service existed, and to ask why that service was created in the first place, to see that the Friedmans are so wedded to their doctrine that they are simply not concerned to enquire seriously into the way in which their recommendations would work or have worked. This is part of what it means to be 'doctrinaire'. Elsewhere in the book, the Friedmans assert that 'the costs of *ordinary* medical care are well within the means of *most* American families' and that 'help for a *few* hardship cases hardly justifies putting the whole population in a straitjacket' — which is their phrase for a system of national health care paid for through taxation.[20] It is the words I have italicized here which indicate the Friedmans' indifference to, and indeed ignorance of, the hardships which the absence of a system of comprehensive health care imposes on the poor. As Nick Bosanquet has written: 'For the New Right, society often seems to be composed of adult men in good health.'[21] That is one reason why the charge of inhumanity is not misplaced.

Equally unempirical is the Friedmans' claim that 'the combination of economic and political *freedom* produced a golden age in both Great Britain and the United States in the nineteenth century.'[22] I doubt if any reputable historian would so readily use a term like 'golden age', nor be so confident in ascribing one to, in effect, a single cause. Once again the real fault lies in the casual combination of an unempirical approach with an indifference to the conditions under which most of the population lived — or died — in this golden age of freedom. If it is the living standards of the majority that we are concerned with, then it is abundantly plain that it has been in the twentieth century, the century of interventionism, and most especially in the period since 1945, the period of Keynesianism, that people in Britain, the USA, and much of the developed capitalist world have begun to enjoy a tolerable standard of life. Like his nineteenth-century forbears, Friedman is so dazzled by the aggregate growth of that period, that he neglects to examine how that wealth was distributed, or who benefited from it. This, once more, is where the harshness of the doctrine is demonstrated.

For the clearest example of this harshness, we must turn to Hayek, who has made a speciality over many years of denouncing the 'mirage' (his term) of social justice. Hayek's primary concern is with freedom, and he claims that 'with reference to a society of free men, the phrase has no meaning whatever.' It is, however, in a casual aside that the full implications of this approach are revealed, when he speaks of 'free competition' as 'precluding all that regard for merit *or need and the like*, on which demands for social justice are based'.[23] Once again I have italicized the tell-tale phrase. Let us grant that the market advocates do have a point when they argue that merit is something very difficult to determine in a would-be objective manner — although it is another thing to accept their conclusion — that the whole idea should be dropped in favour of letting the market determine incomes and rewards. What is so striking is that Hayek should apparently consider 'need' to be an equally dispensable concept. Virtually the whole structure of welfare services and payments has been built up in tacit or explicit recognition of the fact that the market did not, and often cannot, meet the real and tangible needs of people, such as the elderly, the disabled and the mass of the unemployed who, through no fault of their own, cannot support themselves economically. None of this troubles Hayek. For him 'need' is yet another of those pernicious ideas which distort the true freedom of a market economy. To call this inhumane is to say nothing about Hayek himself, who may be as personally charming as Malthus was said to have been. It is to indict a doctrine which remains as rigidly harsh in the hands of its contemporary exponents as it was in those of Malthus and Nassau Senior.

Thus, in political terms, the liberalism represented by Hayek, Friedman and the market theorists, and their disciples among the politicians, is essentially a throwback to Herbert Spencer and the nineteenth century — one which rejects entirely all the insights, adaptations and advances made by the New Liberals and by Keynes — who remains the chief target for attack by Hayek himself, and by many others. Not surprisingly, the political impact of such a doctrine in the late twentieth century is not so much conservative as profoundly reactionary. But then that is what Herbert Spencer was seen to be, even in his own time, a hundred years ago.

The response of liberals in Britain to this revival, and in particular to its local incarnation in the form of 'Thatcherism', has been profoundly depressing to those who would still like to see in organized liberalism a truly progressive and radical movement. A former leader of the British Liberal Party, Jo Grimond, announced in a lecture on 'The Future of Liberalism' given in 1980, that 'Much of what Mrs Thatcher and Sir Keith Joseph say and do is in the mainstream of liberal philosophy.' While a younger liberal, the journalist and historian, Ian Bradley, was, if anything, even more enthusiastic: 'In its rejection of corporatism, its belief in pushing back the frontiers of the state, in its strenuous individualism and its revolt against the collectivist tide . . . it is a profoundly liberal movement. Bradley welcomed what he interpreted as 'a resurgence of the values of Liberal England'.[24]

Denunciations of 'collectivism' and praise of 'individualism' — where have we heard that before? From the *laissez-faire* opponents of the New Liberalism, and even more, of socialism, at the very beginning of the twentieth century. It can hardly provide a platform for radicalism nearly a century later. Nor is there any comfort to be obtained from liberal responses to the welfare state. Grimond complained that 'The Welfare State is not in danger of being abandoned but of being thoughtlessly and endlessly extended', while another prominent liberal, the sociologist Ralf Dahrendorf, declared that 'The welfare state produces the iron cage of bureaucratic bondage'; and, for good measure, repeated the traditional liberal attitude of suspicion towards government and the state: 'there is no such thing as benevolent government. Government is an unfortunate necessity. . . . It is always and by definition liable to encroach on individual liberties. . . . More than that, there is a need for less government.'[25]

Whatever may be said in favour of these attitudes, it cannot be said that they represent anything new or original within the liberal tradition. What is more, it is unlikely that any Thatcherite Conservative would find anything to quarrel with in any of these quoted sentiments — though there are other points, of course, at which all three of these thinkers do distance themselves from Thatcherism. Thus official and proclaimed liberalism in Britain has been alarmingly ready to respond positively to the revival of market theory, and at the same time to respond as if Keynes could be largely forgotten, and Green and Hobhouse and Hobson had never lived.

CONCLUSION

I have not, in this book, attempted to present a carefully 'balanced' view of liberalism, if only because it seemed more necessary, and so more desirable, to redress a balance which, over many years, has been unduly favourable to liberalism. For the fact is that for the most part the presentation of liberalism, its analysis, history and interpretation, has been in the hands of the liberals themselves — with a few exceptions, including, in recent years, writers such as C. B. Macpherson and Robert Paul Wolff.

Not surprisingly, the self-image of liberalism has usually been a flattering one rather than a 'warts and all' portrait. It has been extremely influential. We all tend to associate liberalism with Locke and Mill, with such admirable values as personal liberty and 'the open society', rather than with Malthus and the New Poor Law, with private property and fervent anti-communism. Liberalism is thought of as a benign creed. As Ralf Dahrendorf recently put it, with striking complacency: 'the liberal rarely needs to be ashamed of the realities created in his name as the socialist has to be much of the time.'[26] One of the purposes of this book has been to puncture that particular myth, to drag a few of the skeletons out of the liberal cupboard, and to dwell, from time to time, on the dark side of liberalism: the harshness of its economics, its blind attachment to private property, its typically bourgeois fear of 'the masses', and even of democracy itself. The character of liberalism is, in other words, far more complex, mixed and ambiguous than most liberals are willing to recognize; and its legacy to us is less simply beneficial than is often supposed, as the recent developments discussed in this and the previous chapter must surely make plain.

I have suggested, too, that the historical evolution of liberalism has followed the trajectory which is summed up in the book's title. Liberalism, in eighteenth and early nineteenth centuries, was, at its best, a liberating force. It crusaded against cruelty, superstition, intolerance and arbitrary government. Liberals fought — and some died — for the rights of men (though not women) and of nations. But its dynamism did not survive its nineteenth-century ascendancy. It ran out of ideas and energy. Attempts to revive it through radical reorientation failed. By the mid-twentieth century it had become defensive and conservative, out of touch with and usually hostile to the radical and revolutionary movements of the day, often virtually synonymous with anti-communism, albeit of an intellectually elaborate and sophisticated kind.

Are we then left with the wreck of a once progressive creed and movement from which nothing substantial can be, or deserves to be salvaged? That would be too hasty and sweeping a conclusion. As John Dunn observed of liberalism: 'Even its most savage critics (at least if one excepts Nietzsche) are fundamentally undecided as to whether they have come to destroy liberalism or to fulfil it.'[27] This particular critic is no exception to that rule. I share the view, held by many radicals and socialists, that the best of liberalism is too good to be left to the liberals. It is noticeable, in fact, that radicals and socialists spend much of their time fighting what are essentially liberal battles for liberal causes — such as opposition to racism, or for equality of the sexes — partly because the self-proclaimed liberals are too equivocal or inert to do it themselves; but also because their radicalism or socialism *includes* a commitment to liberal principles such as personal liberty, human rights and equality of status for all human beings regardless of their race or sex. Marx, who was one of the fiercest critics of liberalism, and especially of liberal political economy, also saw socialism as a movement which would 'fulfil' liberalism — that is, give to liberal values such as freedom and rights a more complete and substantial content and meaning than liberalism itself could conceive of. That is the point of the distinction he makes, in his early essay, *On the Jewish Question*, between political emancipation and human emancipation. He did not deny that political emancipation was 'a big step forward'. But it was a limited one, and its limitations were rooted in the liberal individualist conception of human nature: 'not one of the so-called rights of man goes beyond egoistic man, man as a member of civil society, namely an individual withdrawn into himself, his private interest and his private desires and separated from the community.'[28] In the dialectic of history, the role of socialism was both to negate and transcend liberalism; and the relation of socialism to capitalism was to follow the same pattern.

The importance of sustaining this dialectical or, if you prefer, ambiguous attitude towards liberalism is surely underlined by the actual history of socialism and communism in the twentieth century, to say nothing of the sufferings imposed by the countless other illiberal regimes of our age, above all German Nazism. The contempt for 'bourgeois liberalism' expressed by both communist and fascist leaders was not mere rhetoric. It was seriously meant, and we all know something — indeed, too much — of the mass brutalities which that contempt helped to make possible and to inspire. I have myself in this book stressed the bourgeois character of liberalism. That term indicates in shorthand form the source and nature of many of its limitations and shortcomings. They are not to be gainsaid. Yet neither is liberalism to be wholly condemned on account of its bourgeois origins and character, any more than bourgeois culture and bourgeois lifestyles are to be wholly condemned or discarded on that account.

We continue to need the best of liberalism, even while recognizing that liberalism, by itself, is 'not enough'. We need it now more urgently than when I first started work on this book. For the drift towards authoritarianism, and the decay of civil liberties within the capitalist democracies themselves are by now unmistakeable tendencies, making an uneven but steady advance from year to year. In Britain the erosion of the right and practice of trial by jury, the weakening of *habeas corpus* (the principle of no imprisonment without charge or trial), the steady extension of police powers over the citizen, and, most significant of all, the removal of the hard-won rights of trade unions and workers through restrictive legislation — all these developments underline the fragility of liberalism's achievements, even in its traditional heartlands, and make a firm commitment to the best of liberal values and institutions more necessary than ever.

We are still left with a major theoretical and practical problem. It is not one to which I can offer an answer; but nor is it one that can be avoided. It was argued in the first part of this book that liberal *values* are not the core of liberalism, but are themselves dependent upon and derivative from the liberal view of human nature, i.e. individualism. Marx's essay, quoted above, makes the same point. Individualism, it was suggested, is the ontological core of liberalism; and it is in many ways a defective and inadequate way of conceiving of human beings. Many of the gravest weaknesses of liberalism are rooted in the inadequacies of individualism itself. Is it then possible to retain a commitment to the finest values of liberalism without at the same time committing oneself to the individualist conception of human beings on which they have been based, both traditionally and logically? Can human rights and the principle of freedom find a secure basis in a philosophy of human beings which recognizes and stresses their natural and potential sociability, and hence their unity and interdependence, in a way that liberal individualism has never been able to do? To explore these questions lies beyond the scope of this book. But it would be wrong not to acknowledge that they are unavoidably raised by a critique such as this. I can only repeat that we do clearly need a strong and well-founded commitment to the basic rights and freedoms which have been central to liberalism, and that if they are not to be based on liberal individualism, then some other appropriately firm and defensible basis must be found. Radicals have no choice but to move beyond liberalism, while rescuing from the historical and theoretical shipwreck of liberalism itself what they can of its most valuable principles and achievements.

Appendix

A NOTE ON UTILITARIANISM AND LIBERALISM

References to Bentham in a number of chapters raise the question of whether utilitarianism is properly to be considered as a form of liberalism. There are grounds for seeing the two as being at odds with one another. John Stuart Mill's struggle to render his liberal convictions consistent with the utilitarian principles instilled in him by his father and Bentham is famous. The problem, in a nutshell, was how to reconcile the liberal principle of freedom with the utilitarian principle of happiness or pleasure. Suppose that increased freedom did not necessarily lead to an increase of happiness: which principle was to be given priority?

For Bentham there was no doubt as to the answer. His utilitarianism was as consistent as he could make it. The goal was happiness, or pleasure: freedom was only a good in so far as it was a means to that end. But if there were shorter, more efficient routes to happiness, they were preferable: 'Call them soldiers, call them monks, call them machines, so they were but happy ones, I should not care.'[1] He would, it seems reasonable to suppose, have had no great objection to people being manipulated or drugged into a state of happiness. Hazlitt's gibe was by no means misplaced: 'He turns wooden utensils in a lathe for exercise, and fancies he can turn men in the same manner.'[2] His contempt for the notion of natural rights is well known: it was 'nonsense' and '"inalienable and imprescriptible rights" is merely nonsense on stilts.'[3]

This, clearly, is not liberal talk. There was an authoritarian strain in Benthamite utilitarianism which was expressed in the conviction that a science of good government and administration could be based on the rational knowledge of how well-being could be increased and suffering diminished. Those who possessed this knowledge were well equipped to govern. A confidence in their own capacity to do good to, and for, others inspired the Benthamite reformers such as Chadwick and Kay, and was inherited by the Fabians. Thus utilitarianism is one of the sources of the modern British tradition of enlightened reform and administration from above.

Bentham's relation to the liberal tradition is comparable to that of Hobbes, a thinker whom the utilitarians admired and may even be said to have rediscovered. Hobbes's political conclusions were authoritarian, Bentham's were in some respects illiberal; but both thinkers arrive at these conclusions having started out from liberal individualist premises. Bentham, as we saw in chapter 4, was sceptical of all such terms as 'community' and 'the general interest', because he saw society as no more than a collection of individuals, each autonomously pursuing his or her own interest. This is the essence of the liberal individualist conception of society. And this was in turn a variant of his ontological individualism, which recognized single facts as the only reality, and treated all generalities and abstractions as not 'realities *per se*, but an abridged mode of expressing facts'.[4] This, too, is characteristic of liberalism, as we saw in chapter 3.

Bentham also believed that the individual was generally the best judge of where his or her own interest lay. Who, after all, can know better than oneself what gives me pleasure or causes me suffering? Bentham shared the liberal belief in the absolute validity of felt desires and aversions. As Mill put it, 'the sole evidence it is possible to produce that anything is desirable, is that people do actually desire it.'[5] This faith was translated into economic terms by the neo-classical economists later in the nineteenth century. They assumed that, for the purposes of economics, desires or at least 'revealed preferences' are translated into demands in the market, and the degree of desire can be discovered by ascertaining what price people are willing to pay for a commodity. This then replaced older conceptions of 'value': 'The neo-classical theory of *subjective value* or the theory of marginal utility was from its inception purely psychological. It is really just an elaboration of Bentham's hedonistic pleasure-pain calculus.'[6]

If this doctrine is taken to its conclusion, there is no scope for paternalism at any level — for the assumption that others can or do know better than you what your real interests or desires are. So a belief in the ability of the individual to know her own interests, together with an acceptance of the legitimacy of self-interest, tends towards freedom, tolerance and non-interference in both economics and politics. This clearly conflicts with Bentham's practical faith in enlightened and scientific administration and reform; and in this conflict lie the roots of both the interventionist and non-interventionist forms which utilitarian practice was to take.

Bentham's individualism leads him in the direction of Hobbes's view of the natural state of humankind as a war of all against all: 'The boundless range of human desires, and the very limited number of objects . . . unavoidably leads a man to consider those with whom he is obliged to share such objects, as inconvenient rivals who narrow his own extent of enjoyment.'[7] Scarcity engenders competition, and our competitors are looked on as either means or obstacles to the realization of our own objectives. There is thus a natural conflict of self-interests, rather than a natural harmony, and such an analysis points once more in the direction of intervention, if society is to be preserved.

Bentham took the view that 'taken by itself, government is in itself one vast evil', only acceptable as a lesser evil than some others. He believed that 'No law can ever be made but what trenches upon liberty', and that 'To make a law is to do evil that good may come.'[8] Hence, other things being equal, both government and laws should be kept to a minimum. Bentham readily recognized that other things were very often not equal; but he was also in economics a follower of Smith, and so in the economic sphere his basic suspicion of government was supported by a belief in the harmonizing power of the market. Intervention should be confined to non-economic matters.

Behind these problems lurks the larger problem within utilitarianism of the evident tension between the belief, set out by Bentham in the first paragraph of the *Introduction to the Principles of Morals and Legislation*, that individual action is determined by the individual's desire to obtain pleasure and avoid pain for him- or herself, while utilitarianism as a theory of morals sets for its goal the greatest happiness of the greatest number. Mill tried to argue that utilitarianism had to do only with the latter aim, but this is plainly not the case so far as Bentham is concerned. Bentham wished to ground his theory of morals in reality, of what ought to be in what is: happiness is the goal of morals because it is in fact what all people seek for. For that reason he hoped that there would be no dispute about the goal proposed by utilitarianism.

This harmony between actual individual motivation and the ethical goal can only exist if the individual, pursuing happiness for herself, thereby also promotes the general happiness. Smith's 'invisible hand', in other words, must operate throughout human life, and not merely in the economic sphere. Bentham did not believe this. Society could not dispense with government. Egoistic individuals had to be restrained, and the general happiness safeguarded and even promoted by laws and institutions.

It is sometimes assumed that there is a fundamental or complete division between utilitarianism and liberalism, and that the younger Mill, in becoming a liberal, therefore ceased to be utilitarian.[9] Not only does such an approach leave unexplained, however, the remarkable manner in which the two streams of thought have mingled in nineteenth- and twentieth-century Britain. A closer look at Bentham's thought shows that he shared many of the chief characteristics of the liberal outlook: its suspicion of government and laws, its respect for expressed desires, and, beneath everything else, its pervasive and thorough-going individualism — all of which pointed in the direction of freedom and non-interference, even though these were always to be subordinated to the over-riding principle of maximizing happiness. There is, and always has been, a large area of overlap between utilitarianism and liberalism.

Notes

CHAPTER 1: LIBERALISM: ALIVE OR DEAD?

1. Isaiah Berlin: *Four Essays on Liberty* (Oxford University Press, 1969) p. 124.
2. Conor Cruise O'Brien: *Writers and Politics* (Chatto & Windus, 1965) p. xiii.
3. Ibid., p. xv.
4. See Andrew Gamble: 'The free economy and the strong state' in *The Socialist Register 1979* (Merlin Press, 1979) ed. John Saville and Ralph Miliband.
5. Harold J. Laski: *The Rise of European Liberalism* (Allen & Unwin, 1936) 1962 edn, p. 5.
6. Isaiah Berlin: *Vico and Herder* (The Hogarth Press, 1976) p. xxiii.
7. Virginia Woolf: 'Evening over Sussex: reflections in a motor-car', *Collected Essays*, Vol. II (The Hogarth Press, 1966) p. 292.
8. Adlai Stevenson: *Speeches* (André Deutsch, 1952) pp. 117—18.
9. Colin Morris: *The Discovery of the Individual, 1050—1200* (SPCK, 1972) p. 2.
10. Maurice Cranston: *Freedom: A New Analysis* (Longmans, Green, 1953) p. 67. Emphasis in the original.
11. E. M. Forster: *Two Cheers for Democracy* (Edward Arnold 1951) Penguin edn. 1965, p. 70. From an essay on George Orwell.
12. John Plamenatz: *Ideology* (Pall Mall Press, 1970) p. 21.
13. Richard Wollheim: 'The justification of liberalism', *The Listener*, 21 June 1956.
14. Alexander Gray: *The Socialist Tradition from Moses to Lenin* (Longmans, Green, 1946).
15. F. J. C. Hearnshaw: *Conservatism in England* (Macmillan, 1933) p. 20.
16. Alan Bullock and Maurice Shock (eds) *The Liberal Tradition: From Fox to Keynes* (Adam & Charles Black, 1956) pp. liv—lv.
17. J. Salwyn Schapiro (ed.) *Liberalism: Its Meaning and History* (Van Nostrand, 1958).
18. Quoted by Christopher Hill: 'The Norman yoke', *Puritanism and Revolution* (Secker & Warburg, 1958) p. 112.

CHAPTER 2: THE FOUNDATIONS OF LIBERAL INDIVIDUALISM

1. Bhikhu Parekh: 'Liberalism and Morality' in *The Morality of Politics*, ed. Bhikhu Parekh and R. N. Berki (Allen & Unwin, 1972) p. 83.

2. See Steven Lukes: *Individualism* (Basil Blackwell, 1973), especially Part II.

3. E. M. Forster: 'What I believe', *Two Cheers*, p. 84.

4. John Donne: *Complete Poetry and Selected Prose*, ed. John Hayward (Nonesuch Press, 1962) pp. 538, 749.

5. Iris Murdoch: *The Sovereignty of Good* (Routledge & Kegan Paul, 1970) pp. 58, 80.

6. Alasdair MacIntyre: *A Short History of Ethics* (Routledge & Kegan Paul, 1967) p. 173.

7. A chastened and subdued version of this attitude appears in Stuart Hampshire: *Thought and Action* (Chatto & Windus, 1959) pp. 236—7.

8. Alasdair MacIntyre: 'Notes from the moral wilderness, I' in *The New Reasoner*, No. 7, Winter 1958—59.

9. See Alasdair MacIntyre: *Marxism and Christianity* (Penguin, 1971) p. 93, ff.

10. Jean-Paul Sartre: *Existentialism and Humanism*, translated Philip Mairet (Methuen, 1948) pp. 50—1.

11. Ibid., p. 38.

12. Lucien Goldmann: *The Hidden God*, translated Philip Thody (Routledge & Kegan Paul, 1964) p. 229.

13. Pascal: *Pensées*, Appendix to ch. 23, quoted and translated by Stuart Hampshire in *The Age of Reason* (New American Library, 1956) p. 98.

14. *The Diary of Virginia Woolf*, Vol. II, 1920—24, ed. Anne Olivier Bell (The Hogarth Press, 1978) p. 14.

15. In *The Rise of the Novel* (Chatto & Windus, 1957) Penguin edn, 1963, p. 68.

16. Alexis de Tocqueville: *The Ancien Regime and the French Revolution*, translated Stuart Gilbert (Collins/Fontana edn 1966) pp. 120—1.

17. Bentham: *Introduction to the Principles of Morals and Legislation*, ch. 1, para. IV.

18. Aristotle: *The Politics*, translated T. A. Sinclair (Penguin, 1962) p. 29, and see also p. 57.

19. Jean-Paul Sartre: *Being and Nothingness*, translated Hazel E. Barnes (Methuen, 1969) pp. 73—4 and 84.

20. *Existentialism and Humanism*, p. 44.

21. *Being and Nothingness*, p. xxvii.

22. John Locke: *An Essay Concerning Human Understanding*, Book IV, chapter 9, 3.

23. Bacon: *The Advancement of Learning*, quoted in *Nature and Nature's Laws*, ed. Marie Boas Hall (Macmillan, 1970) p. 106.

24. Locke: *Human Understanding*, Book IV, ch. 21, 13, Book IV, ch. 9, 13, and Book IV, ch. 13, 2.

25. Bacon: *First Book of Aphorisms*, XIX, quoted in Hampshire: *The Age of Reason*, p. 25.

26. Leszek Kolakowski: 'Neutrality and academic values', in *Neutrality and Impartiality*, ed. Alan Montefiore (Cambridge University Press, 1975) p. 76.

27. Karl Popper: *The Open Society and Its Enemies*, Vols I and II (Routledge & Kegan Paul, 1945; 4th edn, 1962). See especially Vol I, ch. 10.

28. Bertrand Russell: 'Philosophy and Politics', in *Unpopular Essays* (Allen & Unwin, 1950, 1968 edn) pp. 21—22.

29. Bacon: *Novum Organum*, quoted in Hall, *Nature and Nature's Laws*, p. 449.

30. Thomas Hobbes: *Leviathan*, Part I, ch. 4.

31. Leibniz: *Monadology*, paras. 3 and 18.

32. Locke: *Two Treatises of Government*, Second Treatise, ch. 5, 44.

33. Richard Overton: *An Arrow against all Tyrants* (1646), quoted by C. B. Macpherson: *The Political Theory of Possessive Individualism* (Oxford University Press, 1962), p. 140—1.

34. Hobbes: *Leviathan*, chs. 6, 8.

35. Ibid., ch. 6.

36. See especially Sigmund Freud: *Civilization and its Discontents*, translated Joan Riviere (The Hogarth Press, 1930) and *Beyond the Pleasure Principle* translated James Strachey (The Hogarth Press, 1950, revised edn 1961).

37. Joan Robinson: *Economic Philosophy* (Watts, 1962) Penguin edn 1964, p. 50.

38. Ibid., p. 51.

39. The passages from Bentham and Mill both quoted in Bullock and Shock (eds) *The Liberal Tradition*, pp. 28, 64.

40. See Berlin: *Four Essays on Liberty*, p. 133.

41. The Marquis de Sade: *Justine, Philosophy in the Bedroom and other writings*, translated Richard Seaver and Austryn Wainhouse (Grove Press, 1965) pp. 165—6.

42. Ibid., p. 185.

43. See Robert Paul Wolff: *The Poverty of Liberalism* (Beacon Press, 1968) p. 141.

44. Locke: *Two Treatises of Government*, Second Treatise, ch. 3, 19.

45. See Joan Robinson: *Economic Philosophy*, pp. 19—21.

46. Adam Smith: *Wealth of Nations*, Book IV, ch. 2.

47. David Hume: *A Treatise of Human Nature*, Book III, Part II, Section II.

48. See, for example, the essay by E. M. Forster quoted at the beginning of this chapter.

49. Alexander Pope: *An Essay on Man*, Epistle II, lines 53—4.

CHAPTER 3: THE INDIVIDUAL AND SOCIETY

1. Dwight Macdonald: 'On the Rightness of Mr Berlin', an adulatory review of Isaiah Berlin's *Two Concepts of Liberty*, in *Encounter*, April 1959, p. 82.

2. F. A. Hayek: *The Counter-Revolution of Science* (Collier-Macmillan, 1955) pp. 37—8.

3. Karl Popper: *The Poverty of Historicism* (Routledge & Kegan Paul, 1957) 1961 edn, p. 135.

4. T. D. Weldon: *The Vocabulary of Politics* (Penguin, 1953); see pp. 113—14.

5. Berlin: *Four Essays*, p. 110.

6. *The Poverty of Historicism*, p. 17.

7. Ibid., p. 67. See also p. 79.

8. Hobbes: *Leviathan*. Phrases from chs 6, 11, 17.

9. Quoted in J. W. N. Watkins: *Hobbes's System of Ideas* (Hutchinson, 1965) p. 71.

10. *Mill on Bentham and Coleridge*, ed. F. R. Leavis (Chatto & Windus, 1959) p. 70.

11. E. H. Carr: *What is History?* (Macmillan, 1961) p. 25.

12. William Hazlitt: *Complete Works*, ed. P. P. Howe (Dent, 1933) Vol. 19, p. 305.

13. Ibid., pp. 305—6, 306—7.

14. Freud: *Civilization and its Discontents*, p. 59.

15. Freud: *The Future of an Illusion*, translated W. D. Robson-Scott (The Hogarth Press, 1928) revised edn 1962, p. 2; and *Civilization and its Discontents*, p. 86.

16. John Stuart Mill: *Principles of Political Economy*, quoted in Bullock and Shock (eds) *The Liberal Tradition*, p. 62.

17. Steven Lukes: *Individualism* p. 62.
18. C. A. R. Crosland: *Socialism Now* (Jonathan Cape, 1974) p. 89. See also pp. 65—6.
19. Thucydides: *The Pelopennesian War*, translated Rex Warner (Penguin, 1954) pp. 118—9. And see also Hannah Arendt: *The Human Condition* (University of Chicago Press, 1958) p. 38.
20. These arguments appear in the final pages of *On Liberty*.
21. Ibid., ch. 3 'Of Individuality . . .'
22. E. H. Carr: *1917: Before and After* (Macmillan, 1969) p. 89.
23. This and the next two quotations from Mill are all from *On Liberty*, ch. 3.
24. E. M. Forster: *Two Cheers for Democracy* (Penguin edn) pp. 66, 81, 82.
25. Bertolt Brecht: *Poems 1913—1956* 'Questions from a Worker who Reads', in *Poems 1913—1956*, ed. John Willett and Ralph Manheim (Eyre Methuen, 1976) 1981 edn, pp. 252—3.
26. Forster, *Two Cheers*, p. 76.
27. Thomas Paine: *Rights of Man*, Part II, ch. 1.
28. Roy Jenkins, reported in *The Times*, 24 Jan. 1976.
29. Samuel Brittan in the *Financial Times*, 20 Feb. 1975.
30. Berlin: *Four Essays* footnote, p. 171.
31. Bryan Magee: *Popper* (Fontana/Collins, 1973) pp. 90, 95.
32. Barrington Moore Jr: *Reflections on the Causes of Human Misery* (Allen Lane, 1972) p. 27.
33. In Parekh and Berki; 'Liberalism and Morality', *The Morality of Politics*, p. 85.

CHAPTER 4: LIBERAL VALUES

1. See for example, T. E. Utley, 'Thinking and the Right', *The Spectator*, 9 Oct. 1956; and Stuart Hampshire, 'Human nature in politics' *The Listener*, 3 Dec. 1953.
2. Lord Acton, quoted in Bullock and Shock (eds) *The Liberal Tradition*, p. 121.
3. Stuart Hampshire, 'In defence of radicalism', *Encounter*, Aug. 1955, p. 37.
4. Hobbes: *Leviathan*, chs 14, 21.
5. Berlin: *Four Essays*, pp. 122—3.
6. Cranston: *Freedom*, pp. 26—7.
7. Ibid., p. 67.
8. Berlin: *Four Essays*, p. 173.
9. See, for example Jeremy Thorpe's speech as party leader to the Liberal Party Conference, 1975, as reported in *The Times*, 22 Sept. 1975.
10. Albert Camus, in an interview published in *Encounter*, April 1957.
11. Berlin: *Four Essays*, p. 128.
12. Newman: *Apologia Pro Vita Sua*, Note A. Liberalism (Sheed & Ward, 1948) p. 193.
13. Mill: *On Liberty*, ch. 2.
14. Berlin: *Four Essays*, pp. 171, 39.
15. H. L. A. Hart: 'Are there any natural rights?', *Philosophical Review*, 1955, reprinted in Anthony Quinton (ed.) *Political Philosophy* (Oxford University Press, 1967), p.59.
16. See T. D. Weldon: *Vocabulary of Politics*, pp. 56—61, especially p. 61.
17. Iris Murdoch: 'Against dryness', *Encounter*, Jan. 1961. And see also Kenneth Minogue: *The Liberal Mind* (Methuen, 1963) p. 88.

18. Philip Toynbee: 'The true Left', a review of Raymond Aron's *The Opium of the Intellectuals, Encounter*, Sept. 1957.
19. Robert Paul Wolff: *Poverty of Liberalism*, p. 145.
20. See Forster: *Two Cheers*, p. 78, and pp. 54—5.
21. Bernard Crick: *In Defence of Politics* (Weidenfeld & Nicolson, 1962) Penguin edn, 1982, p. 24.
22. Wolff: *Poverty of Liberalism*, pp. 136—7.
23. Herbert Butterfield: *The Whig Interpretation of History* (1931, Penguin edn 1973) p. 63.
24. See W. H. Morris-Jones's notorious article 'In defence of apathy', *Political Studies*, Vol. II, 1954, where he suggests that the apathetic are 'a more or less effective counter-force to the fanatics who constitute the real danger to liberal democracy'.
25. Paine: *Rights of Man*, ed. Henry Collins (Penguin, 1969), p. 107.
26. Percy Bysshe Shelley: *An Address to the Irish People* (1812, Oriole Chapbooks n.d.) p. 15.
27. Forster: *Two Cheers*, pp. 64, 71.
28. John Fuller: *Epistles to Several Persons* (Secker & Warburg, 1973) p. 40.
29. Thomas Paine: *Common Sense* ed. Isaac Kramnick (1776, Penguin edn, 1976) p. 98.
30. Locke: *Two Treatises of Government*, Second Treatise, ch. 4, 22.
31. Paine: *Rights of Man*, Part II, ch. 1 (Penguin edn., p. 187).
32. Berlin: *Four Essays*, footnote, p. 123.
33. See Lionel Trilling: *The Opposing Self* (Secker & Warburg, 1955) pp. 52—3.
34. C. B. Macpherson: *The Real World of Democracy* (Oxford University Press, 1966) p. 1.
35. Thomas Jefferson: *Notes on the State of Virginia*, in *The Portable Thomas Jefferson*, ed. Merrill D. Peterson (Penguin, 1977) p. 164.
36. See Richard Hofstadter: *The American Political Tradition* (Jonathan Cape, 1962, 1967 edn) p. 4.
37. Letter to Mary Gladstone, 24 April 1881, quoted in Bullock and Shock (eds), *The Liberal Tradition*, p. 124.
38. Matthew Arnold: *Culture and Anarchy*. This observation and his invocations of order and authority occur in the final paragraph of ch. 2.
39. F. A. Hayek: *Studies in Philosophy, Politics and Economics* (Routledge & Kegan Paul, 1967) p.161.
40. Crick: *In Defence of Politics*, p. 62.
41. J. L. Talmon: *The Origins of Totalitarian Democracy* (1952, Sphere Books edn 1970) pp. 46—7.
42. Crick: *In Defence of Politics*, p. 60.
43. Guido de Ruggiero: *The History of European Liberalism* (Beacon Press, 1959) p. 379.
44. D. D. Raphael: *Problems of Political Philosophy* (Pall Mall, 1970) p. 142.
45. I have here repeated in a condensed form some points made at greater length in my article 'Socialism and the idea of science' in Bkikhu Parekh (ed.) *The Concept of Socialism* (Croom Helm, 1975).
46. Stuart Hampshire, 'Russell, radicalism and reason' *New York Review of Books*, 8 Oct. 1970, an exceptionally interesting review of the third volume of Bertrand Russell's *Autobiography*.
47. J. M. Keynes: 'My Early Beliefs', in *Essays in Biography*, Collected Writings, Vol. X, (Macmillan, 1972) p. 446.

48. Edmund Burke: *Reflections on the Revolution in France*, ed. Conor Cruise O'Brien (Penguin, 1968) p. 183.

49. Percy Bysshe Shelley: *A Defence of Poetry*, in *Complete Works of Percy Bysshe Shelley* Roger Ingpen and Walter E. Peck (eds) (Ernest Benn, 1965) Vol VII, p. 134.

50. Keynes: 'My Early Beliefs', *Essays in Biography*, pp. 448—9.

51. William Blake: Annotations to Reynolds's 'Discourses', in *Complete Writings*, Geoffrey Keynes (ed.), (Oxford University Press, 1966) pp. 474—5.

52. See Lionel Trilling: *The Liberal Imagination* (Secker & Warburg, 1951), especially the Preface and 'The Function of the Little Magazine'.

53. Keynes, *Essays in Biography*, p. 447.

54. 'Palinurus' (Cyril Connolly): *The Unquiet Grave* (Hamish Hamilton, 1951 edn) p. 7.

55. Paul Johnson: *The Offshore Islanders*, (Weidenfeld & Nicolson, 1972) pp. 421—2.

56. Talmon: *The Origins of Totalitarian Democracy*, pp. 2, 3.

57. For a fuller critique, see Roy Edgley: 'Reason and Violence', *Radical Philosophy*, 4, Spring 1973. Reprinted in Sephan Korner (ed.) *Practical Reason* (Yale University Press, 1974).

58. J. M. Keynes: *Essays in Persuasion*, Collected Writings, Vol. IX (Macmillan, 1972) pp. 287—8.

59. Ibid., pp. 290—3.

60. J. M. Keynes: *The General Theory of Employment, Interest and Money* (Macmillan, 1936) pp. 374, 380.

61. J. M. Keynes, *Essays in Persuasion*, p. 299.

62. J. M. Keynes, *The General Theory*, p. 374.

CHAPTER 5: THE BEGINNINGS OF MODERN LIBERALISM

1. Colin Morris: *The Discovery of the Individual 1050—1200*.

2. Ibid., p. 65.

3. Eric A. Havelock: *The Liberal Temper in Greek Politics* (Jonathan Cape, 1957).

4. J. B. Bury: *A History of Freedom of Thought* (Oxford University Press, 1913) p. 27.

5. Popper: *The Open Society*, Vol. I, pp. 187, 42.

6. Peter Green: *The Shadow of the Parthenon* (Maurice Temple Smith, 1972) p. 20 ff.

7. Hobbes: *Leviathan*, ch. 21.

8. Peter Green: *The Shadow of the Parthenon*, p. 208.

9. Walter Ullmann: *Medieval Political Thought* (Penguin, 1975) p. 148.

10. Sidney Painter: *Feudalism and Liberty* (Johns Hopkins Press, 1961) p. 14.

11. Ullmann: *Medieval Political Thought*, pp. 148—9.

12. Painter: *Feudalism and Liberty*, p. 248, and see also p. 259.

13. See Wallace K. Ferguson: *Renaissance Studies* (Harper & Row, 1963) p. 38.

14. Quoted in N. Rubinstein: 'Florence and the Despots, *Transactions of the Royal Historical Society*, 1952, p. 21.

15. Myron P. Gilmore: *The World of Humanism* (Harper & Row, 1952, 1962 edn) p. 110.

16. See Lauro Martines: *The Social World of the Florentine Humanists 1390—1460* (Routledge & Kegan Paul, 1963) pp. 299—300.

17. Quoted in *The Renaissance Philosophy of Man*, ed. Ernst Cassirer, et al. (Chicago University Press, 1948) p. 225.

18. Quoted in Raymond Williams: *The Long Revolution* (Chatto & Windus, 1961) p. 6.

19. Rudolf Wittkower: *Architectural Principles of the Age of Humanism* (Alec Tiranti, 1971) p. 14.

20. Quoted in H. R. Trevor-Roper: 'Desiderius Erasmus', *Historical Essays* (Macmillan, 1957) p. 41.

21. Quoted in J. R. Hale: *Renaissance Europe 1480—1520* (Collins/Fontana, 1971) p. 277.

22. See A. G. Dickens: *Reformation and Society in Sixteenth Century Europe* (Thames & Hudson, 1966) p. 117.

23. See Denys Hay: *The Italian Renaissance in its Historical Background* (Cambridge University Press, 1961) p. 117.

24. Erwin Panofsky: *Renaissance and Renascences in Western Art* (1965, Paladin edn, 1970) p. 119.

25. All quotations from *The Livings Thoughts of Montaigne*, presented by André Gide (Cassell, 1939) pp. 51, 41, 118, 98, 96, 120.

26. See E. M. Curley: *Descartes Against the Sceptics* (Basil Blackwell, 1978) ch. 1, especially pp. 16—20.

27. Gide: *Montaigne*, p. 20.

28. Leonard Woolf: *The Journey not the Arrival Matters* (The Hogarth Press, 1969) p. 19.

29. E. M. W. Tillyard: *The Elizabethan World Picture* (1943, Penguin edn, 1963) pp. 130—1.

30. Marlowe quotations from *The Complete Works of Christopher Marlowe*, Vols I, II, ed. Fredson Bowers (Cambridge University Press, 1973).

31. Tillyard: *The Elizabethan World Picture*, p. 27.

32. See Owen Chadwick: *The Reformation* (Penguin, 1964) 1972 edn, pp. 69—70.

33. Both quoted in George H. Sabine and Thomas L. Thorson: *A History of Political Theory* (Holt-Saunders, 1973) p. 388.

34. *Against the Robbing and Murdering Hordes of Peasants* (1525) in *Luther's Works* Vol 46, ed. Robert C. Schultz (Fortress Press, 1967) pp. 49—55.

35. Luther: *Admonition to Peace* (1525) in ibid., p. 39.

36. Quoted in Roland H. Bainton: *Here I Stand* (Abingdon Press, 1951) Mentor edn, n.d. p. 185.

37. Calvin: *Institutes of the Christian Religion*, ed. John T. McNeill (SCM Press, 1961) p. 1486.

38. Ibid., p. 1519.

39. Luther: *Admonition to Peace*, p. 35.

40. Quoted in Bainton: *Here I Stand*, p. 171.

41. Ibid., pp. 169—70.

42. Quoted in H. A. Mason: *Humanism and Poetry in the Early Tudor Period* (Routledge & Kegan Paul, 1959) p. 259.

43. Calvin: *Institutes*, Vol. I, pp. 52—3.

44. Ibid., pp. 208, 197—8.

45. S. F. Mason: 'Science and Religion in Seventeenth-Century England', in *The Intellectual Revolution of the Seventeenth Century* (Routledge & Kegan Paul, 1974) ed. Charles Webster, pp. 202—3.

46. Calvin: *Institutes*, p. 221.

47. Quoted in S. F. Mason: 'Science and Religion', *The Intellectual Revolution*, p. 217.

48. MacIntyre: *A Short History of Ethics*, p. 122.

49. Quotations from Christopher Hill: 'Protestantism and the Rise of Capitalism', *Change and Continuity in Seventeenth-Century England* (Weidenfeld & Nicolson, 1974) pp. 90, 96.

50. Both quotations from *Luther's Works*, Vol. 44, ed. James Atkinson (Fortress Press, 1966) pp. 135, 132.

51. Quoted in Christopher Hill: *Change and Continuity*, p. 191.

52. See Dickens: *Reformation and Society*, p. 164: and H. R. Trevor-Roper: *Religion, the Reformation and Social Change* (Macmillan 1967) 1972 edn, p. 138.

53. See H. G. Koenigsberger and G. L. Mosse: *Europe in the Sixteenth Century* (Longman, 1968) pp. 89, 132.

54. Chadwick: *The Reformation*, p. 398.

55. See Henry Kamen: *The Rise of Toleration* (Weidenfeld & Nicolson, 1967) p. 41.

56. For example, Chadwick: *The Reformation*, p. 191; and Dickens: *Reformation and Society*, p. 131.

57. By Henry Kamen: *Rise of Toleration*, p. 60.

58. Both quotations from Roland H. Bainton: *Studies on the Reformation* (Hodder & Stoughton, 1964) pp. 166, 163.

59. By J. W. Allen: *A History of Political Thought in the Sixteenth Century* (Methuen, 1928) p. 93.

60. Quoted in J. H. Elliott: *Europe Divided 1559—1598* (Collins/Fontana, 1968) p. 231.

61. See Kamen: *Rise of Toleration*, p. 121.

62. See Elliott: *Europe Divided*, pp. 238, 242.

63. Lord Acton: *Lectures on Modern History* (Collins/Fontana, 1960) pp. 167—8.

64. Quoted in Kamen: *Rise of Toleration*, p. 164.

65. Quotations from Bainton: *Studies on the Reformation*, pp. 223—4.

66. See Trevor-Roper: *Religion, the Reformation*, pp. 15—24 and 28—30.

67. Francois Hotman: *Francogallia*, ed. Ralph E. Giesey (Cambridge University Press, 1972), p. 155.

68. Ibid., pp. 286—7, 401.

69. *A Defence of Liberty Against Tyrants*, a translation of *Vindiciae Contra Tyrannos*, with an introduction by H. J. Laski (Bell, 1924), p. 97.

70. Ibid., p. 112.

71. By J. N. Figgis: *From Gerson to Grotius* (Cambridge University Press, 1907) p. 178: and by Acton: *Lectures on Modern History*, p. 161.

72. *De Jure Regni apud Scotos* by George Buchanan (1579), (Richard Baldwin, 1689) p. 9.

73. Ibid., pp. 21, 12, 6, 7.

74. See Henry Kamen: *The Iron Century* (Weidenfeld & Nicolson, 1971), Sphere edn 1976) p. 366.

75. Quoted in *Texts Concerning the Revolt of the Netherlands*, ed. E. H. Kossmann and A. F. Mellink (Cambridge University Press, 1974) p. 234.

76. Ibid., pp. 216—7.

77. See Kamen: *The Rise of Toleration*, pp. 112, 116—8.

78. Quoted in ibid., pp. 147, 149.

79. See Kossmann and Mellink (eds) *The Revolt of the Netherlands*, p. 195.

CHAPTER 6: THE PHILOSOPHICAL FOUNDATIONS OF LIBERALISM

1. Herbert Butterfield: *The Origins of Modern Science* (Bell, 1949) 1957 edn, p. 98.
2. Descartes: *Discourse on Method* and other writings, translated Arthur Wollaston (Penguin, 1960) p. 135.
3. *Turgot on Progress, Sociology and Economics*, translated and edited by Ronald L. Meek (Cambridge University Press, 1973) p. 94.
4. Quotations from Descartes: *Discourse on Method*, pp. 55—6, 44, 36, 37, 174, 45, 96.
5. Hill: *Change and Continuity*, p. 116.
6. Descartes: *Discourse on Method*, pp. 57, 84, 79.
7. Quoted in Hugh Kearney: *Science and Change 1500—1700* (Weidenfeld & Nicolson, 1971) p. 156.
8. Marx: *Capital*, Vol. 1, translated Ben Fowkes (Penguin, 1976) p. 512.
9. Quoted in Jonathan Rée: *Descartes* (Allen Lane, 1974) p. 39.
10. S. F. Mason in Charles Webster (ed.): *The Intellectual Revolution*, p. 203.
11. See Trevor-Roper: *Religion, the Reformation*, pp. 182, 122.
12. Quoted in Jack Lively (ed.) *The Enlightenment* (Longman, 1966) p. 13.
13. See Christopher Hill: *Intellectual Origins of the English Revolution* (Oxford University Press, 1965) Panther edn 1972, pp. 15, 69, 86.
14. Quoted in Basil Willey: *The Seventeenth Century Background* (Chatto & Windus, 1934) Penguin edn 1972, p. 30.
15. See Hill: *Intellectual Origins*, p. 65.
16. Quoted in Marie Boas Hall: *Nature's Laws*, p. 449.
17. Quoted in Hampshire: *Age of Reason*, p. 25.
18. Hall: *Nature's Laws*, p. 8.
19. *The Physical and Metaphysical Works of Lord Bacon*, Joseph Devey (ed.), (Bell, 1891) pp. 14—15.
20. Quoted in Hampshire (ed.): *Age of Reason*, p. 23.
21. *The Dignity and Advancement of Learning*, in Devey (ed.), *Bacon's Works*, p. 30.
22. See Willey: *The Seventeenth Century Background*, pp. 32—3.
23. Blake: *Complete Writings*, p. 398.
24. Quoted by Theodore Redpath: 'Bacon and the Advancement of Learning' in Boris Ford (ed.): *The Age of Shakespeare* (Penguin, 1955) p. 371.
25. See Hill: *Intellectual Origins*, pp. 87—9.
26. See L. C. Knights: 'Bacon and the Seventeenth-Century Dissociation of Sensibility', in *Explorations* (Chatto & Windus, 1946) pp. 95—6.
27. Blake: *Complete Writings*, p. 396.
28. Page references are to the Pelican edition of *Leviathan*, C. B. Macpherson (ed.) (Penguin, 1968) p. 721.
29. Quoted in John Bowle: *Hobbes and his Critics* (Jonathan Cape, 1951) p. 16.
30. Quoted in C. B. Macpherson: *Democratic Theory* (Clarendon Press, 1973) p. 240.
31. See R. H. Tawney: *Religion and the Rise of Capitalism* (John Murray, 1926) 1929 edn, p. 180.
32. MacIntyre: *A Short History of Ethics*, p. 134.
33. Keith Thomas: 'The Social Origins of Hobbes's Political Thought', *Hobbes Studies*, ed. K. C. Brown (Basil Blackwell, 1965).

34. Blake: *Complete Writings*, p. 783.

35. For example, by Berlin in *Four Essays*, p. 123 footnote.

36. Bertrand Russell: *A History of Western Philosophy* (Allen & Unwin, 1946) 1961 edn, p. 584; and Trevor-Roper: *Historical Essays*, p. 242.

37. Isaiah Berlin (ed.) *The Age of Enlightenment* (New American Library, 1956) p. 31.

38. C. B. Macpherson: Introduction to *Leviathan* (Penguin edn) p. 25.

39. All quotations from John Locke: *An Essay Concerning Human Understanding*, ed. Peter H. Nidditch (Clarendon Press, 1975). In this instance, see p. 48.

40. Quoted in Richard Ashcraft: 'Faith and Knowledge in Locke's Philosophy', in *John Locke: Problems and Perspectives*, ed. John W. Yolton (Cambridge University Press, 1969) p. 201.

41. Quoted in Jack Lively (ed.) *The Enlightenment*, p. 35.

42. David Hume: *An Enquiry Concerning Human Understanding*, ed. P. H. Nidditch, (Clarendon Press, 1975) p. 74.

43. For example, Bertrand Russell, in *Unpopular Essays*, p. 22.

44. Spinoza: *Ethics* translated Andrew Boyle (Dent, 1910) 1959 edn, Part I, Propositions XXIX and XXXIII, pp. 23, 26.

45. Ibid., Part II, Propositions XXIX p. 62.

46. Quoted in Hampshire (ed.) *Age of Reason*, p. 174.

47. Ibid., pp. 173, 180.

48. Quotations in this paragraph from Spinoza: *Ethics*, Part I, Definition VII, Proposition XXXII; Part V, Proposition VI; Part III, Proposition VII; Part V, Proposition XL; Part I, Appendix; pp. 2, 25, 205, 91, 222, 36.

49. Quoted in S. F. Mason: 'The Scientific Revolution and the Protestant Reformation', *Annals of Science*, Vol. 9, 1953, p. 66.

CHAPTER 7: EARLY BOURGEOIS LIBERALISM: HOLLAND AND ENGLAND

1. See Christopher Hill: *Puritanism and Revolution*, p. 127.

2. See K. H. D. Haley: *The Dutch in the Seventeenth Century* (Thomas & Hudson, 1972) pp. 36—7.

3. Both quotations from Lewis Samuel Feuer: *Spinoza and the Rise of Liberalism* (Beacon Press, 1958) 1964 edn, pp. 65, 275.

4. Charles Wilson, in *The Dutch Republic and the Civilisation of the Seventeenth Century* (Weidenfeld & Nicolson, 1968) p. 185.

5. Ibid., p. 42.

6. See *The True-Born Englishman* in *Selected Writings of Daniel Defoe*, ed. James T. Boulton (Cambridge University Press, 1975) p. 58.

7. Haley: *The Dutch*, p. 184.

8. Quoted in Feuer: *Spinoza*, p. 62.

9. For these references to Venice see Zera S. Fink: *The Classical Republicans* (Northwestern University Press, 1945) pp. 28 ff., 46, 54.

10. Quoted in G. P. Gooch: *English Democratic Ideas in the Seventeenth Century* (Cambridge University Press, 1927) p. 243.

11. Quoted in Christopher Hill: *Reformation to Industrial Revolution* (Weidenfeld & Nicolson, 1967) p. 19.

12. Both passages quoted in Tawney, *Religion and the Rise of Capitalism*, p. 179.

13. Gerrard Winstanley: *The Law of Freedom and other writings*, ed. Christopher Hill (Penguin, 1973) p. 90.

14. Quoted in Barry Supple: 'Class and social tension: the case of the merchant', in E. W. Ives (ed.): *The English Revolution 1600—1660* (Edward Arnold, 1968) p. 131.

15. Quoted in Ivan Roots: 'Interest — public, private and communal', in R. H. Parry (ed.) *The English Civil War and After, 1642—1658* (Macmillan, 1970) p. 113.

16. Quoted in Hill: *Reformation to Industrial Revolution*, p. 120.

17. Quoted in Christopher Hill: *The World Turned Upside Down* (Temple Smith, 1972) p. 42.

18. Quoted in Hill: *Change and Continuity*, p. 186.

19. Ibid., pp. 219—38.

20. Quoted in Hill: *Reformation to Industrial Revolution*, p. 144.

21. See Kamen: *The Iron Century*, p. 309.

22. Quoted in Hill: *The World Turned Upside Down*, p. 28.

23. John Milton: *Selected Prose*, ed. C. A. Patrides (Penguin, 1974) p. 255.

24. Ibid., p. 259.

25. Ibid., p. 356.

26. In *Lives of the Poets*; in Samuel Johnson: *Selected Writings*, ed. R. T. Davies (Faber & Faber, 1965) p. 334.

27. Milton: *Selected Prose*, p. 335.

28. Ibid., pp. 212, 220, 227.

29. Ibid., p. 213.

30. Ibid., pp. 242, 244, 231.

31. Quoted in Hill: *Change and Continuity*, p. 110.

32. *Selected Prose*, pp. 357, 234, 226.

33. Quotations from Hill: *The World Turned Upside Down*, pp. 19—20.

34. A. L. Morton (ed.) *Freedom in Arms* (Lawrence & Wishart, 1975) p. 252.

35. See ibid., p. 191.

36. Hill: *The World Turned Upside Down*, p. 52.

37. *The Political Theory of Possessive Individualism*, p. 282. See also ch. 3, *passim*, and the Appendix *passim*.

38. Ibid., p. 158.

39. Keith Thomas: 'The Levellers and the Franchise' in G. E. Aylmer (ed.) *The Interregnum* (Macmillan, 1972) p. 71. See also A. L. Morton: 'Leveller democracy — fact or myth?' in *The World of the Ranters* (Lawrence & Wishart, 1970); and Anthony Arblaster: 'Revolution, the Levellers and C. B. Macpherson', in *1642: Literature and Power in the Seventeenth Century*, ed. Francis Barker, et al. (University of Essex, 1981).

40. Macpherson, *Possessive Individualism*, p. 148.

41. Page references for the Putney debates are to the version in A. S. P. Woodhouse: *Puritanism and Liberty* (Dent 1938) 1974 edn. In this instance, see p. 53.

42. G. E. Aylmer: *The Levellers in the English Revolution* (Thames & Hudson, 1975) p. 50.

43. See Keith Thomas, in Aylmer (ed.) *The Levellers*, p. 57. Also *Certain Articles for the Good of the Commonwealth*, in Woodhouse: *Puritanism*, pp. 335—8.

44. Woodhouse: *Puritanism*, pp. 367—8.

45. Quoted in H. N. Brailsford: *The Levellers and the English Revolution* (Cresset Press, 1961) Spokesman Books edn, 1976, p. 324.

46. Winstanley: *The Law of Freedom*, pp. 340, 87.
47. Quoted in Edmund Dell (ed.) *The Good Old Cause* (Frank Cass, 1969) p. 471.
48. Kamen: *The Iron Century* p. 413, and p. 483. See also Emile Lousee: 'Absolutism', in Heinz Lubasz (ed.) *The Development of the Modern State* (Collier-Macmillan 1964) pp. 46—7.

CHAPTER 8: THE EIGHTEENTH CENTURY: WHIGGERY TRIUMPHANT

1. See E. P. Thompson: *The Making of the English Working Class* (Gollancz, 1963) Penguin edn, 1968, p. 29.
2. Quoted in K. H. D. Haley: *The First Earl of Shaftesbury* (Clarendon Press, 1968) p. 739.
3. See Peter Laslett: Introduction to Locke's *Two Treatises of Government* (Cambridge University Press, 1960) Mentor edn, 1965, pp. 37—50. Page references are to this edition.
4. Maurice Cranston: 'John Locke and Government by Consent' in David Thomson (ed.) *Political Ideas* (C. A. Watts, 1966) p. 69.
5. Quoted by Laslett in his Introduction to the *Treatises*, p. 15.
6. Macpherson: *Possessive Individualism*, p. 248.
7. Quoted in Haley: *Shaftesbury*, p. 224.
8. Quoted in J. P. Kenyon: *Revolution Principles* (Cambridge University Press, 1977) p. 49.
9. Cranston in Thomson (ed.) *Political Ideas*, p. 68.
10. Locke: *Epistola de Tolerantia — A Letter on Toleration*, ed. R. Klibansky and J. W. Gough (Oxford University Press, 1968) pp. 133, 135, 131.
11. Kamen: *The Rise of Toleration*, p. 231.
12. Locke: *Two Treatises*, p. 171.
13. Acton: *Lectures on Modern History*, pp. 221, 207—8.
14. See Christopher Hill: *The Century of Revolution 1603—1714* (Nelson, 1961) p. 303.
15. Burke: *Reflections*, p. 112.
16. Quoted in Kenyon: *Revolution Principles*, p. 45.
17. Swift: 'Thoughts on Various Subjects' in *Satires and Personal Writings*, ed. W. A. Eddy (Oxford University Press, 1932) p. 413.
18. 'In general, therefore, the tradition of the English Whigs stood for a gradual, ordered progress . . .', Herbert Butterfield: *The Englishman and his History* (Cambridge University Press, 1945) p. 96.
19. J. H. Plumb: *The Growth of Political Stability in England 1675—1725* (Macmillan, 1967) p. 94.
20. Kenyon: *Revolution Principles*, p. 181.
21. See John Cannon: *Parliamentary Reform 1640—1832* (Cambridge University Press, 1973) p. 30; and Plumb; *The Growth of Political Stability in England*, pp. 72—3.
22. See Plumb, *The Growth of Political Stability in England*, p. 172 and ch. 6, *passim*.
23. Quoted in Kenyon: *Revolution Principles*, p. 175.
24. Marx: *Capital*, Vol. I, p. 885.
25. Quoted in Hill: *Change and Continuity*, p. 201.
26. See Douglas Hay, et al.: *Albion's Fatal Tree* (Allen Lane, 1975) Penguin edn, 1977, p. 18.

27. Hill: *Reformation to Industrial Revolution*, p. 182.

28. Kenyon: *Revolution Principles*, pp. 205—6.

29. E. P. Thompson: *Whigs and Hunters* (Allen Lane, 1975) p. 241.

30. See W. E. Tate: *The English Village Community and the Enclosure Movement* (Gollancz, 1967) p. 130.

31. Ibid., pp. 51, 88; and see J. H. Plumb: *England in the Eighteenth Century* (Pengin, 1950) p. 82.

32. Marx, *Capital*, Vol. I, p. 885.

33. G. E. Mingay: *English Landed Society in the 18th Century* (Routledge & Kegan Paul, 1963) p. 186. And for another benign judgement, see J. D. Chambers and G. E. Mingay: *The Agricultural Revolution 1750—1880* (Batsford, 1966) p. 104.

34. Quoted in Tate, *The English Village Community*, p. 85.

35. Quoted in Hill: *Reformation to Industrial Revolution*, pp. 22—3.

36. Quoted in Marx, *Capital*, Vol. I, footnote p. 892. And see John Prebble: *The Highland Clearances* (Secker & Warburg, 1963) Penguin edn 1969, especially pp. 103—7.

37. Quoted in Kenyon, *Revolution Principles*, p. 113.

38. For quotations from Petty see Eric Roll: *A History of Economic Thought* (Faber & Faber, 1938) 1973 edn, pp. 104, 106.

39. Quoted in E. H. Carr: *The New Society* (Macmillan, 1951) p. 42.

40. Bernard Mandeville: *The Fable of the Bees*, ed. Phillip Harth (Penguin, 1970) p. 294.

41. See Dorothy George: *England in Transition* (1931, Penguin edn 1953) pp. 22, 117.

42. Mandeville: *The Fable of the Bees*, pp. 294, 320.

43. Basil Willey: *The Eighteenth Century Background* (Chatto and Windus, 1940) Penguin edn 1962, p. 99.

44. Swift: *Satires*, pp. 26—7.

45. Quotations from Defoe: *Selected Writings* ed. Boulton, pp. 124, 234, 232, 233—5, 66, 244.

46. Quotations from F. R. Leavis: 'Johnson and Augustanism', *The Common Pursuit* (Chatto & Windus, 1958) p. 100.

CHAPTER 9: THE EIGHTEENTH CENTURY: THE ENLIGHTENMENT

1. *Select Letters of Voltaire*, ed. Theodore Besterman (Nelson, 1963) p. 34.

2. Voltaire: *Philosophical Letters*, trans. E. Dilworth (Bobbs-Merrill, 1961) pp. 48, 52, 61.

3. See Theodore Besterman: *Voltaire* (Basil Blackwell, 1969) 1976 edn, p. 169.

4. Voltaire: *Philosophical Letters*, p. 110.

5. Quoted in Peter Gay: *The Enlightenment, An Interpretation*, Vol. II (Weidenfeld & Nicolson, 1970) Wildwood House edn, 1973, p. 24.

6. Voltaire: *Philosophical Letters*, pp. 26, 32, and see Letter 9.

7. See Thomas L. Pangle: *Montesquieu's Philosophy of Liberalism* (Chicago University Press, 1973) p. 228.

8. Montesquieu: *The Spirit of the Laws*, translated Thomas Nugent (Hafner, 1949) 1966 edn, pp. 321, 314, 151.

9. Quoted in George Rudé: *Europe in the Eighteenth Century* (Weidenfeld & Nicolson 1972), Sphere edn, 1974, p. 126.

10. See Franco Venturi: *Utopia and Reform in the Enlightenment* (Cambridge University Press, 1971) ch. 1 and p. 70.

11. Quoted in Jack Lively (ed.) *The Enlightenment*, p. 15.

12. Quoted in Peter Gay: *Voltaire's Politics* (Princeton University Press, 1959) Vintage edn, 1965, p. 26.

13. Voltaire: *Philosophical Letters*, p. 53.

14. Quoted in Lively (ed.) *The Enlightenment*, pp. 20, 21.

15. See Meek (ed.) *Turgot on Progress*, p. 45.

16. See ibid., p. 48, and Jean le Rond d'Alembert: *Preliminary Discourse to the Encyclopaedia of Diderot*, translated and ed. R. N. Schwab (Bobbs-Merrill, 1963) p. 156.

17. Ibid., pp. 48—9, 29, 5.

18. Voltaire: *Select Letters*, pp. 52—3.

19. Hume: *Treatise*, p. 44.

20. Immanuel Kant: 'What is Enlightenment?' (1784), in *On History* ed. Lewis White Beck (Bobbs-Merrill, 1963) p. 3.

21. See Lively (ed.) *The Enlightenment*, p. 45.

22. See the entry on Atheism in Voltaire's *Philosophical Dictionary*, ed. and translated Theodore Besterman (Penguin, 1971) p. 56.

23. Quoted in Howard Mumford Jones: *Revolution and Romanticism* (Oxford University Press, 1974) p. 171.

24. Hume: *Treatise*, p. 44.

25. Montesquieu on trade: see *The Spirit of the Laws*, pp. 316—7.

26. Quoted in Sidney Pollard: *The Idea of Progress* (C. A. Watts, 1968) Penguin edn, 1971, p. 69.

27. Hume: 'Of Refinement in the Arts' quoted in ibid. p. 64.'

28. Kant: 'Perpetual Peace' in, *On History*, p. 114.

29. See Voltaire: *Select Letters*, p. 147; and H. N. Brailsford: *Voltaire* (Oxford University Press, 1935) 1963 edn, p. 68.

30. Quoted in Pollard: *The Idea of Progress*, p. 72.

31. Kant: 'Idea for a Universal History', in *On History*, pp. 15—16.

32. For Montesquieu on slavery see *The Spirit of the Laws*, p. 235 ff. For Voltaire see Brailsford *Voltaire*, p. 69; and *Candide*, translated Richard Aldington, in Ben Ray Redman (ed.) *The Portable Voltaire* (Viking, 1949) Penguin edn, 1977, p. 282.

33. See, for example, Anthony Strugnell: *Diderot's Politics* (Martinus Nijhoff, 1973) pp. 220, 236.

34. See d'Alembert: *Preliminary Discourse*, pp. 4, 122, 48.

35. Kant: 'Conjectural Beginning of Human History' (1786), in *On History*: pp. 58—9.

36. Cesare Beccaria: *On Crimes and Punishments* (1764) translated Henry Paolucci (Bobbs-Merrill, 1963) p. 69.

37. Pollard: *The Idea of Progress*, p. 51.

38. D'Holbach quoted in Lively (ed.) *The Enlightenment*, pp. 37—8; and Diderot quoted in Strugnell: *Diderot's Politics*, p. 155.

39. Beccaria: *On Crimes*, pp. 43, 42, 32.

40. D'Alembert: *Preliminary Discourse*, p. 10.

41. Norman Hampson: *The First European Revolution 1776—1815* (Thames & Hudson, 1969) p. 18.

42. Hume: *Treatise*, p. 257.

43. Quoted in Norman Hampson: *The Enlightenment* (Penguin, 1968) p. 123.

44. D'Alembert: *Preliminary Discourse*, p. 31.

45. Both quotations in Alfred Cobban: *In Search of Humanity* (Jonathan Cape, 1960) pp. 73, 167.

46. Quoted in Trevor-Roper: *Historical Essays*, p. 264.

47. See Brailsford: *Voltaire*, p. 71, and Gay: *Voltaire's Politics*, p. 222.

48. See Strugnell: *Diderot's Politics*, p. 81.

49. Quoted in Sabine and Thorson: *History or Political Theory*, p. 524.

50. Quoted by Leo Gershoy in Roger Wines (ed.) *Enlightened Despotism* (D. C. Heath, 1967) p. 21.

51. D'Holbach quoted in Cobban, *In Search of Humanity*, p: 165; and Helvetius, in Pollard: *The Idea of Progress*, p. 47.

52. Kant: *On History*, p. 64.

53. Quoted in Brailsford: *Voltaire*, p. 70.

54. De Tocqueville: *The Ancien Regime*, p. 172.

55. See Strugnell: *Diderot's Politics*, pp. 111, 144—151. For the *Nakaz*, see Melvin C. Wren in Wines (ed.) *Enlightened Despotism*, pp. 48—9.

56. See Mary P. Mack: *Jeremy Bentham: An Odyssey of Ideas 1748—1792* (Heinemann, 1962) pp. 362—4.

57. See Lester G. Crocker: *Diderot, The Embattled Philosopher* (Free Press, 1954) 1966 edn, p. 385.

58. Paine: *Common Sense*, p. 120.

59. Quoted in Besterman: *Voltaire*, p. 307.

60. See Gay: *Voltaire's Politics*, p. 15; and Besterman: *Voltaire*, p. 311.

61. See Edna Nixon: *Voltaire and the Calas Case* (Gollancz, 1961) *passim*, especially p. 164.

62. Quoted in Besterman: *Voltaire*, pp. 367, 373.

63. See, for example, the passage quoted in Gay: *The Enlightenment*, Vol. II, p. 4.

64. Gay: *Voltaire's Politics*, p. 293.

65. See Venturi: *Utopia and Reform*, p. 114.

66. Quoted in Christopher Thacker: *Voltaire* (Routledge & Kegan Paul, 1971) pp. 63—4.

67. Voltaire: *Philosophical Dictionary*, (ed. Besterman), p. 44.

CHAPTER 10: AMERICA: THE RIGHTS OF MAN AND THE RIGHTS OF PROPERTY

1. Letter of 21 March 1801, in *The Portable Thomas Jefferson*, ed. Peterson, p. 484.

2. Quoted in Staughton Lynd: *Intellectual Origins of American Radicalism* (Faber, 1969) pp. 22—3.

3. Quoted in Hofstadter: *The American Political Tradition*, p. 16.

4. Quoted in V. L. Parrington: *Main Currents in American Thought*, Vol. I (Harcourt Brace, 1927) p. 282.

5. See Joan Hoff Wilson: 'The Illusion of Change: Women and the American

Revolution', in Alfred D. Young (ed.) *The American Revolution* (Northern Illinois University Press, 1976) pp. 414—18.

6. Quotations from *The Portable Jefferson*, pp. 248, 396, 217, 549.

7. Franklin quoted in Parrington: *Main Currents*, pp. 173—4.

8. See Richard E. Ellis: 'The Political Economy of Thomas Jefferson', in Lally Weymouth (ed.) *Thomas Jefferson — The Man, His World, His Influence* (Weidenfeld & Nicolson, 1973) p. 94.

9. Quotations from Peterson, ed., *The Portable Jefferson*, pp. 356, 558.

10. See Elisha P. Douglass: *Rebels and Democrats* (University of North Carolina Press, 1955) p. 56.

11. Quoted in ibid., pp. 15, 127.

12. Quoted in Jesse Lemisch: 'The American Revolution Seen from the Bottom Up', in Barton J. Bernstein (ed.) *Towards a New Past* (Chatto & Windus, 1970) p. 10.

13. Quoted in Douglass: *Rebels and Democrats*, p. 57.

14. See Eric Foner: *Tom Paine and Revolutionary America* (Oxford University Press, 1977) pp. 131—4.

15. Quotations from Parrington: *Main Currents*, pp. 277, 317.

16. Quotations from Peterson, ed., *The Portable Jefferson*: pp. 534—5, 355, 164.

17. Quoted in Robert A. Dahl: *A Preface to Democratic Theory* (University of Chicago Press, 1956) 1963 edn, p. 7.

18. See Bernard Bailyn: *The Ideological Origins of the American Revolution* (Harvard University Press, 1967) pp. 187—8.

19. See Miriam Schneir: *Feminism: The Essential Historical Writings* (Random House, 1972) pp. 2—4.

20. Samuel Johnson: *Political Writings*, ed. Donald J. Greene (Yale University Press, 1977) pp. 442, 454. For Wesley, see Richard B. Morris: *The American Revolution Reconsidered* (Harper & Row, 1967) p. 76.

21. See Douglass: *Rebels and Democrats*, footnote p. 178.

22. See Bailyn: *American Revolution*, p. 239.

23. Quotations from *The Portable Jefferson*, pp. 14, 214—15, 186, 192—3.

24. Staughton Lynd: *Class Conflict, Slavery and the United States Constitution* (Bobbs-Merrill, 1967) pp. 179—180.

CHAPTER 11: THE MOMENT OF THE FRENCH REVOLUTION:
THE CLIMAX AND CRISIS OF LIBERALISM

1. Quoted in F. O'Gorman: *The Whig Party and the French Revolution* (Macmillan, 1967) p. 45.

2. Quoted in George Rudé: *Revolutionary Europe 1783—1815* (Collins/Fontana, 1964) p. 181.

3. Wordsworth: *The Prelude* (1805 version) Book VI, lines 352—5.

4. De Tocqueville: *The Ancien Regime*, pp. 43—4.

5. Paine: *Rights of Man*, p. 168.

6. Burke: *Reflections*, p. 92.

7. E. Weekley, quoted in Raymond Williams: *Culture and Society 1780—1950* (Chatto & Windus, 1959) p. xiv.

8. See Georg Lukács: *The Young Hegel*, translated Rodney Livingstone (Merlin Press, 1975) p. 10.

9. Marx: *The Eighteenth Brumaire of Louis Bonaparte*, in, *Surveys from Exile*, ed. David Fernbach (Penguin, 1973) pp. 146—7.

10. See Walter Friedlaender: *David to Delacroix* (Harvard University Press, 1952) 1977 edn, pp. 7—8, 14—19.

11. The Abbé Sieyès: *What is the Third Estate?*, ed. S. E. Finer (Pall Mall, 1963) pp. 156, 158, 159.

12. Both quotations from George Rudé: *Robespierre* (Collins, 1975) p. 101. See also pp. 23, 106.

13. Quoted in Alfred Cobban: 'The Fundamental Ideas of Robespierre' in *Aspects of the French Revolution* (Jonathan Cape, 1968) Paladin edn, 1971, p. 140.

14. Rudé: *Robespierre*, p. 96.

15. Sieyès: *What is the Third Estate?*, p. 96.

16. Ibid., pp. 74—5, 78, 85, 161—2.

17. Georges Lefebvre: *The Coming of the French Revolution*, translated by R. R. Palmer (Vintage Books, 1957) pp. 185, 148.

18. Alfred Cobban: *The Social Interpretation of the French Revolution* (Cambridge University Press, 1964) 1968 edn, pp. 40, 52, 65. And see *The Coming of the French Revolution*, pp. 137, 181.

19. Quoted in Norman Hampson: *The French Revolution — A Concise History* (Thames & Hudson, 1975) p. 52.

20. See Rudé: pp. 133, 185; and Cobban: *Aspects of the French Revolution*, p. 168.

21. See R. B. Rose: *The Enragés: Socialists of the French Revolution?* (Sydney University Press, 1965) pp. 86—7; and Gwyn A. Williams: *Artisans and Sans-Culottes* (Edward Arnold, 1968) pp. 43—4.

22. Quoted in Rudé: *Robespierre*, p. 132.

23. See Rose: *The Enragés*, pp. 87, 90, 84.

24. Rudé: *Robespierre*, p. 151.

25. See Rudé: *Revolutionary Europe*, p. 217.

26. Quoted in R. R. Palmer: *The Age of the Democratic Revolution*, Vol. II (Princeton University Press, 1964) p. 152. And see pp. 146—56 throughout.

27. See Richard Herr: *The Eighteenth-Century Revolution in Spain* (Princeton University Press, 1958) 1969 edn, p. 276.

28. Raymond Carr: *Spain 1808—1939* (Oxford University Press, 1966) p. 94.

29. Quoted in Hampson: *The First European Revolution*, p. 155.

30. See Frank MacDermot: *Theobald Wolfe Tone* (Macmillan, 1939) Anvil edn, 1968, p. 53.

31. Quoted in Robert Kee: *The Green Flag* (Weidenfeld & Nicolson, 1972) p. 144.

32. See Irene Nicholson: *The Liberators* (Faber, 1969) pp. 154—5.

33. C. L. R. James: *The Black Jacobins* (1938, Allison & Busby, 1980) p. 57.

34. See ibid., pp. 150, 281.

35. Reprinted with Byron's *The Vision of Judgement* by the Scolar Press, 1973.

36. Trilling: *The Opposing Self*, pp. 52—3.
37. Hugh Ottaway: 'The Enlightenment and the Revolution', in *The Pelican History of Music 3: Classical and Romantic*, ed. Alec Robertson and Denis Stevens (Penguin, 1968) p. 86.
38. Quoted in Alec Harman and Wilfred Mellers: *Man and his Music* (Barrie & Rockliff, 1962) p. 632.
39. See Ottaway 'The Enlightenment', in *The Pelican History of Music, 3* pp. 94—5.
40. John Berger: *Permanent Red* (Methuen, 1960) p. 181.
41. See Gwyn A. Williams: *Goya and the Impossible Revolution* (Allen Lane, 1976) pp. 46—50, 76.
42. I cannot agree with Michael Levey's dismissal of Delacroix and Géricault as political artists in *Rococo to Revolution* (Thames & Hudson, 1966) pp. 236—8.
43. *'Born for Opposition'*, Byron's Letters and Journals, Vol. 8, ed. Leslie A. Marchand (John Murray, 1978) p. 107.
44. *'Between Two Worlds*, Byron's Letters and Journals, Vol. 7, ed. Leslie A. Marchand (John Murray, 1977) p. 63.
45. Quoted in *Byron: Selected Prose*, ed. Peter Gunn (Penguin, 1972) p. 111.
46. *'Born for Opposition'*, ed. Leslie A. Marchand, p. 47.
47. Quoted in Leslie A. Marchand: *Byron: A Portrait* (John Murray, 1971) Futura edn 1976, pp. 415—6.
48. *'For Freedom's Battle'*, Byron's Letters and Journals, Vol. 11, ed. Leslie A. Marchand (John Murray, 1981) p. 32.
49. For useful discussion of Verdi's political dimension, see George Martin: *Verdi, His Life and Times* (Macmillan, 1965), and David R. B. Kimbell: *Verdi in the Age of Italian Romanticism* (Cambridge University Press, 1981) especially 20, 24.
50. Alexander Pushkin: *Selected Works*, Vol. 1, Poetry, translated Irina Zheleznova (Progress Publishers, 1974) pp. 35, 61, 205. See also David Magarshack: *Pushkin: A Biography* (Chapman & Hall, 1967); and Marc Raeff: *The Decembrist Movement* (Prentice-Hall 1966); for the Odeovsky verse, see p. 179.
51. See William Rose: *Heinrich Heine: Two Studies of His Thought and Feeling* (Clarendon Press, 1956) pp. 9, 16.
52. See ibid., pp. 61, 53; and also Max Brod: *Heine: The Artist in Revolt* (Vallentine, Mitchell, 1956) pp. 272, 289.

CHAPTER 12: THE MOMENT OF THE FRENCH REVOLUTION:
CRISIS AND DIVISION

1. Quoted in Mary P. Mack: *Jeremy Bentham*, p. 413.
2. William Hazlitt: 'What is the People?' (1818) in *Complete Works*, ed. P. P. Howe, Vol. VII (Dent, 1932) p. 268.
3. See L. G. Mitchell: *Charles James Fox and the Disintegration of the Whig Party 1782—1794* (Oxford University Press, 1971) p. 178.
4. Quoted by C. W. Parkin in David Thomson (ed.) *Political Ideas*, p. 131.
5. *The Correspondence of Edmund Burke*, Vol. VI, ed. Alfred Cobban and Robert A. Smith (Cambridge University Press, 1967) pp. 30, 71.

6. Quoted by O'Brien in his Introduction to the Penguin edition of the *Reflections* p. 51.

7. See, for example, Mitchell: *Charles James Fox* pp. 198,, 138; and Christopher Hobhouse: *Fox* (John Murray, 1934) 1947 edn, pp. 190—205.

8. See Mitchell: *Charles James Fox* p. 194.

9. Burke: *Reflections* (Penguin edn, 1968) p. 140. Further page references are to this edition.

10. See Frank O'Gorman: *Edmund Burke: His Political Philosophy* (Allen & Unwin, 1973) p. 37.

11. Letter of 26 Feb. 1790, in *Correspondence*, VI, ed. Cobban and Smith, p. 96.

12. Ibid., p. 109.

13. *Thoughts and Details on Scarcity*, quoted in C. B. Macpherson: *Burke* (Oxford University Press, 1890) pp. 56, 59.

14. *Rights of Man* (Penguin edn, 1969) p. 168. Further page references are to this edition.

15. 'Dissertation on First Principles of Government' (1795) in *The Life and Works of Thomas Paine*, ed. W. M. Van der Weyde (Thomas Paine Association, 1925) Vol. 5, pp. 226—7.

16. For both documents, see Eric Foner: *Tom Paine and Revolutionary America*, pp. 226—7.

17. Paine: *Common Sense*, p. 65.

18. See Kramnick's Introduction to *Common Sense*, p. 50.

19. Van der Weyde (ed.) *The Life and Works of Thomas Paine*, Vol. 5, p. 228.

20. Percy Bysshe Shelley: *An Address to the Irish People* (Oriole edn, n.d.) pp. 25—6.

21. For Mary Shelley's note, see *Complete Poetical Works of Percy Bysshe Shelley*, ed. Thomas Hutchinson (Oxford University Press, 1934) p. 588.

22. Mary Wollstonecraft: *Vindication of the Rights of Woman*, ed. Miriam Kramnick (Penguin, 1975) p. 165. Further page references are to this edition.

23. Quoted in Claire Tomalin: *The Life and Death of Mary Wollstonecraft* (Weidenfeld & Nicolson, 1974) pp. 170—1, 95.

24. See John Cruikshank: *Benjamin Constant* (Twayne Publishers 1974) pp. 32, 58, 65.

25. Quoted in Anthony Arblaster and Steven Lukes (eds) *The Good Society* (Methuen, 1971) pp. 88—9.

26. Quoted in Paul H. Beik (ed.) *The French Revolution* (Macmillan, 1970) p. 365.

27. Cruikshank: *Benjamin Constant*, p. 70.

28. Quotations from Cruikshank: *Benjamin Constant*, pp. 18, 64, 21, 56.

29. See ibid., p. 30. Berlin, for example, describes him as the 'most eloquent of all defenders of freedom and privacy', *Four Essays*, p. 126.

30. Antoine Nicolas de Condorcet: *Sketch for Historical Picture of the Progress of the Human Mind*, translated June Barraclough (Weidenfeld & Nicolson, 1955). Further page references are to this edition. In this instance, see pp. 34—9.

31. See Keith Michell Baker: *Condorcet* (Chicago University Press, 1975) pp. 56—7, 243. Also *Condorcet: Selected Writings*, ed. Keith Michell Baker (Bobbs-Merrill, 1976) pp. 9—11.

32. Quoted in Baker: *Condorcet*, p. 330.

33. See *Condorcet: Selected Writings*, ed. Baker, pp. 73, 166, 108.

34. Ibid., pp. 10, 76.

35. Ibid., pp. 97, 102.

CHAPTER 13: LIBERAL POLITICAL ECONOMY: THEORY

1. See Donald Winch: *Adam Smith's Politics* (Cambridge University Press, 1978) p. 81.
2. D. P. O'Brien: *The Classical Economists* (Oxford University Press, 1975) p. 272.
3. See J. B. Brebner: 'Laissez-faire and State Intervention in Nineteenth Century Britain', in *Essays in Economic History*, Vol. 3, ed. E. M. Carus-Wilson (Edward Arnold, 1962) pp. 252—3; G. S. R. Kitson Clark: *An Expanding Society, Britain 1830—1900* (Cambridge University Press, 1967) p. 162; and Ashton quoted in Arthur J. Taylor: *Laissez-faire and State Intervention in Nineteenth-Century Britain* (Macmillan, 1972) pp. 62—3.
4. See Winch: *Adam Smith's Politics*, throughout, but especially, pp. 165, 180—1.
5. See Joseph Cropsey: *Polity and Economy: An Interpretation of the Principles of Adam Smith*, Martinus Nijhoof, 1957) p. viii; and also the quotation from *The Theory of Moral Sentiments* on p. 2.
6. Adam Smith: *The Wealth of Nations* (Dent/Everyman, 1910) Vol. I, p. 306. Further page references are to this two-volume edition.
7. See Joan Robinson: *Economic Philosophy*, pp. 19—23; and Lucio Colletti: 'Mandeville, Rousseau and Smith', in *From Rousseau to Lenin* (New Left Books, 1972) p. 213.
8. See Robert L. Heilbroner: *The Worldly Philosophers* (Allen Lane, 1969) pp. 18, 50—2. I imagine that Heilbroner qualifies as a 'serious commentator'.
9. *The Theory of Moral Sentiments*, quoted in Cropsey: *Polity and Economy*, p. 20.
10. Quoted in Winch: *Adam Smith's Politics*, pp. 68, 58.
11. Quoted in ibid., p. 138.
12. Quoted in Philip Appleman (ed.) *An Essay on the Principle of Population* (Norton Critical edition, 1976) pp. 147—8.
13. See Keynes: *Essays in Biography*, p. 86.
14. Thomas Robert Malthus: *An Essay on the Principle of Population*, ed. Anthony Flew (Penguin, 1970) p. 72. Further page references are to this edition.
15. Appleman (ed): *Essay*, p. 139.
16. Quoted in ibid., p. 154.
17. See Flew's Introduction to the *Essay*, pp. 24—5.
18. See William Hazlitt: *The Spirit of the Age* (Oxford University Press, 1960) pp. 167—8.
19. See William J. Barber: *A History of Economic Thought* (Penguin, 1967) pp. 61—2.
20. Mark Blaug: *Economic Theory in Retrospect* (Heinemann, 1964) 1968 edn, p. 70.
21. John Stuart Mill: *Autobiography*, ed. Jack Stillinger (Oxford University Press, 1971) p. 64; and Patricia James: *Population Malthus* (Routledge & Kegan Paul, 1979) pp. 382—8.
22. Marx: *Capital*, Vol. I, footnote p. 766.
23. Hazlitt: *The Spirit of the Age*, p. 159.
24. Appleman (ed): *Essay*, pp. 135—6.
25. Quoted in Keynes: *Essays in Biography*, p. 90.
26. Charles Dickens: *The Chimes*, in *The Christmas Books*, Vol. I, ed. Michael Slater (Penguin, 1971) p. 171, and see Slater's introduction, pp. 139—41.
27. Keynes: *Essays in Biography*, p. 92.

28. See Raymond G. Cowherd: *Political Economists and the English Poor Laws* (Ohio University Press, 1977) pp. 20, 161—2.

29. *Marx and Engels on Malthus*, ed. Ronald L. Meek (Lawrence and Wishart, 1953) p. 123.

30. Charles Darwin: *The Origin of Species*, ed. J. W. Burrow (Penguin, 1968) pp. 116—17.

31. *The Autobiography of Charles Darwin*, ed. Nora Barlow (Collins, 1958) p. 120.

32. See Burrow's Introduction to *The Origin of Species*, pp. 33—4.

33. See Robert Young: 'Malthus and the Evolutionists', *Past and Present*, no. 43, 1969.

34. David Ricardo: *On the Principles of Political Economy, and Taxation* (1817, Penguin 1971) ed. R. M. Hartwell, p. 390. Further page references are to this edition.

35. Quoted in Patricia James: *Population Malthus*, p. 374.

36. Quoted in Heilbroner: *The Worldly Philosophers* p. 74, and see Ricardo: *Principles*, p. 332.

37. See Lord Robbins: *The Theory of Economic Policy in English Classical Political Economy* (Macmillan, 1952) 1978 edn, p. 104.

38. J. S. Mill: *Principles of Political Economy*, Books IV and V, ed. Donald Winch (Penguin, 1970) p. 314.

39. H. Scott Gordon quoting D. H. Macgregor in 'The Ideology of Laissez-Faire' in A. W. Coats (ed.) *The Classical Economists and Economic Policy* (Methuen, 1971) p. 199.

40. See Coats in ibid., p. 6.

41. Quoted in Robbins: *Theory of Economic Policy*, pp. 101—2.

42. Marian Bowley: 'Nassau Senior and Classical Economics' in Coats (ed.), *The Classical Economists*, p. 61.

43. Quoted in Robbins: *Theory of Economic Policy*, pp. 11—12.

44. For example, O'Brien in *The Classical Economists*, p. 284.

45. See Bentham cited in Robbins: *Theory of Economic Policy*, pp. 104—5, and the Handloom Weavers' Report, summarized by Bowley in Coats (ed.) *The Classical Economists*, pp. 59—62.

46. For Liverpool, see Asa Briggs: *The Age of Improvement* (Longmans, Green, 1959) p. 220. For Speransky, see Hampson: *The First European Revolution*, pp. 161—2.

47. Macaulay, quoted in E. H. Carr: *The New Society*, p. 21.

48. Quoted in Humphrey House: 'The Mood of Doubt', in *All in Due Time* (Hart-Davis, 1955) p. 97, and see the whole essay.

49. See George H. Ford: *Dickens and his Readers* (Princeton University Press, 1955) W. W. Norton, 1965 edn, pp. 102—3.

50. See Asa Briggs: *Victorian People* (Odhams, 1954) Penguin edn 1965, p. 134.

CHAPTER 14: LIBERAL POLITICAL ECONOMY: PRACTICE

1. Quotations from Hill: *Reformation to Industrial Revolution*, p. 135, and from Cowherd: *Economists and the Poor Laws*, p. 245.

2. Quoted in Macpherson: *Burke*, p. 59.

3. Quoted in Hampson: *The First European Revolution*, p. 30. He also cites Burke, p. 28.

4. Quoted in Briggs: *Age Of Improvement*, p. 278.

5. Quoted in Cowherd: *Economists and the Poor Laws*, p. 275.

6. *The Poor Law Report of 1834*, ed S. G. and E. O. A. Checkland (Penguin, 1974) p. 277. Further page references are to this edition of the Report.

7. See Appendix A to the Penguin edition of *Oliver Twist* (Penguin, 1966) ed. Peter Fairclough, p. 483.

8. Dickens: *The Christmas Books*, Vol. I, p. 51.

9. Letter in *Radio Times*, 9 Aug. 1975.

10. *Chartism*, in *Thomas Carlyle: Selected Writings*, ed. Alan Shelston (Penguin, 1971) p. 164.

11. See Cowherd: *Economists and the Poor Laws*, p. 177.

12. See Mark Blaug: 'The myth of the old Poor Law and the making of the new', *Journal of Economic History*, Vol. XXIII, 1963; and 'The Poor Law Report re-examined', *Journal of Economic History*, Vol. XXIV, 1964.

13. See Cecil Woodham-Smith: *The Great Hunger* (Hamish Hamilton, 1962) pp. 74—5.

14. Ibid., pp. 105, 89, 123.

15. Quoted in R. D. Collison Black: *Economic Thought and the Irish Question 1817—1870* (Cambridge University Press, 1960) p. 117.

16. See Woodham-Smith: *The Great Hunger*, pp. 136—7, 381.

17. Quoted in Black: *The Irish Question*, p. 39.

18. Ibid., p. 111.

19. Quoted in Woodham-Smith: *The Great Hunter*, pp. 375—6.

20. See ibid., p. 411.

21. Ibid., pp. 379, 91, 54. And see also pp. 410—11.

22. See Black: *The Irish Question*, p. 244; and Steven Marcus: Hunger and Ideology' in *Representations* (Macmillan, 1976) especially pp. 12—15.

23. Bertrand Russell: *Unpopular Essays*, pp. 24—5.

24. See A. J. P. Taylor: 'Lord John Russell', in *Essays in English History* (Penguin, 1976) pp. 71—2. See also the next essay, 'Genocide'.

25. De Tocqueville: *Journeys to England and Ireland*, quoted in *Industrialisation and Culture, 1830—1914*, ed. Christopher Harvie, et al (Macmillan, 1970) pp. 40—42. Frederick Engels: *The Condition of the Working Class in England 1844* (Panther edn. 1969) pp. 301—2.

26. See Donald Read: *Cobden and Bright* (Edward·Arnold, 1967) p. 6.

27. Quoted in Asa Briggs: *Victorian Cities* (Odhams, 1963) Penguin edn 1968, pp. 119, 126.

28. Quoted in Read: *Cobden and Bright*, p. 95.

29. See John Bright: *Selected Speeches* (Dent/Everyman, 1907) pp. 109, 218—19.

30. Quoted in Ian Bradley: *The Optimists* (Faber & Faber, 1980) p. 40.

31. Quotations from Read: *Cobden and Bright*, p. 107; and Briggs: *Victorian Cities*, p. 103.

32. See Read, *Cobden and Bright*, pp. 33, 65.

33. Paine: *Rights of Man*, p. 234.

34. Read: *Cobden and Bright*, p. 110.

35. Quoted in A. J. P. Taylor: *The Troublemakers* (Hamish Hamilton, 1957) Panther edn. 1969, p. 48.

36. See Read, *Cobden and Bright*, p. 120.

37. See Taylor: *Essays in English History*, p. 48.

38. Quoted in Briggs: *Age of Improvement*, p. 351.

39. Quoted in Read, *Cobden and Bright*, p. 239.

40. Quoted in Keith Robbins: *John Bright* (Routledge & Kegan Paul, 1979) p. 219.

41. Quoted in Read, *Cobden and Bright*, p. 76.

42. Goldwin Smith, quoted in *Industrialisation and Culture*, p. 165.

43. See Robbins, *John Bright*, p. 76.

44. See Briggs: *Victorian People*, p. 209; and Robbins *John Bright*, p. 176.

45. See Robbins, *John Bright*, p. 214, 222, and 233, and Read *Cobden and Bright*, p. 177.

46. See Robbins, *John Bright*, p. 191.

CHAPTER 15: THE FEAR OF DEMOCRACY

1. Quoted in Briggs: *Age of Improvement*, p. 245.

2. See Graeme Duncan: *Marx and Mill* (Cambridge University Press, 1973) pp. 229, 258—60.

3. Macaulay: 'Mill on Government', printed as an Appendix to *John Stuart Mill on Politics and Society*, ed. Geraint L. Williams (Fontana/Collins, 1976). See pp. 388—92. Further page references are to this edition.

4. James Mill: *An Essay on Government*, ed. Currin V. Shields (Liberal Arts Press, 1955) pp. 89, 90.

5. Speech on 'The People's Charter', 3 May 1842, in *The Life and Works of Lord Macaulay*, Vol. VIII (Longmans, 1908) pp. 221, 224.

6. For his views on Burke and Paine, see Joseph Hamburger: *Macaulay and the Whig Tradition* (University of Chicago Press, 1976) pp. 183, 36, 155.

7. Speech of 2 March 1831, quoted in Bullock and Shock: *The Liberal Tradition*, pp. 21, 23.

8. Quoted in Hamburger: *Macaulay*, p. 84.

9. *Life and Works*, VIII, pp. 426, 417. And see Hamburger: *Macaulay*, pp. 134—5.

10. For Acton, see *Lectures on Modern History*, p. 220. For Arnold and Morley, see Hamburger: *Macaulay*, pp. 174—5.

11. See House: *All in Due Time*, pp. 96—7.

12. 'Milton' in *Life and Works*, Vol. V (Longmans, 1903) pp. 4—5.

13. A. J. P. Taylor: '1848', in *Europe: Grandeur and Decline* (Penguin, 1967) p. 28, and see pp. 28—58 throughout.

14. Quoted in Raymond Williams: *Culture and Society*, p. 102.

15. Isaiah Berlin: 'Alexander Herzen', in *Russian Thinkers* (The Hogarth Press, 1978) pp. 207, 194, 201, 200.

16. Isaiah Berlin: *Against the Current* (The Hogarth Press, 1979) pp. 193, 210.

17. Alexander Herzen: *Childhood, Youth and Exile* (Oxford University Press, 1980) p. 24.

18. Alexander Herzen: *From the Other Shore*, (Oxford University Press, 1979) pp. 133, 36—7.

19. Herzen: *Selected Philosophical Works* (Foreign Languages Publishing House, 1956) pp. 578, 549.

20. Herzen: *From the Other Shore*, pp. 68, 59—60.

21. Ibid., p. 63, and Herzen: *Selected Philosophical Works*, p. 549.

22. Herzen: *From the Other Shore*, pp. 93, 3.

23. Ibid., p. 151.

24. Taylor: 'De Tocqueville in 1848', in *Europe: Grandeur and Decline*, p. 44.
25. Tocqueville: *The Ancien Regime*, pp. 142—3.
26. Hugh Brogan: *Tocqueville* (Collins/Fontana, 1973) p. 30.
27. Tocqueville: *Democracy in America*, ed. Henry Steele Commager (Oxford University Press, 1946) p. 6.
28. Tocqueville: *The Ancien Regime*, p. 30.
29. Tocqueville: *Democracy in America*, p. 580, and see also pp. 192—4.
30. See Brogan: *Tocqueville*, p. 68.
31. As Brogan does: *Tocqueville*, p. 21.
32. Giuseppe di Lampedusa: *The Leopard* (Collins/Fontana, 1963) p. 29.
33. See Bradley: *The Optimists*, pp. 155, 151, 158.
34. George Eliot: *Felix Holt, The Radical* (Penguin, 1972) p. 401. Further page references are to this edition.
35. George Eliot: *Daniel Deronda* (Penguin, 1967) pp. 412—3.
36. Matthew Arnold: *Culture and Anarchy*, ed. J. Dover Wilson (Cambridge University Press, 1932) p. 41. Further page references are to this edition.
37. 'Democracy' in *The Portable Matthew Arnold*, ed. Lionel Trilling (Viking, 1949) pp. 454, 465. Arnold invokes Burke in his own support.
38. 'The Function of Criticism at the Present Time', in Trilling, ed.: *The Portable Matthew Arnold*, p. 244.
39. Ibid., pp. 442—3.
40. See Trilling: *The Opposing Self*, p. 53.
41. Berlin: *Four Essays*, pp. 173—4.
42. 'The Spirit of the Age' quoted in Williams (ed.) *John Stuart Mill*, pp. 174—5.
43. Quoted in Duncan: *Marx and Mill*, footnote p. 356.
44. See Mill: *Autobiography*, p. 115, and Williams (ed.) *John Stuart Mill*, pp. 187, 213.
45. Williams (ed.) *John Stuart Mill*, p. 242.
46. See John M. Robson: *The Improvement of Mankind* (University of Toronto Press, 1968) pp. 183—4.
47. See *Essays on Politics and Culture* by John Stuart Mill, ed. Gertrude Himmelfarb (Anchor/Doubleday, 1962) p. 63.
48. Leavis, ed: *Mill on Bentham*, p. 88.
49. Mill: *Autobiography*, p. 138.
50. Himmelfarb (ed.) *Essays*, pp. 209—10; and Leavis, ed: *Mill on Bentham*, p. 148.
51. Quoted in J. H. Burns: 'J. S. Mill and Democracy, 1829—61', in *Mill* (ed.) J. B. Schneewind (Macmillan, 1969) p. 315. An invaluable article.
52. Williams, (ed.) *John Stuart Mill*, p. 182.
53. Mill: *Autobiography*, p. 184.
54. Himmelfarb, (ed.) *Essays*, p. 315.
55. Mill: *Representative Government*, in *Utilitarianism*, p. 288.
56. Mill: *Autobiography*, p. 153.
57. See Himmelfarb (ed.) *Essays*, p. 294; and Burns in Schneewind, ed: *Mill*, p. 142.
58. Berlin: *Four Essays*, p. 182.

59. Mill: *Principles of Political Economy* (Penguin edn) p. 142.
60. Quoted in Pedro Schwarz: *The New Political Economy of J. S. Mill* (Weidenfeld & Nicolson, 1972) p. 162.
61. Mill: *Principles*, p. 159.
62. Ibid., p. 113.
63. See, for example, Williams (ed.) *John Stuart Mill*, p. 328.
64. See Schwarz: *Political Economy*, p. 136, Williams (ed.) *John Stuart Mill*, p. 285; and *Autobiography*, pp. 116, 141.
65. See Williams (ed.) *John Stuart Mill*, pp. 287, 291.
66. See Mill: *Principles*, pp. 353—67.
67. Quoted in John Roach: 'Liberalism and the Victorian intelligentsia', *Cambridge Historical Journal*, 1957, p. 60.
68. Quoted in Bradley: *The Optimists*, p. 228.
69. See Bullock and Shock (eds) *The Liberal Tradition*, pp. 122, 119—120.
70. Ibid., pp. 125, 123.

CHAPTER 16: A 'NEW' LIBERALISM?

1. Quotations from H. C. G. Matthew: *The Liberal Imperialists* (Oxford University Press, 1973) pp. vii, 139.
2. Quoted in Bradley: *The Optimists*, p. 213.
3. L. T. Hobhouse: *Liberalism* (1911, Oxford University Press, 1964) p. 110.
4. Quoted in J. L. Hammond and M. R. D. Foot: *Gladstone and Liberalism* (English Universities Press, 1952) p. 97.
5. Quoted in Melvin Richter: *The Politics of Conscience: T. H. Green and His Age* (Weidenfeld & Nicolson, 1964) p. 210.
6. T. H. Green: *Lectures on the Principles of Political Obligation* (Longmans, 1924) pp. 67, 48.
7. 'Liberal Legislation and Freedom of Contract' in *Collected Works of Thomas Hill Green*, ed. R. L. Nettleship, Vol. III (Longmans, 1888) pp. 371, 386.
8. Ibid., pp. 368, 370—72.
9. Ibid., pp. 375—6, 367, and see Richter: *The Politics of Conscience*, p. 337.
10. See Richter: *The Politics of Conscience*, pp. 289—90.
11. Quoted in David Nicholls: 'Positive liberty 1880—1914', *American Political Science Review*, 1962, pp. 122, 124.
12. Samuel quoted in Richter: *The Politics of Conscience*, p. 340; L. T. Hobhouse: *The Elements of Social Justice* (Allen & Unwin, 1922) p. 83.
13. See Edward David: 'The New Liberalism of C. F. G. Masterman, 1973—1927', in Kenneth D. Brown (ed.) *Essays in Anti-Labour History* (Macmillan, 1974) p. 37.
14. See Michael Freeden: *The New Liberalism* (Clarendon Press, 1978) pp. 255, 1; and Peter Clarke: *Lancashire and the New Liberalism* (Cambridge University Press, 1971) pp. 6, 223, 274—5, 406—7.
15. Quoted in Alan Watkins: *The Liberal Dilemma* (MacGibbon & Kee, 1966) p. 53. For the persisting importance of the free trade issue in the Liberal Party, see

Trevor Wilson: *The Downfall of the Liberal Party 1914—1935* (Collins, 1966) pp. 358—76.

16. Herbert Spencer: *The Man versus the State* (1884), ed. Donald MacRae (Penguin, 1969) pp. 81, 63.

17. See ibid., pp. 169—74, 139—41, 93.

18. L. T. Hobhouse: *Democracy and Reaction* (T. Fisher Unwin, 1909) pp. 86—7, and see p. 103.

19. Hobson and Beveridge quoted in Freeden: *The New Liberalism*, pp. 178, 184—5, and see also pp. 23, 35, 257.

20. See Stefan Collini: *Liberalism and Sociology, L. T. Hobhouse and Political Argument in England* (Cambridge University Press, 1979) pp. 54, 149; and Hobhouse: *Liberalism*, p. 62.

21. Ross McKibbin: *The Evolution of the Labour Party 1910—1924* (Oxford, 1974) p. 244; and see Michael Barker: *Gladstone and Radicalism* (Harvester, 1975) pp. 128—38.

22. Hobhouse: *Democracy and Reaction*, pp. 231, 238; and letter to C. P. Scott of 7 Nov. 1924, quoted in Peter Clarke: *Liberals and Social Democrats* (Cambridge University Press, 1978) p. 237.

23. Ibid., p. 239; and letter of 15 Nov. 1924, quoted in Clarke, *Liberals and Social Demands*, p. 237.

24. Keynes: *Essays in Persuasion*, pp. vii, 325—6, 322.

25. Keynes: *The General Theory*, pp. 379—380.

26. Keynes: *Essays in Persuasion*, pp. 329, 267.

27. Ibid., pp. 258, 297, 309—310, 300.

28. Ibid., pp. 298, 305.

29. See Hugh Thomas: *John Strachey* (Eyre Methuen, 1973) p. 101.

30. John Strachey: *The Strangled Cry* (Bodley Head, 1962) pp. 213—14.

31. See John Strachey: *Contemporary Capitalism* (Gollancz, 1956) p. 253; and R. H. S. Crossman: *The Charm of Politics* (Hamish Hamilton, 1958) pp. 142—3.

32. Keynes and Martin quoted in Clarke: *Liberals and Social Democrats*, pp. 274, 253.

CHAPTER 17: TWENTIETH-CENTURY LIBERALISM:
THE MOOD OF WITHDRAWAL

1. Russell: *Unpopular Essays*, p. 22.

2. E. M. Forster: 'What I Believe', in *Two Cheers for Democracy*, p. 75.

3. Russell: *Unpopular Essays*, pp. 21 and 23.

4. Berlin: *Four Essays*, p. 39.

5. Quoted in Lionel Trilling: *E. M. Forster* (The Hogarth Press, 1944) p. 148.

6. Forster: 'What I Believe', *Two Cheers*, p. 70.

7. Woolf: *The Journey*, p. 10.

8. Forster: 'What I Believe', *Two Cheers*, p. 55.

9. E. M. Forster: *Howards End* (1910), Penguin edn 1941, pp. 27, 121.

10. Forster: *Two Cheers*, p. 64.

11. George Eliot: *Felix Holt*, p. 129.

12. 'The Novels of E. M. Forster', in Virginia Woolf: *Collected Essays*, Vol. I (The Hogarth Press, 1966) p. 345.

13. G. E. Moore: *Principia Ethica* (Cambridge University Press, 1903) 1959 edn, p. 188.

14. Keynes: *Essays in Biography*, pp. 436, 445.
15. Leonard Woolf: *Beginning Again* (The Hogarth Press, 1964) p. 25; and *Sowing* (The Hogarth Press, 1960) p. 86.
16. Woolf: *The Journey*, pp. 18—19.
17. See Trevor-Roper: *Historical Essays*, pp. 35—60, especially pp. 59—60.
18. Keynes: *Essays in Biography*, p. 437.
19. Forster: *Howards End* p. 44.
20. Forster: *Two Cheers* pp. 65—6; and *Howards End* p. 58.
21. Patricia Stubbs: *Women and Fiction: Feminism and the Novel 1880—1920* (Harvester, 1979) p. 210. And see her illuminating analysis of *Howards End*.
22. Rex Warner: *The Professor* (1938, Penguin edn 1945) p. 115. Further page references are to this edition, now unfortunately out of print.
23. Angus Wilson: *The Wild Garden* (Secker & Warburg, 1963) pp. 30—1.
24. Angus Wilson: *Hemlock and After* (Secker & Warburg, 1952) Panther edn, 1979, p. 153. Further page references are to this edition.
25. C. B. Cox: *The Free Spirit* (Oxford University Press, 1963) pp. 133—4.
26. Lionel Trilling: *The Liberal Imagination*, pp. 219, 221.
27. Lionel Trilling: *The Middle of the Journey* (1947) Penguin edn 1977, p. 224. Further page references are to this edition.

CHAPTER 18: COLD WAR LIBERALISM

1. 'Palinurus' (Cyril Connolly) *The Unquiet Grave*, p. 36.
2. Cyril Connolly: *The Condemned Playground* (Routledge & Kegan Paul, 1945) pp. 258—9.
3. *Times Literary Supplement*, 9 Oct. 1953. And see the reviews by A. J. P. Taylor in *The Listener*, 8 Oct. and Philip Toynbee in the *Observer*, 4 Oct. 1953.
4. O'Brien: *Writers and Politics*, pp. 169—73.
5. At least one observer, H. R. Trevor-Roper, noticed this from the start. See Christopher Lasch: 'The Cultural Cold War', in *The Agony of the American Left* (Knopf, 1969) pp. 63—9.
6. Daniel Bell: *The End of Ideology* (Free Press/Macmillan, 1960) 1965 edn, p. 295.
7. See Lasch: 'The Cultural Cold War', *The Agony of the American Left*, pp. 108, 103.
8. See ibid., footnote p. 77.
9. Quoted in Michael Howard: *War and the Liberal Conscience* (1978) Oxford University Press edn 1981, p. 122.
10. Bell: *The End of Ideology*, p. 296.
11. See Garry Wills's 'Commentary' in Lillian Hellman: *Scoundrel Time* (Macmillan, 1976) Quartet edn 1978, pp. 165—6.
12. See Stevenson: *Speeches*, p. 184.
13. Bell: *The End of Ideology* p. 123; Kristol in *Partisan Review*, July—Aug. 1952; and Lasch: 'The Cultural Cold War', pp. 82—3.
14. Quoted in ibid., p. 83.
15. O'Brien: *Writers and Politics*, p. 165; and see David Caute: *The Great Fear* (Secker & Warburg, 1978) pp. 405, 413.

16. Leslie Fiedler: *An End to Innocence* (Beacon Press, 1955) pp. 68, 56. This and some of the other more extreme passages were not included in the *Encounter* version.

17. David Caute: *The Fellow Travellers* (Weidenfeld & Nicolson, 1973) p. 311.

18. Fiedler: *An End to Innocence*, p. 72; and for Kristol, see Lasch: 'The Cultural Cold War', p. 88 footnote.

19. Articles in *Partisan Review*, Jan.—Feb. 1953; and *The New Leader*, 25 Aug. 1952.

20. Caute: *The Great Fear*, pp. 275, 406, 364, 353, 359.

21. Ibid., p. 115.

22. See ibid., p. 60; and for Trilling's view see *The Middle of the Journey*, pp. xx, xxiii.

23. Quoted in Lasch: 'The Cultural Cold War', p. 85.

24. In *Partisan Review*, Sept.—Oct. 1952.

25. See Friedrich's contribution to *Totalitarianism*, ed. Carl J. Friedrich (Harvard University Press, 1954) pp. 52—3.

26. Leonard Schapiro: *Totalitarianism* (Macmillan, 1972) p. 18. And see Raymond Aron: *Democracy and Totalitarianism* (Weidenfeld & Nicolson, 1968) pp. 193—4.

27. Schapiro: *Totalitarianism*, pp. 18, 95.

28. Barrington Moore Jr: *Political Power and Social Theory* (Harvard University Press, 1958) p. 31.

29. See T. W. Mason: 'Labour in the Third Reich 1933—1939' *Past & Present*, 33, 1966; and 'The Workers' Opposition in Nazi Germany', *History Workshop*, 11, 1981.

30. See H. R. Trevor-Roper: *The Last Days of Hitler* (1947) Pan edn 1962, pp. 53—4, and see ch. 1 throughout.

31. See Hannah Arendt: *The Origins of Totalitarianism* (1951, Revised edn Allen & Unwin, 1967) pp. 395, 409.

32. Ibid., p. 458.

33. J. L. Talmon: *Utopianism and Politics* (Conservative Political Centre, 1957) p. 21.

34. Popper: *The Open Society*, Vol. I, p. 159; and Bryan Magee: *Popper* (Fontana/Collins, 1973) p. 90.

35. Introduction to Herzen: *From the Other Shore*, p. xviii.

36. Albert Camus: *The Rebel* (Hamish Hamilton, 1953) p. 175.

37. Berlin: *Russian Thinkers*, p. 217.

38. Norman Cohn: *The Pursuit of the Millenium* (Secker & Warburg, 1957) pp. v, vii.

39. Popper: *Open Society*, Vol. I, p. 163; and *Poverty of Historicism*, pp. 68—9.

40. Berlin: *Russian Thinkers*, p. 193; and *Four Essays*, p. lv.

41. Popper: *Poverty of Historicism*, p. 5; and Popper: *Conjectures and Refutations* (Routledge & Kegan Paul, 1968) 1972 edn, p. 344.

42. Popper: *Open Society*, Vol. 2, p. 101.

43. 'The Eighteenth Brumaire', in *Surveys from Exile*, p. 146; and 'Letter to Mikhailovsky', in *Karl Marx: Selected Writings*, ed. David McLellan (Oxford University Press, 1977) pp. 571—2.

44. E. H. Carr: *The New Society*, p. 16.

45. Edward Shils: 'Ideology', in the *Encyclopaedia of the Social Sciences* (Free Press/Macmillan, 1968) pp. 66, 74.

46. Arendt: *The Origins of Totalitarianism*, p. 471.

47. Bell: *The End of Ideology*, pp. 405, 400.

48. Irving Kristol: 'Teaching in, speaking out', *Encounter*, Aug. 1965.

49. Edward Shils: 'The end of ideology, *Encounter*, Nov. 1955.

50. Bell: *The End of Ideology*, p. 16.

51. Ibid., pp. 393, 402—3.

52. S. M. Lipset: *Political Man* (Heinemann, 1960) p. 406.

53. See the Preface to Raymond Aron: *The Opium of the Intellectuals* (Secker & Warburg, 1957) p. xviii.

54. Sir Lewis Namier: 'Human nature in politics', *The Listener*, 24 Dec. 1953.

55. Talmon: *Origins of Totalitarian Democracy*, p. 4.

56. Arthur Schlesinger Jr: 'On Heroic Leadership', in *The Politics of Hope* (Eyre and Spottiswoode, 1964) p. 21.

57. Lipset: *Political Man*, p. 45.

58. Schlesinger: 'On Heroic Leadership', p. 4; and Dahl quoted in Graeme Duncan and Steven Lukes: 'The New Democracy', *Political Studies*, 2, 1963, p. 163.

59. Joseph Schumpeter: *Capitalism, Socialism and Democracy*, quoted in ibid., p. 167.

60. Jack L. Walker: 'A Critique of the Elitist Theory of Democracy', in *Apolitical Politics*, ed. Charles A. McCoy and John Playford (Thomas Y. Crowell, 1967) p. 201. This useful collection also contains the article by Duncan and Lukes.

61. Quoted in W. G. Runciman: *Social Science and Political Theory* (Cambridge University Press, 1963) p. 75.

62. Quoted in M. I. Finley: *Democracy Ancient and Modern* (Chatto & Windus, 1973) p. 12.

63. See the article by W. H. Morris Jones referred to in ch. 4, note 24.; also Lipset: *Political Man*, p. 32.

64. Crick: *In Defence of Politics*, p. 60.

65. Robert McKenzie: 'Politics of pressure', *Observer*, 14 May 1961.

66. John Plamenatz: 'Electoral studies and democratic theory', *Political Studies*, 1958, p. 9.

67. Robert A. Dahl: *A Preface to Democratic Theory* (University of Chicago Press, 1956) pp. 137, 138, 145.

68. Lipset: *Political Man*, p. 403.

69. Mill: *Representative Government*, p. 217.

70. For example Wolff's critique of pluralism in *The Poverty of Liberalism*; Ralph Miliband: *The State in Capitalist Society* (Weidenfeld & Nicolson, 1968) ch. 6; and the essays reprinted in *Apolitical Politics* (see note 60).

CHAPTER 19: LIBERALISM TODAY

1. John Rawls: *A Theory of Justice* (1971, Clarendon Press, 1972) Further page references are to this edition.

2. Robert Paul Wolff: *Understanding Rawls* (Princeton University Press, 1977) p. 208.

3. Samuel Brittan: *The Economic Consequences of Democracy* (Temple Smith, 1977) p. 271.

4. F. A. Hayek: *New Studies in Philosophy, Politics, Economics and the History of Ideas* (Routledge & Kegan Paul, 1978) p. 109, and footnote p. 77.

5. Brian Barry: *The Liberal Theory of Justice* (Clarendon Press, 1973) p. 32.

6. Ibid., p. 50.

7. Ronald Dworkin: 'Liberalism' in Stuart Hampshire (ed.) *Public and Private Morality* (Cambridge University Press, 1978) p. 122. Further page references are to this essay.

8. See Vinit Haksar: *Equality, Liberty, and Perfectionism* (Oxford University Press, 1979) pp. 162, 186.

9. Robert Nozick: *Anarchy, State, and Utopia* (Basil Blackwell, 1974) p. 230.

10. Peter Singer: 'The Right to be Rich or Poor', in *Reading Nozick*, ed. Jeffrey Paul (Basil Blackwell, 1982) p. 50, and see pp. 50—3.

11. See Barry, *The Liberal Theory of Justice*, pp. 110—11.

12. 'The Faith of a Whig' by G. L. Arnold (a pseudonym of Lichtheim's) *The Twentieth Century*, Aug. 1960.

13. See F. A. Hayek: *New Studies*, p. 209.

14. See Brittan: *Capitalism and the Permissive Society* (Maurice Temple Smith, 1977).

15. Milton Friedman: *Capitalism and Freedom* (University of Chicago Press, 1962) p. 9. Further page references are to this edition.

16. Quoted in Orlando Letelier: *Chile: Economic 'Freedom' and Political Repression* (Race & Class, 1976) p. 6. Letelier was himself murdered, in Washington DC, by agents of the Chilean junta.

17. F. A. Hayek: *New Studies*, p. 143.

18. Samuel Brittan: 'Can Democracy Manage an Economy?', in *The End of the Keynesian Era*, ed. Robert Skidelsky, (Macmillan, 1977) p. 49.

19. Milton and Rose Friedman: *Free to Choose* (Penguin, 1980) pp. 15—16.

20. Ibid., p. 145.

21. Nick Bosanquet: *After the New Right* (Heinemann, 1983) p. 116.

22. M. and R. Friedman: *Free to Choose*, p. 21.

23. F. A. Hayek: *New Studies*, pp. 57—8.

24. Jo Grimond's lecture was published by the Association of Liberal Lawyers. Ian Bradley's *Radical Rebirth?* was published by Holystone Publications, 1981.

25. Ralf Dahrendorf: *After Social Democracy* (Liberal Publications Dept, 1980).

26. Ralf Dahrendorf: *Life Chances* (Weidenfeld & Nicolson, 1979) p. ix.

27. John Dunn: *Western Political Theory in the Face of the Future* (Cambridge University Press, 1979) p. 28.

28. Karl Marx: *Early Writings*, translated Rodney Livingstone and Gregor Benton (Penguin, 1975) pp. 221, 230.

APPENDIX

1. Quoted in Shirley Robin Letwin: *The Pursuit of Certainty* (Cambridge University Press, 1965) p. 182.

2. Hazlitt: *The Spirit of the Age*, p. 18.

3. See Charles W. Everett: *Jeremy Bentham* (Weidenfeld & Nicolson, 1969) p. 58.

4. Leavis, ed.: *Mill on Bentham and Coleridge*, pp. 49—50.

5. Mill: *Utilitarianism* ch. 4, in *Utilitarianism, Liberty, and Representative Government* (Dent, 1910) p. 32.

6. Gunnar Myrdal: *The Political Element in the Development of Economic Theory* (Routledge

& Kegan Paul, 1953) p. 15. And see ch. 4 throughout. See also the passages from Marshall and Edgworth quoted by Joan Robinson in *Economic Philosophy*, pp. 48—9, 65—6.

7. Quoted in Sheldon S. Wolin: *Politics and Vision* (Allen & Unwin, 1962) p. 342. The whole passage quoted by Wolin is very illuminating.

8. See Everett: *Jeremy Bentham* pp. 248—9; and Letwin: *The Pursuit of Certainty*, p. 145.

9. See, for example, Isaiah Berlin's description of Mill as 'a disciple who quietly left the fold', etc. in *Four Essays*, p. 176.

Select Bibliography

I have not included in the Bibliography all the works referred to in the text. Many of them are works of general history, others works of literature or criticism which bear only indirectly on liberalism. Nor have I listed the 'classics' of liberal writing, some of which are discussed in the book. My intention has been to provide a Bibliography to further the interest of the reader in liberalism, and thus I have included some works not specifically referred to in the text.

1 *General*

Hobhouse, L. T., *Liberalism*, Oxford University Press, 1911.
Laski, Harold J., *The Rise of European Liberalism*, Allen & Unwin, 1936.
Manning, D. J., *Liberalism*, Dent, 1976.
Minogue, K. R., *The Liberal Mind*, Methuen, 1963.
Ruggiero, Guido de, *The History of European Liberalism*, Oxford University Press, 1927.

2 *Anthologies*

Bramsted, E. K. and Melhuish, K. J. (eds) *Western Liberalism*, Longman, 1978.
Bullock Alan, and Shock, Maurice (eds) *The Liberal Tradition: From Fox to Keynes*, Adam & Charles Black, 1956.
Schapiro, J. Salwyn, (ed.) *Liberalism: Its Meaning and History*, van Nostrand, 1958.
Simon, W. M., (ed.) *French Liberalism 1789—1848*, John Wiley & Sons, 1972.

3 *Philosophy*

Hampshire, Stuart, *Freedom of the Individual*, Chatto & Windus, 1965.
Lukes, Steven, *Individualism*, Basil Blackwell, 1973.
MacIntyre, Alasdair, *A Short History of Ethics*, Routledge & Kegan Paul, 1967.
Murdoch, Iris, *The Sovereignty of God*, Routledge & Kegan Paul, 1970.

4 *The Early Modern Period*

Acton, Lord, *Lectures on Modern History*, Macmillan, 1906.
Anderson, Perry, *Lineages of the Absolutist State*, New Left Books, 1974.

Aylmer, G. E., (ed.) *The Levellers in the English Revolution*, Thames and Hudson, 1975.

Butterfield, Herbert, *The Origins of Modern Science*, G. Bell and Sons, 1949.
The Whig Interpretation of History, G. Bell and Sons, 1931.

Cassirer, Ernst (ed.) *The Renaissance Philosophy of Man*, University of Chicago Press, 1948.

Feuer, Lewis Samuel, *Spinoza and the Rise of Liberalism*, Beacon Press, 1958.

Fink, Zera S., *The Classical Republicans*, Northwestern University Press, 1945.

Gooch, G. P., *English Democratic Ideas in the Seventeenth Century*, Cambridge University Press, 1927.

Hall, Marie Boas (ed.) *Nature and Nature's Laws*, Macmillan, 1970.

Hill, Christopher, *Change and Continuity in Seventeenth-century England*, Weidenfeld & Nicolson, 1974.
Intellectual Origins of the English Revolution, Oxford University Press, 1965.
Puritanism and Revolution, Secker & Warburg, 1958.
The World Turned Upside Down, Maurice Temple Smith, 1972.

Kamen, Henry, *The Rise of Toleration*, Weidenfeld & Nicolson, 1967.

Kossmann, E. H. and Mellink, A. F. (eds) *Texts Concerning the Revolt of the Netherlands*, Cambridge University Press, 1974.

Lukacs, Georg, *History and Class Consciousness*, Merlin Press, 1971.

Macfarlane, Alan, *The Origins of English Individualism*, Basil Blackwell, 1978.

Macpherson, C. B., *The Political Theory of Possessive Individualism*, Clarendon Press, 1962.

Martines, Lauro, *The Social World of Florentine Humanism 1390—1460*, Routledge & Kegan Paul, 1963.

Morris, Colin, *The Discovery of the Individual, 1050—1200*, SPCK, 1972.

Morton, A. L. (ed.) *Freedom in Arms*, Lawrence and Wishart, 1975.

Tawney, R. H., *Religion and the Rise of Capitalism*, John Murray, 1926.

Trevor-Roper, H. R., *Historical Essays*, Macmillan, 1957.
Religion, the Reformation and Social Change, Macmillan, 1967.

Watt, Ian, *The Rise of the Novel*, Chatto & Windus, 1957.

Webster, Charles (ed.) *The Intellectual Revolution of the Seventeenth Century*, Routledge & Kegan Paul, 1974.

Wittkower, Rudolf, *Architectural Principles in the Age of Humanism*, Alec Tiranti, 1971.

5 *The Eighteenth Century*

Brailsford, H. N., *Voltaire*, Oxford University Press, 1935.

Cobban, Alfred, *In Search of Humanity*, Jonathan Cape, 1960.

Dickinson, H. T., *Liberty and Property*, Methuen, 1977.

Gay, Peter, *Voltaire's Politics*, Princeton University Press, 1959.

Hay, Douglas, et al., *Albion's Fatal Tree*, Allen Lane, 1975.

Kenyon, J. P., *Revolution Principles*, Cambridge University Press, 1977.

Lively, Jack (ed.) *The Enlightenment*, Longman, 1966.

Martin, Kingsley, *French Liberal Thought in the Eighteenth Century*, Ernest Benn, 1929.

Pangle, Thomas L., *Montesquieu's Philosophy of Liberalism*, Chicago University Press, 1973.

Plumb, J. H., *The Growth of Political Stability in England 1675—1725*, Macmillan, 1967.

Pollard, Sidney, *The Idea of Progress*, C. A. Watts, 1968.

Prebble, John, *The Highland Clearances*, Secker & Warburg, 1963.

Strugnell, Anthony, *Diderot's Politics*, Martinus Nijhoff, 1973.

Tate, W. E., *The English Village Community and the Enclosure Movement*, Gollancz, 1967.

Thompson, E. P., *Whigs and Hunters*, Allen Lane, 1975.

Venturi, Franco, *Utopia and Reform in the Enlightenment*, Cambridge University Press, 1971.

6   The American Revolution

Bailyn, Bernard, *The Ideological Origins of the American Revolution*, Harvard University Press, 1967.

Douglass, Elisha, P., *Rebels and Democrats*, University of North Carolina Press, 1955.

Hofstadter, Richard, *The American Political Tradition*, Jonathan Cape, 1962.

Lynd, Staughton, *Intellectual Origins of American Radicalism*, Faber, 1969.

Parrington, V. L., *Main Currents in American Thought*, Harcourt Brace, 1927.

Young, Alfred D. (ed.) *The American Revolution*, Northern Illinois Press, 1976.

7   The French Revolution

Cobban, Alfred, *Aspects of the French Revolution*, Jonathan Cape 1968.
The Social Interpretation of the French Revolution, Cambridge University Press, 1964.

Foner, Eric, *Tom Paine and Revolutionary America*, Oxford University Press, 1977.

Friedlaender, Walter, *David to Delacroix*, Harvard University Press, 1952.

Hobsbawm, E. J., *The Age of Revolution*, Weidenfeld & Nicolson, 1962.

James, C. L. R., *The Black Jacobins*, 1938, Allison & Busby, 1980.

Mitchell, L. G., *Charles James Fox and the Disintegration of the Whig Party, 1782—1794*, Oxford University Press, 1971.

Nicholson, Irene, *The Liberators*, Faber, 1969.

O'Gorman, Frank, *The Whig Party and the French Revolution*, Macmillan, 1967.

Williams, Gwyn A., *Goya and the Impossible Revolution*, Allen Lane, 1976.

8   *Liberal Political Economy*

Black, R. D. Collison, *Economic Thought and the Irish Question, 1817—1870*, Cambridge University Press, 1960.

Blaug, Mark, *Economic Theory in Retrospect*, Heinemann, 1964.

Ricardian Economics, Yale University Press, 1958.

Coats, A. W. (ed.) *The Classical Economists and Economic Policy*, Methuen, 1971.

Colletti, Lucio, *From Rousseau to Lenin*, New Left Books, 1972.

Cowherd, Raymond G., *Political Economists and the English Poor Laws*, Ohio University Press, 1977.

Cropsey, Joseph, *Polity and Economy: An Interpretation of the Principles of Adam Smith*, Martinus Nijhoff, 1957.

Heilbroner, Robert L., *The Worldly Philosophers*, Allen Lane, 1969.

Myrdal, Gunnar, *The Political Element in the Development of Economic Theory*, Routledge & Kegan Paul, 1953.

Robbins, Lord, *The Theory of Economic Policy in English Classical Political Economy*, Macmillan, 1952.

Robinson, Joan, *Economic Philosophy*, C. A. Watts, 1962.

Roll, Eric, *A History of Economic Thought*, Faber, 1938.

Taylor, Arthur J., Laissez-faire *and State Intervention in Nineteenth-Century Britain*, Macmillan 1972.

Winch, Donald, *Adam Smith's Politics*, Cambridge University Press, 1978.

9   *The Nineteenth Century*

Barker, Michael, *Gladstone and Radicalism*, Harvester Press, 1975.

Bradley, Ian, *The Optimists*, Faber, 1980.

Briggs, Asa, *Victorian People*, Odhams, 1954.

Victorian Cities, Odhams, 1963.

Clarke, Peter, *Lancashire and the New Liberalism*, Cambridge University Press, 1971.

Liberals and Social Democrats, Cambridge University Press, 1978.

Collini, Stefan, *Liberalism and Sociology, L. T. Hobhouse and Political Argument in England*, Cambridge University Press, 1979.

Dangerfield, George, *The Strange Death of Liberal England*, 1935, Macgibbon & Kee, 1966.

Hamburger, Joseph, *Macaulay and the Whig Tradition*, University of Chicago Press, 1976.

Hammond, J. L. and Foot, M. R. D., *Gladstone and Liberalism*, English Universities Press, 1952.

House, Humphrey, *All in Due Time*, Hart-Davis, 1955.

Howard, Michael, *War and the Liberal Conscience*, Temple Smith, 1978.

Matthew, H. C. G., *The Liberal Imperialists*, Oxford University Press, 1973.

Richter, Melvin, *The Politics of Conscience: T. H. Green and his Age*, Weidenfeld and Nicolson, 1964.

Taylor, A.J. P., *Europe: Grandeur and Decline*, Penguin 1967.

Essays in English History, Penguin, 1976.

The Trouble Makers, Hamish Hamilton, 1957.

Vincent, John, *The Formation of the Liberal Party 1857—1868*, Constable, 1966.

Watson, George, *The English Ideology*, Allen Lane, 1973.

Williams, Raymond, *Culture and Society, 1780—1950*, Chatto & Windus, 1959.

Woodham-Smith, Cecil, *The Great Hunger*, Hamish Hamilton, 1962.

Young, G. M., *Victorian Essays*, Oxford University Press, 1962.

10 Twentieth-Century Liberalism

Arendt, Hannah, *The Origins of Totalitarianism*, Allen & Unwin, 1951.

Aron, Raymond, *The Opium of the Intellectuals*, Secker & Warburg, 1957.

Bell, Daniel, *The End of Ideology*, Free Press/Macmillan, 1960.

Berlin, Isaiah, *Against the Current*, Hogarth Press, 1979.

Four Essays on Liberty, Oxford University Press, 1969.

Russian Thinkers, Hogarth Press, 1978.

Camus, Albert, *The Rebel*, Hamish Hamilton, 1953.

Caute, David, *The Great Fear*, Secker & Warburg, 1978.

Connolly, Cyril, *The Unquiet Grave*, Hamish Hamilton, 1945.

Cranston, Maurice, *Freedom: A New Analysis*, Longman, Green, 1953.

Crick, Bernard, *In Defence of Politics*, Weidenfeld & Nicolson, 1962.

Dahrendorf, Ralf, *Life Chances*, Weidenfeld & Nicolson, 1979.

Fiedler, Leslie, *An End to Innocence*, Beacon Press, 1955.

Forster, E. M., *Two Cheers for Democracy*, Edward Arnold, 1951.

Freud, Sigmund, *Civilisation and its Discontents*, Hogarth Press, 1930.

Keynes, J. M., *Essays in Biography*, Collected Writings, Vol. X, Macmillan, 1972.

Essays in Persuasion, Collected Writings, Vol. XI, Macmillan, 1972.

Lipset, S. M., *Political Man*, Heinemann, 1960.

Magee, Bryan, *Popper*, Fontana/Collins, 1973.

Popper, Karl, *Conjectures and Refutations*, Routledge & Kegan Paul, 1968.

The Open Society and its Enemies, Routledge & Kegan Paul, 1945.

The Poverty of Historicism, Routledge & Kegan Paul, 1957.

Rawls, John, *A Theory of Justice*, Clarendon Press, 1972.

Russell, Bertrand, *Unpopular Essays*, Allen & Unwin, 1950.

Schlesinger, Arthur, Jnr, *The Politics of Hope*, Eyre and Spottiswoode, 1964.

Stevenson, Adlai, *Speeches*, André Deutsch, 1952.

Talmon, J. L., *The Origins of Totalitarian Democracy*, Secker & Warburg, 1952.

Trilling, Lionel, *The Middle of the Journey*, Secker & Warburg, 1948.

Warner, Rex, *The Professor*, 1938, Penguin, 1945.

Weldon, T. D., *The Vocabulary of Politics*, Penguin, 1953.

Wilson, Angus, *Hemlock and After*, Secker & Warburg, 1952.

Woolf, Leonard, *The Journey not the Arrival Matters*, The Hogarth Press, 1973.

11   *The Revival of Liberal Economics*

Bosanquet, Nick, *After the New Right*, Heinemann, 1983.

Brittan, Samuel, *The Economic Consequences of Democracy*, Temple Smith, 1977.

Friedman, Milton, *Capitalism and Freedom*, University of Chicago Press, 1962.

Friedman, Milton; and Rose, *Free to Choose*, Penguin, 1980.

Hayek, F. A., *New Studies in Philosophy, Politics, Economics and the History of Ideas*, Routledge & Kegan Paul, 1978.

Hayek, F. A., *Studies in Philosophy, Politics and Economics*, Routledge & Kegan Paul, 1967.

Nozick, Robert, *Anarchy, State, and Utopia*, Basil Blackwell, 1974.

12   *Criticism*

Barry, Brian, *The Liberal Theory of Justice*, Clarendon Press, 1973.

Carr, E. H., *The New Society*, Macmillan, 1951.

   What is History?, Macmillan, 1961.

Cox, C. B., *The Free Spirit*, Oxford University Press, 1963.

Dunn, John, *Western Political Theory in the Face of the Future*, Cambridge University Press, 1979.

Finley, M. I., *Democracy Ancient and Modern*, Chatto & Windus, 1973.

Lasch, Christopher, *The Agony of the American Left*, Alfred Knopf, 1969.

McCoy, Charles A., and Playford, John (eds) *Apolitical Politics: A Critique of Behavioralism*, Thomas Y. Crowell, 1967.

Macpherson, C. B., *Democratic Theory*, Clarendon Press, 1973.

   The Life and Times of Liberal Democracy, Oxford University Press, 1977.

O'Brien, Conor Cruise, *Writers and Politics*, Chatto & Windus, 1965.

Trilling, Lionel, *The Liberal Imagination*, Secker & Warburg, 1951.

Wolff, Robert Paul, *The Poverty of Liberalism*, Beacon Press, 1968.

Index

For reasons of space and convenience, I have omitted from the Index the names of 'secondary' authors mentioned in the text, and the names of most minor characters in the drama, (i.e. those mentioned only once in the text) as well as those who belong only incidentally to the history of liberalism.